Human-Computer Interaction Series

Human-Computer Interaction is a multidisciplinary field focused on human aspects of the development of computer technology. As computer-based technology becomes increasingly pervasive - not just in developed countries, but worldwide - the need to take a human-centered approach in the design and development of this technology becomes ever more important. For roughly 30 years now, researchers and practitioners in computational and behavioral sciences have worked to identify theory and practice that influences the direction of these technologies, and this diverse work makes up the field of human–computer interaction. Broadly speaking it includes the study of what technology might be able to do for people and how people might interact with the technology. In this series we present work which advances the science and technology of developing systems which are both effective and satisfying for people in a wide variety of contexts. The human–computer interaction series will focus on theoretical perspectives (such as formal approaches drawn from a variety of behavioral sciences), practical approaches (such as the techniques for effectively integrating user needs in system development), and social issues (such as the determinants of utility, usability and acceptability).

For further volumes:
http://www.springer.com/series/6033

Jörg Müller • Florian Alt • Daniel Michelis
Editors

Pervasive Advertising

 Springer

Editors
Jörg Müller
Deutsche Telekom Laboratories
TU Berlin
Berlin, Germany
hans-joerg.mueller@telekom.de

Florian Alt
Human Computer Interaction Group
University of Stuttgart
Stuttgart, Germany
florian.alt@vis.uni-stuttgart.de

Daniel Michelis
Anhalt University of Applied Sciences
Bernburg, Germany
d.michelis@wi.hs-anhalt.de

ISSN 1571-5035
ISBN 978-0-85729-351-0   e-ISBN 978-0-85729-352-7
DOI 10.1007/978-0-85729-352-7
Springer London Dordrecht Heidelberg New York

British Library Cataloguing in Publication Data
A catalogue record for this book is available from the British Library

Library of Congress Control Number: 2011935526

Printed on acid-free paper

Springer is part of Springer Science+Business Media (www.springer.com)

Contents

Contributors

Alexander Almer JOANNEUM RESEARCH Forschungsgesellschaft mbH, Graz, Austria, alexander.almer@joanneum.at

Florian Alt Human Computer Interaction Group, University of Stuttgart, Stuttgart, Germany, florian.alt@vis.uni-stuttgart.de

Anirban Basu School of Informatics, University of Sussex, Brighton, UK

Christine Bauer Vienna University of Economics and Business, Wien, Austria, chris.bauer@wu.ac.at

Martin Bauer NEC Europe Ltd, Heidelberg, Germany, bauer@neclab.eu

Bo Begole Palo Alto Research Center, Inc., Palo Alto, USA, Bo.Begole@parc.com

Gilbert Beyer Ludwig-Maximilians-University, Munich, Germany, gilbert.beyer@ifi.lmu.de

Ian Brown Oxford Internet Institute, UK, ian.brown@oii.ox.ac.uk

Jorge C.S. Cardoso Portuguese Catholic University, Porto, Portugal, jorgecardoso@ieee.org

Dan Chalmers School of Informatics, University of Sussex, Brighton, UK, D.Chalmers@sussex.ac.uk

Keith Cheverst Lancaster University, Lancaster, UK, kc@comp.lancs.ac.uk

Cees de Bont Delft University of Technology, Delft, The Netherlands, c.j.p.m.debont@tudelft.nl

Berardina De Carolis University of Bari, Bari, Italy, decarolis@di.uniba.it

Susen Döbelt CURE Center for Usability Research & Engineering, Vienna, Austria, doebelt@cure.at

Erica Dubach Spiegler ETH Zürich, Zürich, Switzerland, edubach@ethz.ch

Bernadette Emsenhuber Johannes Kepler University, Linz, Austria, bernadette.emsenhuber@catalysts.cc

Harley Lorenz Geiger Center for Democracy & Technology (CDT), Washington, DC, USA, harley@cdt.org

Hamed Haddadi Queen Mary, University of London, London, UK, hamed@ee.ucl.ac.uk

Benjamin Hebgen NEC Europe Ltd, Heidelberg, Germany, hebgen@neclab.eu

Tristan Henderson University of St Andrews, UK, tristan@cs.st-andrews.ac.uk

Christian Hildebrand University of St. Gallen, St. Gallen, Switzerland, christian.hildebrand@unisg.ch

Pan Hui Deutsche Telekom Laboratories, Darmstadt, Germany, pan.hui@telekom.de

Rui José University of Minho, Guimarães, Portugal, rui@dsi.uminho.pt

Ann Light Northumbria University, Newcastle, UK, ann.light@gmail.com

Miquel Martin NEC Europe Ltd, Heidelberg, Germany, martin@neclab.eu

Elke Mattheiss CURE Center for Usability Research & Engineering, Vienna, Austria, mattheiss@cure.at

Max Meier Ludwig-Maximilians-University, Munich, Germany, max.meier@ifi.lmu.de

Alexander Meschtscherjakov University of Salzburg, Salzburg, Austria, alexander.meschtscherjakov@sbg.ac.at

Florian Michahelles ETH Zürich, Zürich, Switzerland, fmichahelles@ethz.ch

Daniel Michelis Anhalt University of Applied Sciences, Bernburg, Germany, d.michelis@wi.hs-anhalt.de

Thomas Mirlacher University of Salzburg, Salzburg, Austria, thomas.mirlacher@sbg.ac.at

Ingrid Mulder Rotterdam University of Applied Sciences, Rotterdam, The Netherlands
Delft University of Technology, Delft, The Netherlands, i.j.mulder@hro.nl; i.j.mulder@tudelft.nl

Jörg Müller Deutsche Telekom Laboratories, TU Berlin, Berlin, Germany, hans-joerg.mueller@telekom.de

Lucas Paletta JOANNEUM RESEARCH Forschungsgesellschaft mbH, Graz, Austria, lucas.paletta@joanneum.at

Kurt Partridge Palo Alto Research Center, Inc., Palo Alto, USA, Kurt.Partridge@parc.com

Wolfgang Reitberger University of Salzburg, Salzburg, Austria, wolfgang.reitberger@sbg.ac.at

Jon Robinson School of Informatics, University of Sussex, Brighton, UK

Johann Schrammel CURE Center for Usability Research & Engineering, Vienna, Austria, schrammel@cure.at

Sarah Spiekermann Vienna University of Economics and Business, Wien, Austria, sspieker@wu.ac.at

Ursula Stalder Lucerne University of Applied Sciences and Arts, Lucerne, Switzerland, ursula.stalder@hslu.ch

Martin Strohbach AGT Group (R&D), Darmstadt, Germany, mstrohbach@agtgermany.com

Nick Taylor Culture Lab, School of Computing Science, Newcastle University, Newcastle, UK, nick.taylor@newcastle.ac.uk

Manfred Tscheligi University of Salzburg, Salzburg, Austria, manfred.tscheligi@sbg.ac.at

Peter van Waart Rotterdam University of Applied Sciences, Rotterdam, The Netherlands

Delft University of Technology, Delft, The Netherlands, p.van.waart@hro.nl; p.vanwaart@tudelft.nl

Ian Wakeman School of Informatics, University of Sussex, Brighton, UK, ianw@sussex.ac.uk

Chapter 1
Pervasive Advertising

Jörg Müller, Florian Alt, and Daniel Michelis

Abstract As pervasive computing technologies leave the labs, they are starting to be used for the purpose of advertising. *Pervasive Advertising* has the potential to affect everyone's life, but it seems that a knowledge gap is preventing us from shaping this development in a meaningful way. In particular, many marketing and advertising professionals have an expert understanding of their trade, but are unaware of recent advances in pervasive computing technologies, the opportunities they offer, and the challenges they pose. Similarly, many pervasive computing researchers and professionals are on top of the recent technological advances, but lack basic marketing and advertising expertise and therefore an understanding of how their technology can influence these fields. This book is intended to close this gap and provide the means to meaningfully shape the future of pervasive advertising.

1.1   Introduction

The use of pervasive computing technologies for advertising purposes presents huge opportunities and challenges for our future. Pervasive advertising will soon be here whether we like it or not. Its fundamental orientation is being determined now, and

J. Müller (✉)
Deutsche Telekom Laboratories, TU Berlin, Germany
e-mail: hans-joerg.mueller@telekom.de

F. Alt
Human Computer Interaction Group, University of Stuttgart, Stuttgart, Germany
e-mail: florian.alt@vis.uni-stuttgart.de

D. Michelis
Anhalt University of Applied Sciences, Bernburg, Germany
e-mail: d.michelis@wi.hs-anhalt.de

J. Müller et al. (eds.), *Pervasive Advertising*, Human-Computer Interaction Series,
DOI 10.1007/978-0-85729-352-7_1, © Springer-Verlag London Limited 2011

the direction we choose will influence the appearance of urban space for years to come. We are at a crossroads, where a decision must be made that will leave us in a better or worse off position. One direction might create a world clogged with pervasive spam, people being spied upon, or subconsciously manipulated to buy things they do not need. However, the choice exists to take the future in a beneficial direction. This is a world in which pervasive computing actually achieves its positive potential. Where any information we may need, contacts to people we know, and inspiring experiences are provided everywhere and at anytime. This is supported by calm and engaging advertising, which respects our privacy, is honest, and does not manipulate us. These advertisements strike a balance between being calm when we do not need them, and being engaging and inspiring when we want to participate. Our privacy is well protected, and we can inspect our user profiles and change or delete data as we may wish. Some ads persuade us to do things that are in our interests, while unethical persuasion strategies are avoided. The persuasion strategies used are overt, and we have the ability to express our opinion of them. We believe that pervasive advertising has three major challenges that must be addressed; these concern the areas of calm and engaging advertising, privacy, and ethical persuasion.

One major obstacle to addressing these challenges seems to be the considerable number of advertising experts who are largely unaware of pervasive computing technologies and how these will influence and change their business field. They might fear losing revenue if they do not adapt quickly enough to pervasive computing technologies, or might even be tempted to ignore these developments. Furthermore, they know that advertising is an important and necessary activity of any economy, without which most companies would not survive – advertising is simply done well or poorly. On the other hand, there are a considerable number of computer experts who know a lot about pervasive computing but very little about advertising. These individuals may have only experienced advertising as consumers and fear that pervasive advertising will be much more invasive. But they also know that pervasive computing has a lot to offer in terms of automation, interactivity, and ubiquity. As experts from both fields are brought together, synergies will arise that have the potential to greatly improve advertising for all stakeholders.

The chapter aims to narrow the knowledge gap between advertisers and pervasive computing experts by illustrating the core principles of their respective fields. Following an overview of the essential concepts of advertising and pervasive computing, this chapter will propose and address the new technologies, opportunities, and challenges of pervasive advertising. Experts from one or both of these fields are invited to skip the respective introductory sections.

1.2 Advertising

In this introduction we will provide a brief overview of marketing's core principles. Section 1.2.4 will then outline current developments with respect to the context of this book.

1.2.1 Advertising Versus Marketing

The terms advertising and marketing are often used synonymously. Marketing is confused with advertising and selling techniques. This is partly due to the fact that the concepts, strategies, and instruments of marketing are often not visible to the typical consumer. Marketing plays an encompassing role and is integrated into a company's entire value creation process.

1.2.1.1 What Is Marketing?

The American Marketing Association defines marketing as follows:

> Marketing is the activity, set of institutions, and processes for creating, communicating, delivering, and exchanging offerings that have value for customers, clients, partners, and society at large. [1]

This definition shows the broad sweep of the marketing discipline. It also describes three important marketing trends. First, marketing serves more than just the purposes of a given business. It also includes the general activities and institutions beyond the scope of traditional organizations. This conceptual extension takes into account that marketing is no longer conducted by businesses alone, but also by agencies, self-organized groups, or even individuals. Moreover, the classical understanding of marketing is no longer restricted to functional aspects. The conceptual scope is much broader, so that marketing also includes non-functional pursuits, for example, activities that are not necessarily associated with a corresponding output. The second important change is the relationship between companies and customers. Especially in the second half of the twentieth century, marketing is no longer limited to the one-way value delivery from companies to customers. Today, buyers and sellers have entered into long-term relationships that focus on exchange rather than one-sided interaction. In particular, with the intensive use of digital communication technologies, customers have become active participants in the company-client relationship. Thus, they can no longer be described as passive value-recipients. The third significant change concerns the recipients of marketing activities since these are no longer restricted to customers per se, but now also include partners and "society at large." Marketing is increasingly viewed as an exchange between companies, customers, and community groups, where all involved parties see each other as equal partners and adapt their expression accordingly.

1.2.1.2 Marketing and Advertising Are Both Goal-Oriented

The formulation of clear, long-term oriented objectives is an essential part of marketing and advertising.

Superordinate Goals. The defining of marketing objectives is closely related to the formulation of the company's superordinate goals [22]. The first superordinate goal is the business mission that determines the type of services the company will provide. The business mission sets the basic direction for all corporate activities. The second goal is defining the corporate identity, which is most broadly understood as a corporate personality and is manifested in an organization's behavior, communication, and appearance.

Activity Goals. Superordinate objectives help to develop the activity goals related to quality, revenue, and profitability, or to environmental issues. All areas of a company formulate their own objectives in order to achieve these corporate activity goals. In the marketing area these objectives include [11]:

- potential-related marketing objectives such as general awareness, image, customer attitudes, or customer satisfaction;
- performance-based marketing objectives such as sales, market share, number of customers, customer loyalty, and market penetration;
- financial objectives such as revenue, marketing costs, profit, or return on sales.

1.2.1.3 Advertising Is Part of the Marketing Mix

Marketing is based on the marketing mix – a set of marketing instruments that companies use to reach their customers directly. The classical instruments of the marketing mix fall into four areas: product, price, place, and promotion [15].

Product. Product-related instruments are all activities and procedures that take into account the needs and requirements used to design current and future products. In this sense, the product policy encompasses the maintenance of successful products and the planning and realization of product innovations.

Price. The pricing policy is based on the decision related to the type and extent of compensation that customers pay to use the company's services. Price instruments not only refer to the actual price but also discounts, surcharges, or price timing.

Place. Instruments of distribution consist of all measures designed to sell products and services as well as to logistically organize their distribution. Sales measures directly or indirectly target the purchase process. Distribution measures ensure the availability of the product for the customer.

Promotion. Promotion includes all market communication activities of the company. This includes defining communication objectives and target groups, selecting communication channels, and determining the size of the communication budget. Promotional instruments can be divided into "above-the-line" and "below-the-line." Traditional advertising in newspaper, television, radio, cinema, and outdoor advertising are considered "above-the-line" measures; all other new communication tools are considered "below-the-line." Advertising is by far the most important communication tool in the marketing mix [22].

The technological developments in pervasive computing undoubtedly influence all four instruments of the marketing mix. However, the focus of this book concerns the impact of these developments on advertising as an instrument of marketing communication.

1.2.2 Advertising

As shown, advertising is one of four areas of the marketing mix. It is defined traditionally as a mass communication process designed to change the recipient's attitudes and behavior [22].

1.2.2.1 Advertising Definition

Kotler and Keller have formulated a standard definition of advertising that should also define the use of the term in this book:

> Advertising is any paid form of non-personal presentation and promotion of ideas, goods, or services by an identified sponsor. Advertisers include not only business firms but also charitable, nonprofit, and government agencies. [15]

The general goal of advertising is to transmit information to a specific group of recipients in order to achieve the desired effect. Accordingly, the task of advertising is to systematically plan, design, coordinate, and control all communicational activities of an organization with respect to relevant recipient groups in order to contribute to the marketing objectives.

1.2.2.2 Advertising Objectives

Advertising objectives have a direct means-end relationship to overall marketing and business objectives. The achievement of advertising objectives therefore contributes to the fulfillment of higher corporate goals [22].

Advertising objectives should be defined by content, scope, time, and target segment. They can be differentiated into cognitive, emotional, and conative goals as the following categorization of advertising objectives shows [30]:

1.2.2.3 Involvement

Also important to advertising is the concept of involvement: the strength of the relationship of consumers to an object such as a product or a service. Involvement is critical to advertising because it can significantly impact the purchase decision process. The concept of involvement was introduced into the field of advertising research, and has since become a very important means for explaining consumer behavior. The central assumption is that the processing of information depends heavily on the relevance of the information for the consumer. Thus, involvement is a person's perceived relevance of an object based on inner needs, values, and interests [39].

In advertising it is important that involvement varies for different types of products. Here, product involvement is the perceived personal relevance of a product that is determined by the individual's needs and values. Generally, we distinguish between high and low involvement purchases. High involvement purchases are of greater importance to the consumer. They are closely related to personality and self-assessment (e.g., car, house) and therefore characterized by relatively high financial, social, or psychological risks. The majority of most purchases, however, are low involvement purchases that are perceived as less important (e.g., food, facial tissues). Here, financial, social, or psychological risks are low, so that consumers often do not search extensively for information and rarely look for product alternatives. Low involvement will therefore generally lead to a restricted decision making process. The standard approach in advertising is the following: for low-involvement products, advertising generally contains a small amount of information and is repeated frequently; for high-involvement products, advertising contains more information and will be repeated less often [17]. The individual's involvement plays an important role in the categorization of buying behavior.

1.2.2.4 Categories of Buying Behavior

For a comprehensive understanding of advertising, it is important to analyze different decision making processes and their relationship to involvement. Generally, distinctions are made between the following four basic types of purchase decisions [16]:

Extensive decisions are also called real purchasing decisions. The decision to purchase is based on a high cognitive and emotional involvement. Products that trigger extensive choices are usually expensive durable goods, which have a long life. These cause the buyer to check many alternatives before buying. Information demand is particularly high, as buyers usually only have limited experience with the purchase of similar products. The high cost and long life of the product also raises the stakes of a poor purchase.

Habitualized purchase decisions are those purchases for which the purchase decision process is almost automatic. Previous purchases lead to a routine decision making process. Therefore, the buyer does not consciously choose a product or brand. Especially in terms of goods for daily needs, buyers tend to develop their own routines to minimize the emotional and cognitive effort. Between the perceived stimulus and response – the purchase – there is no additional searching for and processing of information. Habitual decision making is characterized by low emotional and cognitive involvement. While routine processes reduce complexity, the buyer's cognitive control is low. An example of this type of decision is daily food shopping at the supermarket.

Impulsive purchase decisions are driven by emotions that strongly influence the decision making process. Unplanned impulse buying is often triggered by strong activating stimuli, which the consumer responds to by making a purchase. Cognitive involvement is low and emotional involvement is high. The buyer therefore makes a decision based on short-term emotional activation and requires only a very small amount of information about the offer.

Limited decisions occur when the decision making process is shortened due to various reasons, for example, when restricted shelf space in a store limits the buyer's choice. This restricts the final decision process to a comparison of pre-selected alternatives.

1.2.2.5 Perception, Attention, and Activation

Due to the abundance of media, an overwhelming number of advertising messages compete against each other. As a result, customer attention is becoming a scarce resource. Thus, disseminating information and getting customers to pay attention both represent fundamental challenges. Difficulty in drawing attention served as a guiding paradigm for traditional advertisers and, for example, led to the establishment of the AIDA model, which describes a basic buying process defined in terms of: Attention, Interest, Desire, and Action [22]. Since attention is the first step in the buying process it plays a very central role in successfully selling products.

Advertising messages can be processed only if the consumer consciously perceives them. Therefore, perception, that is to say the process of interpreting sensory stimuli in a way that is meaningful to the recipient, is a basic tenet of successful advertising. Attention is a prerequisite for perception and is broadly defined as a temporary activation that creates in the individual an awareness of certain stimuli. In sum, perception, attention, and activation are important basic aspects of successful advertising campaigns [19]. Activation describes an individual's inner state of awareness. From a physiological point of view, activation is the stimulation of the central nervous system that leads the human organism into a state of motivation and higher performance. The extent of activation influences the responsiveness, efficiency, and performance of an organism. Performance relates primarily to cognitive processes, such as the acquisition, processing, and storage of information. Activation can generally be triggered in three ways: on a physiological level, on a subjective experience level, and on a motor level. Up to an optimal level of activation the following rule applies: the more powerful the activation, the higher the cognitive performance of the individual and the greater the amount of information that can be processed. However, if the optimal level is exceeded, the organism's responsiveness and efficiency declines. In order to develop sustainable advertising campaigns, it is therefore important not to over-activate. In addition, higher-activation ads are generally remembered longer but the extent of activation has no bearing on whether the ads are perceived positively or negatively. The following rule applies: if the activation of a message is stronger, the consumer will process it more efficiently but qualitative communication success is not necessarily associated with stronger activation [16].

1.2.2.6 Emotions and Experiences

The use of emotions is very common in advertising since people remember situations better based on emotions rather than factual information. In addition, emotional experiences have become an important reason for why consumers choose a particular product or brand [9]. Accordingly, marketers have established the concept of experience marketing [27] that aims to create value from the emotional experience offered by the product or brand. Smoking Marlboro promises the experience of freedom and adventure. The value of the individual experience is defined as a subjective contribution to the quality of the consumer's life. Advertising, therefore, often seeks to awaken emotions in potential consumers. This is based on studies showing that products that trigger emotions are considered more intense, lead to improved processing and memorizing of messages, potentially produce a better brand image, and enable a clearer differentiation from alternative offerings. In communicating emotions, a distinction is made between extent and quality. The *extent* of emotions is relevant when an emotional experience is supposed to activate consumers. As described, activation should lead to higher performance and enable the consumer to process more information. The *quality* of emotions is relevant when a product or brand is supposed to be linked with particular emotions. In the hearts and minds of consumers, specific emotional experiences are to be connected to an offer, and both emotion and offer are to be linked in the long term. Examples of specific emotions are social acceptance, eroticism, freedom and adventure, nature and pleasure, pleasure, happiness, and companionship [16]. A product or brand should thus provide the buyer with selected emotional feelings.

1.2.3   Developing Advertising Programs

The development of advertising programs consists of five steps: setting objectives, establishing a budget, choosing and creating the message, selecting the media-channels, and, finally, evaluating the results. These five steps are known as the "5Ms" of advertising: Mission, Money, Message, Media, and Measurement [15].

1.2.3.1 Mission

Defining the advertising objective is determined by the target market and the positioning established by the organization's marketing strategy. The objective or advertising goal is the desired result of the communication process between advertiser and recipient within a given timeframe. According to the advertiser's needs and aims the objectives can be classified as shown in Table 1.1 into cognitive, emotional, and conative advertising goals.

Table 1.1 Advertising objectives

Cognitive objectives	If the corresponding need is minor, the essential information about the product or service should be communicated. A need is called minor, whenever the recipient is aware that the need is currently present and that it can be satisfied by available offers. In this case, it is often sufficient to communicate the key features of the product
Emotional objectives	Emotional advertising aims to link a product or service with specific emotions that lead to a differentiation from other offerings. Emotions are used primarily in mature markets with technically and functionally interchangeable products (cigarettes, chocolate, etc.)
Conative objectives	Conative objectives are related to actual consumer action. In this case, advertising aims to stimulate potential buyers to buy, order, use, or take action in any other form

1.2.3.2 Money

Defining the budget is generally determined by the product's life cycle, the existing consumer base and market share, competition, buying frequency, and the substitutability of the offer. Of course, the budget varies widely with the media and technologies used.

1.2.3.3 Message

Developing the advertising message and positioning the advertisement is a creative and an analytical task. Using market research, advertisers learn about how, when, and where their target audience will most likely perceive their message. Based on this knowledge they decide the position, frequency, and other aspects of the advertising message. The actual creation of the message, that is to say the design, layout, logo etc. is the creative part of the development process. The latter is just as important for the advertisement's effectiveness: "The ad's impact depends not only on what is said, but often more importantly, on how it says it" [15]. In addition, as postulated by McLuhan, the medium influences the perception of the message [21]. This is of particular interest when new technologies are used to communicate with potential customers.

1.2.3.4 Media

Media types vary in aspects such as reach (percentage of the target market exposed to the medium), frequency (e.g., frequency of message display), or impact (e.g., persuasiveness of the medium). In principle, advertisers try to find the best balance between reach, frequency, and impact on the one hand, and corresponding costs on the other. Among the variety of advertising modes and techniques we would like to highlight out-of-home and point-of-purchase advertising. Both are highly relevant to the field of pervasive advertising.

Out-of-home advertising refers to a range of advertising methods designed to reach people in their everyday environments. Most of these environments are public or semi-public areas in which regular activities such as working, shopping, or traveling take place. Typical environments are shopping malls, airports, train stations, or city centers. Frequent types of out-of-home advertising are described by Stalder in this book.

The term point-of-purchase advertising describes ways to communicate with potential customers during the actual act of purchase. Next to classical in-store TV advertising, other forms of in-store advertising include ads on shopping carts, aisles and shelves, in-store demonstrations, or coupon machines. A significant number of consumer purchase decisions take place at the point-of-purchase. Point-of-purchase advertising has a strong potential to remind consumers of certain offers while making their final decisions as well as stimulating spontaneous purchases.

1.2.3.5 Measurement

The final step is evaluating the results. Has the ad been communicated effectively? In order to measure the communication effect, an advertising objective needs to be set in advance. An advertising objective is, according to Kotler and Keller "a specific communication task and achievement level to be accomplished with a specific audience in a specific period of time" [15]. As described above, these objectives can be classified as cognitive, emotional, or conative.

Different objectives and different advertising media allow different measuring techniques. Whereas measuring the click-through-rate of an online banner is relatively simple, measuring the communication-effect of a newspaper advert is still very complex. This differentiation should be considered when developing new advertising techniques.

1.2.4 Relevant Changes in Advertising

In the previous sections we presented fundamental marketing and advertising concepts as an introduction for the non-specialist reader. The scientific and practical discussion of the ideas presented shows that the central issues are more complex than first set forth.

For example, in addition to the categorizations of "above the line" and "below the line" (Sect. 1.2.1.3), which are rooted in the advertising industry, complementary approaches take into account that the advent of digital technology led to a higher fragmentation of the media landscape and an extensive growth of "touchpoints" between advertiser and consumer. Today, advertisers make use of an increasing variety of promotional instruments that require a more sophisticated categorization. This is especially true for pervasive advertising and many of the new developments we present in this book. Nevertheless, we think the categorizations of "above" and "below the line" provide a useful point of reference that facilitates the linking of standard advertising approaches with new developments.

In contrast to the broad definition of marketing we presented in Sect. 1.2.1.1, the standard definition of advertising as a "paid" presentation and promotion (Sect. 1.2.2.1) seems to have a crucial limitation. The restriction to paid activities means that advertising is limited to a specific type of presentation as well as specific type of distribution. Particularly, the term "paid" refers to advertising that is distributed through channels that are not owned by the "identified sponsor," i.e., the advertiser. The advertiser pays for time or space in an advertising channel operated by someone else in order to present or promote his message to an audience. Hence, the standard definition of advertising implies that advertising channels are always owned by an external operator. Whereas this was mostly the case for mass media channels such as television, newspaper, or radio, the situation has clearly changed with the spread of digital information and communication media. Therefore, in this book, we expand the standard definition to include presentation and promotion through advertising channels owned by advertiser themselves, such as in-store screens or shopping assistance devices.

Accordingly, for scientific and practical work concerning the fundamental concepts presented here, this introduction can only serve as a starting point for a substantive discussion of the latest developments. Some of these developments are presented in detail in the following chapters of this book.

This is of particular importance with regard to the realities of ongoing digitalization. While the digitalization of communication processes continues to progress in business and society, a new wave of digitalization in the field of marketing and advertising can be observed. In recent years, a wide variety of new advertising media, communication channels, business models, and use forms have been established. Now the continuing proliferation of digital communication media leads to far-reaching changes across entire industries. While some industries have been experiencing this change for some time, others have only just begun to respond.

In contrast to the speed at which practical applications have taken hold, it seems that study of "digitalization" in research-based disciplines, such as marketing research, marketing strategy, or online advertising has lagged behind. This is particularly true in marketing and advertising fields. The latest developments in the fundamental concepts presented above define "digital marketing" in very limited ways. Kotler et al. [15], for instance, only describe indirectly the concept of online marketing as an extension of direct marketing. A systematic adjustment or development of the basic theories and models has, for the most part, still not been undertaken [15, 22]. These studies also clearly demonstrate that online marketing activities are usually only assigned to the area of communication (or promotion). This view has been largely influenced by online advertising such as banner ads or search engine advertising that allow a very targeted approach of defined target groups. However, the impact of digital media on the overall marketing mix is usually not taken into account. Such methods typically serve as the core of the underlying business model, such as with eBay or Amazon.

In recent years, the wide availability of digital communication technologies not only led to an extensive cross-linking of companies, such as extended value chains, or electronic data processing [38], in many places consumers also become involved in the internal processes of the value chain itself [34]. The development of social media continues this trend, and transmits it to the great mass of consumers [32]. These consumers take advantage of the open structures of social media in order to participate in the production of (user-generated) content. This applies in particular to the field of advertising [20] but also to the development of new products [12], in which consumers are increasingly involved in more direct ways.

1.3 Pervasive Computing

The following section is intended for readers unfamiliar with pervasive computing. In introducing the field we emphasize the technologies and concepts we consider to be the driving factors behind pervasive advertising. The concept of and term "Pervasive Computing" (we use this term synonymous with "Ubiquitous Computing") goes back to Marc Weiser's visionary paper in the early nineties where he comes to the conclusion that "...the most profound technologies are those that disappear. They weave themselves into the fabrics of everyday life until they are indistinguishable from it" [36]. The manner of working at XEROX Parc at that time served as a precursor to the impending future era of computing in which users are surrounded by multitude computers in everyday situations. Schmidt defines pervasive computing as follows:

> **Pervasive [or ubiquitous] computing** describes the trend that inter-connected computational devices become interwoven with artifacts in our everyday life. Hence, processing, sensing, activation and communication are embedded into devices and environments, making computing an integral part of our life [31].

As myriad numbers of small processors and sensors – integrated not only with household appliances, toys, tools, and clothes but also price labels, receipts, product packages, and shopper loyalty cards – spread throughout our environment, pervasive computing has become the subject of highly progressive research in applied computer science.

In this section a brief historical overview is presented and followed by an illustration of technical advances concerning processing power, storage, networking, sensors, and actuators. The remainder of the section will address concepts of automation, interactivity, and ubiquity, made possible by the previously presented technologies.

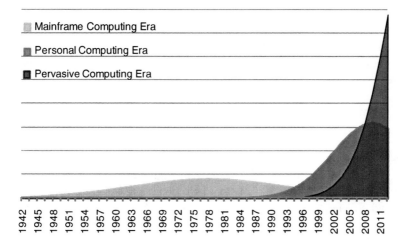

Fig. 1.1 The three eras of computing (Mainframe computing era, personal computing era, pervasive computing era)

1.3.1   Historical Background

According to Weiser, three main eras (see Fig. 1.1) have shaped the computing age thus far [37]. When recalling the *mainframe era*, the image comes to mind of huge computers operated by experts behind closed doors. Computational power was a scarce resource, which had to be shared among fellow users. Mainframe computing is still relevant today (e.g., super computers for weather simulations), but has been largely eclipsed by the PC, whose introduction in the early 1980s ushered in the *personal computing era*. By 1984 as many people were using personal computers as were sharing mainframe computers. Computers became individualized, even intimate devices, which required considerable attention to operate. With the advent of the Internet, people, their PCs, and all kinds of peripheral devices became interconnected, hence creating a distributed medium. The *pervasive computing era*, in which we currently live, is characterized by constant, mass computer use, including the hundreds of computers accessed while browsing the Internet or using a mobile phone, as well as those integrated into cars, buildings, clothes – literally everywhere.

1.3.2   Technical Advances

In the following section we introduce technical advances in processing power, storage, networking, sensors, and actuators that form the basis of the pervasive computing field and are relevant to pervasive advertising.

1.3.2.1 Processing, Storage, and Networking

For a number of years advances in the implementation of computing hardware have led to exponential increases in processing power, storage, and network capabilities. These developmental trends are referred to as Moore's Law (processing power), the Storage Law (storage and memory), and the Fiber Law (network bandwidth). See [4] for a more comprehensive overview. As a consequence of such developments, devices are rapidly getting smaller and more powerful and now surround people in their everyday lives, enabling access at any time and place.

Most importantly, the ability to pack increasing numbers of transistors on an integrated circuit led to a massive boost in computational power that has doubled approximately every 2 years. This trend has continued for more than half a century and still holds true today. The capabilities of many electronic devices are strongly linked to Moore's Law, such as processing power, memory capacity, and even the number and size of pixels in digital cameras. All of these are increasing at exponential rates as well. This has dramatically increased the usefulness of digital electronics in nearly every segment of the world economy. Moore's Law describes a driving force behind technological and social change in the late twentieth and early twenty-first centuries. Apparent today is that processing power, storage, and bandwidth may no longer be a barrier to what computers can achieve in the future. For the most part, the capacities of desktop computers are currently underused, even when writing numerous emails, surfing the Web, or editing images. Hence, increasing processor speed will most likely not increase productivity. Instead creativity, rather than technology, will be the main bottleneck for future system development.

As a consequence of the exponential development described above, the ability emerged to integrate all components of a computer into a single chip (integrated circuit), often referred to as "system-on-a-chip" (SoC) or microcontroller. This chip may contain digital, analog, mixed-signal, and often radio-frequency functions. A typical application pertains to the area of embedded systems. Microcontrollers usually have very limited computational resources and run a single custom program. In modern cars dozens of microcontrollers are used, such as for controlling the engine or windows. Systems-on-a-chip typically use powerful processors, capable of running operating systems such as Linux, and are, for example, used in smartphones.

Popular examples for experimental hardware implementations include Arduino [2] (microcontroller) or the Beagle Board [3] (SoC). Such systems allow different types of sensors and actuators to be hooked up easily, and therefore enable the building of interactive systems in a small form factor.

1.3.2.2 Sensors and Actuators

The increasing prevalence of smart environments requires the integration of more and more sensors for obtaining information on the environment. The information collected is then processed further and used to modify the environment through the use of different types of actuators. Sensors can either be integrated with the infrastructure (e.g., allowing for information to be gathered on weather conditions, traffic congestion, etc.) or personal devices. Mobile phones, for example, now come with many integrated sensors (GPS, cameras, microphones, digital compasses) that enable the user to collect individualized data while controlling access to this information at the same time. The following section provides a brief overview of sensor and actuator technologies.

A range of *optical sensors* (from motion detectors to cameras) are available, which makes possible collecting very simple (motion-related) but also very complex (human-behavioral) information. The (semi-) automatic analysis of camera images is called computer vision. Today, cameras are so inexpensive (they cost only fractions of a dollar to produce) that they can be integrated into virtually any device. With systems-on-a-chip, processing power and storage can be directly integrated with the camera. Hence, integrated systems can be built, which, for example, only output the number of detected faces, therefore preserving user privacy. In order to analyze the three-dimensional composition of a scene, stereo cameras are traditionally used. In addition to the normal camera image, a depth map is calculated that provides the distance of all objects in the camera's visual field. Stereovision relies on good features (e.g., textures) detected in the image and verified in both camera images (similar to the human visual system), and requires considerable processing power. Recently, so-called depth cameras are available, which generate depth maps by illuminating the scene with special (infrared) light. Two general technologies prevail: (1) Time-of-flight cameras (e.g., SwissRanger 4000 by Mesa) use technologies such as modulated light sources in combination with phase detectors to measure how long it takes light to travel from the camera to the object and back to the camera; (2) Structured light cameras (e.g., Microsoft Xbox Kinect®) project a light pattern onto a scene. A vision system then calculates depth information from the distortion of this pattern relative to the objects in the scene. Using depth images, some operations such as background subtraction are much easier than with normal camera images. The recent price decline in depth cameras has also spawned a significant number of applications, such as in gesture control.

Similar to cameras, *microphones* can either provide low-level information requiring only minimal processing (e.g., noise level, base frequency, characterization of sound source) or high-level information (e.g., speech recognition). Microphone arrays can be used to determine the location of sound sources.

Today *location sensors* can be used to obtain information on position, collocation, and proximity of users both outdoors (GPS, GSM, WiFi, etc.) as well as indoors (Ubisense, Optitrack, etc.). Approaches often vary highly in granularity. Indoors, location sensors are typically embedded in the environment, as with the Active Badge system [35]. In the context of advertising, location sensing can be used for tracking purposes, such as the path customers take through the aisles of a supermarket.

To obtain information on direction, orientation, inclination, motion, or acceleration of a device, many mobile phones now come with *accelerometers* and/or *gyroscopes*. Whereas accelerometers measure proper acceleration of a device (relative to free fall), gyroscopes measure orientation and rotation (using the principles of conservation of angular momentum) hence making it possible to accurately recognize movement within a three dimensional space. Accordingly, different types of contexts can be ascertained such as the orientation or movement of the device, whether it is stationary on a table or moving in a car. Acceleration is of particular interest when it comes to analyzing usage patterns.

With the advent of the iPhone there has also been a proliferation of devices using *touch* technologies. In addition to smart phones, more and more displays and tabletops are being equipped with (multi-) touch support. Different technologies are used to create touch surfaces. Resistive touch screens use two flexible sheets coated with resistive material, which can register the precise location of a touch as they are pressed together. For capacitive sensing, a conductive layer is used and a small voltage applied to it, hence creating an electrostatic field. When a conductor such as the human hand comes near or touches the surface, a capacitor is formed and the change in capacitance can be measured from the corners of the panel. Optical touch technologies (such as FTIR) use light sensors / cameras and computer vision to detect fingers and objects on and above surfaces. State-of-the-art technologies also include PixelSense (e.g., Microsoft Surface 2.0), a technology where IR sensors are integrated with the LCD display, hence making it possible to see what happens on top of a surface without using a camera. See [29] for further information on sensor technologies.

Actuators allow information to be output in the form of different representations, for example, via visual, auditory, haptic, or olfactory channels. In the following we introduce the technologies and properties of actuators that address the different channels.

Display technologies include, among others, LCD (liquid crystal displays), plasma displays, projectors, and bendable displays, such as OLED (organic light-emitting diode) displays and e-paper. With the decrease in price of displays, we envision that in the future literally any surface could function as a display with minimal cost. Important properties of displays include size, resolution, readability in sunlight, update frequency, brightness, and flexibility.

For audio presentation, headphones or loudspeakers can be used. Whereas traditional speakers use a horn for increasing the overall efficiency, parabolic loudspeakers use a reflector, resulting in a beam of sound, which can travel farther and be directed to isolated target audiences. Ultrasonic systems use wave interference to create sound that is only audible within small areas, and which can be relatively far from the loudspeakers. When it comes to spatial sound rendering, there are different approaches for generating spatial sound. Whereas stereophonic sound creates the impression of hearing sound from different directions using two independent audio channels, surround sound increases the perceived spaciousness through additional discrete speakers. With both techniques however, the sound essentially comes from one broad direction. In order to create sound coming from arbitrary positions in space, Ambisonics or wave field synthesis (WFS) can be used. WFS mimics natural wave fronts and allows for much larger listening regions than Ambisonics. For example, some large cinemas are currently equipped with WFS. Using WFS, the localization of the sound sources is independent from the listener's position.

Haptics describes the recognition of objects through touch, including tactile perception, proprioception, thermoception, and nociception. For haptics, actuators are used that apply forces to the skin for touch feedback. Such actuators include vibration motors, electroactive polymers, piezoelectric, and electrostatic surface actuation. Haptic actuators are popular in robotics where they serve as the muscles of a robot. Most popular actuators include electric motors, linear actuators, series elastic actuators, air muscles, muscle wires, electroactive polymers, and piezo motors.

Finally, olfactory actuators allow for interaction based on smell. So-called olfactory displays can disseminate odors, hence serving as an olfactory channel between man and computer. For an introduction to olfactory advertising see Chap. 17.

1.3.3 Concepts

The previously mentioned technologies (processing, storage, networking, sensors, actuators) are crucial prerequisites to pervasive computing and make possible its core principles of automation, interactivity, and ubiquity.

1.3.3.1 Automation

With the industrial revolution many work processes were automated; this automation continues today. More and more mechanical and electro-mechanical systems are now computer-controlled, going beyond what we know as mechanization. This enables so-called scale effects, which lead to lower average manufacturing costs per unit relative to increases in output. As a result, prices for products entering the market decrease as higher quantities are produced. An example of this is the fingerprint reader, which was a very specialized device some years ago but can now be integrated with laptops at little additional expense. Today automation is no longer restricted to manufacturing but has found its way into telecommunications (e.g., telephone switchboards), medicine (e.g., electrocardiography), finance (e.g., automated brokering, ATMs), and also advertising (e.g., Google AdSense).

From a computer science perspective, the ultimate automation would be to create artificial intelligence (AI). The term goes back to 1956, when John McCarthy defined artificial intelligence as "the science and engineering of making intelligent machines" [6]. In the beginning the objective was to build a general-purpose AI that can emulate all human cognitive capabilities (strong AI). This was found to be much more difficult than expected, and by now most researchers and engineers have limited their ambitions to use AI technology only to solve very specific problems (weak AI). AI is, among others, concerned with the following sub-problems: problem solving (e.g., search), knowledge representation and reasoning (i.e., logic, inference and planning, dealing with uncertainty), unsupervised machine learning (i.e., finding unknown patterns in a data input stream), and supervised machine learning (i.e., classification into known categories). Computer vision is mainly concerned with extracting and interpreting information from an image that can later be used to solve a task. Exemplary problems in computer vision are recognition (e.g., recognition of an object, identification, or simply detection) and motion analysis (e.g., for tracking purposes). Similar to AI, it is generally not possible to build a general-purpose computer vision system that can recognize arbitrary things. Instead, one needs to define in advance a specific problem to be solved (e.g., finding faces in an image) and can then use computer vision techniques to solve this task. Foundational techniques for many applications are image acquisition (e.g., recording a video stream from a camera), pre-processing (e.g., re-sampling, noise reduction, enhancing contrast, or scaling), feature extraction (e.g., finding lines, edges, or ridges), detection and segmentation (e.g., selecting a set of interesting points), and some final high-level processing (e.g., image recognition, classification). Computer vision can, for example, be used to find and track people in a video stream, for face detection, face recognition (comparing faces to a database of known faces), interaction (e.g., gesture recognition), or activity recognition (e.g., whether somebody is seated).

1.3.3.2 Interactivity

Human-computer interaction (HCI) is concerned with "the design, evaluation, and implementation of interactive computing systems for human use and with the study of major phenomena surrounding them [10]." Since its subjects are man and machine, knowledge from computer science, as well as psychology, communication science, graphic and industrial design disciplines, linguistics, social sciences, etc. are all relevant. The driving goal behind HCI is to improve interaction between users and computers given a certain use context, which usually has a strong impact on the usability of a user interface. Hence HCI draws on methodologies and processes for designing and implementing interfaces, techniques for evaluating and comparing interfaces, developing new interfaces and interaction techniques, and developing models and theories of interaction.

When it comes to interaction, two different types prevail. Traditionally, human-computer interaction focuses mainly on *explicit interaction* where the user tells the computer at some level of abstraction what he expects the computer to do, for example, by directly manipulating an object using a mouse, touch screen, or speech input. Yet, as HCI extends beyond the desktop, *implicit* interaction, that is interaction occurring without the explicit intention or awareness of the user, will become ever more important. Schmidt defines implicit interaction as "an action, performed by the user that is not primarily aimed to interact with a computerized system but which such a system understands as input" [28]. For example, a display may recognize that the audience is smiling and consequently display funny content.

Since the rise of HCI in the eighties, several design methodologies have emerged. *User-centered design* is a design philosophy, which puts the user at the center when designing any computer system. As a result, users, designers, and technical practitioners co-operate in order to address users' wants, needs, and limitations to create a usable system. Norman presented six *principles of user interface design* [25] to be considered during all stages of the design process (visibility, feedback, affordance, mapping, constraint, and consistency).

An important part of HCI is the *evaluation of user interfaces*. Traditionally, empirical measures with regard to usability are time to complete the task(s) and the number of errors made during the task(s). Usability is defined by ISO as "the extent to which a product can be used by specified users to achieve specified goals with effectiveness, efficiency, and satisfaction in a specified context of use." Stated differently, usability is a measure for how easy a user interface is to use. Jakob Nielsen [24] and Ben Shneiderman [33] presented frameworks of system acceptability, outlining learnability, efficiency, memorability, errors, and satisfaction as crucial factors for user interface design. Whereas many traditional interfaces are used to solve concrete tasks, this is often different for advertising. Here, content is often perceived rather passively, or playful interfaces are used as toys. For a general introduction to HCI see [5, 7].

Recent developments in *computer graphics* allow creating impressive images on displays. Computer graphics is a subfield of computer science and is concerned with the methods of digitally synthesizing visual content. Generally, a distinction is made between interactive computer graphics, which may take a few milliseconds to generate an image at most, and non-interactive computer graphics, where the generation of a single image can take up to several hours (e.g., for movies). Two-dimensional and three-dimensional graphics are possible; three-dimensional graphics are also often rendered on a flat screen. For three-dimensional graphics, two general technologies prevail. Rastering techniques (e.g., OpenGL) use mathematical projections to display primitive three-dimensional shapes such as triangles on a flat screen. Similar methods are used to generate shadows, reflections, etc. Ray tracing tries to follow each light ray that hits the screen backwards through the scene to the light sources in order to determine its color. Using rastering techniques, today's massive parallel programmable graphics hardware allows for unprecedented real-time realism in computer graphics.

With the market penetration of the smart phone and other related devices, the notion of layering relevant information into our visual field (*augmented reality, AR*) became a hot topic in HCI. AR describes hereby the live direct or indirect view of the physical world whose elements are augmented with computer-generated, sensory input. In general, AR requires computer vision and object recognition in order for the real world of the user to become interactive and digitally manipulatable. Examples of AR applications include navigation systems that allow views of the road to be augmented with cues on direction, points-of-interest, and upcoming obstacles. Furthermore, social interaction may be augmented in the future by providing additional information about the people we're conversing with by projecting such data onto our glasses.

1.3.3.3 Ubiquity

The ubiquity of pervasive computing technologies is one of their most profound properties. Computers that integrate information processing into everyday objects and activities as well as new generations of the Internet allow people to get in touch with one another at any time and place. Accordingly, this makes information-rich technologies and applications possible and further adds to Mark Weiser's vision of "Ubiquitous Computing".

Mobile and wireless computing devices now come with high-resolution cameras, integrated GPS, and provide easy access to the Internet. Similarly, the TV is also linked to the Internet and is no longer restricted to a single location (at home). As location-independent digital media entertainment becomes available with devices such as smart phones or tablets, younger generations in particular are eager to adopt these technologies.

Beyond mobile devices, more and more processors and sensors are integrated into everyday objects, such as household appliances, tools, toys, and clothes. When linked through wireless networks, they create the so-called *Internet of Things*. This allows users to easily connect to social networks and virtual worlds and makes possible novel forms of applications and services that augment the physical world through new forms of interaction and communication.

1.4 Pervasive Advertising

After decades of development in the laboratories, pervasive computing technologies are finally in a position to reshape our world. Analogous to developments on the Internet, it is our belief that advertising will be the business model that drives pervasive computing. As illustrated above, the goal of advertising is to impart information, evoke emotions, and trigger actions. The properties of pervasive computing (automation, interactivity, ubiquity) make it a powerful tool for achieving these goals. These properties have the potential to change advertising in six main ways: symmetric communication, long tail, experiences, personalization, audience measurement, and automated persuasion.

As stated previously, advertising is defined as any paid form of non-personal presentation and promotion of ideas, goods, or services by an identified sponsor. Pervasive computing environments are saturated with computing and communication capabilities, yet these features are integrated so seamlessly for the user that it becomes 'the technology that disappears.' Based on these definitions, we define pervasive advertising as:

> Pervasive advertising is the use of pervasive computing technologies for advertising purposes.

1.4.1   Pervasive Advertising Technologies

It is our belief that among the technologies developed by pervasive computing, three hold the most initial promise for pervasive advertising: digital signage, mobile phones, and physical computing/robotics. Certainly, the main value will be created not when these technologies are used on their own, but when synergies emerge from their combination.

1.4.1.1   Digital Signage

Digital signage, as developed in pervasive computing, has obvious potential to make out-of-home advertising digital [23]. Stalder and José touch upon this aspect in their chapters on the digital signage advertising market. In a similar vein, de Carolis takes on the issue of displays in fitness clubs, while Taylor addresses displays in villages, and Schrammel and Reitberger displays in public transportation and shops, respectively. Digital signage distinguishes itself most significantly from mobile phones in that the hardware is usually not owned by the audience. The audience is merely passing by or waiting in the vicinity of the display and decides whether to look at or interact with the display. The audience only has limited influence over the content displayed.

1.4.1.2   Mobile Phones

The second most promising technology for pervasive advertising is the smartphone. In contrast to digital signage, mobile phones are owned by individual users. Accordingly, the audience itself decides what content is shown and what applications are installed on the phone. Since the private phone is considered a very personal device, audiences may be more sensitive to advertising. On the other hand, people typically own their phones for long periods of time. Unlike digital signs, which are usually experienced in brief intervals, mobile phone owners carry their devices with them at all times. Smartphones are equipped with a variety of sensors and can store very personal information, such as address books and emails. These properties may enable strong personalization and context adaptivity, as explained in Partridge's chapter. At the same time, this makes privacy protection a goal of primary importance, as Haddadi describes.

1.4.1.3   Physical Computing/Robotics

Beyond digital signage and mobile phones, pervasive computing aims to digitalizing our entire physical environment. This can start from simple markers in the environment (e.g., QR codes or NFC), as explained in Wakeman's chapter. Another aspect is control of lighting and simple robotic devices. An example of this is the Philips smart shop window [14] in which products rest on interactive turntables that rotate to present the products to the audience. Mobile robots, that is, robots that can walk or roll around, can also act as salespersons. For example, Kanda [13] describes a robot that has been used to approach people in front of a shop and lure them inside. Going a step further, such physical computing environments can appeal to all our senses, such as using sound, as shown in Meier's chapter, or even smell, as explained in Emsenhuber's chapter.

1.4.2   Opportunities

Pervasive computing is set to change the face of advertising in major ways. When applied to this field, pervasive computing's automated, interactive, and ubiquitous properties translate into novel forms of advertising. Pervasive advertising distinguishes itself from traditional advertising in six different ways, its unique opportunities include: symmetric communication, the long tail, experiences, personalization and context adaptivity, audience measurement, and automated persuasion.

1.4.2.1   Power to the People (Symmetric Communication)

Classical advertising follows a mass media approach in which a small number of advertisers distribute their advertisements to the masses. This unidirectional communication model produces an asymmetrical distribution of power. All the power is concentrated in the hands of advertisers who decide which ads to show when and where. At best the audience has the option to ignore, protest against, or vandalize the resulting ads. For some people, such an asymmetrical distribution of power creates a feeling of being at the mercy of advertisers.

Since pervasive computing is interactive it offers the opportunity to transfer a significant degree of power to the audience. This fundamentally alters the unidirectional communication model by allowing the audience to communicate opinions directly to advertisers and other audiences. Companies must treat customers as equals. This can benefit both consumers and companies since a closer bond is created between the two and because it allows companies to learn from their customers much faster. Practical examples include the ability of the audience to choose the content they like and even to submit their own content. Eventually, this may lead to a democratization of advertising and the look of public spaces (see van Waart's chapter). Also, social media will foster communication within communities, as Dubach-Spiegler, Wakeman, and Taylor explain in their chapters.

1.4.2.2   Me, Too (The Long Tail)

By definition pervasive computing is highly automated and many things that required individual attention in classical advertising will also become automated. This significantly lowers the cost of and effort needed to produce individual advertising campaigns. Starting a new campaign may be as easy as filling out a few fields on a website and may cost only a few cents. This price decline enables very small companies and even individuals to launch their own tiny, local campaigns. It is important to remember that not only big companies are interested in advertising as the communication of sponsored messages. Even a small restaurant or market stall must advertise, just like anyone who wants to sell an old bicycle. Even someone who wants to surprise his wife at an airport or make a present for a birthday might be interested in displaying something in public, similar to someone who wants to impress his friends. Some examples of how to accomplish this are presented in José's chapter.

1.4.2.3 The 'Wow' Effect (Experiences)

Pervasive computing offers powerful media that respond to all senses. Large, bright displays that surround us create powerful visual impressions, but it is also possible to appeal to our hearing, what we feel, haptics, and even our sense of smell. As Norman [26] explains, there are three levels to interactive computer systems. The lowest level is visceral, in other words, what initial visual impression the technology makes. This can be described as "the first impression." The second level is behavioral, related to the look and feel, and described as "how it feels." The third level is reflective, for example, what we think others think about us when we use it. Since most traditional ads are not interactive, they do not go beyond the first level. Pervasive advertising, however, needs to properly address all three levels. It has a look and feel, and also makes us reflect when we interact with it. These properties make it a much more powerful tool for advertising. Since pervasive computing is all around us, these experiences can follow and surprise us wherever we go. Furthermore, since pervasive advertising is digital, it is very easy to create new experiences all the time. Together, this makes creating a wow-effect possible over and over again. Analog posters will look relatively pale compared to the intense and memorable experiences that can be created with pervasive advertising. Examples of what this can look like are presented in van Waart's chapter.

1.4.2.4 Just for Me, Just for Now (Personalization and Context Adaptivity)

Personalization and context adaptivity are at the core of pervasive computing and provide natural powerful tools for advertising. In personalization / user modeling, computers learn the preferences and behavior models of groups or individuals. This fits naturally with the target groups as a core concept of marketing. It is important to remember that in marketing, target groups are used in different ways: for the development of the product as well as for the placing of the advertisements. The dilemma of advertising traditionally was that the properties defining the target group have to be measurable, and target groups have to be accessible based on these criteria. This restricts them basically to demographics and other easily assessable criteria. Pervasive computing allows many more things to be quantified, thus making it feasible to develop target groups based on measurable demographic criteria or actual behavior. Pervasive computing allows measuring all kinds of things in real time, building user profiles, and adapting advertisements, thus making accessible far more finely tuned target groups. Partridge and de Carolis address these issues in their chapters.

In addition to personalization, adaptation to the context becomes much more fine-tuned because of automation and better sensors. Traditionally, a huge effort was required to post different ads, for example, depending on the weather. Using pervasive advertising, however, such things as advertising ice cream when the sun is shining and umbrellas when it is raining become minor. It can be assumed that when advertisements are much better adapted to the context, for example, when showing products in the hometown context of the audience, they are more effective. Bauer and Strohbach describe in detail how this can be achieved in their chapters.

1.4.2.5 Did You See Me? (Audience Measurement)

Audience measurement has always been an integral part of advertising, mainly because "if you cannot measure, you cannot improve." Any advertising campaign is driven by goals, and goals can only be set according to factors that are measurable. Limited measurement capabilities also limit the scope of what one can try to achieve. Pervasive computing provides powerful sensors for measuring, for example, the actual behavior of people. To see the immense opportunities this provides one only needs to briefly consider the Web. Because clicks are easily measurable, whole new business models and paradigms have emerged. Ads are often paid for on a click-through basis. Campaign success is completely transparent using tools such as Google analytics, enabling advertisers to optimize and cancel campaigns based on live data. Even the fully automated optimization of advertising campaigns is possible, using tools such as Google Website Optimizer, which can automatically run statistical tests on user behavior in different versions of campaigns and optimize the campaign accordingly.

Pervasive advertising makes it possible to apply this entire approach to the real world. User behavior, for example, whether people looked at an advertisement, can be easily measured using computer vision and face detection. Tracking when audiences interact with the ad is basically free, and even such things as eye tracking may soon be ubiquitous. This will allow advertisers to set goals that are far more detailed (e.g., 50% of bald men between 40 and 60 should have read the first sentence in this text block advertising hair implants), and optimize their campaigns in a rapid loop. If it were possible, for example, to track that many people frown and turn away after seeing a specific part of an ad, one might try to find out why and make adjustments. As a result, advertisers can determine which aspects of an advertisement the audience prefers and adapt their campaigns accordingly. Details on audience measurement for digital signage are presented in Schrammel's chapter.

1.4.2.6 Wouldn't You Like This? (Automated Persuasion)

Persuasive technology is defined as "using computers to change what we think and do" [8]. Persuasion stands in opposition to coercion, because no formal pressure is used. Of course, persuasive technology is not only limited to advertising but also has important applications in healthcare and education. It can, for example, help people quit smoking or encourage them to learn. Fogg distinguishes *macrosuasion*, where the whole intent of a product or service is to change intentions and behavior, and *microsuasion*, where persuasion is used to accomplish small steps for a product or service with a different intention. The advantage of computers over traditional media is that they are interactive, and in contrast to human persuaders they are more persistent, allow anonymity, process large amounts of data, use multiple modalities, and are scalable and pervasive. Computers can function as tools, media, or social actors. As tools, they can persuade by reducing complexity, tunneling the user into predefined action sequences, tailoring and personalization, offering suggestions at opportune moments, simplifying the self-monitoring of users, giving users a feeling of being observed, and operant conditioning. As a medium, they can persuade by putting the user into simulations. As a social actor, they can persuade through physical cues such as attractiveness, psychological cues such as similarity to the user, language (e.g. praise), social dynamics (e.g. reciprocity), or by taking social roles (e.g. authority). In order to persuade, a system must be perceived as credible, in other words, that it is trustworthy and possesses expertise.

Since advertising aims to change attitudes and behaviors among other things, it should come as no surprise that persuasive technology is ideally suited to this field. For example, an advertisement might try to persuade a customer to buy a specific product over another, or to promote a general preference for certain kinds of products. An overview of how digital signage can persuade target audiences is presented in Reitberger's chapter.

1.4.3   Challenges

After presenting the foundations of advertising and pervasive computing, and the opportunities of pervasive advertising that result from their merging, we would now like to return to the challenges touched on at the outset. It is our belief that we must solve together the challenges presented by calm and engaging advertising, privacy issues, and ethical persuasion in order to guide the development of the field in a future positive direction.

1.4.3.1   Advertising Needs to Be Calm and Engaging

That technology should be calm and require minimal attention has been a core feature of pervasive computing from its very inception. In their seminal paper on calm computing, Weiser and Brown [37] propose that, when computers saturate the surrounding environment, calm computers will be most effective. Key to this is the effortless sliding of information between the center and periphery of our field of attention. This idea has strongly influenced research for decades, and initially the underlying paradigm was that systems should remain invisible, predict the requirements and wishes of users from data obtained with various sensors, and then 'magically' perform some actions like suppressing phone calls or switching on the light. Over the years, it became clear that predicting what users want through observation alone is very difficult or perhaps even impossible. In response to her observation of these facts Rogers proposed the seemingly oppositional paradigm of engaging computing: computers should provide great experiences and engage users more in how they currently behave.

It is our belief that pervasive advertising should be both calm and engaging. Although this might seem like a contradiction, it is not. Calm advertising means that advertisements should be easy to ignore. Engaging advertising means that ads should provide engaging experiences when one is actively engaging with them. This can be achieved at the same time. A pervasive ad could appear as calm, mildly flowing water when nobody engages with it, and then convert to an engaging mini-game once somebody pays attention. Partridge's chapter provides examples of how context adaptivity can be used to create calmer ads.

1.4.3.2 Privacy Has to Be Guaranteed

Like calm computing, privacy has been an important topic for pervasive and context-aware computing from the beginning. Most systems center on the fair information principles (see chapters by Geiger and Haddadi) of notice/awareness, choice/consent, access/participation, integrity/security, and enforcement/redress. A variety of systems (like pawS) have been proposed to implement these principles in technical systems [18].

In pervasive advertising, there is a huge incentive for advertisers to collect as much user data as possible. Thus, it is crucial that user privacy also be protected. This can happen either through industry self-regulation, lawmaking, or both. The degree to which privacy is protected and guaranteed will determine whether users trust advertisers. Winning such trust requires effort and is also easily lost; guaranteeing user privacy is one of the foremost challenges facing pervasive advertising.

1.4.3.3 Persuasion Needs to Be Ethical

With regard to ethics, Fogg [8] mentions six significant ways in which persuasive technology can be abused. For example: the novelty of the technology may mask the persuasive intent; the positive reputation of computers may be exploited; computers can be proactively persistent; computers control the interactive possibilities; they can affect emotions but are not affected by emotions; and, finally, computers cannot shoulder responsibility.

It is said that intentions as well as methods and outcomes of persuasion can be ethical or unethical. Deception and coercion are always unethical, while operant conditioning and surveillance raise a red flag. Furthermore, it is unethical to persuade vulnerable groups like children. The method proposed to analyze ethics is known as stakeholder analysis, where all stakeholders are listed as well as what they have to lose. It is then evaluated which stakeholder has the most to gain or lose, and the ethics are determined by examining gains and losses in terms of values. Finally, the values and assumptions that are brought to the analysis should be acknowledged.

Persuasion is an integral part of advertising, and ethical use of persuasion is an important challenge facing pervasive advertising. With regard to advertising, it is our belief that any intention to persuade audiences against their own interests is unethical. Similarly, persuasion of vulnerable groups is unethical, as well as all methods that are deceptive, use coercion, operant conditioning, or surveillance. Again, details on persuasion are provided in Reitberger's chapter.

1.5 Conclusion

In this chapter we saw that advertising is any paid form of non-personal presentation and promotion of ideas, goods, or services by an identified sponsor. Advertising aims to inform, evoke emotions, and trigger actions. Pervasive computing describes the trend in which interconnected computational devices are interwoven with artifacts in our everyday life. Pervasive computing enables automation, interactivity, and ubiquity. When pervasive computing technologies are used for advertising purposes, we call this pervasive advertising. The greater effectiveness and efficiency of pervasive advertising over traditional advertising forms will be the key to its success. The six most important opportunities of pervasive advertising include: it shifts more power to audiences and consumers, leading to symmetric communication between them and advertisers. It makes even tiny advertising campaigns viable, leading to a long tail of many small advertisers. It provides much more engaging experiences than traditional advertising. It enables ads to adapt to the audience and the context. It enables detailed audience measurement, and finally, it enables advertisements to employ automated strategies for persuading audiences. We believe that pervasive advertising is coming, and that our greatest responsibility is to shape this development in a meaningful way. We see three important challenges: First, we should strive for calm advertising – ads that do not disturb audiences when they are not interested, while still providing engaging experiences for those who are. Second, we need to respect the privacy of audiences and build privacy-preserving architectures into the foundation of any pervasive advertising system. Third, while advertisements may try to persuade customers, the method of persuasion must always be overt, and may never employ unethical means to achieve its goals. We hope that this book is useful in bringing advertisers and pervasive computing people together and providing a foundation for the approaching era of pervasive advertising.

Acknowledgements We would like to thank Albrecht Schmidt, Bo Begole, Aaron Quigley, Antonio Krüger, and our colleagues from Deutsche Telekom Laboratories for their support. Furthermore, we are indebted to all participants of the pervasive advertising workshop series for their contributions to the field. The research that led to these results also received funding from the European Union Seventh Framework Programme (FP7/2007–2013) under grant agreement no. 244011.

References

1. AMA: American Marketing Association, URL: www.marketingpower.com (2010). Accessed 23 March 2011
2. Arduino Website: http://www.arduino.cc/. Accessed 23 Mar 2011
3. Beagleboard Website: http://beagleboard.org/. Accessed 23 Mar 2011
4. Brown, J.S.: Storytelling: Scientist's perspective. http://www.creatingthe21stcentury.org/JSB2-pace-change.html (2001). Accessed 23 Mar 2011
5. Card, S.K., Moran, T.P., Newell, A.: The Psychology of Human-Computer Interaction. Lawrence Erlbaum Associates, Hillsdale (1983)
6. Crevier, D.: AI: The Tumultuous Search for Artificial Intelligence. BasicBooks, New York (1993). ISBN 0-465-02997-3
7. Dix, A., Finlay, J., Abowd, G., Beale, R.: Human Computer Interaction, 3rd edn. Prentice Hall, Herts (2003). ISBN 0130461091
8. Fogg, B.J.: Persuasive Technology. Morgan Kaufmann, San Francisco (2002)
9. Franzen, G., Bouwman, M.: The Mental World of Brands. NTC Publications, Henley-on-Thames (2001)
10. Hewett, T.T., Baecker, R., Card, S., Carey, T., Gasen, J., Mantei, M., Perlman, G., Strong, G., Verplank, W.: ACM SIGCHI Curricula for Human-Computer Interaction (1992), http://old.sigchi.org/cdg/cdg2.html#2_1. Accessed 23 Mar 2011
11. Homburg, C., Krohmer, H.: Grundlagen des Marketingmanagements: Einführung in Strategie, Instrumente, Umsetzung und Unternehmensführung, 2nd rev. edn. Gabler, Wiesbaden (2009)
12. Howe, J.: Crowdsourcing. Why the Power of the Crowd is Driving the Future of Business. Crown Business, New York (2008)
13. Kanda, T., Glas, D.F., Shiomi, M., Ishiguro, H., Hagita, N.: Who will be the customer?: a social robot that anticipates people's behavior from their trajectories. In: Proceedings of the 10th International Conference on Ubiquitous Computing (UbiComp '08), pp. 380–389. ACM, New York (2008)
14. Kessels, A., van Loenen, E., Lashina, T.: Evaluating gaze and touch interaction and two feedback techniques on a large display in a shopping environment. In Proceedings of the 12th IFIP TC 13 International Conference on Human-Computer Interaction: Part I (INTERACT '09), Gross, T., Gulliksen, J., Paula Kotz\&\#233; Oestreicher, L., Palanque, P., Oliveira Prates, R., and Winckler, M (Eds.). Springer-Verlag, Berlin, Heidelberg,, pp. 595–607 (2009)
15. Kotler, P., Keller, L.K.: Marketing Management, 13th edn. Prentice Hall, Herts (2008)
16. Kroeber-Riel, W., Weinberg, P.: Konsumentenverhalten, 8th edn. Vahlen, Munich (2003)
17. Kuss, A., Tomczak, T.: Käuferverhalten: Eine marketingorientierte Einführung, 4th edn. Lucius & Lucius, Stuttgart (2007)
18. Langheinrich, M.: A privacy awareness system for ubiquitous computing environments. In: Proceedings of the 4th international conference on Ubiquitous Computing (UbiComp '02), Borriello, G., Holmquist, L.E. (eds.). Springer-Verlag, London, UK, pp. 237–245 (2002)
19. Lanham, R.A.: The economics of attention. In: Proceedings of the 124th Annual Meeting. Association of Research Librarians, Austin (1994)
20. Li, C., Bernoff, J.: Groundswell: Winning in a World Transformed by Social Technologies. Harvard Business Press, Boston (2008)
21. McLuhan, M.: Understanding Media: The Extensions of Man. MIT Press, New York (1964)

22. Meffert, H., Burmann, C., Kirchgeorg, M.: Marketing: Grundlagen marktorientierter Unternehmensführung. Konzepte - Instrumente - Praxisbeispiele, 10th edn. Gabler, Wiesbaden (2007)
23. Müller, J., Alt, F., Michelis, D., Schmidt, A.: Requirements and design space for interactive public displays. In: Proceedings of the International Conference on Multimedia (MM '10), pp. 1285–1294. ACM, New York (2010)
24. Nielsen, J.: Usability Engineering. Morgan Kaufmann Publishers, San Francisco (1994). ISBN 0-12-518406-9
25. Norman, D.A., Draper, S.W.: User-Centered System Design: New Perspectives on Human-Computer Interaction. Erlbaum, Hillsdale (1986)
26. Norman, D.A.: Emotional Design: Why We Love (or Hate) Everyday Things, 1st edn. Basic Books, New York (2003)
27. Pine, J., Gilmore, J.: The Experience Economy. Harvard Business School Press, Boston (1999)
28. Schmidt, A.: Implicit human-computer interaction through context. In: Personal and Ubiquitous Computer, vol. 4(2&3), pp. 191–199. Springer, London (1999)
29. Schmidt, A., Van Laerhoven, K.: How to build smart appliances? IEEE Pers. Commun. 8(4), 66–71 (2001)
30. Schmid, B.F., Lyczek, B.: Unternehmenskommunikation: Kommunikationsmanagement aus Sicht der Unternehmensführung. Gabler, Wiesbaden (2006)
31. Schmidt, A., Kern, D., Streng, S., Holleis, P.: Magic beyond the screen. IEEE. MultiMedia 15(4), 8–13 (2008)
32. Shirky, C.: Here Comes Everybody. The Power of Organizing Without Organization. Penguin, New York (2008)
33. Shneiderman, B.: Designing the User Interface, 3rd edn. Addison Wesley, Menlo Park (1998). ISBN 0201694972
34. Tapscott, D., Williams, A.D.: Wikinomics: How Mass Collaboration Changes Everything. Portfolio, New York (2008)
35. Want, R., Hopper, R., Falcao, V., Gibbons, J.: Active badge location system. ACM Trans. Inf. Syst. 10(1), 91–102 (1992)
36. Weiser, M.: The computer of the 21st century. In: Scientific American 265(3), 66–75 (1991)
37. Weiser, M., Brown, J.S.: The coming age of calm technology. In: Denning, P.J., Metcalfe, R.M. (eds.) Beyond Calculation: The Next Fifty Years of Computing. Copernicus, New York (1998)
38. Wigand, R., Picot, A., Reichwald, R.: Information, Organization and Management: Expanding Markets and Corporate Boundaries. Wiley, Chichester (2007)
39. Zaichkowsky, J.L.: Measuring the involvement construct. J. Consum. Res. 12, 341–352 (1985)

Chapter 2
Digital Out-of-Home Media: Means and Effects of Digital Media in Public Space

Ursula Stalder

Abstract Digital out-of-home media and pervasive new technologies are bringing the internet experience into public spaces and stepping up the pace with which brands and products, as well as their virtual representations, penetrate urban environments. This article explores the current phenomenon of pervasive advertising and its underlying perceptions and puts forward a typology for describing a range of applications for the emerging media infrastructure. It argues that the critical dimensions comprise the way in which pervasive advertising and creatives exploit both physical and social contexts by increasingly relying on the effects of illumination, temporality and spatiality.

2.1 Introduction

Technology mediates day-to-day experience in cities more than anywhere else, and pervasive advertising is fast becoming an integral part of such postmodern urban environments. Advertising relies on pervasive digital infrastructures and has become a salient feature in popular culture, where shopping has long since developed into a centrally important activity. The city is reinventing itself as a communication hub in which pervasive advertising generally plays a decisive role in creating an emotionally charged environment that is crucial for shaping the behavior of shoppers, tourists and inhabitants.

From a sociological perspective, these emerging media in public spaces are manifestations of two social trends: continuing digitization and convergence (first pervading and transforming the workplace, then the private sphere, and now the public space), and a societal shift away from consuming goods and service towards

U. Stalder(✉)
Lucerne University of Applied Sciences and Arts, Lucerne, Switzerland
e-mail: ursula.stalder@hslu.ch

J. Müller et al. (eds.), *Pervasive Advertising*, Human-Computer Interaction Series, DOI 10.1007/978-0-85729-352-7_2, © Springer-Verlag London Limited 2011

searching for experiences. While the first trend emphasizes technical developments, as well as the drivers, consequences and controls, the latter focuses on experience as the main marker in this shift towards what is called "experience economy".[1]

The experience society continues where the service society left off – primarily focused on customers' affective responses (and memories) rather than on tangibles and services themselves.[2] Offering experiences as a part of the product has a long tradition in the market. What is new, however, is the increasing importance being put on experience as a product per se, not to mention the growing number of services containing a targeted experience dimension within the vast number of products being offered.

This change in consumer attitude reflects in a paradigm shift in marketing, which is abandoning its emphasis on functional attributes and instead is focusing on creating holistic customer experiences.[3] Brands thus have become symbols for lifestyles in the experience economy that provide stimuli for life plans and emotional states [12, 20, 33]. Furthermore, the proliferation of pervasive media infrastructures in public spaces is only possible in the urban environment, which uses it as catalyst for creating holistic and social brand experiences for all the senses.

A distinguishing feature of the experience economy and its "public spaces"[4] is the abundance and diversity of the media that are being offered and consumed and that define the atmosphere Böhme refers to [5]. Advertising thus structures and defines public space, becoming an everyday phenomenon in itself.

Referring to the concept of "narrative machines" (*Erzählmaschine*) of Legnaro/ Birenheide [17], Guido Zurstiege distinguishes among three types of media that act

---

[1] B. Joseph Pine II and James H. Gilmore coined the term 1999 in their book "The experience economy" [24], defining experiences as a new economy that follows the provision of services, goods, and commodities. In the "experience business", customers are charged for the feeling they get; in the next stage of product evolution, "the transformation business", customers pay for the benefit they receive from spending time there.

[2] Post-materialist consumption has long been an issue, see ibid alt [9, 24, 30].

[3] Bernd Schmitt claims that experiences can be offered strategically. In his book "Experiential Marketing" [28] he states that "experiences are usually not self-generated but induced" and claims that "as a marketer, you provide stimuli that result in customer experiences: you select your 'experience providers'". Unlike conventional function-and-benefit-marketing, which, according to Schmitt, "lacks a fundamental basis and insight understanding of customers', experiential marketing is based on psychological, yet practical, theory of the individual customer and his/her social behavior." Schmitt contends that experiences – depending on their intend effects on the user – may be categorized into various "strategic experiential modules" (e.g. sense, feel, think, act, relate) that can serve as criteria in the design process so as to extend their range (pp. 61, 63).

[4] In this article, the term "public space" refers to public places that are designed for and freely accessible to the public. The starting point is the traditional concept of a place as a tangible, three-dimensional location, regardless of whether it is being administered under public law or privately by a legal entity or natural person. The reasons for using this term is to avoid specialized terms such as "Third Places" [23], "Places", respectively "Non-places" [2], "Other Spaces" as "Utopia" and "Heterotopia" [7], etc. that are highly occupied by discourses.

as drivers [35]: First there are advertising media that stimulate behaviors in visitors revolving around wish fulfillment, transformation and change stories; second there are media such as newspapers, magazines, books as well as portable music players, laptops and tablet PCs that are used in public space not only for information or entertainment purposes but also as social shields, providing relief from excessive demands and reducing on-track conversations; and third there are media that display information as well as regulations and that are specific to the place and thus help define it. These media reduce complexity by suggesting a clearly defined path through the "jungle", besides providing an organizational framework that facilitates social orientation.

Georg Franck identifies a fourth type of media that goes hand-in-hand with the "Invasion of the brands": Surveillance and security media [8]. Mass surveillance is no longer restricted to areas predisposed to promiscuity or crime, such as alleys, parking lots, or public toilets. Instead, public and private organizations frequently use mass surveillance to protect themselves against allegedly dangerous groups, such as terrorists (e.g. at airports), to maintain social control (e.g. at football games or in traffic), or to pursue individual interest (e.g. preventing theft in stores, littering). Private-sector mass surveillance often uses copyright laws and "user agreements" to obtain (typically uninformed) 'consent' to monitor consumers who are within their spaces.

By doing so, Franck emphasizes the less visible aspect that is transforming public space: increasingly dense data space where signals are permanently exchanged [8]. Here, surveillance media use the same digital infrastructure as pervasive advertising media: Information, communication and identification technologies are seamlessly integrated and increasingly available. The latest cameras, which are virtually invisible on account of their small size, allow for real-time image analysis by using facial recognition technology that compares images and behaviors against database records.

This twofold "privatization of public space" by brand images and control mechanisms as found in the private sector has been widely criticized for violating privacy rights, laws, and political and social freedoms because it interferes with the organic and heterogeneous nature of urban life. It reduces cities to places of consumption, transforming them into "non-places" [2] that degenerate into gigantic vending machines [35].

Within marketing research, the scientific analysis of these pervasive digital media infrastructure in public space has only just begun. So far, media studies have made only passing, if any, reference to urban screen media, focusing on media saturation in general and on media abundance in the context of contemporary life in cities.[5] Or, as regards audience measurement, they mainly focus on the realm of traditional "outdoor advertising" or the home (TV, DVD, games, internet for entertainment, etc.) as seen from a consumer perspective.

---

[5] For a critical overview see [14].

One way out of these dead-end approaches is to study the pervasive media infrastructure from the bottom up by examining its concrete forms, their essential characteristics, and gauging their potential for the advertising and brand management industry.

2.2   Media Forms

In the perception of the marketing industry, the predominant business case for digital media infrastructure in public space is mostly restricted to advertising and how the new distribution channels use advertising (content, messages). By focusing less on a given (traditional) business model and more on the common characteristics of the media itself, a field of research opens up that is defined by and centered around a new technology that has long since evolved from a tool into a medium.

In the realm of the public sphere, this digital medium manifests itself in many forms that in essence comprise systems for posting information (news and transport information overlays) on screens, exchanging information (kiosk systems), advertising (billboards), enhancing architectural design (media façades). Furthermore, it serves as a venue for public art (often referred to as "urban screens") in various forms (textual information, moving or still images, light) and on a variable scale. Although they vary strongly as regards their goals, form or scale, they all use digital network technology, which differentiates them from other media in urban environments.

According to Sauter, the digital medium[6] has developed into four physical formats: screen applications, interactive objects and installations, interactive spaces, and interactive architecture, each engaging the user in a different form of interaction [25]. All four types of digital media can be found in public space employed for specific marketing strategies (Fig. 2.1).

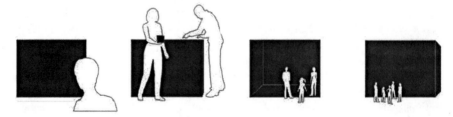

Fig. 2.1   The four physical formats of the digital medium: screen applications, digital objects and installations, media spaces, and media architecture [25]

---

[6] Joachim Sauter describes the digital medium as essentially immaterial, synthetic and virtual and having four distinct qualities: interactivity, multimedia, connectivity, and generativity, through which the content, narrative and form can be represented, expressed and communicated. These four media options define the medium and distinguish it from traditional forms such as print, film, television, each with its own media characteristics, and also from classical art forms such as painting, sculpture, performance, video art [25].

In screen applications, users engage in one-on-one dialogue with a screen (the "text") that is mediated digitally and geared to the user's requirements. When designed with an interface, two-way interactions become possible as a way of processing the input by a user and the subsequent output by the system. These types of digital media are tied to all forms of urban environments, outdoor or indoor, stationary or mobile, small scale (info or ad screen), medium scale (e-boards, public screens), or large scale (media facade), displaying high or low resolution images on a sliding scale.

Digital objects and installations are mostly designed for specific content (e.g. an interactive table). They can host a dialogue between the text (information, message) and one or several parties. In the latter case, the screen functions as interface, e.g. as a touch screen. Well-designed installations allow passive members to observe others in their interaction and thus join in the process of mediation or experience (substitute interaction). In a marketing context, media objects are increasingly used at trade fairs (e.g. *CeBit* in Hannover, the *Autosalon* in Geneva), exhibitions (e.g. *Mercedes Benz* brand museum), or in flagship stores (e.g. *Prada Epicenters*) – enhancing live touchpoints by playfully engaging the customer and offering new brand experiences and service designs.

Media spaces – where digital media decisively impact the space and visitor behavior (e.g. interactive media floors and walls), allowing for immersion and reactive changes – determine visitors' behavior, which in turn determines the "behavior" of the space, generally comprising a multi-user environment designed for a shared experience. The most common aim is to initiate interaction between visitors and the interactive content experience and to facilitate interaction among visitors.

The fourth type, *media architecture* (e.g. a façade enhanced by light or media technology, iconic brand architecture), enhances urban environments by adding a narrative layer. If well done, it increases the value of the physical and social space by adding uniqueness, meaning and authenticity, thus enhancing the status of those who experience it. In marketing strategies, highly medialized architecture helps to build the reputation of locations (cities, neighborhoods) and brands. An excellent example for this is the SPOTS facade of the *Park Kolonnaden* building (*Postdamer Platz*, Berlin) that promoted the real estate company (and their rentals) as well as the value of the site and neighborhood.

2.3   Media Types

Out-of-home media involve at least four different interest groups: The property owner (private or public) looking to optimize the profitability of the property and to maximize rental income from the space; the outdoor media company (media seller) providing the surface for displaying the ads and renting out the space (or time) to clients; the client (media buyer) as tenant/buyer of the available space/time to reach

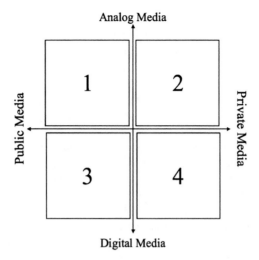

Fig. 2.2 Research framework I: The four media types and the segments of Pervasive Advertising: (*1*) Analog/Public: traditional out-of-home-media e.g. billboards, mega posters or new forms of ambient media; (*2*) Analog/Private: traditional in-store/in-house media, incl. all types of promotional material, interior designs etc.; (*3*) Digital/Public: Adscreens and e-boards of all sizes, indoor and outdoor; and (*4*) Digital/Private: Digital signage media at-store/in-store, as well as media architecture

the audience; and the public administration safeguarding the public interest by means of regulations and licenses/permits.[7]

The potential of the digital medium to develop into different formats for engaging the user in various forms of interaction – cognitive text-user relations, playful interactions, or immersive experiences – can be seen as a prerequisite for deploying specific media in the public sphere (Fig. 2.2).

2.3.1 Public Mass Media

Public or mass media refers to a type of media specifically designed to reach a large audience. The marketing industry uses it for placing advertising by buying media space or time in order to reach relevant audiences.

Commercials displaying moving images in public spaces appeared originally as "a problem-solving tool for the shortcomings of home spectatorship and its possibility

---

[7] Different jurisdictions regulate outdoor advertising to varying degrees and with different reference models, such as traffic safety systems, cityscapes, etc. In general, there is a tendency to prohibit billboards altogether or to prevent new ones from being constructed (e.g., in Zurich 2009), or to ban them within the city (e.g., in Sao Paolo 2007).

to "zap" messages with remote controls or power switches" [19]. Ambient television has given advertisers a reason to imagine the final "captivity" of the audience due to a "lack of competitive separation" [19] in zones without remote controls.

Out-of-home advertising, therefore, addresses consumers who are neither at home nor at work, but in a public or semi-public space or in transit (on the go), while waiting (in-between) in line at the cashier or a medical office, for example, or who are at a specific commercial location, such as in a retail outlet.

2.3.1.1   Adscreens

Adscreens are increasingly common in a range of public spaces, especially in typical urban nodes (e.g. train stations, airports, in public transportation, post offices) and places of entertainment (e.g. bars, restaurants, fitness or music clubs, etc.), and have been accepted by both media buyers and users (Fig. 2.3).

For media buyers, adscreens are complementary media because they are close to buying decision points (the "recency" argument[8]) and thus can leverage situations harboring strong latent viewer attention, e.g. queues (the "captive audiences" argument) as well as reinforce messages from other media (the "crossmedia" argument). Users, on the other hand, have become familiar with traditional ways of experiencing advertising as part of their daily out-of-home experience and are adept at either filtering it out or enjoying its entertainment value (Fig. 2.4).

Adscreens are (other than e-boards) currently set up mostly along traditional lines: Owned by established outdoor advertisers and run by major networks aimed at reaching large audiences that are mostly closed networks, etc. Business models, campaign targeting options and impact measurements are therefore similar to non-digital out-of-home media. It doesn't come as a surprise that new creatives and strategies derived from the digital bases or media characteristics are being used only sparingly. Despite the constraints they face in this market due to the limitations of particular advertising models[9] [11] and the deployment of creative concepts for presenting content in targeted way to specific audiences, ad-screens have successfully established themselves in the modern media landscape.

---

[8]Recency, a "school" of advertising planning, believes that relevance, not repetition, is what makes an ad message effective and that its relevance gains proportionally with the consumer's readiness to buy, i.e. that the prospective buyer's proximity to the actual buying decision or point of sale is crucial. Impact-driven, continuous and creative advertising generally fails to capture consumers' attention because they can screen out the messages that are of no interest. Advertising thus becomes effective only when consumers are ready to buy.

[9] According to José and Soares, there are two emerging trends that are likely to cause a significant development in ad models: First, the move towards interactive displays that can respond to the surrounding spatial environment. Second, the emergence of pervasive display networks in which advertising models can leverage the power of open networks [11].

Fig. 2.3 Adscreens – networked digital billboards – are operated similar to traditional out-of-home media: Selling media time to third-parties by offering large networks for reaching large audiences (**a**) New ePanels, 82″ full HD screens, are replacing the traditional Rolling Stars in major railway stations (scheduled for June 2011) (Photo: © APG/e-Advertising, Zürich); (**b**) A network of adscreens at 77 Tamoil gas stations operated by IP Multimedia (Photo: © IP Multimedia (Schweiz) AG, Zürich)

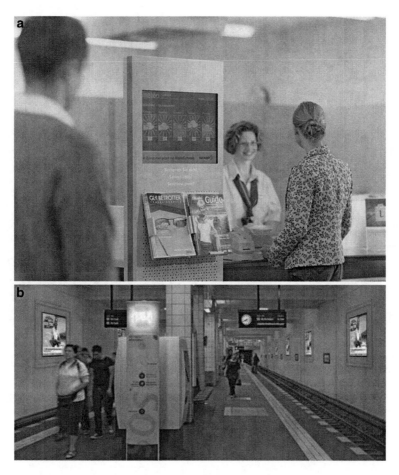

Fig. 2.4 Adscreens potentially replace older (analog) media infrastructures as well as develop new locations and formats for reaching the audience (**a**) Swiss Post's CanalPoste, an advertising network in 236 post offices, offering not only video ads but a full range of crossmedia packages including flyer and staff presentations (Photo: © Die Schweizerische Post, Bern); (**b**) The Digitaler U-Bahnhof Berlin-Friedrichstrasse, the first underground station featuring only digital out-of-home Media (Photo: © Wall AG, Berlin)

2.3.1.2   E-Boards

E-boards are typically much larger and are therefore better integrated into the architectural environment, and they are designed to optimize the size and position available for generating awareness and attention by their audience. While the cost of installing and maintaining them is relatively high, the number of screens that are linked to a network is relatively small. Revenue objectives are nevertheless met by

Fig. 2.5 E-boards – large-scale screens at high-impact sites: Due to their size, e-boards are much better integrated into a particular area than adscreens; the program is also especially developed for a specific environment (**a**) The 65 m² e-board at Zurich Main Station (Photo: © Ursula Stalder, Zürich); (**b**) Big screen at the M&M's WORLD flagship store in New York showing exclusive animation (Photo: © Ursula Stalder, Zürich); (**c**) Interactive mural at New York City's 14th street promoting the launch of Adobe CS3 in 2007 (Photo: © Eric__I_E via flickr.com); (**d**) Forever21's big screen displaying an augmented reality spot during the opening of the new flagship store in 2010 (Photo: © Fastcompany, NYC)

installing such e-boards at high-impact locations with extremely large audiences, and they are particularly suitable for campaigns targeted at the general public and offering a competitive CPT[10] (Fig. 2.5).

Because of their size, e-boards strongly influence the atmosphere of the space where they are installed (and, therefore, are more similar to the newer group of out-of-home-advertising called "Ambient media"). As a consequence of increased visibility, project strategies for getting new e-boards approved invariably lead to mixed programs displaying a range of cultural notes, news headlines, and commercials in an attempt to harmonize interests with financial resources.

---

[10] Cost per thousand (CPT) is a commonly used measurement in advertising. It is used in marketing as a benchmark to calculate the relative cost of an advertising campaign or an ad message in a given medium. Rather than an absolute cost, CPT (or CPM *cost per mille*) estimates the cost per 1,000 views of the ad.

2.3.2 Private Corporate Media

Private or corporate media is a term referring to a system of media production, distribution, ownership, and funding that is dominated by corporations and therefore geared to support companies' strategic goals of maximizing profits rather than serving the public interest (as in the case of public media). These media obviously are based on revenue models that differ from those of public media: third-party commercials are rarely found for competitive reasons, and the revenue model is often linked to long-term brand strategies (image, loyalty) or agreements with business partners (e.g., contribution to marketing costs).

Corporate out-of-home media are traditionally found near stores (e.g., in company-owned parking lots, garages, escalators), in stores (at the entrance, near shelves, at the cashier etc.) and, in a broader sense, include the store itself (interior design, architecture, service design) as well as other touch points (e.g., exhibitions, brand museums, brand lands).

2.3.2.1 Digital Signage

The term digital signage describes a range of digital communication and information media in the retail environment that takes advantage of the digitalization trend that can be observed throughout the retail value chain. These media range from "front-end" promotion, ambient and convenience services, all the way to shopping assistance or services for customers and management help for staff. The reference model here is that of "recency", empirically supported by studies showing that about 70% of purchase decisions are spontaneous while the person is at the shelf [10] (Fig. 2.6).

The increasing amount of information on products and customer behavior enable retailers to offer a more personalized shopping experience, while personalized advertisement and tailored suggestions might potentially benefit both shoppers and retailers. Well-placed and selected advertisement can help to raise satisfaction among retail buyers and increase opportunistic shopping, and thus total revenue, at the same time. The Prada customer card, for example, gives "Epicenter" staff direct access to the stored profiles incl. buying habits of the holder, allowing for a more customized type of service. This might even lead to personalized products that are fully adjusted to the specific needs of each customer [31] (Fig. 2.7).

RFID (radio frequency identification) is seen as a prerequisite system. Transponders can be attached to pallets, clothing shipments or cartons, making it possible to address all items. In the future, RFID is expected to be deployed not only "behind the scene" to optimize logistics and warehouse management, but also at the customer interface where items on the sales floor are tagged with RFID transponders. Such systems are already being tested in a number of pilot projects. In the men's department at *Galeria Kaufhof* in Essen, Germany, for example, readers are installed in dressing rooms and on mirrors to identify the items customers choose

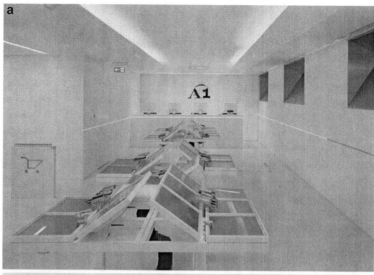

Fig. 2.6 Digital signage – digital retail media, stationary or mobile: The common goal of is to deliver information and services either to customers or to staff (**a**) Telekom Austria "a1 lounge", Vienna (Photo: Rupert Steiner (www.rupertsteiner.com), © mobilkom austria AG & Co KG, Vienna); (**b**) Intel® Intelligent Digital Signage Proof-of-Concept, showcases how digital signage technology can enhance the retail customer experience (Photo: © Intel Corp., Santa Barbara/CA)

and to display the available sizes, colors, and other combinations. The items are then found on smart shelves that send out warnings when inventories run low or displayed on special terminals with details about the products.

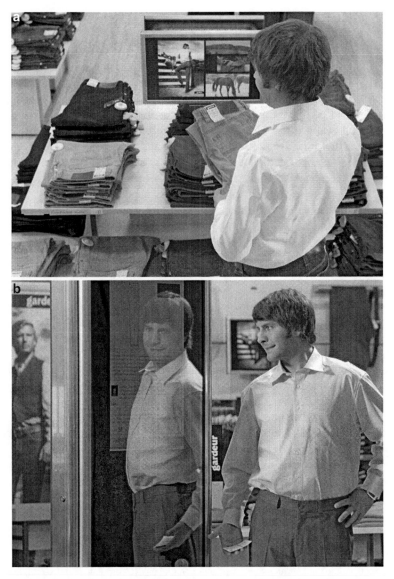

Fig. 2.7 Digital signage when combined with RFID has the potential to create an intelligent environment allowing new service designs on sales floors (**a**) Smart tables and (**b**) Smart mirrors at Galeria Kaufhof in Essen (2007–2008) uses RFID to identify the pieces of clothing customers are trying on and display useful information such as prices, materials and care instructions. On top of that, they also suggest accessories and possible combinations and show which pants go with which shirt (Photos: © Metro AG, Düsseldorf)

2.3.2.2 Brand Architecture

Architecture has long been used to build brands as part of corporate identity programs in multinational corporations, serving as a visual symbol to express a company's culture and personality.[11] While commercials shown on adscreens, e-boards or promotional digital screens have only a short-term effect, brand architecture aims to establish a more lasting impression. Although commercials may trigger an adrenalin rush by means of media-enhanced narratives (plot, storytelling), architecture establishes a sense of individuality and being at ease. According to Barbara Klingmann, architecture has by its very nature "much more long-lasting effects than the ephemeral products of the media because it can manifest ideas about who we are into permanent and tangible forms that endure over time" [13].[12] There are again different forms of mediated architecture employed to establish a brand image in the public's opinion.

2.3.2.3 Media Facades

Media facades – media embedded in architectural facades – comprise components of building envelopes that are animated using digital technology. Krajina points out that this development marks the ultimate separation of a building's two essential purposes: providing shelter and serving as a symbol [14] (Fig. 2.8).

For Klingmann, media facades mark the transition from an "old school" corporate architecture based on the concept of visibility and authority to express power, wealth and financial growth (e.g. BMW's Zylinderhaus in Munich) toward a new concept that is based on interaction and dialogue [13]. The light and media facades of the T-Mobile Headquarter (Bonn), the BIX facade at Kunsthaus Graz or the Park Kolonnaden buildings (Potsdamer Platz, Berlin) are examples of building facades that reflect both the brand's traditional value and the innovation, providing a public interface for interaction with the community (public sphere) and consumers (Fig. 2.9).

---

[11] Corporate architecture, as an integral part of a comprehensive corporate identity program, conveys a firm's core ideas and belief systems by simultaneously providing the symbols, emotional experience, and organizational structure that helps strengthen the perceived corporate values. Unlike conventional architecture, brand environments are not based on an existing physical context but on a holistic corporate identity program designed to represent and support a firm's values and philosophy [6].

[12] Klingmann also observes: "While most architects agree that architecture should create relevant experiences, there is still a lingering confusion about how architecture might compete with, relate to, or distance itself from the noisiness of mediated effects. As digital communication remakes the traditional rhythms of daily life, which is increasingly crammed with sophisticated electronics, many people believe strongly that everything should be action, motion, excitement, and saturation, while countless consumers want nothing more than a seductive oasis." ([13], p. 51)

Fig. 2.8 Media facades – light and media technology embedded in architectural facades – create an interface between the architectural and urban space on one side, the digital and narrative space on the other side (**a**) T-Mobile Headquarters, Bonn, the first permanent media facades worldwide; (**b**) Transparent panel structure with LEDs for Helmut Jahn's concept of a new convention center in Zurich (Photo & rendering: © ag4 mediatecture company, Köln)

Until recently, media facades displayed mainly temporary installations, for cost reasons [25]. In the meantime, the feasibility and sustainability of the technology determines both the awareness and willingness among builders, architects and lighting designers, engineers and media people – including authorities issuing licenses.

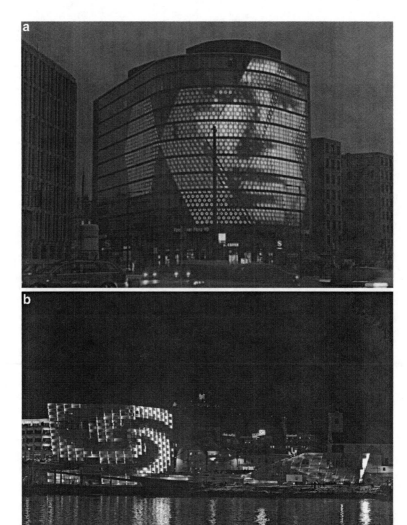

Fig. 2.9 Media facades have substantial influence on both – the visual and the social experience of urban space (**a**) The SPOTS light and media facade at HVB's Park Kolonnaden building, Berlin, showing a curated art program for a period of 18 months (Photo: © Bernd Hiepe, Berlin); (**b**) the Ars Electronica Center AEC media façade, an interactive application with approximately 4,400 individually addressable and adjustable channels, generates a homogeneous interaction with its surroundings, at the same time becoming a distinctive landmark (Photo: Stadt Linz, © Ars Electronica Center, Linz)

Fig. 2.10 Brand Scenographies – three-dimensional multisensual brand presentations: These spatial brand touchpoints aim at stimulating different senses and instincts in order to deepen the experience of a brand (**a**) The Prada Epicenter store in SoHo, New York (Photo: OMA/AMO, © Prada); (**b**) The Mercedes-Benz Gallery, opening 2009 at Berlin's Unter den Linden (Photo: © Ursula Stalder, Zürich)

2.3.2.4   Brand Scenographies and Flagship Stores

Retail architecture increasingly relies on established values and associations, be it the name of a famous architect (Frank Gehry, Herzog & deMeuron), city (Barcelona, New York), or neighborhood (Fifth Avenue or the Meatpacking District in New York City). Nike's temporary "House of Innovations" in Beijing during the Olympic Games or the Chanel Mobile Art Pavilion (designed by Zaha Hadid) exemplifies the more recent trends of using events to build short-term brand presence (Fig. 2.10).

Fig. 2.11 Brand Scenographies are building spaces and stages to tell their stories inviting the consumer to a playful interaction with the brand universe (**a**) Nikes House of Innovations, in the 798 Art Zone in Beijing, telling the most important stories behind some of the most successful Nike products, innovations and technologies during the Olympic games 2008 (Photo: © Inquiringmind Magazine, Toronto); (**b**) Chanel's mobile container for contemporary art by Zaha Hadid, gave the quilted bag, icon of Chanel's heritage, its own means of expression by confronting it with contemporary creation (Photo: © Core77, Inc.)

Flagship stores, brand museums and exhibitions use media and architecture, as well as scenography, in a similar way to build a dialogue with an audience – both externally and internally. In this respect, the store becomes a place of communication, media production, and symbols – including itself – and of intermediality in general [10] (Fig. 2.11).

Brand scenographies become "catalysts" [13] for perceptual values and transformative experiences. The Prada Epicenter stores (New York City, Los Angeles, Tokyo) feature not only sophisticated architectural design for branded fashion goods but an entire program aimed at exploring ways to reinvent the Prada retail experience. Architect Rem Koolhaas argues that "shopping is indeed the last remaining form of public activity", one that inverts the act of consumption, turning the store into a social space[13]: "While presenting a unique brand experience for Prada, the store is first and foremost designed as a social gathering place in which customers can simply enjoy spending time".

2.3.2.5 Brand Lands

Brands and architecture have developed a close relationship over the last decade. Architecture and distinct urban environments are increasingly being integrated into a larger marketing strategy, and the uniqueness of a physical environment (geographical territory) is used to underscore the uniqueness of a brand identity. At the same time, urban planning and architecture borrow increasingly from branding, with the Olympic Games 2008 or the FIFA World Cup 2006 being just two examples. Space/spatiality has become a further marketing asset (Fig. 2.12).

Brand lands are mixed-use centers designed to provide multi-functional customer experiences. They are often close to headquarters and production plants that are closed to the public. Brands lands like BMW Welt in Munich, the Mercedes area around Werk Untertürkheim in Stuttgart Bad-Canstatt or Swarovski's Kristallwelten in Wattens combine a range of facilities and thus anchor the brand in the place.

The physical (natural and man-made) "brandscape" [13] is the result of an artificial spatial manifestation of brand identities and an equally artificial creation of physical space. Marketing will be incorporated into the architectural design process, increasing the tangibility of firms' values by offering places in which to consume experiences. Visual choreography and architecture are thus designed to facilitate experiences in a social context, replacing what would otherwise be a purely commercial environment [13]. In the context of current urban spatial development, brands provide a physical context that re-establishes a connection to a particular territory (Fig. 2.13).

These iconic buildings[14] (signature architecture) are primarily designed to represent values, create moods and provide contrasts. A proven strategy involves

---

[13] Anna Klingmann notes: This blur of highbrow or lowbrow in architecture is echoed in Koolhaas' 'Harvard Design School Guide to Shopping', an 800-page tome on mainstream consumerism. It mainly purports that shopping has become the 'defining activity of public life'. According to one of its contributors, "not only is shopping melting into everything, but everything is melting into shopping" (p. 129). This trend also includes the growing number of signature architects who increasingly use their expertise to blur the distinction between consumerism and elite culture in the form of "shopping architecture." ([13], p. 125).

[14] On the relationship between architecture and branding see ibid alt. [1].

Fig. 2.12 Brand lands – brand communication by means of architecture and territory – generate a distinct experience and lends appropriate dimensions through the uniqueness of the territory, iconic architecture and symbols derived from the brand narratives (**a**) (**b**): The Autostadt, a mixed-use center next to the Volkswagen factory in Wolfsburg, features a museum, an amusement park, seven brand pavilions as well as a customer center, which attracts some two million visitors each year (Photos: © HENN Architekten, München)

Fig. 2.13 Brand lands are the nucleus around which power, cultural values and a certain way of thinking have found expression. They are narrative, designed through consistent adherence to a single theme, anchoring the brand in the real world (**a**) the Mercedes Benz Museum in Stuttgart (Photo: Brigida Gonzales, © Daimler AG, Stuttgart); (**b**) the water-spouting Giant that magically lures visitors into its interior, where 12 Chambers of Wonder ignite beacons of imagination Swarovski Cristal worlds in Wattens, Austria (Photo: Elfie Semotan, © Swarovski AG, Triesen)

co-branding, whereby a corporate brand (e.g. A1, Prada, Guggenheim) is associated with a famous architect (e.g., EOOS, Herzog & deMeuron, Gehry). Architecture is used specifically as a symbol of cultural prestige [34] that relies on technology at all levels, with signs and symbols creating a distinct experience through the use of spatial effects whereby artificial territory provides a spatial (material and social) brand experience.

2.4 Media Characteristics

The nature of new media becomes apparent when staging, rather than hiding, its new properties and at the same time anchoring them in the findings of basic scientific research (social and physical space; pervasive computing [32]; visual communication [15, 21]). This article puts forward a three-vector model for investigating the communicative potential of this digital medium:

1. Screen as light-emitting (output) medium (light emission/illumination);
2. Moving images as the dominant form of communication (movement/temporality);
3. Situatedness of communication/interaction in the social and physical space (spatiality) (Fig. 2.14).

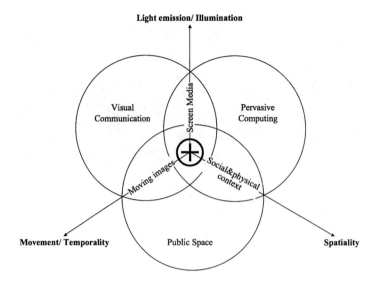

Fig. 2.14 Research framework II: Key vectors suggested for a study of Pervasive Advertising

2.4.1 Screen as Light-Emitting (Output) Medium: Illumination

A common characteristic of all digital out-of-home media is the screen, which serves as the presentation medium.[15] The most desirable brightness of the screen depends on a number of variables, such as the ambient light level and the luminosity of the image source. But in contrast to traditional outdoor media such as billboards, screens actively emit light by means of backlight technology.

Newer display technologies have high luminosity and good contrasts, even under changing or dim conditions. As light and movement (of the images) act as a stimulus enhancement, digital media per se have better chances of being perceived.[16]

---

[15] A digital screen is a data processing and data output device for presenting visual information (pictures or signs), unlike in the case of a projection screen. Flat or curved screens may be deployed depending on the technology used to project the image and the desired geometrical accuracy of the image production, flat screens being the more common of the two. This article disregards projected images mainly because light emitted from screens used as an output device and permanently integrated into urban space is an essential starting point that includes projections only in exceptional cases on account of their mainly temporal nature. Of course this is a subjective point of view that may be challenged.

[16] For the principles of activation theory, see [26]. In cognitive psychology, perception is understood as a process of information processing, in which specific environmental and physical stimuli are selected from a range of other stimuli before they are decoded and combined with prior knowledge. Key features of perception are subjectivity, activity and selectivity. A prerequisite for conscious perception is the willingness to absorb and process information. The capacity to absorb depends on the degree of activation, the "inner alertness"; a temporary increase of activation is referred to as attention [15].

Furthermore, the reflected light itself becomes a form of communication, giving the space a specific aura [29]. Or as Walter Benjamin puts it: "What, at the end, makes advertising so superior to criticism? Not what the moving red neon says – but the fiery pool reflecting it in the asphalt." [3]

2.4.2 Moving Images as the Dominant Form of Communication: Temporality

For Lev Manovich, any screen constitutes a window onto a representation within our normal space, and a digital screen "represents an interactive type, a subtype of the real-time type, which is a subtype of the dynamic type, which is a subtype of the classical type". This "screen genealogy" rests on two ideas: "First, the idea of temporality, whereby the classical screen displays a static, permanent image; the dynamic screen displays a moving image of the past, and finally the real-time screen portrays the present. Second, the relationship between the space of the viewer and that of the representation." [18]

While visual communication research[17] discusses the means and effects of images (as opposed to texts) and film theory discusses the basic code of moving images, Manovich examines the different forms of "new temporality" as "narrative engines" as found in digital media.

However, the effect of moving images – movement in itself as well as visual texts as communication modes – in the context of the public (social, man-made) space creates and simultaneously defines an emotionally charged environment [5].

Located in the public space, the temporality of such movement becomes the boundary between the physical and digital worlds, transforming the *genius loci* beyond what appeals to individual viewers and affecting the experience of everyone who happens to be in the space simultaneously.

The added value for communication lies in this ability to create uniqueness in a fleeting moment.

2.4.3 Situatedness in the Social and Physical Space: Spatiality

When applied to media, experience marketing implies that creating messages people will remember in their daily routines means focusing on the transformative effect a space can have and on the emotions it can trigger through its use, whereby

---

[17] For a summary of visual communication research, see ibid alt. [21]. The findings indicate that images are more easily detected and retained than words, like "quick shots to the brain" [15]. At the same time they are also suitable for public use in various communication modes and usually referred to as (1) autoactive, (2) reactive, (3) interactive, and (4) participatory displays [13, 25, 27].

the atmosphere and other environmental factors, such as light, noise, number of people, etc. and "the surrounding assemblages of signification and stimuli" [14] become prerequisite for success. In terms of "contexts", specialists increasingly refer to an awareness of the complexity of "culture, climate, background, audience and built pattern" on the ground [29]. As Offenhuber purports, design strategies subsume both the planned imagery (that people locally are assumed to be "familiar" with) and the screen as a material object, which may "imitate" other physical objects in close surrounding, such as a bus schedule, or a concrete façade [22].

2.5 Conclusions

From a marketing and branding perspective, these pervasive digital media infra-structures offer much potential to reach, interact and engage audiences in a dialogue and offer opportunities for reaching audiences in new places and situations by means of creative concepts. By using new technology and broadband data networks, per-vasive media offer the means to blend iconic brands, streamlined products, and corporate identity into a single experience. Nike has become a prototypical example of iconic quality marked by uniqueness, the result of standardized mechanisms.

From the perspective of integrated marketing communications, three important trends can be observed that drive this development:

- The trend towards image – moving image – becoming the dominant narrative form of the brand story, cf. "iconic turn" [4];
- The trend towards spatialization of brands against the background of changing consumer behavior, cf. "experience society" [24];
- The trend of shifting away from the reach of a corporate communications orien-tation (mass) toward an involvement orientation (dialogue, encounter communication).

The digital medium, as well as the different media forms, are neutral in essence and can be used to meet strategic goals, and they constitute parts of the message being conveyed. Their characteristics influence the narrative, the means and effects of the message being conveyed – but they are not the story itself. This becomes all the more apparent when examining the immense variety of forms and uses of perva-sive media infrastructure in public space by marketing and brand managers. The fact that pervasive advertising blends with other research fields, thus blurring the distinction to surrounding disciplines, can be seen as a "marker" in the medializa-tion process as put forward by Friedrich Krotz [16].

The spatial dimension of out-of-home media must aim to provide a broader cul-tural context that seizes opportunities to create new organizational structures and social relationships instead of merely devising representational images for clients. In pervasive media, exploiting the potential for enhancing a brand means moving away from the established forms of media communication, and the most cogent arguments put forward by media theorists so far purport that media can be used to transcend spatial and temporal boundaries (Helmmann and [35]).

Pervasive advertising can potentially establish relational frameworks that are both specific and open, that encourage social interaction and engagement, and that are most likely to be defined by new ways of conveying messages: with images (symbolic dimension), narratives (story dimension), places (ecologic and experiential dimension), and communities (social, economic, and political dimension). This will most likely continue to hold true regardless of any specific application.

References

1. Angelil, M.: Die Macht des Brandings. Architektur ge-brand-markt. Architese – Zeitschrift und Zeitschriftenreihe für Architektur **6**, 8–15 (2003)
2. Augé, M.: Non-places: Introduction to an Anthropology of Supermodernity. Verso, London/New York (1995)
3. Benjamin, W.: One way street: this space for rent. In: Jennings, M.W., Eiland, H., Smith, G. (eds.) Walter Benjamin: Selected Writings. Belknap, Cambridge (2003)
4. Boehm, G.: Die Wiederkehr der Bilder. In: Boehm, G. (ed.) Die Wiederkehr der Bilder, pp. 11–38. Fink, München (1994)
5. Böhme, G.: Architektur und Atmosphäre. Wilhelm Fink, München (2006)
6. Calero, C., Ruiz, J., Piattini, M.: Classifying web metrics using the web quality model. Online Info. Rev. **29**(3), 227–248 (2005)
7. Foucault, M.: Of Other Spaces (1967): Heterotopias (1984)
8. Franck, G.: Werben und Überwachen: Zur Transformation des städtischen Raums. In: Hempel, L., Metelmann, J. (eds.) Bild – Raum – Kontrolle: Videoüberwachung als Zeichen des gesellschaftlichen Wandels, pp. 141–155. Suhrkamp, Frankfurt a.M. (2005)
9. Hirschmann, E.C., Hollbrook, M.B.: Hedonic consumption: emerging concepts, methods and propositions. J. Mark. **46**, 92–101 (1982)
10. Jacke, C.: Locating intermediality: socialization by communication and consumption in the popular-cultural third places of the music club and football stadium. Cult. Unbound J. Curr. Cult. Res. **1**, 331–348 (2009)
11. José, R., Soares, A.: Towards new advertising models for situated displays. In: Proceedings of the 3 rd Workshop on Pervasive Advertising, Helsinki, Finland (2010)
12. Kilian, K.: Vom Erlebnismarketing zum Markenerlebnis: Wie und warum Erlebnisse und Marken einander bereichern. In: Herbrand, N.O. (ed.) Schauplätze dreidimensionaler Markeninszenierung: Innovative Strategien und Erfolgsmodelle erlebnisorientierter Begegnungskommunikation, pp. 29–68. Edition neues Fachwissen, Stuttgart (2008)
13. Klingmann, A.: Brandscapes: Architecture in the Experience Economy. MIT Press, Cambridge/London (2007)
14. Krajina, Z.: Exploring urban screens. Cul. Unbound J. Curr. Cult. Res. **1**, 401–430 (2009)
15. Kroeber-Riel, W.: Bildkommunikation. Imagerystrategien für die Werbung. Vahlen, München (1996)
16. Krotz, F.: Mediatisierung: Fallstudien zum Wandel von Kommunikation. VS Verlag für Sozialwissenschaften, Wiesbaden (2007)
17. Legnaro, A., Birenheide, A.: Stätten der späten Moderne – Reiseführer durch Bahnhöfe, 'shopping malls', Disneyland Paris. VS Verlag für Sozialwissenschaften, Wiesbaden (2005)
18. Manovich, L.: The Language of New Media. MIT Press, Cambridge (2001)
19. McCarthy, A.: Ambient Television: Visual Culture and Public Space. Duke University Press, Durham (2001)
20. Mikunda, C.: Marketing spüren – willkommen am Dritten Ort, 2nd edn. Redline, Frankfurt, Wien (2007)
21. Müller, M.G.: What is visual communication? Past and future of an emerging field of communication research. Stud. Commun. Res. J. Swiss Assoc. Commun. Media Res. **2**, 7–34 (2007)

22. Offenhuber, D.: The Invisible Display – Design Strategies for Ambient Media in the Urban Context (2008)
23. Oldenburg, R.: The Great Good Places: Cafés, Coffee Shops, Bookstores, Bars, Hair Salons, and Other Hangouts at the Heart of the Community, 3rd edn. Da Capo Press, New York (1999)
24. Pine, J.B., Gilmore, J.H.: The Experience Economy. Harvard Business School Press, Boston (1999)
25. Sauter, J.: Das vierte Format: Die Fassade als mediale Haut der Architektur (2004)
26. Schachter, S.S.: Cognitive, social and physiological determinants of emotional state. Psychol. Rev. **68**, 379–399 (1962)
27. Schmidt, G.: Medienfassade. Arch + – Zeitschrift für Architektur und Städtebau: Schwellenatlas Von Abfallzerkleinerer bis Zeitmaschine (191/192), p. 77 (2009)
28. Schmitt, B.: Experiential Marketing. Free Press, New York (1999)
29. Schoch, O.: Challenges of Media Integrated Architecture, Categorize the Illusory Real Architecture, 26–29 Sept (2007)
30. Schulze, G.: Die Erlebnisgesellschaft. Kultursoziologie der Gegenwart. Campus, Frankfurt a.M (1992)
31. Spassova, L., Kahl, G., Krüger, A.: User-adaptive Advertisement in Retail Environments. In: Proceedings of the 3rd Workshop on Pervasive Advertising and Shopping, Helsinki, Finland (2010)
32. Weiser, M.: The computer for the 21st century. Sci. Am. **265**(3), 66–75 (1991)
33. Wöhler, K.-H.: Erlebnisgesellschaft – Wertewandel, Konsumverhalten und -kultur. In: Herbrand, N.O. (ed.) Schauplätze dreidimensionaler Markeninszenierung: Innovative Strategien und Erfolgsmodelle erlebnisorientierter Begegnungskommunikation, pp. 3–12. Edition neues Fachwissen, Stuttgart (2008)
34. Zintzmeyer, J., Binder, R.: The power of symbols: brand leadership through visual design. Von der Kraft der Symbole. Markenführung durch visuelle Gestaltung. In: Brauer G. (ed.) Architecture as Brand Communication: Dynaform + Cube. Architektur als Markenkommunikation: Dynaform + Cube (bi-lingual edition), pp. 37–44. Birkhäuser, Basel, Boston, Berlin (2002)
35. Zurstiege, G.: Der Konsum Dritter Orte. In: Hellmann, K.-U., Zurstiege, G. (eds.) Räume des Konsums.Über den Funktionswandel von Räumlichkeiten im Zeitalter des Konsumismus, pp. 121–144. VS Verlag für Sozialwissenschaften, Wiesbaden (2008)

Chapter 3
Meaningful Advertising

Peter van Waart, Ingrid Mulder, and Cees de Bont

Abstract Meaningful design can be defined as putting human values in the centre of the process of designing for meaningful products, services and environments. Brands can make use of pervasive technology in various touchpoints facilitating meaningful brand experiences. Pervasive advertising need to seek for the embedding of brands into the natural living environment of people, in which people can interact any time at any place with brands in an intellectual (symbolic) way with which meaning can be transferred between brand users, an emotional (aesthetic) way by which users will hold a sustainable memory of the experience, as well as a physical (experiential) way in which the immediate conscious and unconscious impact takes place through the interaction with the applied technology.

3.1 Introduction

This chapter reviews advertising from out the idea of meaningful branding: the way in which brands can be of true meaning for people through human experiences. In the second section, the economical developments towards the experience economy are described. Since human values are of great importance for making meaning, the third section outlines how studies on values have led to human centred marketing and design strategies. In section four, semiotic theory offers an adequate description

P. van Waart (✉) • I. Mulder
Rotterdam University of Applied Sciences, Rotterdam, The Netherlands
e-mail: p.van.waart@hro.nl; i.j.mulder@hro.nl

Delft University of Technology, Delft, The Netherlands
e-mail: p.vanwaart@tudelft.nl; i.j.mulder@tudelft.nl

C. de Bont
Delft University of Technology, Delft, The Netherlands
e-mail: c.j.p.m.debont@tudelft.nl

J. Müller et al. (eds.), *Pervasive Advertising*, Human-Computer Interaction Series,
DOI 10.1007/978-0-85729-352-7_3, © Springer-Verlag London Limited 2011

and analyzing approach to detect essential key features of the meaningfulness of pervasive technologies. To illustrate this, a few examples of branded pervasive applications are shown in the fifth section. The final section discusses how meaningful design can be used in the context of pervasive advertising.

3.2 From Advertising Products to Meaningful Branding

Before we discuss what role pervasive advertising could play in today's economy, we give a brief history of marketing and focus on the changing role of brands and their interactions with consumers. This section describes the transformation in the marketing and advertising industry from promoting products in the 1960s and 1970s through branding in the 1980s and 1990s towards the Experience Economy as of 2000.

3.2.1 Industrial Society and Finding Markets for Production

Advertising and branding go a long way back. Ancient tradesman and taverns used outdoor signs describing their goods and prices to inform the audience. Medieval guilds put marks on their product as a quality guarantee to protect them from imitations. However, it was the Industrial Revolution in the eighteenth century that gave advertising the boost to become the industry, as we know it. Industrialization brought large-scale means of production and manufacturers seek ways to sell their fast growing stocks. Advertising became a mean for getting attention from consumers and creating demand for products. Advertising became an industry in itself from the late industrial society. In the Western world economies were driven by consumption as the driver of nations economical success and sense of well-being. Manufacturers produced more and more goods for consumption society and learned to produce products at the lowest costs and the biggest margins. The need to distinct the goods of one manufacturer from another was a major factor in the development of the advertising industry. Advertising agencies emerged to support manufacturers with strategies and campaigns in order to position manufacturers in the competitive field [17]. In general they pushed products to the market by informing consumers of their existence and benefits to create product preference. In this approach, the manufacturer is in the centre of marketing strategy with the purpose of selling and making profit.

3.2.2 Branding and Identity

As production processes improved, it became more difficult for a manufacturer to distinct his products from those of his competitors based on product quality. Also the efficiency of production processes reduced costs, product prices dropped and

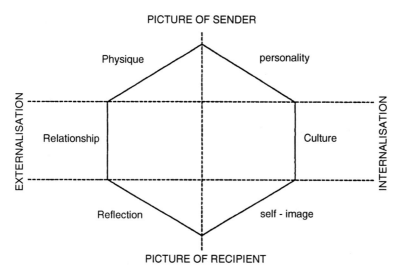

Fig. 3.1 Brand Identity Prism of Kapferer showing six elements that emphasize brand identity

competition on price was getting fierce. And in times of economic growth and wel-fare from the 1950s to the 1990s of the twentieth century, a growing number of people didn't seek for lowest priced products anymore. Until that time, brands were used to distinct a product from others by expressing it's specific product features. But now in this era, manufacturers learned how to develop the economic value of the brand itself.

Also cultural developments in Western society, such as equal chances for men and women, individualization, freedom of choice, sexual liberation, better access to higher education, drove people up to Maslow's pyramid of needs: less people had concerns about basic needs in life because economic prosperity provided endless possibilities to fulfil those needs, and more people grow to self-actualization [32]. Brands were more and more used as way of expressing one's personal preferences and 'way of life', his individual identity. Now that brands could be used as means of expression, manufacturers got the opportunity to expand the symbolic value of their brands as value to consumers.

In the eighties and nineties, brand values became core business in marketing strategies defined as what we nowadays understand as 'branding'. Brand manage-ment experts like Kapferer with his Brand Identity Prism (see Fig. 3.1) and Aaker put brand values and brand equity in the middle of brand strategies [1, 30]. They succeeded in proving that a brand contributes to company revenues (brand equity). Again, in this approach, the manufacturer, specifically his brand, is in the centre of the branding strategy with the purpose to develop brand equity and enlarge the com-pany's profit. However, the era of branding is changing towards a new definition of branding that is much more suitable for future relationships between brands and consumers.

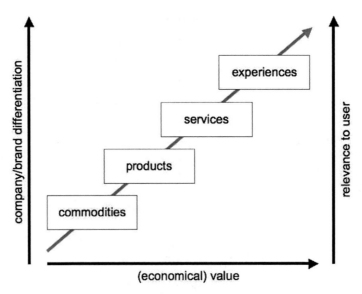

Fig. 3.2 Towards an Experience Economy (Pine and Gilmore) shows how the creation of economical value by companies shifts from commodities to experiences, which are more relevant for users, in order to differentiate from competitors

3.2.3 Experience Economy

Where it were commodities in pre-industrial societies that delivered economical value, industrialisation made manufacturers compete on the quality of products, and modern society produced more and more value from delivering services (see Fig. 3.2). For companies and brands however, it is getting harder to differentiate from each other with products and services because of an endless choice that promises personal freedom, but at the end results in a confused consumer that is not able to value the worth of his choice [50]. Pine and Gilmore described the economical development towards an experience economy [41]. In this experience economy meaningful (brand) experiences can make a difference to consumers, because of the personal relevance for people with regard to their personal values and beliefs, which are the basis of people's consumer behaviour and brand preferences [4, 44] and identity and lifestyle [7].

This economical development shows the transformation of product- and sales-driven organisations, for which cost-reduction and pricing became less and less competing factors, into experience brand-based organisations. The experience brand strategy differs fundamentally from the traditional marketing strategies. Traditional marketing focused on the product or corporate profit, resulting in an advertising industry that Godin [24] calls the TV-industrial complex: buying advertisement space in the media to promote products, sell the products and than use the profit to buy even more advertisement space. At the end this resulted in an advertising rat-race where the companies with the largest budgets end up as the winners of the competition. But what about the relevance for people? Goldhaber [25] proposed that the so-called information economy is actually an attention economy, where attention of consumers became scarce due to the enormous amount of information [12]. Attention can be seen as a scarce resource, which drives economical value. Experience branding differs from attention economy in the way that it put human values as drivers of economical value. From that point of view, attention is triggered when messages are relevant to people, that is, when they adapt to human values of people.

In the current brand experience approach the consumer is in the centre of the brand experience more than ever. In fact, the emphasis is on 'humans', rather than on 'consumers'. Experience brands aim to provide 'meaningful experiences' to people for which a true understanding of human values is required; at the end something can only be of meaning to someone when it comes to what one values in life [41, 52].

In the field of experience branding, also referred to as meaningful branding, the traditional concept of advertising has to be reconsidered. When the product or corporation is no longer in the centre of the marketing strategy, advertisements that solely communicate product features and benefits fail to lead to a meaningful human experience. Without taking into account the personal beliefs and former history of (life) experiences, a true experience won't be likely to appear: an experience has to be constituted by an individual rather than by the experience (brand) provider [41]. Differently put, designers and practitioners cannot design an experience, they just can design *for* an experience [41]. Brand and person really have to interact with each other. Brand experience has a behavioural impact; it affects consumer satisfaction and loyalty towards brands [8].

Another crucial element in experience branding is the concept of 'touchpoints' [31]. A touchpoint is any contact or moment in which one is physically or virtually interacting with a brand. All touchpoints together influence one's brand experience. The orchestration of touchpoints altogether determines the entire expression of brand meaning to a person [8]. Also, a brand experience stretches out over time and space [52, 59]. Touchpoints therefore have to be placed in this time-space continuum.

Consequently, traditional advertising no longer holds in the experience economy. Instead of pushed and seductive advertisements, experience brands need to develop a consistent architecture of touchpoints that is naturally intertwined within the context of a person and that addresses his values. And it is exactly here where pervasive technology can enrich and enforce brand experiences. Some examples of that are shown in Sect. 3.5. Before that, the following section elaborates on how people experience the world around them.

3.3   Human Experience: Meaning and Values

Whereas the previous section explained how in the experience economy brands try to adapt to human values in order to become of meaning to people, the current section elaborates on the process of assigning meaning to things (objects, artefacts as well as other phenomena) and how the marketing and design industry learned to adapt to human values in creating meaningful experiences.

3.3.1 The Meaning of Things

There has been a long tradition of thinking on how people experience reality and how things around them are of meaning to them. From Plato's universal ideas that present themselves in physical entities, via Descartes' dualism to modern philosophy, anthropology, psychology and sociology.

It was Descartes who distinguished the body (the physical existence in the world) from the conscious mind (thinking of the world). From that follows that what the body experiences is being processed by our minds in order to make meaning out of it, based on pre-defined concepts that exist in men. George H. Mead then consequently explained that meaning is not derived from pre-defined concepts but can be seen as a social construction; in order to assign meaning to things around us, we need others to determine what meaning they have to us [34]. Meaning is a result of social interaction rather than of individual psychology. However, what meaning one assigns to a phenomenon is also a result of interpretation, in which personal history and beliefs play an important role.

Dewey argues that no one is a passive observer of the world around him but an active actor that is also influencing his environment [15]. The world of thoughts (mind) and facts (environment) are in interaction with each other. In keeping with Mead and Dewey, Blumer introduced the term symbolic interactionism, and stated three premises [5]:

1. Humans act toward things on the basis of the meanings they ascribe to those things.
2. The meaning of such things is derived from, or arises out of, the social interaction that one has with others and the society.
3. These meanings are handled in, and modified through, an interpretative process used by the person in dealing with the things he/she encounters.

In short, symbolic interactionism states that consciousness is an integral part of both action and interaction. These premises were very useful in describing human-computer-interaction (HCI) from out the users perspective rather than the designer's cognitive approach.

Especially Dourish's contribution for understanding HCI from the user's point of view is interesting for designers of technological artefacts [16]. He describes three aspects of meaning. First, *ontology*, seen as a structure of identities and their relations. Actually, these are the objects around us which we assign meaning to. In HCI ontology occurs in the internal structure of object-oriented software systems or data-structures. Second, *intersubjectivity*, which is about how meaning can be shared as a mutual understanding between people. Between the designer and the user, this is about the interactive system itself and how the designer's intentions are understood by the user. Between users, this refers to how people communicate through the system about how it should be used in what they want to achieve. Finally, *intentionality* refers to the directedness between our mental activities (thinking, remembering, ...) and their meanings. Interestingly, Dourish stresses that computation is fundamentally about the representation of entities in the world of human experience and therefore then "the key feature of interaction with computation is how we act through it to achieve effects in the world" [16].

Additionally, Csikszentmihalyi and Rochberg-Halton argue that people "make order in their selves [...] by first creating and then interacting with the material world". In that point of view, "the material environment that surrounds us is rarely neutral; it either helps the forces of chaos that make life random and disorganized or it helps to give purpose and direction to one's life" [11]. In studying the meaning of things they conclude that meaning is created by the act of perception, that the ability of enjoy one's action (flow, as opposite of alienation) gives value to whatever one is doing. In defining the concept of meaning, Csikszentmihalyi describes three elements to experience meaning [10]. First, one has to have an *ultimate goal* (reason of living). The second is the *resolution* in the pursuit of one's goals (the intention to reach the goals has to be translated into action). When the goal is pursued with resolution and all activities are unified in flow, then these will be followed by the third element called *harmony* that is brought to consciousness. "Purpose, resolution, and harmony unify life and give it meaning" [10].

Among all goals one can have, human values are very important goals for people, which give one direction in life, in what is wrong and right. And things do not have meanings based upon their physical characteristics but as a result from social interaction and personal interpretation. It is the human mind that assigns meaning. One could say that 'meaning is in the mind of the beholder'.

The following sections describe in more detail what human values are, and how these values can be acknowledged in design and marketing processes to create meaningful products and experiences.

3.3.2 Meaning from Human Values

People determine meaning based upon their personal beliefs and values. The social psychologist Milton Rokeach became well-known for his studies of human values. The work of Rokeach in the 1970s and that of Shalom Schwartz from of the 1990s, was gladly adopted in the marketing industry for the possibilities for value-based segmentation models that proved to address human values of consumer segments very well.

Rokeach defines human value as "an enduring belief that a specific mode of conduct or end state of existence is personally or socially preferable to an opposite or converse mode of conduct or end state of its existence" [44]. He distinguishes two kinds of human values: *instrumental values* that reflect modes of conduct and

Table 3.1 Rokeach's instrumental and terminal values

Instrumental values	Ambitious, broad-minded, capable, cheerful, clean, courageous, forgiving, helpful, honest, imaginative, independent, intellectual, logical, loving, obedient, polite, responsible, self-controlled
Terminal values	A comfortable life, an exciting life, a sense of accomplishment, a world at peace, equality, family security, freedom, happiness, inner harmony, mature love, national security, pleasure, salvation, self-respect, social recognition, true friendship, wisdom

Table 3.2 Schwartz Value Inventory (SVI)

Values in terms of their goals	Single values
Achievement	Personal success through the demonstration of competence in accordance with society's standards, e.g., ambition
Benevolence	Preservation and enhancement of the welfare of others in one's immediate social circle, e.g., forgiveness
Conformity	Restraint of actions that violate social norms or expectations, e.g., politeness
Hedonism	Personal gratification and pleasure, e.g., enjoyment of food and leisure
Power	Social status, prestige, dominance, and control over others, e.g., wealth
Security	Safety, harmony, and stability of society, e.g., law and order
Self-direction	Independent thought and action, e.g., freedom
Stimulation	Excitement, novelty, and challenge in life, e.g., variety
Tradition	Respect for and acceptance of one's cultural or religious customs, e.g., religious devotion
Universalism	Understanding, appreciating, and protecting all people and nature, e.g., social justice, equality, environmentalism

behavioural characteristics that are ways of reaching terminal values, and *terminal values* that reflect end states of existence or a desirable end state that an individual would like to achieve. The values that were identified with the Rokeach Value Survey (RVS) are shown in Table 3.1.

Schwartz expanded on Rokeach's value definitions and determined ten basic, universal values together with specific single values that represent them, as shown in Table 3.2 [49].

Rokeach's Value Survey was conducted in the USA only. Schwartz took value research to an international level and measured values in more than 70 countries. Based on that, he formulated six features of values [49]:

1. Values are beliefs linked inextricably to affect. When values are activated, they become infused with feeling. People for whom independence is an important value become aroused if their independence is threatened, despair when they are helpless to protect it, and are happy when they can enjoy it.
2. Values refer to desirable goals that motivate action. People for whom social order, justice, and helpfulness are important values are motivated to pursue these goals.

3. Values transcend specific actions and situations. This feature distinguishes values from narrower concepts like norms and attitudes that usually refer to specific actions, objects, or situations.
4. Values serve as standards or criteria. Values guide the selection or evaluation of actions, policies, people, and events.
5. Values are ordered by importance relative to one another. People's values form an ordered system of value priorities that characterize them as individuals.
6. The relative importance of multiple values guides action. Any attitude or behaviour typically has implications for more than one value.

People act towards things based on how they experience the meaning of things in a perception process constituted by one's reasons to live, their human values. Inspired by this, meaningful design can be defined as putting human values in the centre of the process of designing for meaningful products, services and environments.

Now that value studies like those of Rokeach and Schwartz made clear how values drive human actions, the marketing and advertising industry was keen to apply these insights to adapt to people's preferences and behaviour to seduce them to the act of purchase. The following section describes a few approaches of human-values adaptive methods, ranging from more traditional intentions (making money for the company) to more innovative intentions (making meaningful designs for people).

3.3.3   Values in Marketing and Design

The sociologist Bourdieu describes how groups of people in society distinct themselves from other groups based on their values. In his extensive study he proved how values determine behaviour and lifestyle preferences, including product and brand preferences [7]. In the market research industry Gutman introduced the means-end theory [27, 42]. With this approach it became possible to find the linkage between product characteristics (means), the beneficial consequences of them and finally to consumer's values (end). These analysis provided insights in what the meaning is that people derive from products and brands. An interview technique with which one can disclose the values that determine people's product appraisal is called 'laddering'. With this technique, the interviewer continuously asks interviewees questions such as 'why is that important to you' to climb the ladder from superficial product 'attributes' through their consequences to the underlying values that are in stake. Figure 3.3 illustrates how using the 'laddering'-interview technique, the means-end-chain analysis results in a Hierarchical Value Map. Analysis of the data result in aggregated value clusters that represent the values of a group of product users, and also provides for segmentation of different value segments within this group.

In the marketing industry, human value-based segmentations models were developed by market research agencies, such as LOV and VALS in the USA [29, 56], SIGMA Milieus [3] in Germany and Mentality [21, 55] in the Netherlands. Market research agencies use them to advise clients for human-values centred marketing, communication and product development strategies. These segmentation models

Hypothetical Hierarchical Value Map of Wine Cooler

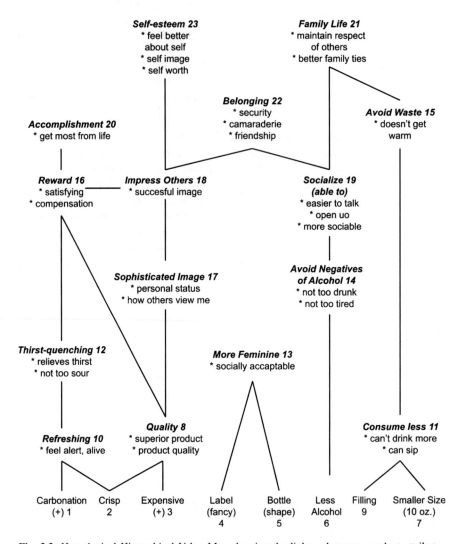

Fig. 3.3 Hypothetical Hierarchical Value Map showing the linkage between product attributes (*1–7, 9*), their consequences (*8, 10–19*) and human values (*20–23*) [42]

proved to be very effective in optimizing targeting and reducing waste: that is, the more precisely one group of specific consumers can be targeted, the less people that do not belong to the target group are exposed to advertisements. That saves a lot of advertising budget from companies. Other innovative approaches aiming at meaningful experiences for people can be found at experience brands (such as Nike and Apple, as described in Sect. 3.5) and in the design industry.

Fig. 3.4 The Model of
Product Emotion showing
how emotions emerge when
stimuli are appraised as being
relevant to one's concerns [13]

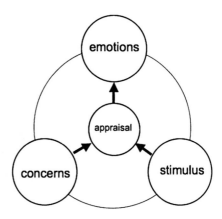

In the design industry, design researchers developed new methods of product and service design that put human values in the centre of the design process, such as context mapping in which users are involved in the design process as experience experts in the context of daily life [47, 53, 54, 57].

Desmet and colleagues studied values in relation to product emotion and argued, referring to Frijda, that values, as one example of concerns that people have, are a factor in the appraisal process of product stimuli [14, 23]. In Desmet's model for product emotion it is made clear how the appraisal of stimuli based on concerns result in an emotional experience [13]. Figure 3.4 shows this model of product emotion and how emotions emerge when stimuli are appraised as being relevant to one's concerns. This is in keeping with Schwartz's statement that values and affect are linked and Modell's description of feeling and emotion as 'markers of value' [35, 49].

Figure 3.5 shows the Brand Relationship Model which is a good illustration of the relationship between brands and people [45, 46]. This model represents clearly the synergy between implicit and intangible brand–human-relationships and explicit and tangible touchpoint design.

With their Elaboration Likelihood Model (ELM), Petty and Cacioppo proved that the more an audience is motivated and is able to process a message, the more the audience is cognitively processing the arguments (ideas, content) in the message [40]. This is what they called the 'central route' that is effective in changing attitude and behaviour of an audience. Personal relevance increases the motivation for central processing. With less motivation and ability, messages are processed via the 'peripheral' route in which the audience is persuaded much more unconsciously based on previous experiences and superficial qualities. Referring to the aforementioned human values studies, advertisements then are more effective when the audience is more motivated as a result of the adaptation of the advertisement to people's human values.

Several researchers describe different levels of information processing in design. Van Gorp noticed that they show similarity because they all distinguish three of such levels [26]. Table 3.3 gives an overview of design models in which the three levels are generalised as how things *feel*, how things *work* and what things *mean*.

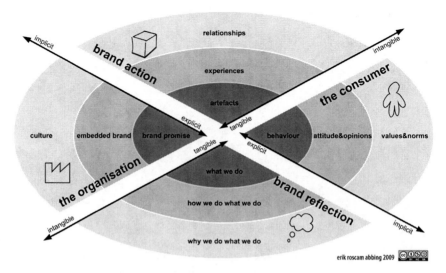

Fig. 3.5 The Brand Relationship Model expresses the brand relationship based on the match between brand values (organisation culture) and human values of the consumer

Table 3.3 Information processing in design models: This table is partly derived from Van Gorp who made a comparative table from emotional design models [24]

Generalisation	Aesthetic: How it *feels*	Experiential: How it *works*	Symbolic: What it *means*
Psychological level	Unconscious	Unconscious/ sub-conscious	Conscious
Forlizzi [20]	Fluent	Cognitive	Expressive
Norman [[37]	Visceral	Behavioural	Reflective
Shedroff [51]	Reflexive	Habitual	Engagement
Highland [28]	Emotional	Physical	Intellectual
Comparative description	Inherent qualities, formal properties, appearance, physical properties, first impressions	Interaction, performance, benefits of use	What it says about ourselves and others, memories, appraisals of motive compliance against goals and concerns
Design discipline	Visual, sensorial designers	Interaction designers, information architects, software engineers	Experience designers, experience branders, artists, story-tellers

It is now merged with new rows with the levels of Shedroff and Highland, and the rows addressing the design discipline and the generalisation. The table shows the similarity between design models in the level of information processing by humans and the according design disciplines

How things feel is related to immediate reactions to the appearance and physical qualities of things. This is also referred to as an *aesthetic experience* [48]. The corresponding design discipline consists of visual designers or sensorial designers focussing on the sensorial experience of things. Designers concerned with *experiential* features, how things work, can be find among interaction designers, information architects, (software) engineers focussing on the construction and mechanics of systems and applications. Another type of designers who are concerned with what things mean are focussing on the *symbolic* experience. Among them are experience designers and designers for brand experiences, but also artists, copy-writers and story-tellers. In keeping with Shedroff and colleagues [52] these differences in experiences will be called *intensity*.

One could say that marketing determines *what to design about* (in terms of meaningful content, brand relationship, and on the level of values) and that visual and interaction designers determine *how to design* (what form, appearance and properties). Based on this, a semiotic perspective seems to be helpful to understand and design for the effects of meaningful pervasive advertising in practice.

3.4 Semiotics and the Branded Symbolic Features of Pervasive Technology

Technology can be of meaning to people based on its appearance, based on its technical-functional characteristics to achieve certain goals but most of all based on its meaningful content that people can exchange through it, similar as people do with television, mobile phones or social media. In experiencing meaning, a distinction can be made between aesthetic experiences as a result from the perception process, and symbolic experiences as a result from the (conscious and unconscious) interpretation in the process of recognising the meaning of things.

Between brand companies and their customers, technology can be of meaning through content that is loaded with brand values, or when things are used as a symbol to express certain values of its owner (like creatives using Apple products). In this way of branding, brand values can give direction to the meaning that is experienced [4, 8, 41, 52].

Technology can be used as instrument to achieve goals or as medium to express and communicate meaning. At the end, meaning depends on the person who assigns meaning. In that way interactive media and technology can be regarded from out a semiotic point of view in which any thing or sign is separated into form, the meaning it refers to, and the meaning that is assigned to it as a result of interpretation. Especially Borgmann succeeded in bridging semiotics and the meaning of technology [2, 6, 36]. O'Neill made an extended study of semiotics and interactive media, also focusing on interactive environments, which is of great use for the pervasive advertising discourse [38].

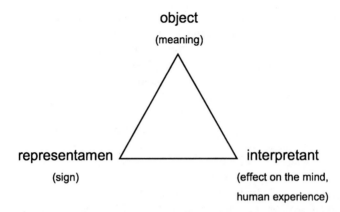

Fig. 3.6 Peirce's triadic sign shows that the interpretant is the effect of on one's mind from a representamen: a sign that refers to a meaning

Figure 3.6 shows the triadic sign of the semiotician Peirce, which describes three distinct parts of a sign [39]. The *object* which is anything that can be represented (things, ideas, concepts), the *representamen* (often called sign) which is representing the object, and the *interpretant*, that is, the effect on the mind of the viewer as a result of the interpretation process.

Peirce identified a large variety of types of signs on the initial categories of sign as an icon, and index and as symbol. Icons represent their objects via a direct likeness or similarity (like a photo, picture or painting that represent a recognisable image of the object). Indices 'indicate' to an object (like shadow indicates that there is light or smoke indicate that there is fire). Symbols refer to their objects by conventions and rules of understanding within a culture. They do not look like their objects (as icons do) nor have they a direct relation to it (as indices do). Books, words, mathematic symbols, as well as computation in terms of Dourish, are examples of symbolic signs [16]. This triadic sign can be used in designing the touchpoints of a brand.

In terms of pervasive advertising, pervasive technology and interactive media offer immense opportunities to become interactive touchpoints. In that way they can act as 'meaningful' media [28]. For centuries, myths and stories, arts, and rituals, respectively addressing the intellect, emotions and physical experience, proved to be powerful 'media' to constitute meaningful experiences. Pervasive and interactive media enable people to constitute brand experiences, individually as well as socially. Technology can function so well that it is not noticed anymore (ubiquitous computing) [58]. One is not aware of the functional aspects of technology and definitely neither of the symbolic aspects of it. Therefore Rogers pleas to actively engage users in designing for the user experience [43]. Moreover, one of the design principles of Dourish in his work on embodied interaction, is that "users, not designers, create and communicate meaning" [16].

Carroll and Mentis claim that "those pervasive systems and applications that enhance social capital as collective goods involving shared goals and values and social norms of reciprocity, are most usable to be of meaning over time" [9]. The value that people experience with YouTube or Flickr or in social networks like Facebook or Twitter, is not so much defined by 'product features' or by 'brand values' but rather their personal values. People use these brands not only because they are useful, but foremost because they are meaningful: people don't share their movie clips, photo's and stories, they enjoy sharing experiences in their social network. The next section illustrates the aforementioned insights with some examples of brand experiences.

3.5 Meaningful Brand Experiences

Key elements of meaningful brand experiences can now be summarized. Some examples of brand experiences are described according to the key elements and compared with each other to give an impression of the effectiveness of the key elements.

3.5.1 Key Elements of Meaningful Brand Experiences in Pervasive Advertising

With the insights from the experience economy, the process of making meaning based on human values, and semiotics, it can be said that the following elements are essential to address when designing for meaningful brand experiences in pervasive advertising:

(A) With regard to *values*, on a symbolic level:

   A1. One or more brand values that are symbolised and adapted to the audience's human values.
   A2. One or more human values that is adapted to.

(B) With regard to the *senses*, on a aesthetic level:

   B1. The appearance in vision, sound, smell, taste and touch, in order to be sensory perceived.

(C) With regard to *physical interaction*, on a functional level:

   C1. The affordance between touchpoint and people.
   C2. The construction of means for physical interaction.

(D) With regard to *social interaction*:

   D1. The interaction between people (as users of the brand) allowed by the touchpoints.

D2. The control people have over the message that is conveyed through the system.

(E)   With regard to *touchpoint orchestration*:

E1.   How the touchpoint is placed in between other touchpoints, on a certain location and on a certain moment.
E2.   How all touchpoints behave over time and space.
E3.   What the balance should be in intensity (how it feels, works, or what it means) of each touchpoint.

The following examples illustrate to what extent brands applied these elements in their brand experience design.

3.5.1.1   Nike+

An interesting example of the use of pervasive technology in experience branding is Nike+. Nike joins efforts with Apple's iPod to come up with a service that enriches people lives in what people value: accomplishment. Nike+is of meaning to people by enriching their experience of challenging themselves. The Nike+iPod Sports Kit uses a sensor in one's running shoe that keeps track of your run (Fig. 3.7). The 'run data' is stored onto the iPod (or iPhone) and also the iPod serves you appropriate music to inspire your running. Back home, the run data can be uploaded to nikeplus. com where you can monitor all your runs and share motivations with other runners.

This example shows that the brand experience is facilitated by the brands Nike and iPod combined with a pervasive application designed for this experience. However, the actual experience is created by individuals themselves. Together these individuals socially interact in a branded running universe in which they share their data, bond with each other in training programs or compete with each other in for instance man versus women competitions. Via the website, people can also create 'challenges' for each other to enhance social interaction. Tangible products are part of the experience. There is a mix between physical activities and digital entities. The brand experience stretches out over time and space. See for details http://nikerunning. nike.com.

3.5.1.2   Google's Integrated Services

Google provides users an integrated service of different applications. At any location and moment, one can use the Internet browser and Google Search for finding, for example, a restaurant (Fig. 3.8). The search result displays the restaurant's address and the smart phone offers the option to activate a routing to it. When one chooses that option, Google Maps is activated, a route is plotted, the current position and the

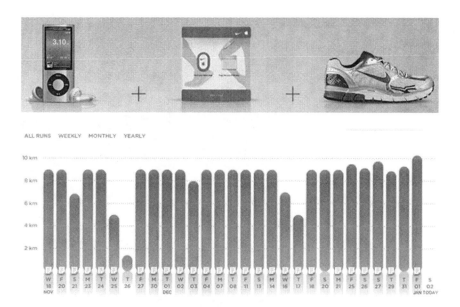

Fig. 3.7 The Nike+kit exist of an Apple device, a sensor and a Nike running shoe, connected to each other, in order to collect data to share with peers online

Fig. 3.8 An example of Google's integrated services: Once a particular restaurant is found via Google Search, Google Maps navigates the user to his destination, in one fluent service

destination are visible, and one can start walking guided by the route on display. The user hardly knows which applications were started after the first one and instead of being busy with starting up and commanding phone applications, one can achieve his primary goal: getting to the restaurant. This can be done anytime anywhere.

Fig. 3.9 Augmented Reality
Ambulance: Passers-by view
themselves at a public display
augmented with a pre-
recorded scene of ambulance
personnel fighting with
aggressive bystanders

3.5.1.3   Augmented Reality Ambulance

In 2010, the Dutch Ministry of Justice in the Netherlands initiated a campaign to
call the audience for action in case of public service personnel is being under attack
of aggressive and violent harassment. In those situations, the bystanders-effect
appears and people don't react or intervene in the situation. The campaign consisted
out of public screens that showed a runtime videostream of the city square that was
crowded by the audience, that was also augmented with a previously filmed
bluescreen fragment of public servants of an ambulance that were under attack of
aggressors (Fig. 3.9). The screen was placed at places in the city with large crowds.
A video registration of the scene showed that the audience was immersed by the
appearance of the screen. Yet, it should be doubted if the audience was impressed

Fig. 3.10 Passers-by are
attracted by the ESPN
Interactive Shopping Front,
that invites them to catch the
ball of a football player and
share their scores with other
participants nation-wide
Source: monstermedia.net

by the message that was conveyed or the novelty or surprise effect of the technological
application. The registration shows however, that people started interaction by
discussing the images on the screen [18].

3.5.1.4   ESPN Football Shopping Front

Monster Media teamed up with Wieden + Kennedy and MacDonald Media to create an
interactive storefront in some larger cities in the USA, to promote Monday Football of
sports television station ESPN. The video registration on YouTube of this campaign
shows a store front with public displays that attract passers-by with some visual clues
and triggers them to challenge a virtual football quarter back on screen (Fig. 3.10). The
virtual player throws a ball and the viewer has to reach for it as if he was catching the

Fig. 3.11 Audience on city square cheering during a FIFA World Cup Soccer match broadcasted on a large public display (Source: http://www.avpoint.nl)

ball. Sensors detect the activity of the viewer (if it was a catch or not) and the viewer scores points. At the end, the viewer can enter his name on a touch screen to be displayed on a list of high scores that is displayed in each city, and the final message is shown promoting Monday Football.

The video registration shows a very active viewer being immersed in the match with the virtual player. Around him passers-by have stopped to witness the match, and they even started to cheer to support the viewer who's playing the match [19].

3.5.1.5 FIFA World Cup Soccer

In 2010, the FIFA World Cup Soccer tournament took place in South Africa. Television stations worldwide broadcasted the matches live. Not even earlier, so many huge public displays arised at city centres in so many European countries, enabling large crowds of people to enjoy soccer matches all together. News reports on these phenomena showed a vast crowd totally immersed into the match that was broadcasted, engaged in emotions all together (Fig. 3.11).

3.5.2 Comparative Matrix of Interactive Pervasive Brand Experiences

To get insight in how the key elements identified earlier in this section map to the brand experience examples, a comparative matrix is shown below. Mind that this is based on assumptions and observations rather than empirical measurements (Table 3.4).

Table 3.4 Comparative matrix of interactive pervasive brand experiences

Key elements	Nike+	Google	Ambulance	ESPN	WC Soccer
(A) Values					
(A1) Brand value	Accomplishment Self-respect	Openness Challenging	Social respect Obedience	Accomplishment	World at peace Accomplishment
(A2) Human value	Accomplishment Pleasure Self-respect	Comfortable life Independent Freedom	World at peace National security	Accomplishment Pleasure	Exciting life Social recognition Happiness
(B) Senses					
Vision	+	+	+	+	+
Sound	+	−	−	−	−
Smell	−	−	−	−	−
Taste	−	−	−	−	−
Touch	+	+	−	+	−
(C) Physical interaction					
(C1) Affordance	+	+		+	
(C2) Construction	+	+		+	
(D) Social interaction					
(D1) Interaction between people	+	−	−	+[a]	+[a]
(D2) People in control of message	+	+	−	−/+	−
(E) Touchpoint orchestration					
(E1) Placement	+	+	−	+	−
(E2) Time-space behaviour	+	+		−	
(E3) Intensity					
Feels	+	−	+	+	+
Works	+	+	−	+	−
Meaning	+	+	−/+	+	+

[a]Though not through pervasive system

The matrix shows that Nike + with his products and services addresses most of the key elements. It excels on the time-space aspect of the brand experience. Also Google performs well at the time-space aspect. Nike + involves quite a few senses for its brand experience. Although FIFA, exposed on a public display in an environment, is actually not interactive at all, and also weak on the time-space aspect, the event is of important meaning to the audience but that is more to be attributed to the match itself (high involvement of viewers) rather than the pervasive technology of its interactions. The augmented reality ambulance does not address many key elements: it hardly involves the senses, no interaction is possible, and it is doubtful if the message will have the effect that it is supposed to have.

It is to be assumed that the more key elements are addressed, the more meaningful the brand experience is. However, not all elements seem to be of equal importance: the FIFA event had quite an impact although it addressed very few key elements.

3.6 Conclusions and Discussion

People act towards things based on how they experience the meaning of things in a perception process constituted by one's reasons to live, their human values. Meaningful design then can be defined as putting human values in the centre of the process of designing for meaningful products, services and environments. When applied to brands, we speak of meaningful branding.

Meaningful brands can only express themselves to people in a way that they respect and endorse people's choices and lifestyle as expression of their personal values and beliefs. This is in keeping with the vision of pervasive computing, which foresees novel scenarios of highly interactive environments in which communication takes place between single users and devices, between devices and devices, and between users and users. Moreover, technology becomes increasingly invisible and personal. Who fears technology that is of personal meaning? The fear for annoying or even pestering people is, in a way, superfluous in the paradigm of meaningful branding. When adapted to human values from without the brands authentic brand values, brands really have the opportunity to contribute to people's life.

Brands can make use of pervasive technology in various touchpoints facilitating meaningful brand experiences (co-)created by people themselves. Pervasive technologies could be of great importance of the time-space aspect of brand experiences. Therefore, pervasive advertising needs to seek for the embedding of brands into the natural living environment of people, in which people can interact any time at any place with brands in an intellectual (symbolic) way with which meaning can be transferred between brand users, an emotional (aesthetic) way by which users will hold a sustainable memory of the experience, as well as a physical (experiential) way in which the immediate conscious and unconscious impact takes place through the interaction with the applied technology. This is then what we can call pervasive *meaningful advertising*.

Although pervasive technology seems very suitable for enriched meaningful brand experiences, a few remarks can be made.

With pervasive touchpoints all the time everywhere that stimulate the brand experience of people, the idea of advertising should be reconsidered. The brand experience perspective acknowledge all brand expressions, whether these are the product, the call centre, the retail store or the advertisement, as part of an holistic environment in which one comes to experience. Few brands already act as experience brands and align their touchpoints to really be of meaning to people. But larger industries tend to hold on to more classic branding strategies that not specifically focus on people's meaningful experiences. Meaningful branding needs innovation in these industries in the entire branch of manufacturers (advertisers), media agencies, advertisement and communication agencies and media owners. As long as classic marketing and branding perspectives persist, stakeholders are reluctant to change.

In the end, many issues need further investigations. For example, the effects of pervasive brand messages on the experience of meaning are hardly investigated. Also the effect of interaction between brand and single users as well as brand users in between on brand experience needs further research. And then, how will answers to these questions lead to design principles for designing meaningful pervasive brand experiences?

References

1. Aaker, D.: Managing Brand Equity. Free Press, San Francisco (1991)
2. Achterhuis, H.: Technology and the good life? and the empirical turn for philosophy of technology. In: Techné: Research in Philosophy and Technology, 6(1), 93–109 (2002)
3. Ascheberg, C., Uelzhoffer, J.: Transnational consumer cultures and social milieus. Int. J. Market Res. 41(1), 47–59 (1991)
4. Batey, M.: Brand Meaning. Routledge, New York (2008)
5. Blumer, H.: Symbolic Interactionism: Perspective and Method. University of California Press, Berkeley (1969)
6. Borgmann, A.: Holding on to Reality: The Nature of Information at the Turn of the Millennium. University of Chicago Press, Chicago (1999)
7. Bourdieu, P.: Distinction: A Social Critique of the Judgement of Taste. Routledge, London (1984)
8. Brakus, J.J., Schmitt, B.H., Zarantonello, L.: Brand experience: What is it? How is it measured? Does it affect loyalty? J. Market. 73, 52–68 (2009)
9. Carroll, J.M., Mentis, H.M.: The useful interface experience: the role and transformation of usability. In: Schifferstein, H.N.J., Hekkert, P. (eds.) Product Experience. Elsevier, Amsterdam (2008)
10. Csikszentmihalyi, M.: Flow: The Psychology of Optimal Experience. Harper & Row, New York (1990)
11. Csikszentmihalyi, M., Rochberg-Halton, E.: The Meaning of Things: Domestic Symbols and the Self. Cambridge University Press, Cambridge (1981)
12. Davenport, T.H., Beck, J.C.: Attention Economy. Harvard Business School Press, Boston (2001)
13. Desmet, P.: Designing Emotions. TU Delft, Delft (2002)
14. Desmet, P., Hekkert, P., Hillen, M.G.: Values and emotions; an empirical investigation in the relationship between emotional responses to products and human values. In: Proceedings of Techné: Design Wisdom 5th European Academy of Design conference, Barcelona, Spain (2004)
15. Dewey, J.: Art as Experience. Perigree, New York (1934)

16. Dourish, P.: Where the Action Is: The Foundations of Embodied Interaction. MIT Press, Cambridge (2001)
17. Fennis, B.M., Stroebe, W.: The Psychology of Advertising. Psychology Press, Hove (2010)
18. For more details see http://www.youtube.com/watch?v=uDTdHG_FytM Accessed 23 Mar 2011
19. For more details see http://monstermedia.net/portfolio.php?id=291 Accessed 23 Mar 2011
20. Forlizzi, J., Ford, S.: The building blocks of experience: an early framework for interaction designers. In: Designing Interactive Systems 2000 Conference Proceedings, pp. 419–423, New York (2000)
21. Franzen, G.: The SWOCC Book of Brand Management Models. SWOCC, Amsterdam (2006)
22. Franzen, G., Bouwman, M.: The Mental World of Brands. NTC Publications, Henley-on-Thames (2001)
23. Frijda, N.H.: The Emotions. Cambridge University Press, Cambridge (1986)
24. Godin, S.: Purple Cow: Transform Your Business by Being Remarkable. Penguin, New York/London/Toronto (2003)
25. Goldhaber, M.H.: The attention economy and the net. First Monday 2(4), http://www.firstmonday.org/issues/issue2_4/goldhaber (1997). Accessed 23 Mar 2011
26. Gorp, T. van.: Understanding design for emotion models. http://www.affectivedesign.org/archives/199 (2007). Accessed 23 Mar 2011
27. Gutman, J.: A means-end chain model based on consumer categorization processes. J. Market. 46(2), 60–72 (1982)
28. Highland, M., Yu, G.: Communicating inner experience with video game technology, In: Heidelberg Journal Religions on the Internet, 2008 vol. 03.1, pp. 267–289 (2008)
29. Kahle, L.R., Beatty, S.E., Homer, P.M.: Alternative measurement approaches to consumer values: The List of Values (LOV) and Values and Lifestyle Segmentation (VALS). J. Consum. Res. 13(3), 405–409 (1986)
30. Kapferer, J.N.: Strategic Brand Management: New Approaches to Creating and Evaluating Brand Equity. Kogan Page, London (1992)
31. Mager, B.: Service design. In: Erlhoff, M., Marshall, T. (eds.) Design Dictionary. Birkhauser Verlag AG, Basel (2008)
32. Maslow, A.H.: A theory of human motivation. Psychol. Rev. 50(4), 370–396 (1943)
33. McCarthy, J., Wright, P.: Technology as Experience. MIT Press, Cambridge (2007)
34. Mead, G.H.: In: By Morris, C.W. (ed.) Mind, Self, and Society. University of Chicago Press, Chicago (1934)
35. Modell, A.H.: Imagination and the Meaningful Brain. MIT Press, Cambridge (2006)
36. Mullins, Ph.: The problem of meaning and Borgmann's realist response. In: Techné: Research in Philosophy and Technology, 6(1), 46–68 (2002)
37. Norman, D.A.: Emotional Design – Why We Love (or Hate) Everyday Things. Basic Books, New York (2004)
38. O'Neill, S.: Interactive Media: The Semiotics of Embodied Interaction. Springer, London (2008)
39. Peirce, C.S.: Collected Papers of Charles Sanders Peirce, vols. 1–6, 1931–1935, Charles Hartshorne and Paul Weiss (eds.) vols. 7–8, 1958, Arthur W. Burks (ed.) Harvard University Press, Cambridge (1931–1935, 1958)
40. Petty, R.E., Cacioppo, J.T.: Communication and Persuasion: Central and Peripheral Routes to Attitude Change. Springer, New York (1986)
41. Pine II, B.J., Gilmore, J.H.: The Experience Economy: Work Is Theater & Every Business a Stage. Academic Service, Boston (2000)
42. Reynolds, T.J., Gutman, J.: Laddering theory, method, analysis, and interpretation. J. Advert. Res. 28(1), 11–31 (1988)
43. Rogers, Y.: Moving on from Weiser's vision of calm computing: engaging UbiComp experiences. In: Dourish, P., Friday A. (eds.) Proceedings of Ubicomp 2006, LNCS 4206, pp. 404–421, 2006. Springer, Berlin (2006)
44. Rokeach, M.: The Nature of Human Values. Free Press, New York (1973)

45. Roscam Abbing, E.: Brand-Driven Innovation: Strategies for Development and Design. AVA Publishing, Lausanne (2010)
46. Roscam Abbing, E., van Gessel, C.: Brand-driven innovation. Des. Manag. Rev. **19**(3), 51–58 (2008)
47. Sanders, E.B.N., Stappers, P.J.: Co-creation and the new landscapes of design. Codesign **4**(1), 5–18 (2008)
48. Schifferstein, H.N.J., Hekkert, P.: Product Experience. Elsevier, Amsterdam (2008)
49. Schwartz, S.H.: Universals in the content and structure of values: Theoretical advances and empirical tests in 20 countries. In: Zanna, M. (ed.) Advances in Experimental Social Psychology. Academic, San Diego (1992)
50. Schwartz, B.: The Paradox of Choice: Why More Is Less. HarperCollins, New York (2004)
51. Shedroff, N.: Experience Design 1.1. http://www.experiencedesignbooks.com (2009). Accessed 23 Mar 2011
52. Shedroff, N., Diller, S., Rhea, D.: Making Meaning: How Successful Businesses Deliver Meaningful Customer Experiences. New Riders Publishing, Berkeley (2006)
53. Sleeswijk Visser, F.: Bringing the Everyday Life of People into Design. TU Delft, Delft (2009)
54. Sleeswijk Visser, F., Stappers, P.J., van der Lugt, R., Sanders, E.: Contextmapping: experiences from practice. Codesign **1**(2), 119–149 (2005)
55. Spangenberg, F., Lampert, M.: De grenzeloze generatie en de eeuwige jeugd van hun opvoeders. Nieuw Amsterdam Uitgevers, Amsterdam (2009)
56. SRI Consulting Business Intelligence: Understanding U.S. Consumers. SRI Consulting Business Intelligence, Menlo Park (2006)
57. Stappers, P.J., van Rijn, H., Kistemaker, S., Hennink, A., Sleeswijk Visser, F.: Designing for other people's strengths and motivations. Adv. Eng. Inform. **23**, 174–183 (2008)
58. Weiser, M., Brown, J.S.: The coming age of calm technology. http://www.ubiq.com/; hypertext/weiser/acmfuture2endnote.htm (1996). Accessed 23 Mar 2011
59. Wheeler, A.: Designing Brand Identity: A Complete Guide to Creating, Building, and Maintaining Strong Brands. Wiley, Hoboken (2006)

Chapter 4
Activity-Based Advertising

Kurt Partridge and Bo Begole

Abstract This chapter discusses Activity-based Advertising, an approach to more accurately target advertisements by inferring a consumer's activities. This chapter begins with some of the important characteristics of advertising, and explains the incentives held by consumers and marketers. We explain why consumer and advertiser interests are not necessarily at odds, and briefly survey some existing targeting technologies that benefit both. We then describe the vision and benefits of activity-based advertising, and describe how it can advance targeting technologies even further. We finish with a methodology for evaluating activity-based advertising technologies, and present some initial results of activity-based advertising's potential.

4.1 Advertising Benefits and Deficiencies

From the moment a customer walks into a store, a good salesperson will assess the prospect of making a sale by estimating the customer's likely needs, preferences, and spending level. Some sales people will ask direct questions, using a "hard sell" approach that is usually off-putting to customers. Other sales people use the "soft sell" approach, reading between the lines of the customer's responses and behaviors to gain deeper insight without annoying the customer. But even before they interact, a good salesperson will make an "educated guess" based solely on how the customer looks and behaves. Some physical characteristics are useful filters for some product categories, such as gender for clothes. Other clues are less telling or perhaps misleading, such as the richest hotel guest who dresses shabbily [3]. A wise salesperson also knows that appearances can be deceiving and will seek more information

K. Partridge (✉) • B. Begole
Palo Alto Research Center, Inc., Palo Alto, USA
e-mail: Kurt.Partridge@parc.com; Bo.Begole@parc.com

J. Müller et al. (eds.), *Pervasive Advertising*, Human-Computer Interaction Series,
DOI 10.1007/978-0-85729-352-7_4, © Springer-Verlag London Limited 2011

to avoid mishandling a prospective customer. No single clue tells the whole story and putting these clues together to form a reliable picture requires much experience in deduction and perception of human nature.

It is not easy to be a good salesperson, because during the sales process, buyers and sellers have competing goals. The buyer wants to spend as little as possible, and the seller wants to acquire as much as possible. However, they also share an objective: satisfying the buyer's needs with available merchandise and services. And to get there, they must exchange their complementary knowledge. The buyer has at least a vague notion of what she wants, but does not know the full range of available options. The seller knows what he has available, but not what would optimally fit the buyer's criteria.

Advertising is a way for sellers to share their information with consumers. Advertisements educate consumers about product options, they show solutions to major and minor problems in life, they inform about evaluation criteria, they compare product features to those of the competition, and they point out when competitors are misleading. They accomplish all this with a brevity of content and efficiency of consumer attention, and often manage to do so while providing entertainment and funding other valuable services at the same time.

Despite these benefits to consumers, advertising is unpopular. An April 2004 New York Times article [5] reports the results of a survey by marketing research firm, Yankelovich, in which 65% of respondents state that they "are constantly bombarded with too much" advertising and 69% said they "are interested in products and services that would help them *skip* or *block* marketing" (emphasis added).

So, if advertising is a form of communication, providing at least *some* beneficial information to consumers, why does the majority of the population hold it in contempt? Perhaps it is too much of a "hard sell" approach. In the Yankelovich survey, 54% of respondents stated they "avoid buying products that overwhelm them with advertising and marketing." 61% said they agreed that the amount of advertising and marketing to which they are exposed "is out of control." A report from Forrester Research agreed, citing "clutter, interruption, and irrelevance as the key reasons for [consumer] frustration" [10].

Given the negative impressions held by so many consumers, why do marketers continue to subject us to such advertising? Why do societies tolerate these costs on our attention? The most likely reason is that there is little or no economic impact from the negative effect of advertisements. Although seeing an advertisement can be a waste of time, no advertiser must pay extra for frustrating a consumer (however, see [16] for an approach to optimize outdoor advertising by having some advertisers pay more for advertisements with greater attentional costs). Untracked costs such as these are referred to as negative externalities. As we have seen in other industries such as energy, when an industry does not pay directly for the costs of negative externalities, the industry will not self-regulate to minimize the negative effect. There's little negative *economic* effect from being irritating, and in some cases, negative publicity can lift sales.

No doubt there are a few cases where the cost of an advertisement's negative impression causes some customers to deliberately boycott the product, hurting the product economically. For some individual products, the result of bad advertising might even cause the product to fail. However, at the aggregate level of all businesses and all consumers, we see that the costs of the negative externalities are not born by the advertisers so that the economic gains outweigh the economic costs.

So if advertisers are not paying the full costs, and if advertising is effective, is there any incentive for advertisers to address consumer concerns about advertising? There is. Kim's report indicates that consumers are increasingly blocking all advertisements. Unless the advertising industry can figure out how to make advertising less frustrating, consumers will shut out advertising completely. If this happens, advertisers won't be able to educate consumers about their products, market efficiencies will drop, content providers will be unable to fund their services, and consumers will overall be less well-served than they are today.

To make advertising less overwhelming, less cluttering, less interruptive, and more relevant requires understanding the consumer's state of mind and needs in detail. Advertising cannot be a one-way channel. It must perceive and understand, guiding the consumer to a purchase like a good salesperson.

In this paper, we present a new approach to targeting that infers person's real-world activities to personalize the content and timing of advertisements, referred to as activity-based advertising. This type of targeting is possible today because of the rapid technological advances in smartphones, and their unprecedented adoption by the general public. We show how this new form of targeting differs from existing technologies, and describe a methodology for evaluating systems that use it. To begin, we first describe the elements of successful targeting technology.

4.2   Elements of Successful Targeting

The previous section explained why both consumers and advertisers wish that advertising were "better targeted." From an advertiser's perspective, the advertisements should only reach consumers who are likely to buy. From the consumer's perspective, they should only be exposed to advertisements that will make a difference to them.

What makes targeting good? We propose four elements of good targeting that can be remembered by the acronym FFTT, "Find," "Filter," "Time," and "Tailor."

- **FIND consumers with a need for the advertised product or service**. The product or service advertised must address a consumer's perceived need. This need must be *known* to the consumer. If a consumer doesn't perceive a need for the product or service, they will not buy it. This need doesn't have to necessarily be theirs, because they may buy the product as a gift that addresses someone else's need. Also, the need may be a future, anticipated need rather than an immediate one. In addition to being known, the need must also be *inadequately fulfilled*. If the consumer is already satisfied with their solution to a need, then they will be reluctant to try alternatives. They will also quickly lose interest in advertisements for products that they see as inferior.

- **FILTER the found consumers for those able to buy**. The consumer must have the means to buy the product. If they are nowhere near a place where the product is sold, or if they don't have the cash on hand, or if they are ineligible (such as below the minimum age to rent a car), there is little value in advertising to them, despite their need for it.
- **TIME the ad delivery for a receptive context**. The consumer must be willing and able to read, watch, or listen to the advertisement. Many activities are not conducive to ad presentation. The reasons may be social (directing attention away from a conversational partner may be impolite), or safety (watching a TV commercial while driving is dangerous), or internal (diverting attention from the user's current action means not accomplishing the user's goal as quickly). Participants are more receptive if they are relaxed and not doing anything that would incur a cost if their attention wanders. It is difficult even for a human observer to judge whether a consumer's context makes them "interruptible" [9], but if properly assessed, the context could provide a helpful cue for improving this targeting dimension.
- **TAILOR the content to the consumer**. Every advertisement must attract and then maintain the consumer's attention. Even consumers with the same needs and context can appreciate different styles of humor and presentation. Tailoring the content also uses the advertisement's content limits efficiently to educate the consumer about the product's superior features so the consumer can recognize the need and value, and educate the consumer about where to buy the product.

An advertisement can still succeed if some of these elements are neglected. After all, television advertisements do not filter for affordability or tailor content for every consumer. However, the better an advertisement addresses these elements, the more likely it is to succeed. Accurate targeting benefits advertisers because they waste less money, and consumers because they are exposed to fewer messages that waste their time.

4.3   Targeting Technologies

Targeting is no easy task. As we explained in Section 1, advertisers often get it wrong, annoying a consumer rather than motivating them to buy. To target well, an advertiser must understand the consumer in tremendous detail, knowing their likes and dislikes, what products they already own, what image they want to achieve, and what they already know. Advertisers may have to know more about their customers than the customers know about themselves.

Different technologies have developed for performing targeting. In this section, we survey the existing technologies, and their strengths and weaknesses in addressing each of the targeting elements listed in the previous section. While technological advances have made targeting increasingly accurate, no technology today comes close to the kind of targeting a salesperson can do. As we will show, there are many opportunities for improvement.

4.3.1 Demographic Targeting

One of the most common forms of targeted marketing is demographic. Demographics describe measurable characteristics about target audiences that are correlated with needs and desires for particular products and services. Typical demographics include gender, age, marital status, occupation, income, and neighborhood. When a marketer wants to target, they identify the demographics associated with the product, and then search for content providers that have readers, viewers, or listeners of the content that match the target demographics. Demographics are the traditional way that targeting is performed for newspapers, radio, television, and direct-mail marketing.

Obviously, demographic targeting is imperfect. Because of individual differences, no advertisement will be suitable for everyone. A luxury car advertisement in an investment magazine might appeal to some, but it would not appeal to those ineligible to drive or who are otherwise not in the market for a car (perhaps having just bought a different car). In short, although an advertisement may be relevant, it might not be useful.

Another problem with demographic targeting is that it may miss people in the market that do not match the demographic. Someone who does not manage the finances, but does play a role in the car purchase decision would be an appropriate target for the advertisement, but not reached through the investment magazine channel.

4.3.2 Psychographic Targeting

Demographics provide only an approximation of a person's interests. Savvy marketers long ago switched away from simple demographic segmentation to more *psychographic* segments based on lifestyle (including access to financial resources), political, religious and other personal choices. The Nielsen Company has created a list of 66 distinct market "segments" that group people of similar likes, lifestyles, and purchase behaviors. Introduced in 1976 and updated periodically, Nielsen's PRIZM list contains groupings with descriptive names such as "Young Digerati," "Kids & Cul-de-Sacs," "Traditional Times," and "Crossroads Villagers" to categorize the breadth of lifestyles in the US. By combining data from a variety of sources, Nielsen is able to estimate the psychographic composition of each US zipcode region [20].

This kind of segmentation helps marketers more directly target their products. The marketer does not have to figure out the demographic characteristics of their prospective customers. Instead, the psychographic profile practically tells them whether the customer would be interested in their product.

However, PRIZM is still not accurate enough for many purposes. As with demographic targeting, psychographic targeting doesn't indicate whether the user has already purchased the item, or whether they have already been exposed to the advertising message. How could a system do better? A salesperson that knew the prospect's PRIZM score could use it as a starting point, much like an initial judgment based on the customer's clothing. But the salesperson would quickly apply other techniques, such as noticing what products the customer appeared to be interested in, and engaging the customer in a conversation to pinpoint their needs.

4.3.3 Search Targeting

Search targeting bundles ads on the same topic as the results of a keyword query entered into the search engine. This form of targeting does a much better job of addressing all four targeting elements. Consumers are not only explicitly stating the topic they want information about, but they are also telling the system that such information would be useful and that they are ready to receive the information. And for some products, the question of how to buy is simplified because the consumer can complete the purchase online.

Although search advertisements make up a majority of the search revenue, not every search query arises from a commercial intent. This may also be true of other non-search interactions consumers have with their computers, such as when they are keeping up with their social network or email, or trying to find the address to a friend's house. However, effective advertisements can still be delivered to such users through the technique of behavioral targeting.

Behavioral targeting looks beyond the user's immediate interactions to their interaction history. If a user recently purchased a plane ticket, then they might be interested in things to do while on their trip. A system that noticed the plane ticket purchase could present tourist-related advertising in the destination city, even if the user was doing a search for completely unrelated terms. Behavioral targeting can collect data from all sites on which an advertising network delivers ads. By tracking these streams of clicks, demographic and psychographic algorithms can classify the categories that matter to groups or individuals. Google, Yahoo, and several other services offer these kinds of analytics to advertisers by tracking "cookies" placed on web pages that display advertisements brokered by them [8]. In a survey conducted for the Search Engine Marketing Professional Organization and released in Feb 2009, 75% of advertisers reported that they would be willing to spend 13% more on average for behaviorally targeted advertisements [24]. Another agency, eMarketer, projects near-exponential growth in behaviorally targeted online advertising from $775M in 2008 to $4.4B by 2012.

Despite all its advantages, digital advertising has its limits. Not every product need can be inferred from a search query or pattern of visiting web sites. For example, consumers often spend money on packaged goods and food items that they don't research on the web first. For items that are more likely purchased offline, online advertising generally has no way to know whether consumers are near a place where they can be bought. And finally, digital advertisers often have a limited understanding of a consumer's context and receptivity. Although because they are using a computer, consumers are naturally receptive, digital ads do not proactively identify receptive situations and deliver advertising at those times.

4.3.4 Mobile and Location-Based Targeting

Mobile advertising is a relatively recent sub-category in the advertising industry and growing fast. In June 2009, Gartner research [6] projected spending in mobile advertising to climb from less than $1B in 2009 to over $13B by end of 2013. Mobile advertising comprises many segments, including SMS advertisements, ads inside mobile games, and the traditional digital ad categories of search, and display alongside content.

From a targeting perspective, however, the location-based mobile advertising segment is especially interesting. In the classical location-based advertising scenario, a coffee shop, usually Starbucks, issues coupons to consumers that are near their retail establishments. This technique is often called "geofencing" because it targets any consumer who can be located within a geographic area.

Some observers have criticized the "Starbucks" example as being naïve. They point out that consumers are mostly likely already aware of the Starbucks locations in their neighborhood. Although consumers may redeem the coupons if offered them, these consumers may have been near Starbucks because they had already intended to go into the store. So the coupons would not increase sales at all, and instead would cut into profit margins.

Nevertheless, many retailers, including Starbucks, have recently begun experimenting with campaigns just like these [14]. They may be trying out the new technology, hoping that even if some coupons are delivered to regular customers that they bring in enough new customers that they are worth the discount given.

Of course, any marketer using location-based advertising would prefer to target more accurately than just by location. They would prefer to know more about the customer, including her current needs for the retailer's products or services, her past history buying from the retailer and their competition, her present schedule and whether it permits a visit to the retailer, and whether her current context would permit her attention to be directed to an ad. Fortunately, smartphones have additional sensors for location, motion, sound, and lighting that make it possible for the phone to determine and provide details of the user and the situation in which the phone is being used. As we will explore more fully below, this aspect of smartphones – that they can observe and interpret the user's situations and activities *over time* – means that many of the elements of targeting can be fulfilled more extensively than other technologies have been able to.

4.3.5   Other Targeting Techniques

This brief tour of targeting techniques is not and cannot be complete. Many organizations keep customer databases and through analysis and cross-correlations have developed a number of industry-specific marketing approaches. The above approaches can also be combined together with these and other solutions to make superior hybrid approaches.

Although not the topic of this paper, social networking is a significant trend that makes more accurate targeting possible. Through social networking, it is possible to identify a person's interests because interests are influenced by and highly correlated with the product interests of their friends. Although social networking makes the connections between people explicit, algorithms for recommending items have existed for decades to predict items that people will like based on similarities in explicit rankings for products like movies, restaurants, etc. According to VentureBeat's Matt Marshall [13], 35% of Amazon's sales come from personalized recommendations.

4.4   Activity Inferencing and Forecasting

The new targeting technologies presented in the previous section have been made possible by new technologies. In this section, we describe activity inference, a new emerging technology that is just beginning to be applied to advertising. In short, the idea is that by using sensors on the phones, it is possible to determine a user's activity, and from this, some aspects of their needs, purchasing opportunity, and context can be inferred for the present and future. In some cases, these inferences can also direct content tailoring.

Over the past decade, researchers in the field of ubiquitous computing have been inventing algorithms that combine information from a variety of sensors to determine transportation modes (walk, bike, run, train, car, etc.), mechanical actions (hammering, screw-driving, etc.), activities of daily living (making meals, using the bathroom, etc.), and office-work activities and temporal patterns (presence and availability at different times of day). Although these techniques are not as accurate as humans can be at sensing activities, they are accurate enough to be able to improve targeting in advertising systems.

Generally speaking, the concept of "activity" is not clearly defined. Here, by "activity" we mean how a person would answer the question "what are you doing?" Of course, the computer representation of an activity is likely to be different from a person's explanation. We do not want to make a particular assumption about the representation here, but it could be a bag (set) of words, a single variable that is assigned from a well-defined taxonomy from a time-use study (see, for example, the taxonomy of over 400 activities in the American Time Use Survey), or it could be a highly structured representation such as the one described in Activity Theory, a sociological theory of human behavior that specifies the actions performed by actors upon objects, determined by roles, and mediated by tools and the societal framework that provides a context [12].

4.4.1 Activity Inference

Regardless of the representation, activity inference determines from one or more data sources what it is that a person is likely doing at any time. Some activity inference algorithms provide only a "best guess." Others compute a distribution over activities with a low-entropy distribution indicating that the estimate is very certain, and a high-entropy distribution indicating uncertainty.

How can activities be detected and predicted? Human behavior can be inferred through a variety of means, from on-phone sensors to infrastructure sensing to data provided directly or indirectly by the user. Here is a quick survey of some of the relevant sensing technologies available on a user's phone.

1. GPS. Location is a critical predictor of human activity. In fact, according to the American Time-Use Survey, 50% of all activities (coarsely defined) reported by individuals can be correctly determined from location alone. When combined with other readily-available information, such as the day of week and time of day, the accuracy rate improves to around 60% [18].
2. Alternative location-sensing technologies. Cellular radio, WiFi, Bluetooth, and even FM radio signals can be used to estimate the user's location. While not as accurate as GPS, these alternative technologies can be useful in acquiring a GPS fix more quickly, and in determining the user's position when the GPS signals cannot be observed. This is often the case indoors, although GPS signals do work indoors surprisingly often [11].
3. Audio. Microphones are useful for determining when a person is in a conversation, which is crucial for knowing when he or she can't be interrupted. A phone that stores a model of the user's voice can analyze the audio to determine if the phone's owner is speaking, which can be useful for distinguishing between a live conversation and other ambient noise like from a radio or TV.
4. Motion sensors such as an accelerometer. Accelerometers are especially good at determining when someone is walking if the phone is carried on their body. Walking patterns can help distinguish among two or more neighboring venues that cannot otherwise be identified through GPS [1]. They also can be useful for identifying the exact moment a person walks inside a store, because people naturally slow down at store boundaries [25]. This is particularly important if the GPS signal can be picked up both outside and inside the store without much signal strength degradation, or if it cannot be picked up in either place.
5. Orientation sensors. Orientation can be important in particular situations. For example, if the user's location within a grocery store is known, it is still not clear what product they are interested in. Knowing the direction that the user is facing helps narrow down the user's interest much further.

6. Wearable cameras. New technologies such as wearable cameras make it possible to passively collect images of a user's environment. This could further narrow down a user's activity or object of attention.

In addition to sensors on the phone, sensors in the environment can detect human activity as well. These sensors have already become useful in applications like digital signage for identifying faces and recognizing expressions. They could also be used more generally to infer user behavior, although they face the challenges of reliably identifying the sensed user and of providing sufficient value at the place of installation to justify their cost. One particularly useful data source, however, is purchase events, discussed in more detail below.

These technologies are especially interesting because they do not require any effort or intervention from the user. Users may also provide data that assists activity inference. User-provided data is different from data that is directly collected from sensors because it requires natural language processing to interpret text that is primarily intended for use by people, not by machines.

Many people keep calendars to remind themselves about events. Calendar events typically contain a short label that is a sufficient reminder for the person. This label can sometimes be interpreted to directly suggest the activity. In other cases, the label may name a person or place. In these cases, the activity itself may not be determined directly, but the label contents can be used to connect this activity to other times with the same label. Finally, a calendar entry may explicitly list other people involved in the activity because they were also listed in an email message used to set up the calendar entry. A system can then determine from the list of people invited the sort of an activity that may be occurring, and in some cases, textual analysis techniques like Latent Dirichlet Allocation can identify discussion keywords topics.

Consumers may also explicitly provide information about their location through checkin services like Foursquare, Gowalla, Loopt, and social networks supporting such a feature like Facebook Places. This can be more reliable than a calendar entry. A calendar entry may refer to a regularly scheduled event that the user doesn't always attend, or to an event scheduled by others that the user does not plan to go to. Checkins, however, must be performed at (or at least very close to) the place that the user says that they are. Having an explicit confirmation has significant marketing value because GPS is not yet reliable enough to distinguish adjacent stores, or among stores inside a single building. A checkin can also provide additional information about an activity that is not included in a GPS reading. However, checkins are not reliable, because the user may forget to checkin, and it has not yet reached the same acceptance level among the general population as other technologies. According to a Forrester Research report [17], around 80% of all location-based social network users are male.

Finally, activities may be determined by analyzing text that contains plans for the future. In a preliminary study of text messages among college-age students in Singapore [2] we found that roughly one in ten text messages contained information related to planning for future events. These text messages can be analyzed for text keywords and grammatical structures that experts have identified as indicating future plans. Once the plans have been extracted from these structures, an automatically-constructed calendar entry can be added to when the system believes an event will happen. An alternative mechanism works without experts, and uses machine learning to identify the relationship between keywords and word n-grams and the act of manually adding a calendar entry. Once the relationship is known, then the system can infer a user's future activities from similar messages, even if the user does not explicitly add the calendar entry.

Activity inference algorithms typically work by using machine learning algorithms over a labeled set of data to identify the pattern of features that determine activity. For more information, see [7] for a general description of machine learning, or [23] to see examples of how these techniques can be applied to activity inference.

4.4.2 Activity Forecasting

Activity forecasting refers to making an inference about a person's activity at a future time. Probabilistic machine learning techniques that work well for inference also work well for forecasts. Typically they cannot make a completely accurate prediction from data about the present, so extending the techniques to make predictions about the future is not hard.

However, because the system does not have direct data about the time that the forecast is to be made, the inference algorithms are limited in the sources of data available. They can still use the time of data and day of week as a predictive feature, because that is an input to the forecast. They also can extrapolate sequences from present data based on temporal models that have been constructed from observing past data. For example, a system might notice that a person has a typical pattern of going from home to school to drop off their children, then to work, and then to the grocery store, and then home. If this knowledge is incorporated into a statistical model, then by knowing that a person is at work, a system could make a reasonable prediction that the user would go to the grocery store, and then home. The system could make this prediction even if the user had an unreliable work schedule and the "home-to-school-to-work-to-grocery store-to-home" pattern did not happen on every day.

Another technique for forecasting is to use information about the user's social group. By observing where a user goes and where their contacts go, it may be possible for a system to determine patterns of correlation. If the system can infer that a contact is highly likely to perform an activity in the future, then it may be possible for it to infer that another person in that contact's social group will also perform the same activity, even if there is no direct evidence about that other person's future behavior.

4.5 Activity-Targeted Advertising

Intuitively, there should be value in delivering advertisements tailored to people's activities. Just as content-bundled ads are effective because people are interested in things that they read, activity-based ads can be valuable because people are interested in the work they do, the sports they play, the types of restaurants they frequent, and the hobbies they enjoy. Furthermore, just as search-based ads are effective because the searcher is in a state to receive information, activity detection can infer times when people are more receptive to attaining information versus times when they are too busy to be bothered. In addition, location-based behavior tracking can even anticipate future opportunities for acting on a received advertisement and optimize the timing of the presentation.

On the other hand, search-based advertising already performs far better than previous advertising models (e.g., bundling ads with content) so why add even more complexity to advertising systems by inferring activity? Here's why: advertisers can reach customers even *before* they resort to searching for information. Before they are even aware that they have an interest in a product, advertisers can reach people who have a latent, unexpressed need for a product or service category, influencing them *before they've already made a decision* of what to purchase.

There are several aspects of activity inferencing that enhance the effectiveness of advertising.

4.5.1 Advertising Products Related to User Activities

An activity may directly suggest a product. For example, a user going to a golf course may be interested in golf clubs, golf balls, etc. An activity may also suggest an opportunity to buy a variety of goods or services. Going to a grocery store creates an opportunity for a customer to fulfill several needs.

In some cases, the role must be determined as well as the activity. Someone at a golf course could be a player or a greens keeper. Someone visiting a patient at a hospital has very different product interests than if she were a patient herself. The role of the user at a place distinguishes activity-based advertising from conventional location-based advertising, which does not consider role.

4.5.2 Forecasting Locations and Activities

Another distinction from location-based advertising is that many of the best opportunities lie not in advertising products related to the user's current location or activity, but to *predicted future* locations and activities. During the current activity, the consumer's attention is likely on their activity, not on a media device. In addition, consumers may make purchase decisions before the activity starts. For both these reasons, it is important to deliver advertising related to activities before the activities start.

Patterns are especially helpful for predicting future activities. While users vary in how predictable their activities are, even users with exceptionally high appetites for variety tend to have more stable patterns about the *types* of products and services they prefer [22]. For example, a user may never go to the same restaurant twice, but they still may eat out nearly every night.

4.5.3   Timing the Presentation of Advertisements

Once future activities have been predicted, the system must decide. Should an advertisement be presented, and if so, which advertisement? Making this decision means considering all the possible futures and optimizing ad presentations and assignments over this and all future opportunities.

Additional data sources beyond activity are important in the ad-placement decision. Purchase history is particularly useful, because purchases indicate whether advertising is effective or not. Knowing not only when the user made a purchase, but their contextual and ad exposure history at the time of the purchase can lead to much more accurate ad placement decisions.

Using activity, purchase history, and demographic and psychographic data, the system can optimize its presentation by constructing a model of the user's current cognitive state. Are they happy? Relaxed? Upset? Frustrated? Bored? These situations affect the kind of ad that should be presented, and the way it is presented. These states can be estimated from the user's activity stream along with other data such as sentiment mining of user communications.

4.5.4   Optimizing Exposure to Advertisements

Also important is to model the user's exposure to an advertisement. If the user has viewed the advertisement recently, then a repeat exposure may have no additional effect. Or if the user has been over-exposed, then another presentation may just frustrate him or her further. In traditional media, individual exposure rates can only be estimated based on reach and frequency, but in a pervasive advertising environment, individual exposures may be directly counted. Unlike web advertising, a system that pervasively monitors ad presentation can track user exposure to campaign advertising across channels, thereby better estimating ad exposure.

To sum up, activity inference provides an abstraction for concentrating data that is coming from multiple sensors and other sources to target advertisements to user behavior. It brings advertising technology one step closer on the road from simple demographic modeling of users to highly personalized, individual tailoring of the delivery of the right information at the right time.

4.6 Is Activity-Based Advertising Effective?

We have explained in the preceding pages how activity inference and prediction could help target advertising better. But does it actually improve targeting, the consumer experience, and the value to advertisers? Is activity inference accurate enough? Do consumers have a more positive reaction to ads that use activity-targeting?

While a rigorous evaluation of any new technology is critical to its adoption, there are many challenges in evaluating an activity-based advertising system. All pervasive computing systems are difficult to evaluate [4]. Because the system must learn the user's patterns, it takes time before enough data has been collected to make an accurate inference. Each user also has their own individual activity patterns; it is difficult to isolate individual variables because there is so much user-to-user variation. Mobile development platforms also have more challenges than traditional digital systems. The devices have less memory and processing power, limited battery life, and there are many competing platforms to choose from. Users may not always carry their devices, which means that a phone may not be able to observe the user's entire day [19]. Finally, researchers are actively inventing new activity inference techniques, so the results of an evaluation performed today may not reflect the ultimate potential of the technology.

How, then, do we test an activity-based advertising system? One approach is to fake it. Instead of investing a large amount of technical resources to prototype an activity-detection system, we developed smartphone software to randomly ask the user, "What are you doing now?" We used their answers in place of a working activity recognition system.

For purposes of experimentation, we recruited 19 coworkers who were willing to carry phones with this software (named PEST, the Proactive Experience Sampling Tool) for 3 days [21]. They gave answers like "catching up on some school work," "talking to Mom," and "waiting in line." We sent each of these responses to Amazon's Mechanical Turk system where online workers do small pieces of work for small amounts of money. This service provides a way to simulate artificial intelligence before it has been developed (as Amazon puts it, "*artificial* artificial intelligence"). The workers proposed products or services to be used along with the user's given activity description. The user was then presented with an ad that was either randomly selected, or one that was matched to the worker's product recommendation. The user then rated both the usefulness and the relevance of the ad on a scale from one to ten, and compared the user ratings for activity-based ads to randomly selected ads.

Relevance is the degree to which information is related to the consumer's desires or needs. An irrelevant ad describes a product or service the consumer has no need or interest in. Usefulness is the degree to which the information changes how the user satisfies their desire or need. A useless ad may be relevant, but may not affect the consumer's opinion of the product or competitors' products. Of course, these definitions are vague and imprecise, but we generally share a sense that things can be relatively *more* or *less* relevant and useful to an individual.

Fig. 4.1 Activity-targeted ads were significantly more relevant than randomly targeted ads over all activity types, but not necessarily more useful

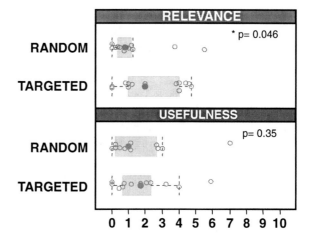

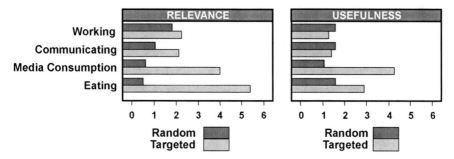

Fig. 4.2 Activity-targeted ads are more useful than random ads for activities except when the user is engaged in work or communication

The aggregated results showed that the study participants found the activity-targeted advertisements to be significantly more relevant than random advertisements over all types of activity (Fig. 4.1). However, the users did not find the advertisements to be more useful. But when segmenting the activities into different types (Fig. 4.2), activity-targeted advertisements were considered more useful in activities other than work-related or communication-related activities.

In interviews following the experiment, participants gave several suggestions for how to improve the advertising mechanism, including being more sensitive to the user's context and only advertising during idle times, targeting needs that could be inferred from activities rather than directly targeting activities themselves, infer probable future web queries and target advertisements to those projected queries, and allow users to rate advertisements and use those ratings to select better advertisements in the future.

We believe that the low usefulness scores, particularly when the user was working or communicating, arise because the system was interruptive. Although it may have been possible to tailor the content according to the user's context of working or communicating, by not respecting the user's context, users were frustrated by the system's efforts to attract their attention. We suspect that low "usefulness" scores in our evaluation would have turned into relatively low attention in a deployed system.

This evaluation has provided a preliminary methodology for evaluating activity-based advertising. While much more work is needed to show that targeting algorithms can be effective, particular from an advertiser perspective, the results do show that it is possible to get more relevant targeting with only a little bit of information, and for some categories, more useful targeting as well.

4.7 Privacy

Targeting technologies raise important questions about the privacy of user data, and the potential for abuse of that information. Systems that collect and analyze real-time data about people's locations and activities pose real danger as illustrated by a short-lived 2010 web site, "pleaserobme.com," which became famous for aggregating foursquare.com users' self-reported location to indicate when people were not at home. Add the ability to predict where users are likely to be, and the risks become even greater. Criminals could use this information to plan crimes.

To address this concern, systems that process such user data must be secure. Security analyses should be performed by a team separated from the general engineering team, and there should be mechanisms in place for security problems to be reported and patches quickly deployed to running systems.

Even if their personal data is secured, people have some discomfort with the idea that other institutions may collect and store information about them. Many of these people may not trust advertisers in general, fearing that the advertisers will trick them into making a purchase contrary to their interests.

To mitigate the concerns, some organizations such as the Mobile Marketing Association have adopted opt-in policies to give consumers the control needed before new advertisement technologies can be regarded positively [15]. Activity-based advertising must also give users opt-in control, and in a way that makes the effects of the choice very clear to the end user. Some users will not want activity-targeted advertisements. However, some consumers will appreciate the benefits that activity-based ad targeting can provide, whether in the form of fewer poorly targeted ads, or as coupons that they appreciate. These consumers will need to have enough trust in the technology operators to make the entire system effective and profitable. If the industry can obtain this trust, through targeting appropriately, enough consumers will opt-in to make the activity-targeted advertising technology worthwhile.

4.8   Conclusion

No one likes ineffective advertising. Consumers hate that their attention has been wasted and, even though the consumers' wasted attention does not carry a direct economic cost, advertisers have no desire to waste their money paying for irrelevant or useless advertisements. Effective advertising includes four elements: finding consumers in the market, filtering for those who can act on the advertisement, timing the delivery to when the consumer is receptive, and tailoring the content to the consumer's individual preferences and needs. Traditional targeting methods include demographic and psychographic segmentations of a market. Modern targeting includes search-based advertising, behavioral targeting, and location-based advertising.

Activity-based advertising is a new targeting technique that provides the four key elements of effective advertising by using sensing and inferencing technologies to infer what a person is doing. Activity inferencing provides insight into a consumer's interests and state of mind, making it potentially as effective as search-based advertising, but in situations where the user has not explicitly provided information to the system. An activity-based advertising system can detect a person's latent needs and interests in product or service category based on what they do. It can also detect times when a person is more receptive to information, potentially in advance of the person sitting down to search for a product.

Like other forms of behavioral targeting, activity-based advertising raises the concern of encroachment on personal privacy. Exposing deep details about one's individual life is only warranted if the benefits outweigh the risks. Experiments at PARC have found that activity detection is more useful for certain product categories (food and media) than for others, and that the timing of the presentation is as important as the content. However, we caution that only the individual can make the cost-benefit decision, and that systems must provide opt-in as a bare minimum measure.

Activity-based advertising is still a new technology, only recently enabled by the widespread adoption of smartphones. The capability will certainly grow as our lives are increasingly filled with sensors, including in-vehicle telematics, in-building smart energy consumption, on-body health monitoring, and other forms of machine perception. Current advertising is insensitive to the consumer, and obtrusive and annoying like a pushy, hard-selling salesperson. The goal of activity-based advertising is to make advertising more adaptable to the customer's actions and receptivity, and bring it closer to the experience of working with a helpful, knowledgeable, friendly salesperson.

Acknowledgements Matthias Sala co-designed, implemented, and ran the PEST user study while an intern at PARC. Many of the ideas in this chapter emerged out of discussions with the PARC research community, particularly Dan Greene, Maurice Chu, and Alan Walendowski.

References

1. Azizyan, M.: SurroundSense: mobile phone localization via ambience fingerprinting. In: Mobicom 2009 (2009)
2. Bellotti, V.: Activity-based serendipitous recommendations with the Magitti mobile leisure guide. CHI 2008, Florence (2008)
3. Binkley, C.: The gatekeeper: how posh hotel sizes up guests. Wall St. J., 10 May 2007, p. D1 (2007)
4. Carter, S., Mankoff, J.: Challenges for Ubicomp evaluation. Technical Report, Electrical Engineering and Computer Sciences, UC Berkeley (2004)
5. Elliott, S.: The media business; advertising; a survey of consumer attitudes reveals the depth of the challenge that the agencies face. The New York Times. http://www.nytimes.com/2004/04/14/business/media-business-advertising-survey-consumer-attitudes-reveals-depth-challenge.html (2004). Accessed 23 Mar 2011
6. Gartner.: Dataquest insight: consumer location-based services, subscribers and revenue forecast, 2007–2013. http://www.gartner.com/DisplayDocument?id=1035015 (2009). Accessed 23 Mar 2011
7. Hastie, T., Tibshirani, R., Friedman, J.H.: The Elements of Statistical Learning. Springer, New York (2003)
8. Helft, M.: Google to offer ads based on interests. NY Times. http://www.ny-times.com/2009/03/11/technology/internet/11google.html (2009). Accessed 23 Mar 2011
9. Hudson, S., Fogarty, J., Atkeson, C., Avrahami, D., Forlizzi, J., Kiesler, S., Lee, J.C., Yang, J.: Predicting human interruptibility with sensors: a wizard of Oz feasibility study. In: Proceedings of CHI 2003. ACM, New York (2003)
10. Kim, P.: Consumers love to hate advertising. Forrester Research (2006)
11. Kjærgaard, M.: Indoor positioning using GPS revisited. In: Pervasive Computing 2010. Springer, Berlin (2010)
12. Kuutti, K.: Activity theory as a potential framework for human-computer interaction research. In: Nardi, B. (ed.) Context and Consciousness: Activity Theory and Human Computer Interaction, pp. 17–44. MIT Press, Cambridge (1995)
13. Marshall, M.: Aggregate Knowledge raises $5M from Kleiner, on a Roll. http://venturebeat.com/2006/12/10/aggregate-knowledge-raises-5m-from-kleiner-on-a-roll/ (2006). Accessed 23 Mar 2011
14. Mobiadnews.: Starbucks Starts Location-based Messaging Ads with O2. http://www.mobiadnews.com/?p=4967 (2010). Accessed 23 Mar 2011
15. Mobile Marketing Association.: Mobile Advertising Guidelines. http://mmaglobal.com/policies/global-mobile-advertising-guidelines (2009). Accessed 23 Mar 2011
16. Müller, J., Krüger, A: Competing for your attention: negative externalities in digital signage advertising. In: Proceedings of Ambient Information Systems, workshop paper (self-published), Toronto (2007)
17. Parrish, M.: Location-based social networks: a hint of mobile engagement emerges. Forrester Research (2010)
18. Partridge, K., Golle, P.: On using existing time-use study data for ubiquitous computing applications. In: Proceedings of Ubicomp 2008. ACM, New York (2008)
19. Patel, S., Kientz, J., Hayes, G., Bhat, S., Abowd, G.: Farther than you may think: an empirical investigation of the proximity of users to their mobile phones. In: Proceedings of Ubicomp 2006. ACM, New York (2006)
20. Rosenberg, M.: You Are Where You Live: Claritas PRIZM NE System Sorts ZIP Codes into 66 Clusters. http://geography.about.com/od/obtainpopulationdata/a/claritas.htm (2006). Accessed 23 Mar 2011
21. Sala, M., Partridge, K., Jacobson, L., Begole, B.: An exploration into activity-informed physical advertising using PEST. In: Proceedings of Pervasive 2007. Springer, Berlin (2007)

22. Simonson, I.: The effect of purchase quantity and timing on variety-seeking behavior. J. Market Res. **27**, 150–162 (1990)
23. Tapia, E.M.: Activity recognition in the home using simple and ubiquitous sensors. Masters Thesis, MIT (2004)
24. The SEMPO Annual State of Search Survey.: Summary Results: http://www.sempo.org/learning_center/research/2008_execsummary.pdf (2008). Accessed 23 Mar 2011
25. Underhill, P.: Why We Buy: The Science of Shopping. Simon & Schuster, New York (2000)

Chapter 5
A Standard for Digital Signage Privacy

Harley Lorenz Geiger

Abstract Privacy controls are essential for digital signage to maintain consumer trust as the medium continues to assimilate identification and interactivity technologies. Unless the industry adopts robust self-regulation, it is likely to face consumer backlash and reactive government regulation that may stifle innovation. The digital out-of-home industry as a whole should commit to comprehensive privacy standards based on the Fair Information Practices.

5.1 Introduction

Digital signage, also known as "digital out-of-home" or DOOH, is a communications medium characterized by a dynamic display presenting messages in a public environment [13]. A common example of digital signage media is a flat screen television displaying a loop of advertisements in retail stores. Other digital signage units take the form of kiosks, projectors or billboards. The units appear in a broad range of settings, including in shopping malls, hospitals and doctors' offices, public transportation, gas stations, restaurants, government facilities and public schools. The messaging content is often controlled via computer, enabling one master location to control many networked units.

The medium is a prominent part of the shift in communications and advertising away from traditional offline media [11]. Digital signage has rapidly grown into a multibillion-dollar industry over the past decade. Despite the economic downturn, industry forecasts predict growth at double-digit rates for the next 3–5 years [18]. There were an estimated 630,000 displays in the United States in 2007, though there are many more worldwide, particularly in China [16].

H.L. Geiger (✉)
Center for Democracy & Technology (CDT), Washington, DC, USA
e-mail: harley@cdt.org

J. Müller et al. (eds.), *Pervasive Advertising*, Human-Computer Interaction Series,
DOI 10.1007/978-0-85729-352-7_5, © Springer-Verlag London Limited 2011

Until recently, a shortcoming of digital signage as an advertising medium was the challenge in determining how many and what kind of individuals see a given display unit. This made it difficult for advertisers to measure the size of their audience and price ad time on digital signage networks accordingly. This problem also makes it relatively difficult to target ads to specific audience demographics or psychographics, which is a cornerstone of modern advertising.

To overcome these obstacles, the digital signage industry is exploring several technologies that will improve audience measurement and interactivity. Depending on the system, these enhancements often obtain a range of information about consumers. Some of the technologies have the ability to identify individual consumers, track them as they move from place to place and store detailed information about their preferences and activities. These emerging technologies include:

- *Facial recognition*: Increasingly, digital signage units use facial measurement technology to discern certain characteristics about a person looking at the display. This is perhaps the most common method, with one company claiming to have scanned more than 400 million people to date [27]. Some systems, while not yet configured to identify individuals, can calculate a passerby's age, gender, and race, and determine how long an individual watches the display. The advertisement on the screen can then change to match the consumer's profile. Other systems note only gender, and still others merely count the number of faces that see the screen (gaze-tracking).
- *Mobile marketing*: A rising number of digital signage units interact in various ways with portable devices, particularly mobile phones. Some units communicate with phones via SMS messaging and Bluetooth to send rich content (like ringtones or movie trailers) to consumers. Other units enable consumers to download a coupon, play games, or enter contests through their mobile phones. Given the broad range of potential applications for mobile marketing and digital signage, industry analysts predict the two media will grow together.
- *Social networking*: Some digital signage units provide access to social networks like Facebook, Twitter and Flickr through the Internet or apps on consumers' mobile devices. In some applications, consumers can send user-generated messages, photos and other content to specific digital signage screen locations in real time. Some long-view predictions see consumers consulting friends about clothing purchases through retail-based digital signage screens over social networks.
- *Radio Frequency Identification (RFID)*: The most common use of RFID in digital signage features RFID-enabled shelves that prompt nearby digital signage units to display advertisements related to the products on the shelves. Other digital signage systems air ads triggered by shopper loyalty cards equipped with RFID [28].
- *License plate scanners*: In a 2009 advertising pilot, digital billboards along a UK highway displayed personalized advertisements to passing cars. Roadside cameras scanned license plates and ran the numbers through the Driver and

Vehicle Licensing Agency. The billboard then displayed the license number and the best type of motor oil for that make and model of car. Public outrage and questions about whether the pilot's use of motor vehicle registration data for marketing violated UK privacy laws led to the pilot's abrupt shutdown [17].

Digital signage uses other technologies, such as GPS, to a lesser extent, and more have potential to combine with digital signage to create interactive experiences for consumers. Clearly digital signage can integrate many technologies to collect a broad range of consumer data in various contexts. Although the privacy recommendations in this document is intended to offer suggestions for present and future digital signage data collection practices, the significant innovation digital signage has shown in the past will likely lead to hitherto unforeseen business models.

5.2   The Time Is Right for a Digital Signage Privacy Framework

Using identification and interactivity technologies, the digital signage and mobile industries are taking the Internet experience into the physical world. In doing so, digital signage has established a burgeoning offline version of the behavioral advertising that currently occurs online – the practice of tracking consumers' activities in order to deliver advertising targeted to the individual interests [33]. Deployed to enough locations in digital signage units, such a practice may well be profitable to the industry, just as behavioral advertising has proven profitable on the Internet. Privacy invasion associated with digital signage is not rampant because only a small percentage of digital signage units have audience measurement, identification or interactive capabilities. However, the industry trend is clearly toward greater adoption of measurement, identification and surveillance capabilities, not less.

The usefulness of audience data to marketers and the increasing cost effectiveness of sophisticated equipment will encourage the digital signage industry to collect detailed consumer data. Interactivity has been named a key driver of digital signage growth in 2010 [9]. In January 2010, Intel and Microsoft announced a joint effort to develop digital signage that can emulate the ability of online retailers to identify returning customers and tailor advertisements to them based on their shopping histories [6]. Coordinating online and offline behavioral advertising will be especially natural to companies like Focus Media Holding. Focus Media owns an extensive Internet advertising network and also operates the largest digital signage network in China, with more than 190,000 screens [14].

Consumers and companies are already wary of the privacy implications of identification and consumer profiling technologies in digital signage. Comments to blog posts and news articles on facial recognition in digital signage indicate many consumers have little faith that digital signage companies will protect consumer data [25]. Some industry figures have said that companies must guarantee consumer privacy [15], while others have cited privacy issues as an obstacle to using facial recognition technology for advertising purposes [10]. A New York Times article on billboards with facial recognition prompted a major digital signage company to publicly defend its privacy practices [22]. Public backlash and possible violations of existing privacy laws have already led to the discontinuation of some digital signage advertising projects, as with the billboard which scanned UK license plates.

The reaction to this form of digital signage marketing parallels the controversy associated with online behavioral advertising. A 2009 study of consumer attitudes towards behavioral advertising found two-thirds of Americans "definitely would not" allow marketers to track them online, even if the tracking is anonymous [31]. The study also found 90% of young adults reject advertising tailored to them based on offline activities. Facebook members have revolted several times over uses of their information on the social networking site, persuading Facebook to repeatedly revise its privacy policies and the information management tools it provides to its users [8].

In 2009, the U.S. Federal Trade Commission (FTC) issued self-regulatory guidelines for online behavioral advertising [33]. The soon-to-be Chairman stated the guidelines may be the last clear chance the industry had to show it would effectively protect consumer privacy in the absence of stricter legislation [19]. The U.S. Congress has held multiple hearings on the issue, and members of Congress have repeatedly called for privacy legislation to regulate how consumer information is collected, used and shared for marketing [1].

Given this environment, digital signage companies should proactively adapt their practices to be transparent and minimally intrusive, and to afford consumers control over how their information is collected and used. Incorporating privacy into the fabric of digital signage business models and data management practices is the best way to prevent privacy risks before they arise [3]. It will be less expensive for digital signage companies to integrate privacy controls now, while identification technologies are still relatively new to the industry, than it will be to retrofit privacy protections onto existing systems. How digital signage companies handle the privacy issues they face today will affect the way the public, regulators and advertisers perceive the medium, as well as the industry's direction in the future. The industry should prove its dedication to privacy protection to reduce the risk that the public will consider interactive digital signage a disrespectful intrusion.

In 2010, the Point Of Purchase Association International (POPAI), a trade association, released a first generation set of privacy guidelines for digital signage [26]. POPAI's Code of Conduct is an excellent start for industry self-regulation. In particular, the Code's section on cross-channel and cross-domain marketing contains several good privacy protections, such as the requirement that a consumer re-opt in each time he or she enters a new venue where cross-domain marketing takes place. However, the Code does not articulate a full set of Fair Information Practices, nor does it suggest digital signage companies establish a comprehensive privacy framework. The POPAI Code is a sound foundation for the digital signage industry, but the industry should not limit itself to the Code's recommendations.

5.3   Protection Should Go Beyond Directly Identifiable Information

Some privacy protection frameworks, including many industry guidelines, typically extend only what was traditionally considered "personally identifiable information" (PII). PII was thought to include only information that can be directly linked to an individual's identity. However, it is increasingly being realized that the distinction between PII and non-PII is becoming much less meaningful in light of data analytic capabilities. Researchers have demonstrated that individuals can still be identified from records stripped of traditional identifiers [24]. The FTC supports extending privacy protection to information beyond that which only directly identifies individuals [33].

The best approach for companies is to evaluate all the data they collect on a spectrum ranging from directly identifiable to "pseudonymous" to aggregated, providing different levels of privacy protection corresponding to the sensitivity of the information involved [4].

Directly identifiable data includes what was once referred to as PII:

- Name
- Address
- Telephone number
- Date of birth
- Social Security Number
- Driver's license number
- License plate number
- Email address
- Bank, credit card, or other account number
- Biometric data, such as unique data points captured via facial recognition systems
- Images of individuals.

In addition to directly identifiable data, companies should extend protection to any data that could reasonably be associated with a particular consumer or a particular consumer's property, such as a smart phone or other device [33].

The term *"pseudonymous data"* refers to information associated with a unique identifier. Although pseudonymous data does not directly identify an individual, pseudonymous data can be traced to an individual's identity with relative ease. This type of data includes, but is not limited to

- RFID codes: RFID chips frequently come with a uniquely identifiable number, which can individualize any property to which the chip is attached.

- Device identification numbers, such as IP address, Mac address, Bluetooth number, Near Field Communication number, International Mobile Equipment Identity number.
- Internet username, such as the name with which one uses to posts to a discussion forum.
- Social networking data, including login information and friend lists.
- User-generated data: data generated knowingly by an individual, such as search terms, posts in discussion forums and data input into social networking profiles.

Whether a data element will reasonably identify an individual will depend on the context in which the data was collected. When determining the privacy practices necessary for handling pseudonymous data, companies should consider the availability of other data sets [21]. An individual's identity may be reasonably inferred by combining pseudonymous data with, for example, records of purchases from credit or loyalty cards, security surveillance systems, or aggregated location data which reveals unique habits or travel patterns.

Aggregate data includes information about multiple individuals that cannot reasonably be used to directly identify or infer the identity of a single individual. The most prominent example of this in digital signage may be facial qualification, where the demographics of individuals passing by a digital sign are compiled over time, but unique biometric data points and images of individuals are not saved. Even though aggregate data may not be directly identifiable or re-identifiable, companies should incorporate privacy practices – particularly transparency – into their collection of such data. Many consumers object to covert behavioral targeting even if it is done on an "anonymous" or aggregate basis [31].

5.4   Policy Framework and Models

Privacy standards for digital signage should be based on the widely accepted Fair Information Practices (FIPs). These internationally recognized principles are reflected (although often incompletely) in many privacy laws in the U.S. and are also the basis of more comprehensive privacy laws internationally, such as the European Union's Data Protection Directive. We believe the FIPs are equally well-suited as the basis for digital signage privacy guidelines. Recently, the U.S. Department of Homeland Security (DHS) adopted a modern and comprehensive formulation of these principles [32]. These are the FIPs as set forth by DHS:

- Transparency
- Individual Participation
- Purpose Specification
- Data Minimization

- Use Limitation
- Data Quality and Integrity
- Security
- Accountability

The online behavioral advertising industry has partially incorporated the FIPS into various self-regulatory guidelines. These include the guidelines issued by the Network Advertising Initiative and by the Interactive Advertising Bureau. However, the guidelines of the online advertising industry fall short in key areas, so the digital signage industry should not merely mimic them [5]. Nevertheless, the industries share the practice of targeting advertisements to consumers based on their activities. This makes it worthwhile for digital signage companies to familiarize themselves with the privacy frameworks of their online counterparts.

Digital signage companies and their affiliates may also find relevance in existing frameworks for the technologies they use. For example, digital signage companies that utilize mobile marketing should use the Mobile Marketing Association (MMA)'s Global Code of Conduct as a baseline on which to build [23]. Similarly, digital signage companies that use RFID should integrate the standards of relevant trade associations or privacy groups [2]. None of these frameworks is perfect, and some are deficient in certain areas, but they may serve as a starting point for companies to develop their own policies.

With reference to existing models, and drawing on the comprehensive DHS framework, we recommend that the digital signage industry develop a privacy framework along the following lines:

5.4.1   Transparency

Digital signage data collection and use should be transparent. Generally, there are two important ways for digital signage companies to do this. First, digital signage companies should develop privacy policies and publish them on their websites. Second, digital signage companies should give consumers notice at the location in which the digital signage unit is placed. Transparency through notice and a public privacy policy is the responsibility of not just the technology vendors, which are unfamiliar to consumers, but also the digital signage network operators and the owners of the establishments at which the signage is located.

5.4.1.1   Privacy Policies

Privacy policies serve an important role. Internally, the process of developing a privacy policy forces a company to assess its data collection practices and develop rules for the custodianship of the data it collects. Companies should publish privacy policies to their websites, even if they collect nothing but aggregate data. A privacy policy should describe in concise, specific terms:

- What consumer data is collected,
- How the data is collected,
- The purposes for which the data is used,
- With whom the data is shared,
- How the data is protected,
- How long the data is retained, and
- The choices that consumers have with respect to their data.

Once the policy is set, data should not be collected, shared or used in any way contrary to the published privacy policy. In some cases, the data management practices of the digital signage company may overlap with the practices of another company, such as when digital signage integrates with mobile marketing or social networking applications. The digital signage privacy policy should underscore how these services interact.

Numerous digital signage companies already publish privacy policies. For example, some of the policies of companies using facial recognition state they do not retain images or identify individuals [7]. Similarly, some companies that integrate digital signage and social networking publish privacy policies [20]. However, existing policies vary greatly in detail, and not all digital signage services specify what they do with personal information.[1] A privacy policy alone is not enough, however, and many consumers confuse the mere existence of a policy with substantive privacy protections [30].

5.4.1.2   Notice

At present, many digital signage companies are completely unknown to consumers, so consumers are unlikely to look for the privacy policies posted on the websites of digital signage companies. Even if consumers come to know the names of digital signage companies, current practices give consumers little hint as to what company is responsible for a given digital signage display. The challenge for the industry is to find a way to present meaningful notice at the point of data collection. Such notice is fundamental to transparency and individual participation.

Consumers should be given clear, prominent notice of digital signage media units that collect consumer data at the physical location in which the unit operates. To the extent possible, the notice should appear conspicuously on or close to each

---

[1] The Marketplace Station [29]. The policy makes no reference of the data collection systems integrated into some of Marketplace Station's screens. See Digital Signage Today [12].

digital signage unit that is collecting the information.[2] One notice should not cover, for example, an entire supermarket, but instead should be at each sensor and associated digital signage screen within the supermarket. There should be no secret receivers, cameras or sensors used exclusively for marketing.

The precise manner in which companies provide notice may differ based on physical environment, equipment and other factors, but we conceptualize two layers of notice: a notice at the entrance of the data collection area and a notice on digital signs that collect consumer data.

First, companies should provide a notice near the entrance of a data collection area (i.e., in the breezeway of a supermarket using digital signs that record age and gender). This is to alert the consumer that data collection is occurring prior to the consumer entering the area.[3] The notice need not be large, but it should be easily readable to consumers.

Second, companies should display a notice on or near each digital signage screen associated with consumer data collection. This notice can be a physical sign, such as a small placard. The notice can also be mixed in intermittently with the media content. If the notice appears intermittently, it should remain on screen long enough for consumers to read it.

- For standalone signage units, an intermittent notice message should preferably be displayed an equal number of times to the network ID interstitial – the message that identifies the digital signage network or operator. However, if the network ID occurs less than four times an hour, a physical sign should be used. Alternatively, the notice could be displayed once per average consumer dwell time – the time the consumer spends near the unit.
- If multiple screens are networked together in one location, another option would be to display the notice once per average consumer trip. Here the goal would be to display the notice on multiple screens simultaneously at least once during the average time a consumer spends in the data collection area.

In addition, the operators of the establishment in which the unit is located should maintain an on-site hard copy of the digital signage company's full privacy policy.[4]

---

[2] The POPAI Code permits one notice to cover one establishment. See POPAI Code of Conduct, p. 8. However, we believe a notice should be provided at each screen. One discreet notice in an isolated location within a large retail store full of labels competing for consumers' attention is insufficient to provide notice for a digital signage network collecting data throughout the store.

[3] This alone would be insufficient because consumers often do not observe signs like these (i.e., the max capacity sign in a supermarket), which can defeat the point of the notice. If consumers don't observe the notice, they don't perceive the data collection as transparent and there is no positive effect on consumer trust. Hence, the second layer of notice – on the digital signs themselves – should give consumers an additional opportunity to become aware of the data collection.

[4] Since companies' privacy policies are online, most consumers are likely unable to access them in the store. Also, consumers without Internet access should have the opportunity to read the privacy policy elsewhere. Keeping a hard copy in the establishment in which the sign is located is the most practical way for consumers to easily review the privacy policy offline.

The notice message should – at minimum – describe:

- What information the location's digital signage system collects,
- For what purpose the information is used,
- Whether any directly identifiable or pseudonymous information is combined with other data, such as purchases or third party marketing data, and
- How the consumer may access the privacy policy of the digital signage unit operator (such as the company's website).

Therefore, a typical notice message might read: *This Company Name digital sign uses a camera to estimate your age and gender in order to make advertisements more relevant to you. No images or identifying information about you is collected or stored. For more information, visit* www.companyname.com/privacy *or see the store manager.*

Generic notices like "These premises are under video surveillance" are not sufficient. Consumers have come to assume such notices to relate to security measures, not marketing. Such notices do not provide accurate notification of the more comprehensive data collection, sharing and usage associated with marketing. If a digital signage unit is used for both security and for marketing, or if security information is used for marketing, the notice (and privacy policy) should clearly disclose this.

In cases where digital signage units interact with consumers' devices, such as with smart phones via Bluetooth, a comprehensive notice should also be delivered directly to the consumers' devices. This should be the norm when the digital signage unit or the consumer initiates the interaction.

5.4.2   Individual Participation

The FIPs principle of "individual participation" embodies two concepts: the right to consent to the collection and use of data and the right to access to data that has been collected about oneself. The robustness of the individual participation protocol required varies depending on the sensitivity and identifiability of the information collected and the use to which it is put. Similarly to the POPAI Code, we conceptualize digital signage audience measurement and interactive marketing as occurring on three general levels:

- Level I: *Audience counting.* Information related to consumers is gathered on an aggregate basis and not used for tailoring advertisements. No retained information, including images, links to individuals or their property. Example: facial recognition systems that track gazes or record passerby demographics, but do not store facial images or contextualize ads.
- Level II: *Audience targeting.* Information related to consumers is collected on an aggregate basis and is used for tailoring contextual advertisements to individuals. No retained information, including images, links to individuals or their property.

Example: facial recognition systems that record passerby demographics and contextualize ads accordingly.

- Level III: *Audience identification and/or profiling.* Information related to consumers is collected on an individual and aggregate basis and is used for tailoring advertisements. Information linked to individual identity or an individual's property (such as a mobile phone) is retained. Example: using digital signage networks for social networking, RFID tracking, mobile marketing.

5.4.2.1   Consent

Consumers should have a ready means to choose whether their data is collected for advertising purposes. The means will differ between digital signage systems and services. Levels I and II (described above) should implement opt-out consent. At minimum, opt-out consent can be accomplished via notice by giving consumers an opportunity to avoid a particular digital signage unit. Level III requires opt-in consent, which should be issued after the consumer has the opportunity to examine the applicable privacy policy.

Consumers should be able to exercise control over what information is collected, which marketing messages they receive, and which other companies and parties may see the data. The consent should be persistently honored until the consumer alters his or her choice, and the consent should also be revocable at any time. To the extent possible, opt-in consent protocol should be granular without also being confusing to consumers. One way to strike this balance is to offer various privacy control options, but to also offer an easy means to opt-out or opt-in to all the choices at once.

5.4.2.2   Access

Consumers should have the ability to view and/or correct any directly identifiable data collected about them for digital signage marketing. Digital signage companies should designate an internal point person to receive and process consumer complaints and questions. Companies should specify, in their privacy policies, a ready and inexpensive means for consumers to submit questions, complaints, and requests to access their data.

5.4.3   Purpose Specification

The purpose specification principle requires a company to think through its data collection and use practices and to specify how the company intends to use the data it is collecting. The purposes to which consumer data will be put should be specified not later than at the time of collection. Properly applied, the principle should lead companies to minimize the collection of unnecessary data, which is the next principle.

5.4.4 Data Minimization

Through privacy policies and guidelines, individual companies and the digital signage industry as a whole should commit to limit their data collection and retention to only the minimum necessary to achieve specified ends.

Digital signage companies should collect and use the minimum amount of consumer data necessary to deliver their services. For example, there is no need to use a license plate number when a car's make and model will do [17]. In most cases, it may not be necessary to retain consumer data for future use beyond the delivery of a contextual advertising message. For example, there is no need to maintain persistent records of phone numbers or Bluetooth addresses when a company does not seek an ongoing relationship with the individuals associated with that data. When a digital signage company does retain consumer information, that retention should last no longer than is needed to serve the purpose for which it was collected, as specified in the privacy policy.[5] If a consumer opts-out or cancels a service, the associated information should be destroyed.

5.4.5 Use Limitation

Consumer data should not be shared for any uses that are incompatible with the purposes specified in the company's privacy policy. Transfers of consumer data to any third parties or affiliates should be transparent, specified in advance to consumers and may require opt-in consent [26].

5.4.6 Data Quality and Integrity

Digital signage companies should, to the extent practicable, ensure consumer data they collect is accurate, relevant, timely and complete. Allowing consumers to access and edit data collected about them is one of the best mechanisms for ensuring data quality and integrity. Companies should establish a consumer complaint process that enables consumers to dispute inconsistencies in collected information and to notify the company if the consumers' consent choices are not being honored.

---

[5]The POPAI Code recommends that image or biometric data "should be stored for up to 3 months or the maximum period allowed by law." See POPAI Code of Conduct, Pg. 6. It is unclear whether POPAI means that the data should be stored no longer than that period, or whether POPAI recommends that the data be stored regardless of whether there is a business need for it, so long as the law allows it.

5.4.7   Security

Digital signage companies should exercise reasonable and appropriate efforts to secure information collected about consumers. In so doing, a company should maintain a standard information security program appropriate to the amount and sensitivity of the information stored on its system. Such a security program should include processes to identify and address reasonably foreseeable internal and external risks to the security, confidentiality, and integrity of information. Collected consumer data should be accessible only to those company employees who must use the data to perform their job functions.

The nature and extent of security required will largely depend on what kind of collection technology is employed and what consumer data is retained. Unnecessary consumer data should be destroyed via secure methodologies. The best data security is for a company not to possess consumer data in the first place.

5.4.8   Accountability

There has been substantial criticism of self-regulation of the behavioral advertising industry because of a lack of accountability for noncompliance. Digital signage companies who collect and use consumers' information should establish internal accountability mechanisms. These mechanisms should ensure strict compliance with companies' privacy policies, as well as laws and other applicable privacy protection requirements.

Companies should maintain a written procedure for processing and responding to consumer complaints. Companies should provide privacy and security training to all employees, contractors and affiliates who collect and use consumers' information. There should be meaningful penalties for violations, especially willful or chronic noncompliance.

The digital signage industry may also consider empowering one or more trade associations with independent oversight functions to monitor compliance and offer privacy management guidance for individual companies. The organization that takes on these functions should provide a dispute resolution forum for consumers and articulate clear benchmarks for companies to evaluate the efficacy of their privacy practices.

5.5   Conclusion

Privacy can be an enabler – not an impediment – to the development of digital signage as an industry and a communications medium. If companies are willing to incorporate strong privacy protections into their business models, then the industry has the opportunity to enter a new era of responsible, consumer-friendly, interactive out-of-home marketing. By adopting strong privacy protections early on, the digital signage industry can avoid the ire of regulators and the embarrassment of advertisers. There's also the matter of consumer trust: It's far easier to keep than to win back.

Acknowledgement An earlier version of this paper was first published by the Center for Democracy & Technology in March 2010 (available at www.cdt.org). This paper formed the basis of a set of digital signage privacy standards I wrote for the Digital Signage Federation, a U.S.-based trade association, in February. 2011 (available at www.digitalsignagefederation.org).

References

1. Boucher, R.: Behavioral ads: the need for privacy protection, The Hill, http://thehill.com/special-reports/technology-september-2009/60253-behavioral-ads-the-need-for-privacy-protection (2009). Accessed 23 Mar 2011
2. Center for Democracy & Technology Working Group on RFID.: Privacy Best Practices for Deployment of RFID Technology, http://old.cdt.org/privacy/20060501rfid-best-practices.php (2006). Accessed 23 Mar 2011
3. Center for Democracy & Technology.: Online behavioral advertising: industry's current self-regulatory framework is necessary, but still insufficient on its own to protect consumers. http://www.cdt.org/report/online-behavioral-advertising-industrys-current-self-regulatory-framework-necessary-still-ins (2009a). Accessed 23 Mar 2011
4. Center for Democracy & Technology.: The role of privacy by design in protecting consumer privacy. http://www.cdt.org/content/role-privacy-design-protecting-consumer-privacy (2009b). Accessed 23 Mar 2011
5. Center for Democracy & Technology.: Threshold analysis for online advertising practices. http://www.cdt.org/privacy/20090128threshold.pdf[accessed (2009c). 23 Mar 2011
6. Clark, D., Wingfield, N.: Intel, Microsoft offer smart-sign technology, Wall Street Journal, http://online.wsj.com/article/SB10001424052748704055104574652742982646768.html (2010). Accessed 23 Mar 2011
7. Cognovision.: Privacy policy. http://cognovision.com/privacy.php (2007). Accessed 23 Mar 2011
8. Coursey, D.: After criticism, facebook tweaks friends list privacy options, PC world. http://www.pcworld.com/businesscenter/article/184418/after_criticism_facebook_tweaks_friends_list_privacy_options.html?loomia_ow=t0:s0:a41:g26:r32:c0.000691:b23490248:z0 (2009). Accessed 23 Mar 2011
9. Digital Signage Expo: Capital Network's research identifies customer interaction as key digital signagetrendfor2010,http://www.digitalsignageexpo.net/DNNArticleMaster/DNNArticleView/tabid/78/smid/400/ArticleID/2312/reftab/66/Default.aspx (2009b). Accessed 23 Mar 2011
10. Digital Signage Expo.: Question of the month, http://www.digitalsignageexpo.net/Resources/QuestionoftheMonth/September09.aspx (2009c). Accessed 23 Mar 2011
11. Digital Signage Expo.: VSS forecast shows major shifts in communications industry growth patterns. http://www.digitalsignageexpo.net/DNNArticleMaster/DNNArticleView/tabid/78/smid/1041/ArticleID/1854/reftab/67/t/VSS-Forecast-Shows-Major-Shifts-in-Communications-Industry-Growth-Patterns/Default.aspx (2009a). Accessed 23 Mar 2011
12. Digital Signage Today.: Cognovision integrates with BroadSign for automated digital signage campaign analytics. http://www.digitalsignagetoday.com/article.php?id=22115 (2009). Accessed 23 Mar 2011
13. Digital Signage Resource.: Digital Signage Terms Glossary. http://www.digitalsignageresource.com/digital-signage-glossary-ofterms.asp?modes=3&col=term&term=digital_signage. Accessed 23 Mar 2011

14. Focus Media.: Company Overview. http://www.focusmedia.cn/en/aboutus/companyoverview. htm. Accessed 23 Mar 2011
15. Gerpa, B.: Digital signage networks must guarantee viewer privacy, The Digital Signage Insider. http://www.wirespring.com/dynamic_digital_signage_and_interactive_kiosks_journal/ articles/Digital_signage_networks_must_guarantee_viewer_privacy-569.html (2008). Accessed 23 Mar 2011
16. InfoTrends.: InfoTrends study shows strong growth up ahead for digital signage. http://www. capv.com/public/Content/Press/2007/06.06.2007.html (2007). Accessed 23 Mar 2011
17. Leake, C.: Drivers' details sold by DVLA are used in bizarre roadside adverts for Castrol, Daily Mail. http://www.dailymail.co.uk/news/article-1216414/Now-drivers-details-sold-DVLA-used-bizarre-roadside-adverts-Castrol.html (2009)
18. Lebovitz, R.: Forecasts show digital out-of-home still on track for growth, Digital Signage Expo. http://www.digitalsignageexpo.net/DNNArticleMaster/DNNArticleView/tabid/78/smid/ 1041/ArticleID/2249/reftab/67/t/Forecasts-Show-Digital-Out-of-Home-Still-on-Track-for-Growth/Default.aspx (2009a). Accessed 23 Mar 2011
19. Leibowitz, J.: Concurring statement to federal trade commission staff report: self-regulatory principles for online behavioral advertising. http://www.ftc.gov/os/2009/02/P085400behavadl eibowitz.pdf (2009b). Accessed 23 Mar 2011
20. LocaModa.: Privacy policy. http://locamoda.com/legal/privacy_policy (2010). Accessed 23 Mar 2011
21. Malin, B., Sweeney, L.: How (not) to protect genomic data privacy in a distributed network: using trail re-identification to evaluate and design anonymity protection systems. J. Biomed. Inform. 37, 179–192 (2004)
22. MediaBuyerPlanner.: TruMedia: Facial Recognition Boards will never record, share data. http://www.mediabuyerplanner.com/entry/34111/trumedia-facial-recognition-boards-will-never-record-share-data (2008). Accessed 23 Mar 2011
23. Mobile Marketing Association.: Global code of conduct. http://www.mmaglobal.com/ codeofconduct.pdf (2008). Accessed 23 Mar 2011
24. Ohm, P.: Broken promises of privacy: responding to the surprising failure of anonymization. http://papers.ssrn.com/sol3/papers.cfm?abstract_id=1450006 (2009). Accessed 23 Mar 2011
25. Patel, N.: TruMedia says its facial-recognition bilboards will never record video, it won't share with cops – user comments, engadget. http://engadget.com/2008/06/10/trumedia-says-its-facial-recognition-billboards-will-never-record/#comments (2008). Accessed 23 Mar 2011
26. POPAI Digital Signage Group.: Best practices: recommended code of conduct for consumer tracking research. http://www.popai.com/pdf/2010dscc.pdf (2010). Accessed 23 Mar 2011
27. Quividi.: Automated Audience Measurement. http://www.quividi.com/ (2011). Accessed 23 Mar 2011
28. Swedberg, C.: French jean boutique adopts RFID to boost loyalty, RFID Journal. http://www. rfidjournal.com/article/articleview/3472/1/1 (2007). Accessed 23 Mar 2011
29. The Marketplace Station.: Privacy Policy. http://www.themarketplacestation.com/pri-vacy. html. Accessed 23 Mar 2011
30. Turow, J., Hoofnagle, C.J., Mulligan, D.K., Good, N., Grossklags, J., Law, S.: The FTC and consumer privacy in the coming decade. http://www.ftc.gov/bcp/workshops/tech-ade/pdfs/ Turow-and-Hoofnagle1.pdf (2006). Accessed 23 Mar 2011
31. Turow, J., King, J., Hoofnagle, C.J., Bleakly, A., Hennessy, M.: Contrary to what marketers say, Americans reject tailored advertising and three activities that enable it. http://papers.ssrn. com/sol3/papers.cfm?abstract_id=1478214 (2009). Accessed 23 Mar 2011
32. U.S. Department of Homeland Security.: The fair information practice principles: framework for privacy policy at the Department of Homeland Security. http://www.dhs.gov/xlibrary/ assets/privacy/privacy_policyguide_2008-01.pdf (2008). Accessed 23 Mar 2011
33. U.S. Federal Trade Commission.: FTC staff report: self-regulatory principles for online behavioral advertising. http://www.ftc.gov/os/2009/02/P085400behavad-report.pdf (2009). Accessed 23 Mar 2011

Chapter 6
Targeted Advertising on the Handset: Privacy and Security Challenges

Hamed Haddadi, Pan Hui, Tristan Henderson, and Ian Brown

Abstract Online advertising is currently a rich source of revenue for many Internet giants. With the ever-increasing number of smart phones, there is a fertile market for personalised and localised advertising. A key benefit of using mobile phones is to take advantage of the significant amount of information on phones – such as locations of interest to the user – in order to provide personalised advertisements. Preservation of user privacy, however, is essential for successful deployment of such a system. In this chapter we provide an overview of existing advertising systems and privacy concerns on mobile phones, in addition to a system, MobiAd, which includes protocols for scalable local advertisement download and privacy-aware click report dissemination. In the final section of this chapter we describe some of the security mechanisms used in detecting click-through fraud, and techniques that can be used to ensure that the extra privacy protections of MobiAd are not abused to defraud advertisers.

H. Haddadi (✉)
Queen Mary, University of London, London, UK
e-mail: hamed@ee.ucl.ac.uk

P. Hui
Deutsche Telekom Laboratories, Darmstadt, Germany
e-mail: pan.hui@telekom.de

T. Henderson
University of St Andrews, UK
e-mail: tristan@cs.st-andrews.ac.uk

I. Brown
Oxford Internet Institute, UK
e-mail: ian.brown@oii.ox.ac.uk

J. Müller et al. (eds.), *Pervasive Advertising*, Human-Computer Interaction Series,
DOI 10.1007/978-0-85729-352-7_6, © Springer-Verlag London Limited 2011

6.1   Introduction

Advertising is one of the largest revenue sources of many Internet giants. Targeted and personalised advertisements, provided by advertising brokers such as Google and Microsoft, are displayed on designated advertisement slots on websites that in return receive payment from the advertising network. Google's advertising revenue in 2010 was over $28 billion and is only expected to increase over time [15].

The mobile phone advertising market is also becoming increasingly significant. There are currently over three billion mobile phone subscribers in the world. Surveys from Gartner and Telsyte group suggest that nearly a third of these are using smart phones, with the smart phone market increasing at a rate of nearly 50% last year [6]. With modern smart phones having 3G and wireless connectivity, GPS and Wi-Fi localisation capabilities, a wide range of social networking applications and web-browsing abilities on large touch LCD displays, there is a fertile market for targeted and personalised advertising. Naturally, handset manufacturers have recently launched a series of advertising platforms which leverage the users' choice of websites, activities, music and social activities to present them with targeted advertisements.

There are a large number of technical, legal and user-related obstacles to overcome on the path to a successful mobile advertising strategy. The use of sensitive, personal information kept on the phones can raise privacy concerns, and successful and accurate profiling and personalisation of advertisements will depend strongly on advertising networks assuaging consumers' privacy concerns over targeted advertisements [41]. Mobile phones in general have also less bandwidth, processing power and screen size when compared to ordinary computers. Hence any advertisements must be smaller, downloaded less frequently and have low processing requirements. The profiling tasks must also require limited computation and storage access to preserve battery life.

This chapter describes MobiAd, a system for personalised, localised and targeted advertising on smart phones. Utilising the rich set of information available on the phone, MobiAd presents the user with local advertisements in a privacy-preserving manner. Advertisements are selected by the phone from the pool of advertisements which are broadcast on the local mobile base station or received from local Wi-Fi hotspots. In this manner, the user only needs to download advertisements which are relevant to his interests, and are for items and services in his locality. Information about advertisement views and clicks are then encrypted and sent to the advertisement channel via other mobile phones and intermittent Wi-Fi hotspots, in a delay-tolerant manner. In this system, other nodes and the network operator cannot discover which advertisements were viewed. Likewise, the advertisement provider cannot determine which users viewed which advertisements and only receives aggregate information. MobiAd allows businesses, both local and global, to target users narrowly and directly, without compromising users' privacy. It also improves the scalability of advertisement distribution by using a local broadcast frequency with geo-targeted advertisements.

In this chapter we also discuss the security issues surrounding online advertising, such as click fraud, where a weblog publisher continuously clicks on the advertisements displayed on his own website in order to make revenue. Detecting click fraud is a relatively new area of research. In its simplest form, the broker can perform threshold-based detection. If a web page is receiving a high number of clicks from the same IP address in a short interval, these clicks can be flagged as fraud. The detection gets complicated if the clickers are behind proxies or globally distributed. We present *Bluff Ads* [18], a set of advertisements which are designed to be detected and clicked only by machines, or poorly trained click-fraud work force. These advertisements are targeted at the same audience profile as the other advertisement groups, however their displayed text is totally unrelated to the user profile. Hence they should not be clicked on by the benign user. This simple set of advertisements, mixed with ordinary advertisements, work as a litmus test, or a "CAPTCHA" for the user's legitimacy. If a high number of Bluff ads are clicked, the user is deemed to be flagged as suspicious. Another form of Bluff ads is a set which contain specialised text but they are not targeted to a specific profile and are randomly displayed. This group helps in detecting click-fraud when the botnet builds up a fake profile to harvest relevant ads.

6.2 Advertising and Privacy

Despite the fertile market for advertising, there are not many dedicated advertising networks for mobile phones. There are a few services for serving advertisements on mobile websites. For instance, AdMob is a service which provides advertisements for more than 15,000 mobile Web sites and applications around the world. AdMob stores and analyses the data from every advertisement request, impression, and click and uses this to optimise advertisement-matching in its network [2]. However the methods used are in no way privacy-aware or localised. This limits the scalability of the system as advertisements have to be served individually at the time of browsing. This is not an issue in general for desktops, but on a mobile phone numerous HTTP connections could slow down the browsing experience.

Adnostic [40] and Privad [16] are also newly-proposed private advertising systems for ordinary browsers. They work on the basis of downloading all of the relevant advertisements offline and showing them at appropriate times. The core ideas of these systems are similar to MobiAd from a privacy perspective. Operation in a mobile environment, however, brings a range of challenges on dissemination of advertisements, capturing reports and scalability. We have attempted to address these issues by using a range of solutions such as DTN for report collection and 3G broadcast channel for advertisement dissemination. MobiAd is also resistant to collusion between advertisers and network operators, as the DTN anonymisation strategy would prevent the origin of the clicks being easily traced.

Recently, Apple and Microsoft have also entered the mobile advertising market. Apple launched the *iAd* service [20], on which they will perform a range of standard targeting options including demographics, application preferences, music and movies choice and location. All of this information will be kept by Apple and will be used to target advertisements to relevant customers. Google use advertisements throughout their Android smartphone operating system, while Microsoft also envisage a similar service on the Windows Mobile platform. Having such detailed profile information at a content provider or handset provider's disposal is a clear threat to users' privacy. There are some suggested solutions for managing cookies and trackers, but they usually require detailed analysis of the cost-benefit trade-offs [13].

The concept of mobile or pervasive advertising has been researched for several years, e.g., [34]. Mobile advertising systems have been built and studied using existing technologies such as Bluetooth [1] to test their viability. User studies have also been carried out on simple mobile advertising scenarios, such as the sale of ringtones [29], that indicate that users who are exposed to such advertising do indeed purchase the advertised services. M-system has also been introduced by Komulainen et al. [24] as a permission based advertising for the use of local retailers and consumers. In this system, service provider hosted the system and gathered and updated databases of consumers. The m- advertisers or their advertising agencies created and sent the m-ads by using the advertising tool. However the profile information was provided by consumer and kept up-to-date in the central database. They found that almost all users find privacy a concern in this system which could potentially be compensated by monetary or entertainment value. However, retailers naturally had great interest in use of the system.

But despite this interest in the area, we still lack high-quality data about how, where, and when consumers are willing to allow mobile advertising, or indeed if they would be willing to allow their smartphones or other mobile devices to be used to transport such advertising content. One factor in this dearth of useful data is the general difficulty in capturing data from smartphone users. New measurement studies have recently been conducted [9, 11, 36] and testbeds built [35], but these tend to concentrate on network-level data such as traffic statistics, rather than user-level data such as willingness to participate in content sharing.

A second factor is that collecting data from advertising networks is fraught with difficulties itself. Guha et al. [17] outline the challenges in measurement, including differences between measurement clients, due to noise from DNS load-balancing, and the churn of advertisements. These difficulties become even more challenging in a mobile environment: a user study that proposed to measure and collect data from mobile users in a mobile advertising environment would no doubt have even more variations in advertising, given differences between users in locations, activities, behaviours and networks.

One solution might be to combine passive measurement with an active user study, allowing experimental participants to verify the types of advertisements being received, and the contexts, behaviours and experiences under which they are willing and unwilling to view, click on, or distribute such advertisements. One mechanism for doing this might be to use the Experience Sampling Method, where participants combine a diary study with signal-contingent alerts which trigger questions [25]. For instance, a participant could be detected near a shopping centre or restaurant, and this might trigger questions about their advertising preferences. Experience Sampling has been combined successfully with mobile devices, e.g., [27, 5, 3], but care should be taken before implementing a large-scale mobile advertising ESM study. For instance, the ethical, legal and privacy implications of collecting mobile location and advertising data need to be considered [19], and mechanisms for ano-nymising data accordingly need to be designed, especially given the number of related datasets that have been subsequently deanonymised by researchers [31].

There are a number of solutions for avoiding click fraud and performing better advertisement. One suggestion is to charge based on user's actions, i.e., the publisher gets a premium only after the successful conversion of the advertisement, meaning the user's visit to the advertiser's website and performing an action such as buying an item or signing up for a service. There are a number of basic attempts at such an approach by means of tracking cookies, however these efforts make up a negligible portion of the current advertising revenue on the Internet.

Juels et al. [23] propose a cryptographic approach for replacing the pay-per-click model with one in which pay-per-action (e.g., shopping) can attract premium rates and unsuccessful clicks are discarded. in this system, the users which make a purchase are identified by the network of advertisers as premium advertisers. The client browsers use a coupon instantiated by third party cookies or issued by the attestor upon redirection. The disadvantage of this method is the ability of malicious attacker, possibly an advertiser, to use a botnet and replay the coupons numerous times, for a large number of cooperating publishers. This will then force the syndicator either discount all those replays, or removing those clients from the system with valid coupons. In both cases, the advertisement income is minimised. It also allows for the syndicator and the attestor (ad broker and middle box) to profile the users accu-rately including their spending budget. They also indicate that most standard click fraud techniques remain unsolved today. Despite early suggestions of this method, it has not been implemented on a large scale as it requires trust between advertisers and publishers.

Some advertisers have suggested the use of anonymised ISP data streams for verification of clicks and for better user profiling. Attempts to do so, such as Phorm, have been unsuccessful due to user privacy concerns. Privacy reasons also prevent brokers from releasing their server logs and click data to advertisers and their agents for deep inspection of the click rates. Other solutions include use of human-invisible advertisements to act as traps for botnets, but these can easily be ignored by a simple visibility test in botnet design.

Immorlica et al. analyse the click-fraud learning algorithms to compute the esti-mated click-through rate [22]. They focus on a situation in which there is just one advertisement slot, and show that fraudulent clicks can not increase the expected payment per impression by more than $o(1)$ in a click-based algorithm. The complexity of the inferred algorithm and the need for click-through rate estimation, however, would make it impractical as it also deviates from the pay-per-click model, to pay-per-view model, which is the least desired model in the modern advertisement world where bidding for space is of critical importance.

6.3   Internet Targeted Advertising Basics

Before introducing our MobiAd system, we first characterise today's advertising systems. These can be broken down into four major components: *advertisers*, *publishers*, *clients*, and *brokers*.

Advertisers wish to sell their products or services through advertisements. Publishers (e.g., news and review websites, personal weblogs) provide opportunities to view advertisements, for instance by providing space for advertising banners. Clients are the devices that show publisher web pages and advertisements to users. Brokers (e.g., Google or Yahoo!) bring together advertisers, publishers, and clients. They provide advertisements to users, gather statistics about which advertisements were shown on which publisher's pages, collect money from the advertisers, and pay the publishers.

Figure 6.1 illustrates the most popular advertising model on the Internet today. Advertisers specify their advertisements and bids (how much the advertiser is willing to pay for views and clicks of the ads) to the broker. When a publisher provides banner space to the client on a web page, a request goes to the broker, asking it to fill in the banner space with appropriate advertisements. The provider makes the decision as to which advertisements to place based on a number of criteria such as the keywords for the web page, personalisation information about the client (usually persistent cookies on client machine), the keywords of the advertisement, and the bid associated with the advertisement. It then delivers the advertisement to the

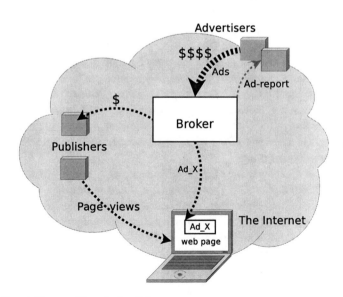

Fig. 6.1 Targeted keyword-based advertising

client, informs the advertiser of the advertisement's views and clicks, and charges the advertisers and compensates the publishers accordingly.

6.4   MobiAd Architecture

In this section we present an overview of the MobiAd system architecture. Figure 6.2 presents an example of some of the components of the MobiAd advertising system. The main components of the system are:

- *Advertisers*: The advertising providers aim to reach a specific groups of users based on requirements such as sex, age, interests and location. They provide the advertisement texts, targeting information, bidding budgets and potentially a landing page for the clicks.[3]
- *Network Operator*: The network operator provides the infrastructure for disseminating the advertisements, collecting reports and locating users. In return they receive a share of revenues.
- *Content Provider*: Content providers, such as news sites and blogs, provide online services and materials which are of interest to users. Alongside their main

Fig. 6.2 Targeted localised advertising

---

[3] We elaborate in Sect. 6.7 why a landing page is not essential.

content, they provide advertising boxes where personalised advertisements can be displayed to the user. Social networking sites such as Facebook are a particular type of publisher, with access to detailed profile information on their users that can be used for targeting.

- *Ad Provider*: The ad providers (e.g., Google or Microsoft) are the interface between the advertisers, operator and content providers. They gather advertisements from advertisers, provide advertisements for the users in the publisher websites, collect view and click reports, bill the advertisers and compensate the publishers and the network operator.
- *Profiling Agent*: The agent gathers relevant information for profiling users. It also downloads and filters relevant advertisements, displays them to the user at appropriate and convenient times and prepares click and view reports for billing purposes.

By using detailed profiling and data-mining techniques in addition to sensed mobile information such as users' locations, MobiAd provides new opportunities for localised and personalised advertising. In terms of privacy protections, some of these components are also similar to traditional advertising systems (such as Google's AdWords program) or newly proposed privacy-aware systems such as Adnostic [40] and Privad [16]. The key difference in our system, however, here is the fact that mobility and use of local advertisement distribution and Delay Tolerant Networks (DTN) [12] provide a simple and scalable advertisement distribution and privacy-preserving click-report mechanism, while addressing many of the numerous challenges for profiling and advertisement placement on a mobile device with limited screen size and battery life. The network operator also plays a more central role as it needs to broadcast advertisements in a localised manner and collect and forward reports. The lower bandwidth, battery life and display size of mobile phones prevent us from downloading, sorting and showing a large number of advertisements on the user's phone. Hence in MobiAd we focus on displaying a lower number of advertisements, but with higher targeting and a focus on local advertisements that would particularly benefit from the user's location information.

In the next sections we expand on the key individual components, their roles and operation strategies.

6.5   Profiling and Incentives

The most important objective of MobiAd is to serve relevant and interesting advertisements to the user. Since the mobile phone's battery life and display size and general browsing time are currently reduced compared to the average personal computer, it is crucial to use the advertisement display opportunities effectively. In order to do this, users' interests and profiles should be maintained on user handsets, while allowing the user to configure and delete their interest categories. This is also in compliance with requirements and recommendations of most regulatory organisations and privacy advocates.

6.5.1 Maintaining the User Profile

There are many rich sources of profile information on a typical smartphone, from email and browsing activities to social networking and shopping sites. This information is in essence an aggregation of information from the user's web history, application caches and keyword extractions from activities on social networks and email. Users are likely to have different privacy sensitivities regarding these various data sources, and should be allowed to control which are included in profiling activities. Browsing behaviour can be used to update profiles at lower processing cost using server-side pre-categorisation of URIs into interest segments [40].

The profile and the associated software work in cooperation in a similar manner to Google's Gmail or persistent cookies from search engines and advertising providers. In MobiAd, however, the profile does not leave the user's handset and the software platform picks up the appropriate advertisements from the broadcast channel.

As a further protection the profile is an aggregate view of user interests rather than a detailed history, reducing the risk of information leakage. Such aggregated information can exclude information about sensitive matters such as medical interests, trade union membership and religious beliefs. This builds user trust in the system, reduces the potential for this information to be accessed for unauthorised purposes, and enables easier compliance with data protection laws such as the European Union's Data Protection Directive [10].

In this design, user profiles are kept solely and securely on the handset. The profile must be visible to the user but unobtainable by other applications. The isolation of information between different applications is readily available on popular smart phones. Profiling tasks can be done while the phone is idle. The extent and depth of categorisation is dependant on the different regions and users, e.g., Google keeps 700 categories in a 3-level hierarchy, while Amazon has over 65,000 categories. We envisage that a MobiAd client can maintain an extensive database of interests, locations, mobility patterns and daily habits. Such detailed information would enable the relevant advertisements to be easily filtered and directed to the user.

6.5.2 User Incentives

The MobiAd system is clearly beneficial to advertisers and network operators, but why would users install such an application? Users have an incentive to install and utilise most applications if there is a marginal entertainment or financial benefit for them. iPod touch users download an average of 12 apps a month and spend 100 min a day using apps [32]. Android and iPhone users download a similar number of apps every month and spend a similar amount of time using the apps [2]. On a new iPhone app, users have been reported to be searching daily for money saving vouchers and local promotions [7]. Hence the intention is that useful services would encourage the users to download the client which could also act as a privacy information centre on their phone.

For the MobiAd system, we are exploring a range of advertisement benefits to the user, location-based and independent. Location-based benefits could include offers and coupons for local businesses and retailers. Independent long-term benefits could include informative applications, such as suggesting events and activities which could be off interest to the user and are not necessarily advertised. In addition, network operators may pre-install this type of software on handsets, or offer incentives to users (such as discounted monthly fees) for them to use MobiAd. In this way the costs of carrying other user reports can also be compensated by the *availability* of a user's handset for carrying traffic and hence contributing to the anonymisation process. Another incentive could be a small percentage cut payment from the advertising click revenue for the report carriers, in an aggregate manner, so as to avoid the network operator or the advertiser being able to trace the origin of the clicks.

6.6 Dissemination and Reporting

6.6.1 Advertisement Dissemination

Dissemination of advertisements in a mobile environment is different from the desktop environment. In MobiAd, the focus is on local advertisements that are relevant to the user. Location information can be obtained using GPS, Wi-Fi or network provider information from the handset. While users may roam in and out of mobile cells and thus affect advertisement download rates, it has also been shown that there are limits to predictability of location of users at given times [37]. We therefore do not rely heavily on prefetching all the relevant advertisements to the user, apart from at locations such as home and work where they appear frequently.

The optimal data dissemination strategy should avoid constant data download, but be ready for unpredictable arrival of the user into new areas. The MobiAd agent on-handset should be able to classify locations that are frequently visited (using a list of GPS positions most frequently visited), such as the route from home to work, weekend hotspots and such like. The advertisements for these locations could be prefetched when there is wireless connectivity and stored for longer periods, to minimise data transfer costs and battery utilisation on the handset.

When a user enters a new location where the relevant advertisements have not already been prefetched, she can receive all local advertisements using technologies such as Multimedia Broadcast and Multicast Services (MBMS) [28]. MBMS is a new service offered on GSM and UMTS networks and uses multicast distribution in the core network that enables an interaction between the handset and the network which can be used for distributing advertisements and collection of reports. MBMS enables network operators to distribute all the local advertisement texts simultaneously to all cell phone users within each transmitter's coverage area using a single shared transmission broadcast. As cell coverage is expected to be in order of a few hundred meters, the text advertisements within each cell should not exceed a few kilobytes (a few hundred local advertisements, each having around 100 characters of text) which is a reasonable amount of data transfer for all modern smart phones to deal with. If one channel is used at each cell tower to broadcast locally-relevant ads, all phones could listen to all channels and just select relevant advertisements without revealing which advertisements are of interest and shown to the user. If more privacy is required, protocols such as SlyFi [14] could be used to provide anonymous sniffing capabilities for downloading advertisements from local Wi-Fi hotspots. However since all the local advertisements can be downloaded from Wi-Fi hotspots, the hotspot service provider is not able to classify the users, as they cannot find out which advertisements were displayed. The number of broadcast advertisements even in busy metropolitan areas could be limited by a combination of network operator and ad provider using an auction mechanism to limit the number of location-targeted advertisements through raising their price. Hence we opted for local flooding for the current design.

It is also possible for the advertising network to suggest a shortlist of relevant advertisements within specific advertisement frames, resulting from centrally-available context and pricing information [40]. One may also consider using Tor [39] for ad dissemination or report collection, however Tor requires a real-time interactive channel that consumes significant amounts of power. MobiAd's transmission of advertisement reports does not need a real-time interactive anonymous channel. By relaxing this requirement, we can reduce power use.

6.6.2 Billing

At the end of each billing cycle, advertisers are billed by the advertising network for advert displays and click-throughs. MobiAd uses a cryptographic protocol developed by Toubiana et al. that allows clients to notify the network of advertisement impressions without leaking user interest information [40].

Figure 6.3 provides an overview of the public key encryption stages of the click reports. The advertisement report will be encrypted using the advertising provider's public key, so only the advertising provider can open the report. Advertisement clicks will then be anonymised, as the advertising provider can identify the advertisement which was clicked, but does not know who clicked on the advertisement. Likewise, the network operator knows a report was received, but does not know what advertisement was clicked on. MobiAd also uses a one-time pseudorandom number in order to avoid replay clicks. This is similar to the reporting mechanism used in Privad [16]. We avoid using more sophisticated methods such as Tor due to the complexity of running such CPU- and data-intensive systems on mobile phones.

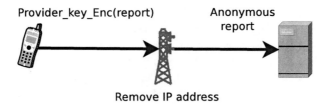

Fig. 6.3 Encrypting click reports

6.6.3 Report Collection Using DTN

As advertisers are generally billed using information on cost-per-impression or cost-per-click, there needs to be a return path for clients to report these data (without leaking information on user interests). To further protect users against attempts to link reports to user behaviour, we take a similar approach to onion routing [8] using the DTN paradigm.

DTN was originally designed for interplanetary communication, where the delays can be several minutes or longer [4], and then was adapted to solve intermittent connectivity problems in daily life. Furthermore, it has been recently shown that by leveraging the delay of transmission, DTN can improve the anonymity of wireless communication from physical localisation (e.g., triangulation) [26]. Onion routing is an approach to achieve anonymous communication by routing messages through several intermediate relays before reaching their destinations, and so the probability of revealing the source node of a message is significantly reduced. As shown in Fig. 6.4, the MobiAd agent system is designed to report on advertisement views and clicks, while preserving the privacy and anonymity of users.

In MobiAd, we use DTN to route advertisement reports to several intermediate relays before they are finally passed to the cellular network. DTN relies on mobile peer-to-peer store-and-forward (using Wi-Fi or Bluetooth connections) and hence there is no additional monetary cost on top of the cellular network cost. Here for further privacy consideration we have three requirements: (1) the relays should have certain social in-correlation with the social network, which prevents identity reverse engineering from the social relationship, (2) if possible, the final location of the final hop to the cellular network should have certain geographical distance from the original location of the report, (3) we want a certain delay (but not too long for billing purpose) between the time when the report is first sent out from the source and the time when it is finally sent to the network.

To better guarantee successful delivery, we use two-copy forwarding instead of a single copy [38] for the reports, which means that the source will make a duplicate copy of the report and send them separately to two different relays. The report will not be further duplicated during the multiple-hop transmission. To achieve the social in-correlation criteria, we take an anti-social network approach as opposite to the social-based approach introduced in BUBBLE Rap forwarding [21], where a mobile device will periodically scan the environment and detect the devices belonging to its

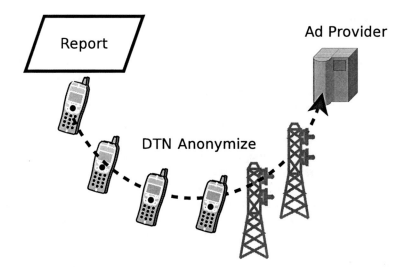

Fig. 6.4 Collecting reports via a Delay-Tolerant network

social community. But here we obfuscate the sender's social network by adding random nodes, including friends and strangers, as relays instead of socially-close nodes [33]. In this way the social network of a node cannot be easily identified by an attacker who monitors all the forwarded packets in a cell network where a node is frequently present.

In order to preserve the location and temporal privacy, we will set the number of hops before the last hop to the cellular network to be 3 (so in total 4 hops). Based on the seminal work on 6-degree of separation by Milgram et al. [30], 4 hops should be a reasonable distance in order to scramble the social correction, and long enough for the message to have enough temporal delay and geographical distance from the source. There may be energy consumption issues due to excessive wireless scans for efficient DTN routing, but since delay is not a main concern for the delivery of the advertisement reports, we do not need to scan the environment so frequently.

While taking all these measures into consideration, it is theoretically possible for an advertiser or the network operator, through long-term monitoring of the mobile user, to determine which advertisement reports have a geographical correlation with the user's location. This is due to the user's routes following a specific home-work-home pattern for most of the days. In order to overcome this, MobiAd can employ a system where base stations follow a similar approach to the DTN system proposed before forwarding the reports for, for example reports from a specific region or town could be forwarded all over the country, or they could be presented to the advertising provider in aggregate form. In this way the advertising provider cannot build an accurate estimate of number of phones and their geographic correlation in specific regions. We are currently working towards categories of attack scenarios by the advertisers, advertising provider, network operator and content provider and plan to address these issues in future work.

6.7 Security and Privacy Challenges

MobiAd is privacy-aware, but several security and privacy challenges remain. An open question is whether users that click on advertisements should be taken directly to an advertiser's URI; redirected to an advertiser site via an intermediate URI hosted by the ad provider for click-through measurement and fraud protection, as commonly happens in today's advertising networks; or to content also distributed using an anonymous channel, to further limit the potential for linking users to specific interests. In general usage the click-through rate for adverts is extremely low, so sending users directly to advertisers' sites is much less privacy-intrusive than building detailed server-side user profiles. Users may anyway voluntarily provide further information to advertisers at this point, particularly if they make a purchase. However, particularly privacy-sensitive users may make use of a service such as Tor to reduce linkage of their browsing behaviour to any long-term identifier (such as an IP address). Care needs to be taken to reduce the ability of malicious advertisers to gain information on users who click-through an advert that is targeted at extremely small numbers of individuals – both in terms of interests and in frequently-visited locations such as homes and work places.

Careful attention also needs to be paid to client-side implementation details to prevent information leakage. Advertisements need to be carefully isolated within display pages using mechanisms such as identically-sized iframes, to prevent client-mediated communications between publisher and advertiser. This may preclude the inclusion of active content such as Flash ads [40].

Mobile handsets are less frequently shared than PCs, and hence information is less likely to leak between users of the same equipment. However, care must be taken to protect profiles using a PIN or password from access by other people with physical access to a handset. The possibility of coerced access – such as by parents to their children's handset profile – must also be considered, which is a further reason for storing only aggregate information and excluding sensitive personal data categories.

An issue outside the scope of MobiAd is users' reactions to highly-targeted adverts, even with guarantees that behavioural profiles remain entirely private to the individuals they describe. Advertisers may need to tread carefully in targeting adverts for products such as low-fat foods that to some users may raise concerns that they have been unfairly categorised, or suggest lifestyle problems. A possible mechanism to address the first concern would be transparency in explaining to users why they had been shown any given advert. Many countries also have laws that ban discriminatory treatment of individuals based on certain characteristics that might be inferred from behavioural profiles. For sensitive advertisements we envisage that no reports need to be collected in order to minimise any privacy leaks. Even the landing pages of such advertisements could be provided using a Content Distribution Network (CDN), or they can be pre-fetched using the DTN system. We are dealing with the privacy issues in more detail for future work.

6.8 Detecting Click Fraud

One of the main reasons that online advertising platforms keep detailed logs of user clicks on adverts is to detect instances of fraud. In this section of this chapter we describe some of the mechanisms used in such click-through fraud, and techniques such as Bluff Ads that can be used to ensure the extra privacy protections of MobiAd are not abused to defraud advertisers.

For fraud detection, one can add some untargeted ads, or as we refer to them, Bluff ads to the advertisements displayed to the user. These are real advertisements, but served randomly. Every time the user visits a publisher page, we serve the user with probability $p(i)$ with profiled advertisements, and with probability $[1-p(i)]$ with other, non related Bluff ads. The brokers' entire advertising model is based on the idea of showing only the most relevant advertising content. If displayed advertisements are poisoned with context-free advertisements on a frequent basis, benign users will perceive this as the broker doing a poor job at finding relevant advertisements. Hence, the Bluff/real ratio must be set in a way that the user's browsing experience and advertising quality perception is not greatly affected. For example, a user living in Iran should not ideally be presented with special offer advertisements on beer during Oktoberfest. But it might not unreasonable to be shown car adverts, though his profile has no indication of his interests in driving. In practice, the Bluff ads should be authentic advertisements of different advertisers, spread in the network and shown randomly, but never charged for.

The Bluff ads serve two purposes. First, they give the user "comfort" that he is not being watched too closely and monitored too deeply. Secondly and more importantly, they help identify fraud clickers and eliminate them from the system. These fraud agents are just clicking for publishers, or against a specific advertiser.

6.8.1 Using Bluff Ads

We now address different forms of click-fraud attacks and those on user privacy, and we briefly describe how the Bluff ads will help minimise them.

6.8.1.1 Profiling the Customer

The Bluff ads will prevent publishers and advertisers from narrowly targeting the client as it is not possible to know whether the viewed advertisement was a Bluff or not. Unless the publishers work in large groups together which will also increase the difficulty level for them. The advertisers can naturally profile users easier, however that is not avoidable as ultimately users; interests lead to revenue generation for the advertiser and broker. If the broker notices that a specific web page covers many categories it can ignore that website altogether. In the case of content aggregators the broker can put specific emphasis on pages visited during client's browsing session.

6.8.1.2 Publisher Fraud

The most common case is where a publisher has hired a large botnet to perform clicks for it. This can be easily realised from the frequency of the clicks. In this case the publisher ID and the Bluff/real ratio for publishers can inform the broker of this attack. If the Bluff/real ratio is higher than an average user, it is indicative of a bot being in operation.

6.8.1.3 Attacks on Advertisers

These can again be identified by the a combination of simple threshold sampling and Bluff/real ratio of the advertisements. If most of the clicks from a host are targeted towards a single advertiser, there will be an obvious trend in their Bluff/real ratio. If the attacker decides to poison the statistics by clicking on random other advertisements, the ratio will be affected again. Many large advertisers today use specialised agencies to monitor their incoming traffic and identify spammers and click-fraud users, who tend to visit often but spend no time on the advertiser website. These users are also identifiable if they come from same IPs with frequent visit counts (simple threshold detection). The advertisers' agents can hence pass a list of fraud suspects to the broker who will remove them from the billing system.

6.8.1.4 Attacks on Publisher

These are the most difficult attacks, when a publisher is under attack from another source. Such attacks happen when reliable publishers, such as CNN, who use advertising brokers, are under attack in order to damage their relationships with the advertisers and providers and ultimately eject them from the competition scene when bidding for advertising space on the page. It is possible to detect such attacks by examining the Bluff/real ratio for the advertiser and publisher pair and identify these if the frequency of views/clicks is less than a certain time threshold. Distributed attack on publishers are a new form of attack and further research is needed to determine solutions for detecting these in detail.

6.9 Summary

In this chapter we presented the MobiAd system architecture, a system for delivering personalised, localised and private yet scalable mobile advertisements. In this system, advertisements are locally broadcast to users within mobile cells, appropriate advertisements are shown to the user and view and click reports are collected using a DTN system, preserving the privacy and anonymity of the user. MobiAd provides an opportunity for using the significant amount of information on users' smart phones for targeted advertising while protecting their privacy.

We also presented a brief overview of the current challenges in detection of click-fraud in online advertising. We presented a simple detection strategy, Bluff ads. These are sets of irrelevant advertisements displayed amongst user's targeted advertisements, which should not be clicked on by an authentic user. Together with threshold detection, IP address monitoring and profile matching techniques, Bluff ads can be used to make it raise the bar for botnet owners to train their software, or a human operator. The Bluff ads also may have a comfort factor of decreasing the user's negative perceptions by reducing the number of accurately targeted advertisements. We are currently working on deployment of Bluff advertisements on a large advertising service.

References

1. Aalto, L., Göthlin, N., Korhonen, J., Ojala, T.: Bluetooth and WAP push based location-aware mobile advertising system. In: Proceedings of the 2nd International Conference on Mobile Systems, Applications, and Services (MobiSys), pp. 49–58. ACM, New York (2004). doi: 10.1145/990064.990073
2. AdMob: Admob mobile metrics report. http://metrics.admob.com/wp-content/uploads/2010/02/AdMob-Mobile-Metrics-Jan-10.pdf (2010). Accessed 23 Mar 2011
3. Ben Abdesslem, F., Parris, I., Henderson, T.: Mobile experience sampling: reaching the parts of Facebook other methods cannot reach. In: Proceedings of the Privacy and Usability Methods Pow-Wow (PUMP). British Computer Society. http://scone.cs.st-andrews.ac.uk/pump2010/papers/benabdesslem.pdf (2010). Accessed 23 Mar 2011
4. Burleigh, S., Hooke, A., Torgerson, L., Fall, K., Cerf, V., Durst, B., Scott, K., Weiss, H.: Delay-tolerant networking: an approach to interplanetary internet. IEEE Commun. Mag. **41**(6), 128–136 (2003). doi: 10.1109/MCOM.2003.1204759
5. Consolvo, S., Walker, M.: Using the experience sampling method to evaluate ubicomp applications. IEEE Pervas. Comput. **2**(2), 24–31 (2003). doi: 10.1109/MPRV.2003.1203750
6. Cozza, R.: Forecast: Mobile Communications Devices by Open Operating System, Worldwide, 2008–2015, http://www.gartner.com/DisplayDocument?ref=clientFriendlyUrl&id=1619615
7. Crompton, B.: Tech Deals: Moneysupermarket Launches iPhone App. http://www.pocket-lint.com/news/34077/deals-moneysupermarket-launches-iphone-app (2010). Accessed 23 Mar 2011
8. Dingledine, R., Mathewson, N., Syverson, P.: Tor: the second-generation onion router. In: Proceedings of the 13th USENIX Security Symposium, pp. 303–320. USENIX Association, Berkeley (2004)
9. Do, T.M., Perez, D.G.: By their apps you shall understand them: mining large-scale patterns of mobile phone usage. In: Proceedings of the 9th International Conference on Mobile and Ubiquitous Multimedia (MUM). ACM, New York (2010). doi: 10.1145/1899475.1899502
10. European Parliament: Directive 95/46/EC of the European Parliament and of the Council of 24 October 1995 on the protection of individuals with regard to the processing of personal data and on the free movement of such data. OJ. L. **38**(281), 31–50 (1995)
11. Falaki, H., Lymberopoulos, D., Mahajan, R., Kandula, S., Estrin, D.: A first look at traffic on smartphones. In: Proceedings of the 10th Annual Conference on Internet Measurement (IMC), pp. 281–287. ACM, New York (2010). doi: 10.1145/1879141.1879176

12. Fall, K.: A delay-tolerant network architecture for challenged internets. In: SIGCOMM '03: Proceedings of the 2003 Conference on Applications, Technologies, Architectures, and Protocols for Computer Communications, pp. 27–34. ACM, New York (2003). doi: 10.1145/863955.863960

13. Freudiger, J., Vratonjic, N., Hubaux, J.P.: Towards privacy-friendly online advertising. In: Proceedings of W2SP 2009: Web 2.0 Security and Privacy. http://w2spconf.com/2009/papers/s2p1.pdf (2009). Accessed 23 Mar 2011

14. Greenstein, B., McCoy, D., Pang, J., Kohno, T., Seshan, S., Wetherall, D.: Improving wireless privacy with an identifier-free link layer protocol. In: MobiSys '08: Proceeding of the 6th International Conference on Mobile Systems, Applications, and Services, pp. 40–53. ACM, New York (2008). doi: 10.1145/1378600.1378607

15. Google Advertising Revenue: http://investor.google.com/fin_data.html Accessed 23 Mar 2011

16. Guha, S., Reznichenko, A., Tang, K., Haddadi, H., Francis, P.: Serving ads from localhost for performance, privacy, and profit. In: HotNets-VIII: Proceedings of the Eighth ACM Workshop on Hot Topics in Networks. http://conferences.sigcomm.org/hotnets/2009/papers/hotnets200%9-final27.pdf (2009). Accessed 23 Mar 2011

17. Guha, S., Cheng, B., Francis, P.: Challenges in measuring online advertising systems. In: Proceedings of the 10th Annual Conference on Internet Measurement (IMC), pp. 81–87. ACM, New York (2010). doi: 10.1145/1879141.1879152

18. Haddadi, H.: Fighting online click-fraud using bluff ads. ACM SIGCOMM Comput. Commun. Rev. 40(2), 21–25 (2010). doi: 10.1145/1764873.1764877

19. Henderson, T., Ben Abdesslem, F.: Scaling measurement experiments to planet-scale: ethical, regulatory and cultural considerations. In: HotPlanet '09: Proceedings of the 1st ACM International Workshop on Hot Topics of Planet-Scale Mobility Measurements, pp. 1–5. ACM, New York (2009). doi: 10.1145/1651428.1651436

20. iAd service: http://advertising.apple.com/ Accessed 23 Mar 2011

21. Hui, P., Crowcroft, J., Yoneki, E.: BUBBLE rap: social-based forwarding in delay tolerant networks. In: MobiHoc '08: Proceedings of the 9th ACM International Symposium on Mobile ad Hoc Networking and Computing, pp. 241–250. ACM, New York (2008). doi: 10.1145/1374618.1374652

22. Immorlica, N., Jain, K., Mahdian, M., Talwar, K.: Click fraud resistant methods for learning click-through rates. In: Deng, X., Ye, Y. (eds.) Internet and Network Economics. Lecture Notes in Computer Science, vol. 3828, pp. 34–45. Springer, Berlin/Heidelberg (2005). doi: 10.1007/11600930_5

23. Juels, A., Stamm, S., Jakobsson, M.: Combating click fraud via premium clicks. In: SS'07: Proceedings of 16th USENIX Security Symposium on USENIX Security Symposium, pp. 1–10. USENIX Association, Berkeley (2007)

24. Komulainen, H., Ristola, A., Still, J.: Mobile advertising in the eyes of retailers and consumers – empirical evidence from a real-life experiment. In: Proceedings of the International Conference on Mobile Business, p. 37. IEEE Computer Society, Washington (2006). doi: 10.1109/ICMB.2006.31

25. Larson, R., Csikszentmihalyi, M.: The experience sampling method. New Dir. Methodol. Soc. Behav. Sci. 15, 41–56 (1983)

26. Lu, X., Hui, P., Towsley, D., Pu, J., Xiong, Z.: Anti-localization anonymous routing for Delay Tolerant network. Comput. Netw. 54(11), 1899–1910 (2010). doi: 10.1016/j.comnet.2010.03.002

27. Mancini, C., Thomas, K., Rogers, Y., Price, B.A., Jedrzejczyk, L., Bandara, A.K., Joinson, A.N., Nuseibeh, B.: From spaces to places: emerging contexts in mobile privacy. In: Ubicomp '09: Proceedings of the 11th International Conference on Ubiquitous Computing, pp. 1–10. ACM, New York (2009). doi: 10.1145/1620545.1620547

28. MBMS: Multimedia Broadcast/Multicast Service (MBMS); Stage 1, 3GPP Specification. http://www.3gpp.org/ftp/Specs/html-info/22146.htm (2010). Accessed 23 Mar 2011

29. Merisavo, M., Vesanen, J., Arponen, A., Kajalo, S., Raulas, M.: The effectiveness of targeted mobile advertising in selling mobile services: an empirical study. Int. J. Mob. Commun. 4(2), 119–127. http://www.metapress.com/content/4RE0HR5YAARJC061 (2006). Accessed 23 Mar 2011

30. Milgram, S.: The small-world problem. Psychol. Today **1**(1), 61–67 (1967)
31. Ohm, P.: Broken promises of privacy: responding to the surprising failure of anonymization. Soc. Sci. Res. Network Working Paper Series. http://ssrn.com/abstract=1450006 (2009). Accessed 23 Mar 2011
32. Oliver, S. iPod touch users spend more time using apps than those with iPhones. http://www.appleinsider.com/articles/10/02/25/ipod_touch_users_spend_more_time_using_apps_than_those_with_iphones.html (2010). Accessed 23 Mar 2011
33. Parris, I., Henderson, T.: Privacy-enhanced social-network routing. Comput. Commun. In Press, Corrected Proof, Available online 19 November 2010, ISSN 0140-3664, doi: 10.1016/j.comcom.2010.11.003. (http://www.sciencedirect.com/science/article/pii/S0140366410004767)
34. Ranganathan, A., Campbell, R.H.: Advertising in a pervasive computing environment. In: WMC '02: Proceedings of the 2nd International Workshop on Mobile Commerce, pp. 10–14. ACM, New York (2002). doi: 10.1145/570705.570708
35. Shepard, C., Tossel, C., Rahmati, A., Zhong, L., Kortum, P.: Livelab: measuring wireless networks and smartphone users in the field. In: Proceedings of The 3rd Workshop on Hot Topics in Measurement and Modeling of Computer Systems (HotMetrics). http://hotmetrics.cs.caltech.edu/pdfs/paper12_final.pdf (2010). Accessed 23 Mar 2011
36. Shye, A., Scholbrock, B., Memik, G.: Into the wild: studying real user activity patterns to guide power optimizations for mobile architectures. In: Proceedings of the 42nd Annual IEEE/ACM International Symposium on Microarchitecture (MICRO 42). ACM, New York, USA, pp. 168–178. doi:10.1145/1669112.1669135, http://doi.acm.org/10.1145/1669112.1669135 (2009)
37. Song, C., Qu, Z., Blumm, N., Barabasi, A.L.: Limits of predictability in Human mobility. Science **327**(5968), 1018–1021 (2010). doi: 10.1126/science.1177170
38. Spyropoulos, T., Psounis, K., Raghavendra, C.: Efficient routing in intermittently connected mobile networks: the single-copy case. IEEE/ACM Trans. Netw. 16, 1 (February 2008), pp. 63–76. doi:10.1109/TNET.2007.897962, http://dx.doi.org/10.1109/TNET.2007.897962 (2008)
39. Torproject Website: http://www.torproject.org/ Accessed 23 Mar 2011
40. Toubiana, V., Narayanan, A., Boneh, D., Nissenbaum, H., Barocas, S.: Adnostic: privacy preserving targeted advertising. In: Proceedings of the 17th Annual Network and Distributed System Symposium. Internet Society, San Diego (2010)
41. Turow, J., Hennessy, M.: Internet privacy and institutional trust. New Media Soc. **9**(2), 300–318 (2010). doi: 10.1177/1461444807072219

Chapter 7
Opportunities and Challenges of Interactive Public Displays as an Advertising Medium

Rui José and Jorge C.S. Cardoso

Abstract Advertising is often the key element in the business case for public display networks. However, this is still a limited medium in its support for key advertising concepts, such as targeting or impact assessment. This chapter analyses how the evolution of the medium is creating the opportunity for re-shaping advertising models for Digital Signage. In particular, we consider how the increasing availability of sensing and interaction opportunities may generate the necessary digital footprints that will help to characterise advertising opportunities in Digital Signage and measure impact. A generic footprint model would enable advertising models to be specified at a higher level of abstraction, enabling them to be applied across global display networks composed by very diverse display types, managed by many different entities, and serving many different purposes. We propose a design space that relates the multiple types of digital footprints that can be generated with multiple modes of campaign targeting and impact assessment, providing the ground for a fundamental shift from advertising based on measuring attention to advertising based on active engagement with people.

7.1 Introduction

Public digital displays are an increasingly ubiquitous element in our visual culture. We can find them in all sorts of public and semi-public spaces, where they can be serving multiple types of informative purposes. However, the main driver behind most deployments has been their use as an advertising medium. Digital Signage has

R. José (✉)
University of Minho, Guimarães, Portugal
e-mail: rui@dsi.uminho.pt

J.C.S. Cardoso
Portuguese Catholic University, Porto, Portugal
e-mail: jorgecardoso@ieee.org

J. Müller et al. (eds.), *Pervasive Advertising*, Human-Computer Interaction Series,
DOI 10.1007/978-0-85729-352-7_7, © Springer-Verlag London Limited 2011

attracted much interest as a marketing tool because displays can be close to shopping decision points, they can leverage on situations of strong attention availability, e.g. queues, and they can reinforce messages from other media. Advertising is thus almost always an integral part of their business case, which revolves around the revenue obtained from selling screen real estate and time to advertisers. In many cases, this revenue is indeed the sole purpose for setting up the network, but even if that is not the case, advertising is still very often an important way to off-set deployment costs and to guarantee the sustainability of the services.

While the revenue generated from advertising in these networks has been steadily increasing, and the medium continues to attract the interest of marketers, the evolution of this market has been somewhat restrained by key limitations of the medium with major implications for advertising. The first is that most public displays offer very little in ways of interacting with and responding to the people around them. This absence of systematic interactive or sensing features means that displays fail to produce meaningful traces of how they are used. The second is that the advertising process is essentially based on selling undifferentiated screen real estate within the scope of a single display network. As a result, there is no significant impact assessment and targeting is limited to the selection of the display networks in which the campaign is to be placed. Without effective solutions to these key issues, digital agencies will not embrace Digital Signage as a mature and worthy advertising medium with which they can have a clear and sustainable Return on Investment (ROI). Moreover, web marketing has been generating solid advertising models that are enabling that medium to become increasingly central in marketing strategies. The sophistication of web advertising provides an inspiring model for other digital media, but it also means that marketers will have increased expectations regarding the advertising models for Digital Signage and other digital media. Failing to live up to those expectations could potentially mean the fallout of the respective business case. These concerns have been widely acknowledged by the Digital Signage industry, which has been making an effort to address them, mainly through more advanced audience metering techniques. Also, a large number of patents have been filled in recent years on targeted advertising for public displays, including major companies such as Google, Microsoft, IBM, NEC or HP, reflecting a significant interest in this topic. With this quickly evolving landscape, there are many challenges to be addressed, but there is also a major potential for a significant evolution of Digital Signage towards more mature advertising models.

In this chapter, we discuss the opportunities and challenges for the evolution of Digital Signage towards a mainstream advertising medium for public spaces. We start by introducing key advertising concepts and how they are addressed across different advertising media. We then analyse the properties of Digital Signage and discuss how this medium can evolve to meet the increasingly high expectations of marketers. We then introduce the concept of digital footprint as a high-level abstraction for representing the traces left behind when people implicitly or explicitly interact with Digital Signage. This is the basis for a design space that associates various sensing and interaction features with the types of advertising functionality they can enable.

7.2 Pervasive Networks of Public Displays as a New Advertising Medium

Advertising is a key element of the promotion mix of companies and covers a wide range of communication tools in order to inform and persuade. As in any other form of communication, advertising effectiveness depends on understanding the communication process (encoding, decoding and feedback) and elements (sender, receiver and media). Developing an advertising process involves at least four major steps, namely: setting advertising objectives; budget; message; and media [15]. Advertising will thus occur as part of advertising campaigns with specific communication goals that should determine the structure of the campaign, its intended audience, its duration, and the media used to support it, very often more than one. A specific budget will delimit the range of opportunities to be considered and will necessarily lead to optimisations that are able to produce more results with fewer costs. The economic valuation of advertising opportunities needs to be established based on the size, characteristics and situation of the potential audience. Impact assessment will measure the reaction of the target segments to the message of the campaign. Measuring the effectiveness of the campaigns is crucial for control and for validating the return on the investment. When performed in real time, impact assessment may also enable the campaign strategy to be adapted on the fly, according to the reactions it is generating. The execution of campaigns, especially in digital media, is normally supported by some type of campaign management service that supports the campaign specification (what to present in what circumstances), the actual delivery of the adverts (generating impressions and tracking actions) and some type of analytics (reporting on the results of the campaign).

A key part of the advertising process is thus the identification of the segments that are the primary targets for the message and the ability to direct the message to this target audience. This delivery of the right message to the right audience and in the right context is essential because it allows campaigns to be executed in a much more cost-effective way. If an advert is only shown to those people or in those situations for which it might be more relevant, it is much more likely to produce sales. A targeting process can be very diverse and refined, depending on the availability of information about the targets and the contexts in which they are consuming the message. With the emergence of digital media, marketers are increasingly empowered with a very rich set of information about people and their behaviour, enabling a broad range of new targeting techniques that may include not only the selection of the targets, but also the dynamic adaptation of the message to increase its relevance.

Demographic targeting is the classical segmentation approach that considers properties such as the age group, gender, the residential area or the education level. Demographic data can be a reasonable predictor for consuming behaviour and requires less information than other approaches.

Behavioural targeting tries to model people based on their past behaviour. It can be extremely sophisticated, depending on the number and nature of the behavioural data sources, and it has become increasingly important with web advertising, where it is often possible to collect substantial information about browsing patterns. For example, with information about previous visits to other web sites, normally obtained through cookies, advertisers can much more easily select the most relevant adverts to show to that person when entering another web site. Retargeting is another form of behavioural targeting whereby a person is shown adverts from a previously visited web site. The idea is that a person who has already demonstrated a certain level of interest on the products of that web site is more likely to generate sales.

Geographic targeting is also an important parameter for segmentation. With a small business running a local campaign this may involve selecting local media or global media with support for fine-grained geographical scoping. In global campaigns on digital media, geographical targeting may be used to adapt the message to different locations, considering for example the respective country, local language or time of the day.

Contextual targeting involves selecting places for the adverts that are related in content to the products. For example, a magazine about video-games would be a relevant context for an advert about a new video game. A web-site about babies would be a relevant context for adverts about baby food. Targeting occurs, not only because the message is being directed to people who seem to have an interest in those topics, but also because it is presented at a time when they are actively thinking about them. Contextual targeting may also explore not only the type of place where the advert is being shown, but also its potential credibility with the audience or even the affinity that people may have with that place.

7.2.1 Advertising Models Across Other Media

Advertising models have evolved very significantly in recent years, especially with the new possibilities emerging from the web, but audiences and impact can be expressed very differently depending on the supporting medium. Multiple advertising models have thus emerged to address the specificities of each medium. This section analyses several advertising media, uncovering their approaches regarding targeted advertising, impact assessment and advert valuation. This will frame our discussion on the advertising models for Digital Signage.

7.2.1.1 Television

Television is a medium with solid and well-established advertising models that have sustained and driven that industry for many years. Audience measurement is a high-profile activity strongly associated with the prestige of the TV shows. The measurement unit is the number of exposures by time unit, with the audience data being gathered through phone surveys, diaries or even dedicated audience metering devices that detect and communicate which channels are being watched. Advertisers want their adverts to be seen by as many people as possible, but they also want to optimise the process by focusing more on their main target groups. Therefore, audience data is complemented with demographic data about viewers, enabling audiences to be determined, not only as a global number, but also according to multiple demographic parameters, such as gender, income, age and residential area. As a result, the valuation of adverts also considers the type of viewers. As certain segments may be more valued than others, a larger audience does not necessarily correspond to a higher price. Impact assessment, albeit limited, is typically achieved through surveys on brand recall.

7.2.1.2   Static Displays

Static displays differ from the other media being analysed in that they are an example of a static medium. With static media it does not really matter when people are watching because the message always remains the same. Therefore, audience measurement is mainly based on measuring foot traffic. This can be achieved manually or using people counters, small sensors that can count the number of people that walk through doors or virtual gates. Even though this is not effective in determining how many persons are actually paying any attention to the display, it is still effective enough to establish a reasonable valuation model for this medium. More elaborate techniques may also include visits to assess display visibility and obtain refined demographic data about visitors [23].

7.2.1.3   Web

The emergence of the web raised many challenges, but also immense opportunities for advertising. What clearly distinguishes the web from other media in this analysis is its inherently interactive nature, and the consequent ability to obtain rich information about user context and behaviour. As a user visits particular web sites or places search queries for particular keywords, these actions can be used to infer interest in particular topics and select appropriate adverts or sponsored links. These characteristics were first explored by Google AdWords and Google AdSense to address two fundamental issues that had previously undermined web advertising: establishing a valuation for adverts and assessing their impact. The first issue involves determining which ads may be closer to the interests of the potential audience in order to target advertisements. The main alternatives include the geographic location, the context of the page being visited or some knowledge about user behaviour. The second issue involves assessing impact by determining which ads have actually managed to lead people into the desired action. In the web this is mostly achieved by measuring Click-Through Rates (CTR).

Despite being a relatively new medium, the web has now become a thriving environment for the emergence of new and sophisticated advertising models with implications for other digital media. The first is that exposure is no longer seen as the single or even the main element in determining the valuation of adverts. The focus has shifted from merely determining who receives the message towards measuring how many people were interested or even how many people actually bought something. This immediate feedback also means that it is now possible to try many different campaign strategies and evaluate on-line which ones are more effective. As a consequence, valuation models have also evolved from the traditional Pay-per-Impression, based on exposure, to models based on the achieved impact, such as the Pay-per-Click (PPC), in which payment is determined by the number of clicks generated by the advert. The economic value associated with each click as well as the allocation of advertisements to specific advertising opportunities are typically managed by automated bidding systems. The allocation algorithms try to maximise the value generated to all the parties involved by seeking to allocate adverts to the opportunities that maximise the generation of clicks, while subject to the limitation of capital available for the campaign.

Another major characteristic of web advertising is that it can benefit both large traffic web sites as well as the small blog page. The PPC model and the automated media planning system have created the ground for open and automated campaigns in which any web site can benefit from advertising revenue and any campaign can reach any web site. A web site does not need to attract a high volume of traffic to be considered a relevant advertising medium. Through affiliate programs, even a small website can offer relevant advertising opportunities and generate advertising revenue, as long as it performs well in attracting some niche segment.

7.2.1.4 Social Networking Sites

Social Networking Sites (SNS) have extended even further the already immense possibilities of web advertising by enabling campaigns targeted at very refined user profiles. Campaigns are mainly centred on the demographics of users, which may include detailed elements such as geography, age, job, company size or gender. Information about preferences or likes and the overall history of previous actions are also increasingly part of the targeting process. Additionally, social networks are particularly strong enablers for Relationship Marketing in which a brand aims to promote longer term and stronger ties with consumers in a way that extends far beyond traditional marketing messages.

7.2.2 Specificities of Digital Signage as an Advertising Medium

The evolution of the Digital Signage landscape in terms of technology, scale, openness and cooperation models provides a promising path towards the evolution of the medium and its support for more sophisticated advertising models. In particular, we consider two main evolutions that will provide fundamental contributions towards that objective: the emergence of open advertising markets for public displays and the systematic availability of sensing or interaction features.

Currently, the Digital Signage advertising market is very fragmented. There are many isolated display networks, each providing its own separate set of advertising opportunities and negotiation procedures. An advertiser who wants to create a large campaign may need to individually negotiate with multiple network operators to buy advertising space.

As a result, only large networks can have the necessary scale to be of any interest to advertisers. This limitation is being addressed with the emergence of advertising aggregators, such as SeeSaw, BookingDOOH, Vukunet, Argo Digital Solution or AdCentricity. These services collect information about the advertising opportunities across multiple display networks and provide a media planning service for matching adverts with advertising opportunities. This is opening the opportunity for automated allocation across multiple networks and for a global and open market for advertising in Digital Signage.

Systematically enriching Digital Signage with sensing and interaction capabilities represents the other major step towards new advertising models for Digital Signage. Public displays, whether digital or not, can be watched without generating any information on their usage, but without such information there can be no effective solution to the key issues of targeted advertising and impact measurement. Displays that react to the presence of people and offer them the possibility to interact will strongly enhance the user experience by enabling people, not just to be exposed to adverts, but to engage with content in a much more meaningful way. This increased engagement will implicitly or explicitly generate information for characterising social contexts and the advertising opportunity they represent. Even considering that the resulting information may never be as rich as click-through patterns on the web, it would still represent a major step forward when compared with the idea that displays are just to be seen by passive observers.

These evolutions may take the advertising models for Digital Signage one step closer to the rich advertising models supported by web advertising. However, one key observation from the analysis of advertising models across other media is also that the characteristics of the medium are central to the evolution of the respective advertising models. Therefore, despite the major role played by web advertising in setting the expectations for Digital Signage, we must also understand the specificities of Digital Signage and their implications in defining what the most appropriate model might be.

7.2.2.1   Proximity

Public displays are part of a physical and social environment that strongly determines their communication context. This means that not only geographic location, the type of venue, or the demographics of visitors should be considered for targeted advertising, but also other physical and social proximity elements. For example, two places sharing a significant percentage of visitors may be targeted in an integrated way enabling the mutual exchange of adverts or providing the ground for Life Pattern Marketing approaches [33] in which the same message is reinforced by being present, even if slightly adapted, in the multiple locations that a person may visit throughout the day. Also, nearby displays may act collectively to provide a consistent and strongly situated user experience, such as dynamic guidance services [30] that suggest directions to nearby businesses.

7.2.2.2 Place-Sensitive

While web browsing is essentially an individual activity, Digital Signage is part of a social and physical setting in which adverts are seen in a shared environment. An effective advertising model must acknowledge the role of Digital Signage as an element with a potentially strong impact in shaping the places where the displays are located. It should, therefore, give the people responsible for the place increased control over the nature of the adverts displayed. If those adverts are not aligned with the place's values, practices or commercial strategies, their public presentation may become a source of embarrassment.

7.2.2.3 Generate Engagement

It has been argued in this chapter that a strong user engagement will be crucial for stronger advertising models in Digital Signage. However, achieving the type and level of user engagement that will enable audience characterisation and impact assessment is not very natural for this medium. It will require specific approaches for bringing people into interacting with public displays in ways that are both meaningful for people and relevant for advertising. Examples may include specific types of games, quizzes or polls, specifically designed for that purpose or models of shared control over the display in which increased engagement is rewarded with increased control. It may also mean that content adaptation should go beyond targeted advertising and be extended to other forms of content. Adaptive content will make the display more valuable to people, which will be more willing to express their preferences to influence displayed content rather than displayed adverts. For example, the ability to select content may enable targeted adverts to be injected into the selected content, while being valued by people.

7.2.2.4 Crowd Targeting

Public displays will typically have multiple simultaneous users and the adaptation process must consider the best strategy for dealing with the potentially varied interests expressed by those people. This generates a trade-off between the selection of adverts based on a profile combing the multiple interests of the multiple persons present and the selection based the use of each individual profile, one at the time [2].

The first is a balanced approach, but faces the risk of not really matching anyone's specific interests. The second approach can be targeted for each individual, but it raises additional privacy issues and may conflict with the idea of Digital Signage as a place-making tool.

7.3 A Design Space for Advertising in Digital Signage

This section will now consider how we can map multiple forms of sensing and interaction into the characterisation of advertising opportunities and their assessment. The challenge is that Digital Signage is likely to support multiple interaction modalities, from mobile technologies to touch-sensitive surfaces, and also multiple types of interaction semantics, in many cases associated with specific applications. Making sense of the myriad sensing and interaction events that can occur across a display network requires higher-level abstractions that are independent from the specific affordances or the semantics of the interaction offered by particular displays. Such abstractions should be able to play for Digital Signage a similar role to the one that click-through patterns and search phrases play for the web.

We propose a design space created around the concept of digital footprint as an abstraction for representing the traces left behind when people implicitly or explicitly interact with Digital Signage. A digital footprint focuses on the nature of the information generated about the interaction itself and abstracts away from the particular interaction modality being used or the particular application semantics in which the interaction occurred. They aim to represent preferences, characteristics and behaviour, regardless of how they are expressed. We have structured digital footprints around four main categories: presence sensing, self-exposure, user-generated content and actionables, as represented in Table 7.1.

These categories represent not only different types of interaction, but also increasingly higher levels of engagement with the display system.

The design space that we propose associates the various types of sensing and interaction features with the type of digital footprint they can generate and maps these into the types of advertising functionality they can enable. This should inform Digital Signage creators about the relationship between sensing and interaction features and their possible role in the advertising process.

We will now describe these footprints in more detail, analysing how they can be generated and how they can contribute to the advertising process.

Table 7.1 Digital footprints

Presence sensing (Detection, Characterisation, Identification)	Being physically there
Self-exposure	Explicitly managing exposed identity
User-generated content	Pushing content to the system
Actionables (Interactive, External)	Responding to the system

7.3.1 Presence Sensing

The ability to implicitly collect information about the presence of nearby people is an important element for characterising situations. Despite its stronger potential for generating rich information about usage, interaction events are necessarily sparser than presence events, as there will normally be many more people present than those actively engaged with the display at any given moment. Presence sensing is thus critical to enable targeted advertising to occur even when there is no one interacting. Presence sensing may involve increasingly complex levels of presence information, more specifically: the ability to simply detect presences (detection), the ability to characterise those presences (characterisation) and the ability to associate presences with unique entities across multiple sessions (identification).

7.3.1.1 Presence Detection

Presence detection is the most basic level of presence information in which the system is simply able to detect whether or not there is someone nearby, and possibly at what distance. Multiple off-the-shelf sensors can be used for this purpose. Distance to the display can be determined by combining presence sensors with different sensing ranges or using distance sensors that report distance. Computer vision techniques, such as frame differencing, can also be used to sense movement.

Information about the presence of someone near a display, even without knowing who or how many, can mainly be used as a trigger for presenting specific content, and particularly as part of an attraction loop designed to entice people to interact when passing-by. In Community Wall [11] frame differencing was used as part of the presence detection system to prevent the display from changing content while someone was reading from it. Knowing the distance can be important for the display system because there is normally a strong correlation between distance and the awareness level that people may have about the display. If they are in a short distance, it is much more likely that the display is currently the focus of their attention. In the Range whiteboard [14], for example, an infrared distance sensor was used to determine the distance of people using a whiteboard application.

The digital footprint generated by a presence detection mechanism is essentially a presence/absence pattern that may only provide a very basic characterisation of the place in terms of people flow.

7.3.1.2 Presence Characterisation

Presence characterisation is the ability to count and possible determine particular characteristics about the presences detected near the display, which broadly corresponds to the concept of audience measurement. A vast range of audience measurement technologies has been emerging to estimate, not only the number of people in front of a display, but also to determine their attention span or inferring some type of characteristic about them, such as age or gender [25, 32]. This normally involves placing a video camera on the display, typically on the top and facing the audience, and processing the images to generate reports about the number, attention span, and characteristics of viewers. In an attempt to set industry standards for these reports, the Digital Place-based Advertising Association (DPAA) (formerly OVAB) has produced a guidelines document that describes the Average Unit Audience as "the number and type of people exposed to the media vehicle with an opportunity to see a unit of time equal to the typical advertising unit" [29]. These guidelines have a clear focus on what is normally called the Opportunity to See (OTS) and on three qualifying characteristics associated with that opportunity: Presence, Notice and Dwell time.

Audience metering techniques are very important for the Digital Signage industry because they may help to justify and valuate advertisement investment. However, they assume a model in which the objective is simply to estimate the number of people potentially exposed to an advert, without considering what their real engagement might be. Presence characterisation can also be used for targeting adverts according to the characteristics of the current audience, as for example in the case of the Eye Flavour that selects adverts based on age and gender [21].

7.3.1.3 Presence Identification

Presence identification is the ability to identify unique identities within presences and thus recognise different visits by the same person. A common approach involves the use of a personal device as a proxy for the person. Bluetooth has been extensively used for this purpose, as it is widely available and enables many mobile phones to be discovered and uniquely identified through their Bluetooth address. Radio Frequency Identification (RFID) tags can also be used. They are small and can easily be incorporated into many existing artefacts, as exemplified by the IntelliBadge system [8] in which conference participants were given RFID augmented badges and then tracked through the conference rooms. A display would then generate several visualisations of the resulting data.

Presence identification raises considerable privacy issues and therefore it should only occur as part of a process in which people are informed and value the extra functionality that the existence of this information may be providing. The ability to enable or disable presence identification according to the circumstances would be equally important. This is a point in which Bluetooth, which allows discovery to be easily disabled, takes considerable advantage over RFID tags.

The digital footprints resulting from presence identification correspond to individual presence information and open many new opportunities for the advertising process. They may serve to build individual profiles that characterise people according to their presence patterns, e.g. regular visitors vs. first-time visitors. They can be used to optimise advertising by selecting adverts that have not yet been shown to the people that are currently present, as exemplified by the BluScreen system [28] that uses Bluetooth detection to avoid showing advertisements to users more than once. If a network of displays is involved, presence identification may also serve to show some variant of the same advert to the same person at different locations, thus reinforcing the message, or to select adverts based on where the person has been before. The existence of multiple sensing points would also enable new forms of impact assessment. For example, it may be possible to measure how many people who have been shown an advert about a nearby store will then go to that store, or simply how the number of first-time visitors has increased as the result of a campaign.

7.3.2   Self-exposure

Self-exposure is the ability of the display system to collect information that people have explicitly created to represent their characteristics, preferences or personal tags. This personal information can take many forms, such as a reference to a user's personal webpage, the user id in a Social Networking Site or a purposely created profile. Self-exposure should also be seen as way for people to take control over how their identity is projected in the public space by the Digital Signage. It should be part of a process whereby people expose something about them because they understand and value the implicit response of the display to that self-exposure. Moreover, the intended level of self-exposure may be strongly influenced by a broad range of circumstances. Therefore, a key feature for self-exposure mechanisms is some type of control on how that exposure should occur at any given moment. This means not just the ability to enable or disable presence detection, but also the ability to dynamically manage self-exposure in a way that is easily controlled and understandable. Self-exposure differs from presence in the sense that it is an explicit act of identity management, while with presence we assume that all the information was implicitly generated. It differs from interaction in the sense that there is no pre-established connection between self-exposure and a specific type of reactive behaviour by the display system. Potentially, different display systems may react very differently to the same form of self-exposure, or even the same system may also react differently under different circumstances.

Self-exposure may be achieved by combining presence identification with the *a priori* definition of a user profile that is associated with the identity. In Proactive Displays [18], users attending a conference registered their affiliation, interests and personal webpage before the conference day and were given RFID augmented conference badges at the conference site. Throughout the conference, several displays reacted to the nearby participants showing and creating associations between their profiles and creating opportunities to socialise. A limitation of this approach is that people could not easily change their profile, and had no control over what information to expose at any given moment. Another alternative is the use of a personal information device running a custom application to manage and expose a profile. This application can connect automatically, or on demand, to the display system and communicate users' preferences. This can be exemplified by the Hello.Wall [24], a system in which people would carry a *ViewPort* device (a modified PDA) to communicate with an ambient display. Similarly, in the Camera-Phone [31] system, a custom mobile application can be configured with personal information that is made automatically available to the display system when a user interacts with it. One advantage of these approaches is that the information is always available to be updated by its owner and it may be possible to have greater control on how to manage self-exposure, but they have the disadvantage of requiring a dedicated application. The use of Bluetooth names to express self-exposure, as explored by Jose [13] and Davies [9], is an opportunistic alternative that is easily available on almost any device. It allows people to enter predefined commands in the Bluetooth name of their mobile phone. When that person approaches a display, these commands can be obtained and interpreted as part of the person's preferences. For example, Ribeiro [27] has shown how tags exposed this way by multiple people could be used to select from the Internet content feeds for presentation on a local display.

In all the previous examples, there was the assumption that information would be specifically created for the purpose of influencing a display system. However, a very promising alternative is to explore connections with the many Social Networking Sites where people already have extensive descriptions about themselves and their preferences. WhozThat [3] uses the SNSs profiles of people nearby to create context information that can then be used to support spontaneous interactions or drive the music selection. People are expected to use a mobile phone running an identity sharing protocol that will advertise their on-line identities to the other nearby devices. This system does not consider the use of Digital Signage or any explicit selection of which information to share, but it is an example of using SNSs profiles as a sort of personal data aura that can be used to mediate digital self-exposure. Böhmer and Müller [4] conducted a study on the exhibition of SNSs profiles in public settings. Using mockup images they asked people about their willingness to expose profile information in two types of what they called social signs. The first was a personal social sign projected around the person and showing parts of the respective profile. The second was an interpersonal sign, projected in such a way to link two people and representing some type of connection between them, such as having a mutual friend or sharing an interest. The study provides an interesting example of the type of identity projections that can be generated by these connections with SNSs.

Information associated with self-exposure footprints can be very varied. In its simplest form, the result may be just a list of keywords generated from multiple forms of preferences expression. However, with access to profiles, much more structured information can be obtained. The potential of self-exposure in the advertising process is particularly relevant for targeted advertising, where depending on the type of information collected, it may support multiple forms of targeting, such as demographic, contextual or behavioural.

7.3.3   User-Generated Content

User-generated content is the ability of the system to accept content originating from the users of the display. This is achieved by allowing people to post their own content for publishing at the display, either directly or indirectly through a reference to the content (e.g. a URL). Many displays have been created that support some variant of this feature. WebWall [10], for example, allows people to submit content using SMS, email or a web interface. The Plasma Poster [7] system supports content (photos, text, web pages) submission through two interfaces: email and a web form. MMS has also been extensively used as an input interface for display systems. For example, the Joe Blogg project [16] includes a display designed in the form of an interactive artwork where people can send pictures and text messages through MMS or SMS. Bluetooth can also be used to push content to a display system using either standard OBEX exchanges or custom mobile applications. Both Hermes [6] and Snap and Grab [17] use the OBEX feature to enable users to send pictures and other media to a display. In both cases, the user just selects the content on his mobile phone, selects the "send via Bluetooth" command and selects a particularly named device. An example of a custom Bluetooth application for sending content is Touch & Interact [12], which allows users to choose a picture in their mobile phone and touch the display in the position they want to place that picture. The main advantage of a custom application is that it can be built to interact specifically with a given display, thus allowing a richer and more convenient interaction. For example, the application may be able to automatically determine the Bluetooth address of the display system, alleviating the user from the task of manually searching for nearby devices and selecting the correct device name. The application may also be able to determine beforehand what type of content is acceptable by the display system, impeding the user from sending content that will be rejected. OBEX on the other hand, has the obvious advantage of not requiring the installation of any additional software in the mobile device, and thus enable more opportunistic interactions. Also, from a developer's perspective, OBEX is more attractive because, given the multitude of different devices, it is often the case that multiple versions of the application have to be created to deal with the hardware and software variants in devices. Also, these applications must be somehow distributed to users which may be yet another barrier to usage.

When generating content to a display, users are implicitly associating that content with that particular place. The nature of the digital footprints generated by such process depends on the type of content. However, the analysis of the content and its meta-data should produce a relevant characterisation of that place and its local practices. This is already common on the web, where a vast and sophisticated range of techniques has been emerging to analyse user-generated content. For example, tags in Flickr images have been used to extract place semantics [26], and tweets have been used to determine mood and emotions [5]. If displays were able to generate enough content from users, similar techniques could also be applied to generate footprints that would be very relevant for targeted advertising processes.

7.3.4 Actionables

Content on Digital Signage is often some type of actionable, a message or an interactive feature intended to cause people to act [20]. Actionables provide a specific demand for action, such as downloading a content item, selecting one of several available options or reading a 2D code from the display. An actionable footprint represents a reaction to one of those actionables.

Generating this type of footprint requires some mechanism for tracking the actions taken and also some type of system-wide reference for the actionables, e.g. a URL or some unique Id. The existence of a unique reference that can be tracked system-wide separates actionables from the myriad interactive features that may exist in a display system and which in many cases will not be meaningful outside the specific application in which they are available.

Actionables may provide one of the most promising paths for advertising in Digital Signage. They enable several forms of automated impact assessment and advert valuation, ultimately leading to something similar to the pay-per-click concept. When considering how to generate actionable footprints, we need to take into account two major types of actionable: interactive actionables in which the reaction occurs within the system and can thus be automatically detected by the system; and external actionables in which the action that the actionable is promoting occurs outside the context of the display system and cannot be tracked directly by the system itself.

7.3.4.1 Interactive Actionables

Interactive actionables are invitations to interaction that can be interpreted by the system. They involve giving users some type of control and being able to track their options. Allowing people to pull content from the display system is a common example of an interactive actionable. Knowing who has downloaded which items enables the system to infer interest on the content items that are being offered. Giving people some type of control over the system behaviour may also be used to generate interactive actionables. For example, Jukola [22], which allows people in a bar to vote on the next music to be played by selecting music from a list, is an example of a system that could generated this type of footprint. Rating content items allows people to explicitly say they like or dislike an item. Ratings give the display system information about the popularity of content items. It is also possible to conceive a Games With A Purpose approach [1] in which all sorts of polls, quizzes, questionnaires, or games are designed to provide engaging experiences, while allowing the display to collect users' preferences and interests. These actionable footprints may be anonymous or identifiable depending on the interaction mechanism provided, but the key point is that the meaning of the reactions can be interpreted system-wide and not just within the scope of a particular application.

7.3.4.2 External Actionables

With external actionables, the intended action is to occur outside the scope of the display system, and therefore, the system is unable to automatically assess their efficiency. At best, their efficiency can be assessed through some type of off-line mechanisms, such as the collection of redeemed coupons.

MobiDiC [19] is an example of the use of digital coupons in public display advertisement. The public display shows adverts with coupons that people can photograph with their mobile phone and redeem at the associated shop to receive the announced item. The time and location where the ad was displayed is encoded in the coupon. When the coupon is redeemed and the shop owner enters the code back to the system, the specific advert and display are identified and the aggregated results can tell how successful the advert was.

7.3.5 Analysis

Our goal with this design space was to inform the process of mapping multiple types of sensing or interactive features in Digital Signage into specific advertising models. The digital footprints that have been presented support the first part of that mapping. By focusing on the essence of the information generated from sensing and interaction features, they provide a framework for reflecting on the meanings of interaction without being caught by the specificities of any particular interaction mechanisms. In this final analysis, we discuss the second part of that mapping, which is to describe what types of digital footprints may be needed to support specific pervasive advertising goals. We hope that, by making the relationship between advertising goals and footprints more explicit, this framework may contribute to focus the design of public displays on the data generation objectives, while avoiding the pitfalls of focusing too much on a particular application or interaction technique.

Table 7.2 presents a summary of these mappings. Several types of advertising goals are listed and associated with the specific types of digital footprint that could support them.

Based on this framework, Pervasive Advertising solutions may start by setting their specific goals, consider the digital footprints that the display systems may need to generate, and finally conceive sensing or interactive features that are capable of generating the appropriate information while providing an adequate user experience. This last step should also consider that these different digital footprints are not completely independent from each other. They are more like a stack of increasingly richer information about the audience of a public display. For example, availability of presence characterisation also generates presence detection. Presence identification is implicit in self-exposure and identifiable interactive actionables. The correct choice of the interactive features may optimise the generation of the most appropriate set of digital footprints.

Table 7.2 Mapping between advertising goals and digital footprints

Advertising goals	Digital footprints
Attraction loops	Presence detection can trigger specific content to get people's attention.
Audience measurement	Presence characterisation may provide sophisticated reports about viewers and their attention.
Demographic targeting	Presence characterisation may infer basic demographic information from presences, but self-exposure and specific actionables may generate even richer information, given that they involve people explicitly saying something about themselves.
Contextual targeting	Self-exposure and specific actionables may generate keyword sets and other types of aggregate descriptions that will help to dynamically characterise the context of a public displays in ways that are relevant for contextual targeting, such as hot keywords, social situations or on-going local activities.
Behavioural targeting	Presence identification and identifiable actionables generate rich information about people's behaviour and enable multiple types of behavioural targeting. Presence identification will mainly revolve around presence patterns, possibly at multiple locations, whereas action-ables will revolve around expressed preferences inferred from actions.
Optimise individual exposure	Presence identification supports several types of optimisations related with specific individuals, from avoiding repetitions to purposely generating periodic repetitions for reinforcement.
Impact assessment	Actionable footprints provide the most appropriate measure for engagement and therefore for really understanding the reaction of people to the message.

7.4   Conclusions

Advertising models define key properties of the advertising process within a particular medium. More specifically, they should address key issues such as how to target the message to the most relevant opportunities and how to measure the impact of a campaign. Advertising models for Digital Signage are still very limited regarding these two key points, especially when compared with the rich and sophisticated web advertising models that are increasingly part of the mainstream advertising industry. Interactive displays and the emergence of open display networks are two trends that will necessarily re-shape the medium and will also open entirely new possibilities for advertising.

We have presented a design space that maps between interaction mechanisms and their contribution to the generation of digital footprints that are relevant for targeted advertising. While this design space has been conceived mainly for Digital Signage, many of these same concepts would also apply to other situated forms of situated marketing, such as Bluetooth Marketing. Overall, the emergence of a generic footprint model would represent a fundamental shift from advertising based on measuring attention to advertising based on active engagement with people. This would in turn provide a major contribution to overcome some of the most fundamental limitations in current models for advertising in Digital Signage.

Acknowledgments Jorge Cardoso has been supported by "Fundação para a Ciência e Tecnologia" and "Programa Operacional Ciência e Inovação 2010" POCI 2010, co-funded by the Portuguese Government and European Union by FEDER Program and by "Fundação para a Ciência e Tecnologia" training grant SFRH/BD/47354/2008. The research leading to these results has also received funding from the European Union Seventh Framework Programme (FP7/2007-2013) under grant agreement no. 244011.(PD-Net).

References

1. Ahn, L., Dabbish, L.: Designing games with a purpose. Commun. ACM **51**(8), 58–67 (2008)
2. Alt, F., et al.: Adaptive user profiles in pervasive advertising environments. In: Proceedings of the European Conference on Ambient Intelligence, Salzburg, pp. 276–286 (2009)
3. Beach. A., et al.: WhozThat? Evolving an ecosystem for context-aware mobile social networks. Network IEEE. **22**(4), 55, 50 (2008)
4. Böhmer, M., Müller, J.: Users' opinions on public displays that aim to increase social cohesion. In: Proceedings of the 6th International Conference on Intelligent Environments, Kuala Lumpur, Malaysia, pp. 255–258 (2010)
5. Bollen, J., Pepe, P., Mao, H.: Modeling public mood and emotion: Twitter sentiment and socio-economic phenomena. CoRR, abs/0911.1583, 2009 (2009)
6. Cheverst, K., et al.: Exploring bluetooth based mobile phone interaction with the hermes photo display. In: Proceedings of the 7th International Conference on Human Computer Interaction with Mobile Devices & Services, Salzburg, vol. 111, pp 47–54. ACM Press, New York (2005)
7. Churchill, E.F., Nelson, L., Denoue, L., Helfman, J., Murphy, P.: Sharing multimedia content with interactive public displays: a case study. In: Conference on Designing Interactive Systems: Processes, Practices, Methods, and Techniques, Cambridge, pp. 7–16 (2004)
8. Cox, D., Kindratenko, V., Pointer, D.: IntelliBadge. In: First International workshop on Ubiquitous Systems for Supporting Social Interaction and Face-to-Face Communication in Public Places, Seattle (2003)
9. Davies, N., Friday, A., Newman, P., Rutlidge, S., Storz, O.: Using bluetooth device names to support interaction in smart environments. In: Proceedings of the 7th International Conference on Mobile Systems, Applications, and Services, Krakow, pp. 151–164 (2009)
10. Ferscha, A., Vogl, S.: Pervasive web access via public communication walls. In: Proceedings of the 1st International Conference on Pervasive Computing (Pervasive 2002), Zurich, 2002. Springer LNCS, vol. 2414, ISSN: 0302-9743, pp. 84–97, Springer-Verlag London, UK (2002)
11. Grasso, A., Muehlenbrock, M., Roulland, F., Snowdon, D.: Supporting communities of practice with large screen displays. In: O'Hara, K., Perry, M., Churchill, E., Russell, D. (eds.) Public and Situated Displays – Social and Interactional Aspects of Shared Display Technologies, pp. 261–282. Kluwer, Dordrecht (2003)
12. Hardy, R., Rukzio, R.: Touch & interact: touch-based interaction of mobile phones with displays. In: MobileHCI '08: Proceedings of the 10th International Conference on Human Computer Interaction with Mobile Devices and Services, Amsterdam, pp. 245–254 (2008)
13. Jose, R., Otero, N., Izadi, S., Harper, S.: Instant places: using bluetooth for situated interaction in public displays. Pervasive Comput. IEEE **7**(4), 52–57 (2008)

14. Ju, W., Lee, B.A., Klemmer, S.R.: Range: exploring implicit interaction through electronic whiteboard design. In: CSCW '08: Proceedings of the ACM 2008 Conference on Computer Supported Cooperative Work, San Diego, pp. 17–26 (2008)
15. Kotler, P., Armstrong, G.: Principles of Marketing, 8th edn. Prentice Hall College Division, Englewood-Cliffs (1998)
16. Martin, K., Penn, A., Gavin, L.: Engaging with a situated display via picture messaging. In: CHI '06 Extended Abstracts on Human Factors in Computing Systems, Montreal, pp. 1079–1084 (2006)
17. Maunder, A., Marsden, G., Harper, R.: Creating and sharing multi-media packages using large situated public displays and mobile phones. In: Proceedings of the 9th International Conference on Human Computer Interaction with Mobile Devices and Services, Singapore, pp. 222–225 (2007)
18. McDonald, D.W., McCarthy, J.F., Soroczak, S., Nguyen, D.H., Rashid, A.M.: Proactive displays: supporting awareness in fluid social environments. ACM Trans. Comput. Hum. Interact. **14**(4), 1–31 (2008)
19. Müller, J., Krüger, A.: MobiDiC: context adaptive digital signage with coupons. In: Tscheligi M., et al. (eds.) Ambient Intelligence, Salzburg, vol. 5859, pp. 24–33. Springer, Berlin/Heidelberg (2009)
20. Müller, J., Paczkowski, O., Krüger, A.: Situated public news & reminder displays. In: Proceedings of European Conference on Ambient Intelligence, Darmstadt (2007)
21. NEC.: NEC Launches Eye Flavor, Japan's First All-in-One Digital Signage Board with Face Recognition Technology. http://www.pr-inside.com/nec-launches-eye-flavor-japan-s-first-r1030399.htm (2009). Accessed 9 Nov 2010
22. O'Hara, K., Lipson, M., Jansen, M., Unger, A., Jeffries, H., Macer, P.: Jukola: democratic music choice in a public space. In: Proceedings of the 5th Conference on Designing Interactive Systems: Processes, Practices, Methods, and Techniques, pp. 145–154 (2004)
23. Philport, J.C.: TAB Eyes On: Out of Home Media Measurement. http://www.eyesonratings.com/images/pdf/recent-publications/TAB-Eyes-On-OOH-Media-Measurement-by-Philport.pdf (2007)
24. Prante, T., et al.: Hello.wall – beyond ambient displays. In: Adjunct Proceedings of UbiComp 2003, Seattle, pp. 277–278 (2003)
25. Quividi.: Quividi: Automated Audience Measurement of Billboards and Out Of Home Digital Media. http://www.quividi.com/ (2010). Accessed 9 Nov 2010
26. Rattenbury, T., Naaman, M.: Methods for extracting place semantics from Flickr tags. ACM Trans. Web **3**(1), 1–30 (2009)
27. Ribeiro, F. R., Jose, R.: Autonomous and context-aware scheduling for public displays using place-based tag clouds. In: Augusto, J.C., Corchado, J.M., Novais, P., e Analide, C. (eds.) Ambient Intelligence and Future Trends-International Symposium on Ambient Intelligence (ISAmI 2010). Advances in Intelligent and Soft Computing, vol. 72, pp. 131–138, Springer (2010)
28. Sharifi, M., Payne, T., David, E.: Public display advertising based on bluetooth device presence. In: Mobile Interaction with the Real World (MIRW 2006) in conjunction with the 8th International Conference on Human Computer Interaction with Mobile Devices and Services, Dublin (2006)
29. Spaeth, J., Singer, S., Hordeychuk, M.: Audience Metrics Guidelines. Digital Place-Based Advertising Association. http://www.dp-aa.org/guidelines.php (2008). Accessed 9 Nov 2010
30. Strohbach, M., Kovacs, E., Martin, M.: Towards pervasively adapting display networks. In: 1st International Workshop on Pervasive Advertising, Held in Conjunction with Pervasive 2009, Nara (2009)
31. Toye, E., Madhavapeddy, A., Sharp, R., Scott, D., Blackwell, A., Upton, E.: Using Camera-Phones to Interact with Context-Aware Mobile Services. University of Cambridge, Computer Laboratory, Cambridge (2004)
32. TrueMedia.: TrueMedia: iTALLY: Opportunity to See (OTS) People Counter. http://www.trumedia.co.il (2010). Accessed 9 Nov 2010
33. Zweben, M.: Life pattern marketing: a new way to reach people out-of-home. SeeSaw Networks. http://www.seesawnetworks.com/services/whitepapers/life-pattern-marketing/ (2007). Accessed 9 Nov 2010

Chapter 8
Conceptualizing Context for Pervasive Advertising

Christine Bauer and Sarah Spiekermann

Abstract Profile-driven personalization based on socio-demographics is currently regarded as the most convenient base for successful personalized advertising. However, signs point to the dormant power of context recognition: Advertising systems that can adapt to the situational context of a consumer will rapidly gain importance. While technologies that can sense the environment are increasingly advanced, questions such as what to sense and how to adapt to a consumer's context are largely unanswered. In this chapter, we analyze the purchase context of a retail outlet and conceptualize it such that adaptive pervasive advertising applications really deliver on their potential: showing the right message at the right time to the right recipient.

8.1 Introduction

As pervasive computing technologies (radio-frequency identification, sensors, ambient displays, networked video-systems, etc.) become more reliable and cost efficient, retailers are exploring ways to leverage them for new services. 'Pervasive Commerce' promises retailers the ability to reach out to customers electronically, at any time and anywhere in physical space. The goal is to influence purchase decisions at the right moment and in an efficient way. Because the point of sale is still the site for 91% of earned revenue (compared to only 9% in web-based e-commerce) [19] and 75% of purchase decisions [1], advertising within retailers' business premises is key for marketing success.

C. Bauer (✉) • S. Spiekermann
Vienna University of Economics and Business, Wien, Austria
e-mail: chris.bauer@wu.ac.at; sspieker@wu.ac.at

J. Müller et al. (eds.), *Pervasive Advertising*, Human-Computer Interaction Series,
DOI 10.1007/978-0-85729-352-7_8, © Springer-Verlag London Limited 2011

Still, reaching out to the customer in the right spot (where he or she makes a purchase decision) may not be enough. In recent years, advertising effectiveness has suffered dramatically. Consumers have become blind to promotional messages as they are overwhelmed by their quantity. Only personalization mechanisms seem to promise the ability to break through the information clutter. Yet, current approaches to personalization face an identity crisis themselves. Thought leaders point to the limits of socio-demographic customer segmentation and market basket analysis. *"Using the demographics of a male, over 40, and with an income above a million euro would lead to both Prince Charles and shock-rocker Marilyn Manson; this cannot be it"*, as an expert of the Metro Group – Europe's leading retailer – points out [35].

But what could be better than profile-driven personalization? Signs point to the dormant power of context recognition for personalization, particularly advertising adaptivity [28, 39]. Personalization mechanisms for websites (e.g., [2, 39]) and mobile applications [42] have used contextual information for years. Recommendation systems like Amazon's 'customers who bought' suggestions are popular (e.g., [2, 42]); one of Google's key success factors is that it can powerfully adapt advertisements to a user's context (e.g., language, location, current search interest, etc.). It appears that consumers' context-specific preferences, goals, and behaviors have become an integral part of how advertisements work online [39]. Why not transfer this context-adaptivity to the physical world, for instance, to the retail outlet?

Few applications for context-adaptive advertising in the 'offline world' exist. Many retailers still use paper-based promotional material in their retail outlets and are only beginning to upgrade to digital displays ('digital signage'). Experiences with this new advertising display medium are positive. Retailers such as the British supermarket chain Tesco or Spar in Germany increased sales between 25% and 60% by using digital point-of-sale advertisements [30, 32]. However, the way digital advertisements are presented is still driven by the traditions of the advertising market: Spots produced for TV are often recycled in stores. Content scheduling, display times and the order of material shown as well as pricing are based on pre-purchased sequence blocks and upfront media planning. The online concept (or 'Google Model') of scheduling and charging for advertisements in real time, on the basis of market demand for specific consumer contexts and response rates, is currently unseen in physical outlets.

Present media planning practices are partly driven by business realities. Advertising agencies still need to adapt their processes and business models to new opportunities. In addition, technical challenges are partially responsible for the small number of context-adaptive systems in physical commerce environments. Despite grand visions for contextual computing at large (e.g., [8, 17, 18]), research on context-adaptive systems is scattered and prototype-driven. In the field, the research community works on different individual problems that need to be solved in different phases of system construction (i.e., data collection challenges, data aggregation, adaptivity, etc.). However, no holistic and systematic methodology has outlined how a context-adaptive system, such as an advertising system, should actually be constructed. System designers find it difficult to elicit user requirements for these systems because challenges arise from implicit or indirect interaction with the system. Users often only interact with the system indirectly, while engaged with another primary task. For example, a person who is shopping may perceive an adaptive advertising screen only in the periphery. As a result, engineers often do not know what data they should collect and how they should combine them in a way that creates a meaningful adaptive service. User-centered designers, meanwhile, gather information by interviewing users about their tasks. But what should users be asked in the context of advertising, when they tend to perceive advertising screens only in the periphery? Requirements engineering in the field is still the result of a few user interviews combined with a dose of engineers' gut feeling rather than of a systematic approach.

Against this background, the present chapter pursues three goals: First, we propose a high-level process model for context-adaptive service development. This model provides a structured overview of the step-by-step challenges involved in the provision of pervasive, context-adaptive advertising services. Furthermore, the model allows for a better understanding of the current research landscape for contextual computing.

We then turn to the first phase of context-adaptive service construction, a phase we call "conceptualization of context". Systematic context conceptualization is a system development phase that has not been defined yet for adaptive system design. It aims to help engineers in the early requirements engineering phase understand what information they should collect and combine. We introduce and define the conceptualization of context and argue for its importance because this process deconstructs a personalization situation into measurable and logically disjunctive information units. We strongly believe that an upfront conceptualization of context is vital for engineers working to understand the full bandwidth of a given service environment; with this understanding, engineers can compose meaningful adaptive applications. By describing in detail how we conceptualized context for pervasive advertising, we propose one possible methodology for this phase.

Finally, we outline a concrete context model for context-adaptive retail advertising.

8.2 The Process of Context Adaptivity

In computer science, researchers use context to relate information processing to aspects of situations in which such processing occurs [38]. Researchers aim to relate tasks and devices to the situation of usage in which they are embedded. Context-adaptive systems have been studied from myriad angles, with researchers employing various terminologies. However, it is often unclear whether 'context-aware' or 'context-sensitive' systems are the same as 'context-adaptive' ones. Computer science researchers in the field tend to give different names to similar problems while concentrating on working architectures, prototypes and toolkits [4, 12, 21] and data capture and aggregation challenges [15]. Little systematization of these diverse activities has occurred. As real-world deployments emerge, a more structured view

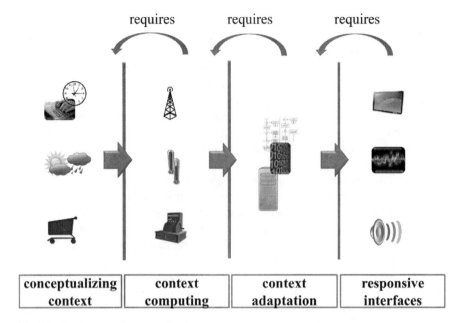

Fig. 8.1 The process of context adaptivity

of the field's activities and achievements may be beneficial. To engineer market-driven requirements, researchers must understand the relationships and dependencies between the various technical components of an adaptive system. We therefore set out by proposing a process model for context adaptivity that integrates the different research threads of context-aware computing; this model also provides an overview of the sequence of challenges engineers face when designing a fully functional and meaningful adaptive service (such as contextual advertising).

As depicted in Fig. 8.1, there are four phases of challenge.

The first step is to 'conceptualize context': to systematically identify the full spectrum of context variables that can be used to meaningfully interpret a specific adaptive service. In the second step of the process, 'context computing', relevant sources of context information are identified and collected. The stored context information is used to trigger events that mark the beginning of the 'context adaption' stage of the process. The goal of this phase is to intelligently adapt to the context that has been detected. Adaptivity mechanisms then use an algorithm to translate the captured context into the desired action. Finally, in the responsive interfaces stage, the computed personalization action is operationalized and presented.

In the following sections, we describe the four phases of adaptive service engineering in more detail and comment on what these phases imply for the realization of pervasive advertising scenarios.

8.2.1   Conceptualizing Context

To seamlessly support a user's activities, one must understand context from various viewpoints [9]. "How are dimensions of context identified, quantified, and interrelated for each situational purpose?" [9]. The first step to answering this question is to conceptualize context.

> We define context conceptualization as *the process* by which a personalization situation is deconstructed into measurable and logically disjunctive information units, all of which must be combined to create an adaptive service.

Some scholars already work to deconstruct and identify disjunctive information units. Common information categories used to understand context include a user's location and environment, the identities of nearby people and objects (entities), and changes to those entities [11, 36]. Schmidt et al. [38] tried to systematize information categories for mobile systems. They relate context information to two domains: human factors and the physical environment, both in the broadest sense. They then operationalize human factors as information about users themselves, their social environment and their tasks. Likewise, the physical environment is described by location, infrastructure, and physical conditions.

Bradley and Dunlop [9] take a multi-disciplinary approach to context, integrating linguistics, psychology, and computer science. Combining and building upon existing models from these three domains, they distinguish the world of the 'user' from that of the 'application'; for both, they consider 'incidental' and 'meaningful' context. In a circular layer that surrounds both worlds, they add a third 'contextual' world, which they break down into six dimensions: task, physical, social, temporal, cognitive and application's context.

But are these categorizations of information units valid? That is, are they complete, adaptable and usable for all kinds of service contexts? We challenge these categorizations, because we believe that an understanding of the context situation and the identification of available and meaningful information for adaptive service delivery can only be achieved as the result of a *process* methodology. Predefined information categories, which may be more or less complete depending on the situation, are insufficient.

Conceptualizing context for pervasive advertising, for example, involves thinking about the context of the advertiser, the brand, and promotion and inventory levels.

Another possible consideration is the stage in the buying process in which consumers find themselves at the moment an advertisement is displayed. Yet none of these variables are considered by existing information taxonomies.

Against this background, we will suggest and demonstrate below (Sect. 8.3) one methodology we used to conceptualize the context for pervasive adaptive advertisement services. This approach may be reused for other application domains and can amend and replace existing information categories.

8.2.2 Context Computing

After all potential variables of context adaptivity are listed, context computing [16] is responsible for the actual identification, collection, transformation, interpretation, provision and delivery of context information [13].

To identify and collect relevant information sources, we use sensors and other context sensing technologies [33] such as radio- frequency identification (RFID), global positioning system (GPS) and eye-tracking. Context sensing is the most basic computational level of context computing [33].

Low-level context information obtained by sensing must be transformed, structured, aggregated and interpreted (context transformation) to be represented in an abstract context world model (context representation) [16]. Contextual augmentation [33] such as tagging [12, 16] combines context transformation and interpretation. This technique provides an opportunity to extend information about the environment with additional information. This is achieved by associating the particular context with related digital information [33]. The context information is stored in a centralized or decentralized fashion and is used to trigger context events (context triggering) [16].

The following example illustrates this phase in the context of pervasive advertising: A person is identified via a loyalty card, which is scanned by a cashier. The company-owned databases are searched for relevant information about that particular user. Using an eye-tracker, the system recognizes that two eyeballs are looking at the display next to the cashier. Combining the information from the loyalty card scan and eye-tracking, the system interprets that this particular person's attention is drawn to the display. This information could then trigger a response such as the display of a specific advertisement.

8.2.3 Context Adaptation

Context-adaptivity mechanisms take the 'results' of context computing and 'react' to this context based on a defined algorithm. We can distinguish three categories of algorithms: the presentation of context information to a user (e.g., showing the current time), the automatic execution of a service (e.g., personalized content), and the tagging of context to information to support later retrieval [12, 13].

Many scholars refer to the tailoring of products, services or content to consumer needs as 'personalization' [29]. And an overlap between the literature on context adaptivity and personalization cannot be denied. From a large body of information sources, personalization provides only the information that is relevant to an individual or group [23]. Personalization is used as a means to better satisfy consumer needs and increase customer loyalty. On the Web, the technique is typically based on consumer information [2] such as specified preferences, past purchases, historical visit patterns or click stream data. The consumer who may be interested in (parts of) the contextual data from a sensory system or applications can leverage contextual knowledge by adapting their behavior to integrate seamlessly with the consumer environment [33].

Personalization as it is lived in electronic commerce contexts today spans a wide range of approaches, techniques, and applications. Tuzhilin [41], for instance, differentiates between personalized search, personalized content, personalized recommendation, personalized pricing and personalized communication. Personalized search aims to offer search results that are tailored to a user's preferences and needs. Personalized content refers to presenting information to a user that is relevant to him or her in the most suitable way. Personalized recommendation systems recommend products based on user preferences. Personalized pricing offers products or services at a price that meets the expectations of a specific consumer.

Any of these services could be transferred to the world of offline advertising. For example, a terminal next to an advertisement for a concert hall could be used to search for tickets. Search results may be tailored to a tourist's stay in a particular town. An electronic leaflet on a shopping cart could adapt its contents based on consumer preferences such as a desire for organic food. Displays may be used to recommend products based on a consumer's past purchases. Digital price tags may present personalized pricing based on the number of articles in a consumer's shopping cart. And displays may adapt advertising based on a consumer's mood. Realizing these context-adaptive services, however, entails new challenges such as dynamic data exploitation and real-time adjustment to contextual factors like consumer preferences and behavior [14].

8.2.4 Responsive Interfaces

We can differentiate between two kinds of interfaces in the environment: those for input and those for output. If applications are to act *instinctively*, they have to support multimodal interaction. Multimodal interaction utilizes a number of different communication channels or modalities to enable interaction between humans and computers, either in terms of input or output [31].

For context-adaptive systems, the input is context. In the field of human-computer interaction (HCI), we identify context as something that can be obtained through explicit interaction or implicit interaction. Explicit interaction relies on explicit input and output by the user (e.g., involving a command-based or graphical user interface). Implicit interaction, in contrast, occurs without the explicit awareness of the user [22]; the system 'understands' an action as input also when the user's primary aim is not to interact with the system [37].

Traditionally, HCI has focused on the principle of explicit interactions. However, the principles that govern desktop computing interactions cannot be adopted for applications that "populate the rest of our lives" [22]. Instead, implicit interactions become increasingly important [22, 37]. Essentially, there are two kinds of implicit interaction. One kind involves an exchange that occurs outside the attentional foreground of the user (background interaction). The other kind involves an exchange in which the system initiates action by drawing the user's attention; for example, the system might inform the user about a computation or ask for a user response (foreground interaction) [22].

The output of a context-adaptive system targets one or more of the five human senses: sound, sight, smell, taste, and haptic perception. Output systems of devices have greatly improved in recent years; notable features include stereo audio output and high-resolution color screens, even on mobile phones or display systems for wearable computers [37].

Human-computer interactions that demand the user's attention (foreground interaction) produce interactive output during the adaption process. In pervasive advertising, even an interaction that eludes the user's attention during processing (background interaction) finally leads to the interaction with a user's attention because the adaptation process results in the presentation of an advertisement.

The degree of human attention towards output can be manipulated by adjusting the output's perceptional prominence. Interaction design research investigates how to manipulate human attention when users are engaged in some other primary task [22]. This research finds that systems can attract attention by using disruptive mechanisms or non-obtrusive techniques [10].

8.3 Early-Phase Requirements Engineering for Context Adaptive Advertisement and How to Conceptualize Context

All traditional system design and development methodologies include a requirements engineering phase [25]. Here, stakeholder interests are collected. Business expectations are formulated and potentially drawn from the strategic goals of a company or system operator. The tool-level tasks of users are also analyzed [40].

When engineering requirements for context-adaptive services, however, it is difficult to describe people's implicit or indirect interaction with context-adaptive services or determine user requirements. How can users relate to a context that they do not explicitly interact with? That they often relate to or see only in the periphery? That they do not pay attention to? And how can engineers determine what information they should collect and combine to create a meaningful adaptive service if they cannot interview users?

Moreover, many commercial adaptive services rely on existing company data such as inventory data, promotion data, etc. Very little requirements engineering research has investigated how existing databases should be combined for ad-hoc service delivery.

To overcome these challenges, we argue that context-adaptive services need an 'early' requirements engineering phase that aims to 'conceptualize' context.

Conceptualization of context identifies the full spectrum of measurable and logically disjunctive information units available and/or required for a meaningful service.

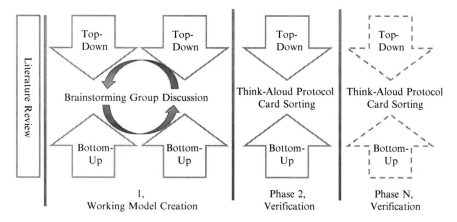

Fig. 8.2 Methodology for conceptualizing context. The top-level domain is broken into its compositional subsystems (*top-down*) while individual base elements are pieced together to form grander systems (*bottom-up*)

We believe that the full business potential of an adaptive service can only be recognized when this full spectrum or 'information landscape' is available (see Fig. 8.3 for an overview). Furthermore, from our perspective, prototyping only makes sense when this 'information potential' of a service has been identified.

In the following sections, we support our argument by describing the information landscape for pervasive advertising services. We methodologically conceptualize context for this service category and thereby show how this exercise promotes meaningful understanding of an adaptive service environment (before delving into prototyping).

Our approach to conceptualizing context is both top-down and bottom-up (Fig. 8.2). The top-down approach is informed by a literature review and involves reflecting on the overall dimensions of the system under review. In contrast, the bottom-up approach considers information types and availabilities in each of the identified dimensions.

We used these two perspectives to analyze the service context in three phases, refining our analysis each time.

8.3.1 First Phase of Context-Model Development: Working Model Creation

In the following section, we describe how we contextualized the pervasive advertising domain. In doing so, we outline a methodology that may be useful for early-phase requirements engineering in other domains as well.

Our first step was to identify relevant literature from the multidisciplinary (computer science, psychology, business) domain of context (for a multidisciplinary

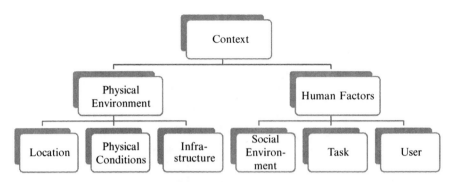

Fig. 8.3 Starting point – Schmidt et al.'s context information categories [38]

approach to context also see [9]). We chose the context model by Schmidt et al. [38] as a starting point for the conceptualization of the pervasive advertising domain. Figure 8.3 provides an overview.

Schmidt et al. [38] distinguish context related to human factors from context related to the physical environment. On a second level, they operationalize human factors as information about users themselves, their social environment, and their tasks. The physical environment includes information about location, infrastructure, and physical conditions.

8.3.1.1 Top-Down Conceptualization of Advertising Adaptivity

We began the first phase of context conceptualization by challenging the applicability of Schmidt et al.'s model to the pervasive advertising context. Top-down brainstorming and group discussions led to (a) a *refinement* of their model *for the advertising context* and (b) an extension of the model to *embrace all stakeholders*. More concretely, refining the top-level information taxonomy consisted of renaming the 'human factors' category to 'consumer's environment'. The refined category refers to the concrete human user type that is targeted by the service in the model. We also opted for consumer '*environment*' because the term is more precise than 'factors' when embracing social issues at lower levels of the taxonomy. Furthermore, we decided that the entity delivering the service, here the company advertising its products, should be reflected in the pervasive advertising model. To acknowledge this additional stakeholder involved in the service delivery, we added a high-level category called 'advertiser's environment'.

On the second level of the model abstraction, we kept five of the six information categories proposed by Schmidt et al.: consumer profile, social environment, task, location, and conditions [38]; however, we again renamed and amended them. Most importantly, we found that Schmidt et al.'s context framework lacks a differentiation between 'manipulable' and 'non-manipulable' environmental conditions. 'Manipulable' conditions are environmental states that the service operator can influence (e.g., light

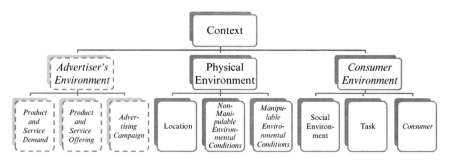

Fig. 8.4 Schmidt et al.'s model with extensions (in *dotted lines*) and refinements (in *italics*) for the pervasive advertisement context

conditions in a shop). 'Non-manipulable' conditions cannot be manipulated: they result from natural factors such as outdoor temperature. From the perspective of the service operator or engineer (for whom the requirements engineering is performed), this distinction is important: the two information categories entail different consequences for the application's operations and strategic design. Non-manipulable environmental conditions are passively sensed or observed and may or may not be used as input data for the adaptive service at hand. For example, the weather outside a retail store could serve as an input to determine whether or not to show an ice-cream advertisement inside. In contrast, manipulable environmental conditions can be actively designed for the adaptive service experience. For example, the temperature inside of a store could be tuned to correspond to the outdoor level. If it is hot outside (non-manipulable) and hot inside (manipulable), the probability of ice-cream purchases would probably be higher than if air-conditioning cooled the inside of a store. This example demonstrates that manipulable environmental conditions are a powerful means to strategically design an adaptive service.

Finally, three additional information categories emerged that belong to the advertiser's environment category: product and service demand, product and service offering, and the advertising campaign itself, which is the object of the adaptive service delivery. Figure 8.4 provides an overview of the refinement of the model.

8.3.1.2 Bottom-Up Conceptualization of Advertising Adaptivity

Specifying and amending generic context models does not produce a sufficiently thorough conceptualization of context. To specify "context feature space on the third level" [38], we need to understand context from the consumer's situational perspective. Accordingly, we consider the specific situation in which the adaptive advertising service is provided to the consumer and try to consolidate all the specific information types needed to support service adaptivity.

To inform discussion about the specific information units needed for service delivery, we used situational scenarios involving adaptive advertisement services. One scenario focused on a hair-coloring product designed to cover grey hair. Ideally, an advertisement for this product should be specific to a customer's sex, age and hair color. Such an advertisement should only be displayed on a public display when few people other than the advertisement's target are near the display. It should be shown at the moment when the respective customer is near hair-styling shelves. And it should only be shown if the respective product is on the shelf (or at least in stock).

However, the gap between such situational detail and the broader information categories identified in Fig. 8.4 made plain that conceptualization of context requires further structuring. We therefore introduced a hierarchical specification of the top-down information categories on three levels: a macro, micro and situational level.

The macro level is valid for all model applications. It should be considered as a further refinement of the information categories in Fig. 8.4, but specific to the pervasive advertising context. For example, the task of a consumer is specified as 'shopping', while the location of the service is the region where an advertisement is launched.

The micro level then filters this macro level information category and helps apply it to a specific application environment (e.g., a specific store in a region that has specific climate conditions, specific clientele, etc.). The specific application environment is embedded in the macro environment. Accordingly, the specific application environment supplies more detailed information than the macro factors.

Finally, the situational level describes an 'adaptive incident' or 'moment of service delivery' that happens in the application environment. For example, a female consumer with blond hair, age 18, is supposed to see a hair-color advertisement on a display integrated in a Douglas store shelf in the first district of Vienna.

For context-adaptivity, the situational level is eventually determining, as systems have to adapt to the actual conditions at the scene at the moment of service delivery. Still, understanding the micro and macro level has proven useful for identifying the full spectrum of available information sources.

Figure 8.5 provides an overview of the structuring approach, summarizing an excerpt of the pervasive advertisement context model we developed.

8.3.2 Second Phase of Model Development: Working Model Verification

The second phase of model development aimed to verify the working model by applying a strict methodology. We invited five academic experts to serve as participants. On a plain wall, the context model was depicted with sticky notes, with each model item written on a single note.[1] Participants were briefly informed about the context of the research, the first level of the model and the concept of the macro, micro and situational level. When a participant did not understand the meaning of a term, brief clarification was given. To avoid priming, no other questions were

---

[1] Additionally, the participants had a printout of the working model at their disposal. The interviews were held in German, while the model on the sticky notes and printout were in English.

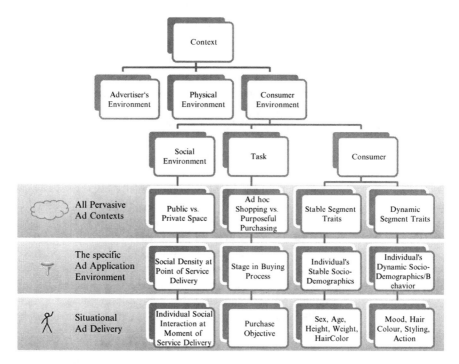

Fig. 8.5 Specifying high-level information categories for a context-adaptive service situation

answered. Participants were encouraged to present ideas for renaming a category or introducing a new one.

Participants were first asked to interpret the overall working model (top-down conceptualization) while thinking-aloud so that their thoughts could be captured. They were also instructed to rearrange the sticky notes or introduce new ones until they were satisfied with the model.

In a second exercise, participants were asked to classify a specific advertising adaptivity situation according to their rearranged working model (Bottom-up Verification of Advertising Adaptivity). For this purpose, we told them to assume that a fully functional pervasive advertising system would be installed in a store. We asked them to recall one of their last shopping experiences in a physical store and imagine that they encountered a context-adaptive advertisement. Again, they then had the opportunity to rearrange the sticky notes or introduce new ones until they felt that they could accurately classify the situation.

The think-aloud exercise, which lasted 191 min, was audio taped and transcribed. The interviewer took additional notes on paper.

The result of this two-sided approach of card sorting was a rephrasing and rear-rangement of many of the categories on all three (macro, micro, and situational) levels. The next section presents each part of the context model we developed for pervasive advertising. This model incorporates all changes initiated by the expert exercise. Figure 8.9 depicts the consolidated end result of the model.

8.4   A Context Model for Adaptive Advertising

Following the method described in Sect. 8.3, we outline the conceptualized context for an adaptive digital advertising service. The full model is depicted in Fig. 8.9. It presents the spectrum of measurable and logically disjunctive information units that are available to design adaptive advertisement services.

Note that the model only represents what can be measured on a macro, micro and situational level. The model does not contain information about how measurement should be performed, whether information sources are accessible, or how the measured information could be combined to extract additional meaning from it. This information would be part of the later adaptation phase of the context adaptivity process.

In describing the context model's details, we presume that networked digital displays (digital signage) are spread out in retail outlets and other public and semi-public spaces and are being used as an interface to transmit highly personalized context-adaptive advertising messages. Digital displays can be mounted onto shelves, hang from ceilings, be part of a shopper's cart or meet him or her at waiting points, such as sales counters. We also presume that many current hurdles associated with reliable data collection and aggregation as well as dynamic content delivery have been resolved.

We are aware that the description of the context model for adaptive advertising is in parts highly futuristic from the perspective of today's operations. That said, we believe that our assumptions are realistic and that, due to the increasing availability of context-sensitive technologies, this model could soon be realized for advertising at the point of sale.

8.4.1   Data Involved in Grasping the Advertiser's Environment

Naturally, a conception of context for advertising has to include the advertiser's perspective, as the advertiser is the key stakeholder and service operator in this context. At the macro level, advertisers have three core information categories that capture their operational environment and should drive adaptive advertisement delivery (Fig. 8.6): the current market demand as reflected in the consumers' shopping basket (at the macro level), the products and services that the advertising company offers, and an advertising campaign that may promote specific products or services.

8.4.1.1   Product and Service Demand

On the macro level of consumer demand, the typical shopping basket consists of a set of items purchased by an average customer during an average shopping occasion. The methodological toolbox that enables researchers to study the composition

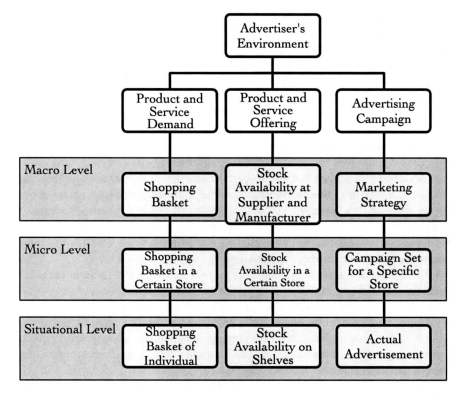

Fig. 8.6 Excerpt of the context model specifying the conceptualization for the advertiser's environment

of such product bundles is referred to as market basket analysis and is typically done at the national level [26, 27]. On a micro level, the shopping basket can be broken down for a certain store; i.e. on the basis of purchase data. On the situational level, measurements can relate to an individual shopper; for instance, one can measure the actual contents of a shopping cart.

In one scenario, a market basket analysis computes high demand for rye bread by an average customer. The system recognizes that a particular customer does not have rye bread in her shopping cart. In a next step, based on a certain algorithm (predefined in the adaptivity phase), the system presents an advertisement for rye bread on a nearby display.

8.4.1.2 Product and Service Offering

The macro level describing an advertiser's offer should typically recognize the availability of goods and services. General availability on the market (at the macro level) may be more abundant than availability at a specific site (micro level) or on a shelf (situational level).

This factor can be operationalized in an advertising scenario; for example, a woman who wears size 4 shoes enters a shop and sees a pair of red shoes. The system is aware that this shoe model is out of stock in shoe size 4 in this particular shop. In a next step, the adaptivity algorithm could then, for example, cause the display to show an advertisement for a similar red-colored shoe model that is available in size 4.

8.4.1.3 Advertising Campaign

An advertising campaign is a series of advertisements that share a single idea and message. It includes information that is adapted to the context in contextual advertising and also serves as context itself. Typically, advertising campaigns appear in different media across a particular time frame [5].

On a macro level, we consider a retailer's marketing strategy, which provides the frame for any kind of advertising activities.

The micro level involves the campaign set for a specific site. This level considers which advertisements (out of the set of advertisements of a whole campaign) should actually be displayed and identifies controls for possible restrictions.

The situational level deals with the actual advertisements displayed. For example, there may be a '2 for 1' discount campaign or a reduced price policy for products nearing their expiration date. In a purchase situation, a consumer may encounter one of these campaigns.

For instance, a system may be configured to the marketing policy of an advertiser. In this advertiser's particular advertising campaign, there are three different advertisements for the same product. The system detects that one of these advertisements interferes with the retailer's marketing policy, which forbids showing advertisements with offensive language during morning hours. Engaging in advertising adaptation, the system would then make only the two remaining advertisements available during morning hours.

Note that advertising campaigns may increase the demand for products and services and may, therefore, lead to reduced availability of those products and services. This kind of mutual influence between different information dimensions is not analyzed as part of the conceptualization of context. Instead, this logic is part of a later step in the adaptivity process (context adaptation).

8.4.2 Physical Environment

The physical environment refers to all elements that characterize the physical surroundings (Fig. 8.7).

One of the most discussed environmental factors for computing context is location. Furthermore, we distinguish between manipulable and non-manipulable environmental conditions.

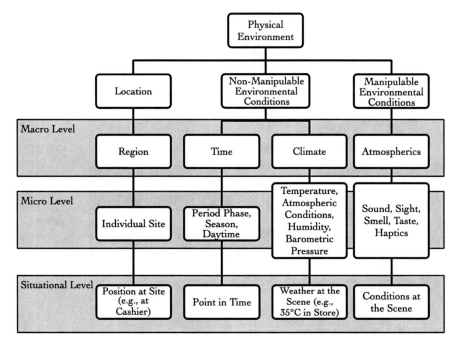

Fig. 8.7 Excerpt of the context model specifying the conceptualization for the physical environment

8.4.2.1 Location

Beyond being an aspect of the physical environment, location is frequently used to approximate more complex contextual factors [38]. For instance, geo coordinates may give information about the social environment or infrastructure at a location. As with the advertiser's environment, deductions that lead to additional information in this way are not part of the conceptualization phase.

We take a sociological approach to location. A site with a public display in Vienna and a site with the same kind of display in Paris are unlikely to look the same. Even two stores from the same retailer in two distinct districts within a city may differ significantly, as the subcultures visiting these stores vary. On a macro level, we therefore view location from a regional perspective, considering the people and their preferences in the particular region. For example, residents of the first district in Paris traditionally have a higher socioeconomic status than those of the 18th district. On a micro level, we then distinguish a specific site within a region by identifying its particular 'microcosm' [3]. For instance, a specific store may correspond to the average store in the region or be an 'outlier'.

On the situational level, we are even more specific within the microcosm of a site and refer to the actual position of a consumer in the store at hand (e.g., in front of the cashier, next to the refrigerated display case). Obviously, a consumer will respond differently to impulse advertisements in front of cashiers than to the same advertisements in one of the aisles where no impulse goods are sold. Actual adaptation, however, is part of a later step in the adaptivity process. The conceptualization of context involves only a consideration of location on a macro, micro and situational level for system development.

8.4.2.2 Non-manipulable Environmental Conditions

This category refers to environmental conditions that are naturally produced, such as time and climate. Advertisers cannot manipulate these conditions, but can use them to their benefit.

Time. Temporality can refer to particular points in time or general time periods [6]. A point in time – for instance, 7 p.m. on a particular day – can inform the characterization of an advertisement situation. On a higher level, relevant time periods include seasons (e.g., summer, winter, Christmas, Easter) and special time periods such as Valentine's Day.

The conceptualization of a system may consider time of day as a relevant parameter. In a later step – the phase of context computing – a system could be equipped with a clock. The adaptation mechanism could then act on a schedule and, for instance, prioritize organic product advertisements between 3 and 5 p.m. on weekdays.

Climate. Weather is most commonly associated with temperature, rain and wind force. However, weather refers to more factors. On a macro level, we consider climate as a generic, broad factor. On a micro level, we may consider a wide range of variables such as temperature, wind force, wind-chill factor, air humidity, barometric pressure, rain or snowfall and cloudiness; we may also consider forecasts for changes in any of those variables. On a situational level, the weather determinants act in combination. While the micro level still considers the factors generally, in this level we observe the situation in a very specific setting (at a particular site at a particular point in time). While wind force, for instance, may be weak in a region, it might be much stronger right in front of a public display; this factor might imply that the area where the display is located is a chillier place than one would expect.

Let us, for instance, assume that ice-cream advertisements are most effective when the recipient feels warm and that they are not effective at all when the recipient is cold. An adaptivity mechanism could foresee to show ice-cream advertisements only when the temperature is high enough at the particular site. This, in turn, requires a consideration of climate in the conceptualization phase.

8.4.2.3 Manipulable Environmental Conditions

Atmospherics is perhaps the most studied manipulable contextual element for retail environments [7]. It can affect consumers' attitudes in various ways. For instance, retailers seek to create an atmosphere that promotes cross-buying [34]. Cross-buying is defined as buying other products and services as opposed to buying more of what

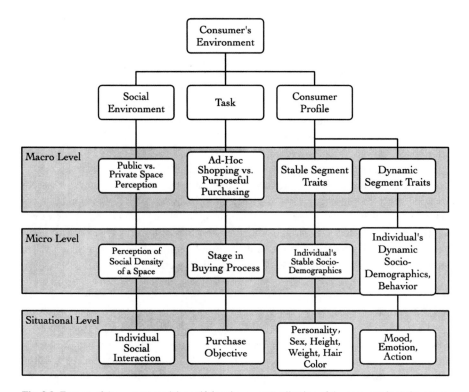

Fig. 8.8 Excerpt of the context model specifying the conceptualization of the consumer's environment

a consumer bought before [24]. We consider atmosphere at the macro level of our conceptualization. On a micro level, we include atmospheric determinants at a site including the temperature, air quality, sound, (functional) music and odor [7]. On a situational level, again, these determinants act in combination at a particular site at a particular point in time. For instance, the system may detect that the consumer in front of a display is in a bad mood. Accordingly, it spreads scents of essential oil to put her in a happy mood.

For adaptive advertising, considering the effects of atmospherics is part of the conceptualizing phase. After these effects are identified, the system can act on them in the adaptation phase. Considering these effects, the system may present advertisements that fit the given atmospherics or create the desired atmospherics so that the presented advertisement will be effective.

8.4.3 Consumer's Environment

The consumer's environment subsumes all elements concerned with the consumer. As outlined above, we consider the consumer him or herself, the consumer's social environment [6] and his or her primary 'task' (Fig. 8.8).

8.4.3.1 Social Environment

Social environment refers to an individual's perception of a space. On a macro level, we consider whether a space is perceived as public or private. Further distinctions of space perception, such as meeting points or points of transfer, can be found in Hillier [20].

On a micro level, we refer to the social density of the respective space. A strong aspect of how individuals perceive a space is whether other people are around. If other people are around, their number and level of interaction with an individual influences that individual's perception of the space.

On a situational level, we consider an individual's interaction with passersby, co-shoppers, or a retailer's employees as situational context. For example, a system detects that a couple is gazing at a display and is aware that they sympathetically interact. Accordingly, it presents an advertisement showing a couple (thus representing a similar situation) and introducing a new product in an emotional way. This form of adaptivity mechanism can only be implemented when social density had been considered during the phase of conceptualizing context.

8.4.3.2 Task

On a macro level, we consider the task a consumer is engaged in when viewing a display. Naturally, there is a difference between viewing an advertisement while driving a car to work (no shopping intention) and viewing it in a shop. In a shop, the consumer might want to buy something specific (purposeful purchasing) or might just be looking around, the latter of which could lead to an ad-hoc purchase.

On a micro level, we consider the buying process. Every stage of a buying process (needs recognition, information search, evaluation, purchase, post-purchase) defines different consumer goals (i.e., shapes a different context) and triggers different consumer behavior [34]. Consequently, the toeholds for effective advertisements are distinct in each stage of the buying process.

On a situational level, we consider an individual's purchase objective, such as the specific product sought (Fig. 8.9).

For instance, a system may detect that a consumer is evaluating a printer she wants to purchase. Accordingly, it can launch printer advertisements on the nearby display; these advertisements can include a range of printer products with detailed properties, prices or even specifications. For this example, it is crucial to consider the stages of the buying process during context conceptualization. Context conceptualization is the basis for the identification of adequate measures in the context computing phase.

8.4.3.3 Consumer Profile

Personalized advertising is typically based on some kind of consumer profiling. Consumers are classified into segments based on various personal traits. Here, we distinguish between stable and dynamic segment traits.

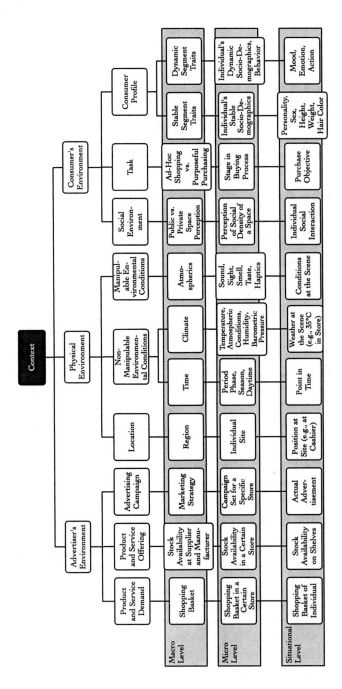

Fig. 8.9 Conceptualized model of context for pervasive advertising

Stable Segment Traits. On the situational level, stable traits include those variables of a profile that cannot be changed in a specific adaptive advertisement moment (e.g., sex, height) or evolve very slowly over a consumer's lifetime (e.g., personality traits, age, social status). On the micro level, we consider the consumer profile of an advertiser's target group. This profile characterizes the typical audience of the advertiser.

For instance, let us assume that a clothing retailer's target group is defined as men in their forties. Let us further imagine that a site where a large display is situated is typically frequented by women in their late thirties. In the advertising adaptation phase, this information could be combined and interpreted to produce a new target group for the advertising: women who buy clothes for their husbands. In this case, the thorough conceptualizing of the 'stable segment traits' variable strongly contributes to the development of an effective adaptivity mechanism.

Dynamic Segment Traits. Puccinelli et al. [34] argue that dynamic factors such as affect, mood, emotions, and feeling clearly influence all stages of the consumer buying process. They further claim that consumer affect may trigger affect-congruent memories. Pervasive advertising can call on this influence by manipulating such factors to its advantage.

Accordingly, we consider unstable, dynamic consumer variables that allow advertisers to trigger affect-congruent memories with their advertisements. On the macro level, we refer to the dynamic traits of the (market) segment. The micro level includes the unstable traits that customers may encounter. Such traits include socio-demographics and individual behavior.

On a situational level, we consider all unstable parameters – such as mood, emotion or attention – that may vary while a consumer is, for instance, visiting a store. The situational level draws from the range of unstable parameters and applies relevant ones to the specific situation of a consumer in a particular moment. For instance, when the system recognizes that a consumer is very emotional, it may display an emotional advertisement for a hedonistic product instead of product information.

8.5 Conclusions and Outlook

In today's advertising industry, context plays an increasingly important role. Existing adaptive advertising systems tend to account for individual dimensions without considering the big picture.

The key for any adaptive system is a thorough conceptualization of context, which considers the various aspects of context information. Taking a top- down and bottom-up approach, we have demonstrated the importance of viewing various kinds of context from different angles and integrating stakeholders' perspectives.

In this chapter, we provided a comprehensive context model for adaptive pervasive advertising. Among academic experts, the model has proven useful and coherent. In a next step, we will evaluate whether this model can be meaningfully applied. The in-depth description of the methodology should inspire scholars to take a similar approach for system design.

Against this background, we emphasize that a model of context is a dynamic process rather than a product. The long-term goal is to provide a fully integrated model; currently, the model (Fig. 8.3) presents context categories on all levels without fully integrating them. Still, it provides a basis for future development.

While we will never be able to compile a complete list of context variables, research needs to undergo a continuous process of conceptualization. We have provided a basis for pervasive advertising. For further advancement, researchers are encouraged to apply our context model for pervasive advertising to other adaptive advertising applications in retail.

References

1. 42media MediMax: Der moderne Vorreiter der Elektronikfachmarktbranches (2010)
2. Adomavicius, G., Tuzhilin, A.: Toward the next generation of recommender systems: a survey of the state-of-the-art and possible extensions. IEEE Trans. Knowl. Data Eng. **17**(6), 734–749 (2005)
3. Anderson, S.J., Volker, J.X., Phillips, M.D.: Estimating intermarket retail sales flows on a comparative county, MSA and statewide benchmark basis, Proceedings of American Society of Business and Behavioral Sciences Conference (ASBBS 2000), 17–21 February, Las Vegas, NV, ASBBS, pp. 139–144 (2000)
4. Baldauf, M., Dustdar, S., Rosenberg, F.: A survey on context-aware systems. Int. J. Ad. Hoc. Ubiquitous Comput. **2**(4), 263–277 (2007)
5. Belch, G.E., Belch, M.A. (eds.): Advertising and Promotion: An Integrated Marketing Communications Perspective, 5th edn. Irwin McGraw-Hill, Boston (2001)
6. Belk, R.W.: Situational variables and consumer behavior. J. Consum. Res. **2**(3), 157–164 (1975)
7. Bitner, M.J.: Servicescapes: the impact of physical surroundings on customers and employees. J. Market. **56**, 57–71 (1992)
8. Black, D., Clemmensen, N.J., Skov, M.B.: Supporting the supermarket shopping experience through a context-aware shopping trolley. In: 21st Annual Conference of the Australian Computer-Human Interaction Special Interest Group: Design: Open 24/7, Melbourne, 23–27 Nov 2009. ACM, pp. 33–40. doi:10.1145/1738826.1738833 (2009)
9. Bradley, N.A., Dunlop, M.D.: Toward a multidisciplinary model of context to support context-aware computing. Hum. Comput. Interact. **20**(4), 403–446 (2005)
10. Cutrell, E., Czerwinski, M., Horvitz, E.: Notification, disruption, and memory: effects of messaging interruptions on memory and performance. In: Hirose M., (ed.) Human-Computer Interaction (INTERACT 2001), Tokyo, 9–13 July 2001, pp. 263–269. IOS Press, Oxford (2001)
11. Dey, A.K.: Context-aware computing: The cyberDesk project. In: AAAI '98 Spring Symposium, Palo Alto, California, 23–25 Mar 1998, pp. 51–54 (1998)
12. Dey, A.K., Abowd, G.D.: The context toolkit: aiding the development of context-aware applications. In: Workshop on Software Engineering for Wearable and Pervasive Computing (SEWPC 2000), part of 22nd International Conference on Software Engineering (ICSE 2000), Limerick, 6 June 2000 (2000)
13. Dey, A.K.: Understanding and using context. Pers. Ubiquitous Comput. **5**(1), 4–7 (2001). doi:10.1007/s007790170019
14. Eriksson, C.I., Åkesson, M.: Ubiquitous advertising challenges. In: 7th International Conference on Mobile Business (ICMB '08), Barcelona, 7–8 July 2008. IEEE Computer Society, pp. 9–18, doi:10.1109/ICMB.2008.19 (2008)

15. Ferscha, A., Vogl, S., Beer, W.: Ubiquitous context sensing in wireless environments. In: Kacsuk, P., Kranzlmüller, D., Németh, Z., Volkert, J. (eds.) Distributed and Parallel Systems: Cluster and Grid Computing. Springer, New York (2002)
16. Ferscha, A., Holzmann, C., Oppl, S.: Context awareness for group interaction support. In: 2nd International Workshop on Mobility Management & Wireless Access Protocols in Conjunction with International Conference on Mobile Computing and Networking (MobiWac '04), Philadelphia, 1 Oct 2004. ACM, doi:10.1145/1023783.1023801 (2004)
17. Ferscha, A., Swoboda, W., Wimberger, C.: En passant coupon collection. In: Fischer S., Maehle E., Reischuk R., (eds.) 2nd International Workshop on Pervasive Advertising (in Conjunction with Informatik 2009), Lübeck, pp. 3911–3925, 28 Sept – 2 Oct 2009a (2009)
18. Ferscha, A., Vogl, S., Emsenhuber, B., Spindelbalker, R.: SPECTACLES – autonomous wearable displays. In: Adjunct Proceedings of 13th International Symposium on Wearable Computers (ISWC '09), Linz, Vienna, Austria, 4–7 Sept 2009b. OCG (2009)
19. Handelsverband. (2010) Distanzhandel gewinnt an Bedeutung [Electronic Version], from http://www.handelsverband.at/16238.html [Last Accessed 27 July 2011]
20. Hillier, B.: The common language of space: a way of looking at the social, economic and environmental functioning of cities on a common basis. J. Environ. Sci. (China) 11(3), 344–349 (1999)
21. Hong, J.-Y., Suh, E.-H., Kim, S.-J.: Context-aware systems: a literature review and classification. Exp. Syst. Appl. 36, 8509–8522 (2009). doi:10.1016/j.eswa.2008.10.071
22. Ju, W., Leifer, L.: The design of implicit interactions: making interactive systems less obnoxious. Des. Issues 24(3), 72–84 (2008)
23. Kim, W.: Personalization: definition, status, and challenges ahead. J. Object Technol. 1(1), 29–40 (2002)
24. Kumar, V., George, M., Pancras, J.: Cross-buying in retailing: drivers and consequences. J. Retail. 84(1) (2008)
25. Kurbel, K.E.: The Making of Information Systems: Software Engineering and Management in a Globalized World. Springer, Berlin (2008)
26. Manchanda, P., Ansari, A., Gupta, S.: The "shopping basket": a model for multicategory purchase incidence decisions. Market. Sci. 18(2), 95–114 (1999). doi:10.1287/mksc.18.2.95
27. Mild, A., Reutterer, T.: An improved collaborative filtering approach for predicting cross-category purchases based on binary market basket data. J. Retail. Consum. Serv. 10(3), 123–133 (2003)
28. Müller, J., Exeler, J., Buzeck, M., Krüger, A.: Reflective Signs: digital signs that adapt to audience attention, Proceedings of 7th International Conference Pervasive Computing (Pervasive 2009), 11–14 May, Nara, Japan, Springer, pp. 17–24 (2009)
29. Mulvenna, M.D., Anand, S.S., Büchner, A.G.: Personalization on the net using web mining. Commun. ACM 43(8), 123–125 (2009)
30. NEC Display Solutions: Vergleichsstudie SPAR Markt Füssen/Kempten: Umsatzsteigerungen mit Retail Signage Systemen im Einzelhandel. Retail Signage & Public Displays, NEC Studie (2006)
31. O'Grady, M.J., Ye, J., O'Hare, G.M.P., Dobson, S., Tynan, R., Muldoon, C.: Implicit interaction. In: International Workshop on Instinctive Computing, Pittsburgh, 15–16 June 2009. Lecture Notes in Artificial Intelligence (LNAI). Springer Heidelberg, Germany (2009)
32. Page, B.: Dunnhumby renames Tesco TV: rethinks approach to content [Electronic Version]. aka.tv - retail. Retrieved 30 June 2010, from http://www.aka.tv/articles/article.asp?ArticleID= 1143 [Last Accessed 27 July 2011] (2007)
33. Pascoe, J.: Adding generic contextual capabilities to wearable computers. In: 2nd International Symposium on Wearable Computers, Pittsburgh, 19–20 Oct 1998, pp. 92–99. doi:10.1109/ ISWC.1998.729534 (1998)
34. Puccinelli, N.M., Goodstein, R.C., Grewal, D., Price, R., Raghubir, P., Stewart, D.: Customer experience management in retailing: understanding the buying process. J. Retail. 85(1) (2009). doi:10.1016/j.jretai.2008.11.003

35. Rehme, F.: From challenge to chance: challenges in a changing society. In: Innovative Technologien im Handel, St. Wendel, 1 June 2010. Innovative Retail Laboratory, DFKI, St. Wendel, Germany (2010)
36. Schilit, B.N., Theimer, M.M.: Disseminating active map information to mobile hosts. IEEE Netw. **8**(5), 22–32 (1994)
37. Schmidt, A.: Implicit human computer interaction through context. Pers. Technol. **4**(2–3), 191–199 (2000)
38. Schmidt, A., Beigl, M., Gellersen, H.-W.: There is more to context than location. Comput. Graph. J. **23**(6), 893–902 (1999)
39. Smith, S.: Sharing the wealth: is contextual advertising the new gold rush for content providers? EContent **27**(4), 22–27 (2004)
40. Te'eni, D., Carey, J., Zhang, P.: Human Computer Interaction: Developing Effective Organizational Information Systems. John Wiley, Hoboken (2007)
41. Tuzhilin, A.: Personalization: the state of the art and future directions. In: Adomavicius, G., Gupta, A. (eds.) Business Computing: Handbooks in Information Systems, vol 3. Emerald, Bingley (2009)
42. Yuan, S.-T., Tsao, Y.W.: A recommendation mechanism for contextualized mobile advertising. Expert Syst. Appl. **24**(4), 399–414 (2003). doi:10.1016/S0957-4174(02)00189-6

Chapter 9
Managing Advertising Context

Martin Strohbach, Martin Bauer, Miquel Martin, and Benjamin Hebgen

Abstract This technological chapter provides an overview of how real-world knowledge and context information can be integrated in pervasive advertising applications. Often developers of such applications integrate sensing technologies directly into their application. This has two consequences. First, developers need to learn how to interface, use and manage potentially distributed sensors for each individual sensing technology. Second, applications are hard to evolve, e.g. when a better sensing technology is available, the application must be modified so that it can interface with the new technology. As a solution to this problem we describe a methodology that facilitates the integration of sensing technologies and provides an overview of context management tools that are suitable for pervasive advertising applications. The presented methodology is extracted from previous research in context-aware systems and our own research in pervasive advertising. For a case study based on our Context Management Framework (CMF) we describe an application using public digital displays. We illustrate how the methodology can be applied for more effective development of pervasive advertising applications.

9.1 The Challenge: Using Sensor and Context Information

It is an intrinsic property of pervasive advertising applications that they rely on knowledge about the physical environment in which they operate. For instance in research, public displays are often used to show personalized advertisements

M. Strohbach (✉)
AGT Group (R&D), Darmstadt, Germany
e-mail: mstrohbach@agtgermany.com

M. Bauer • M. Martin • B. Hebgen
NEC Europe Ltd, Heidelberg, Germany
e-mail: bauer@neclab.eu; martin@neclab.eu; hebgen@neclab.eu

J. Müller et al. (eds.), *Pervasive Advertising*, Human-Computer Interaction Series,
DOI 10.1007/978-0-85729-352-7_9, © Springer-Verlag London Limited 2011

with the objective of making advertising more effective and show more relevant information to potential customers [20]. Such applications require sensors to detect the proximity of passers-by. Obtaining additional information, e.g. about the current activity of nearby people allows even further customization. Other examples include interactive display installations that engage potential customers with advertised products [12] or contextualized advertisements on mobile phones [23].

A common problem of such applications is the effective integration of appropriate sensing technologies in the application. Ideally an application developer should be able to simply specify what information is required and get some notifications about changes in the real world to which the application needs to adapt. Caring about individual interfaces and specific technologies or solving distribution and communication problems are practical problems that have to be solved, but are typically of secondary importance to integrators and researchers that are interested in the application itself.

From previous research [5, 8, 37] it is well known how common distributed middleware abstractions can effectively speed up development and provide a better degree of reusability. Nevertheless, pervasive advertising applications are often developed as vertical applications in which sensing technologies are directly integrated in the application. As a consequence developers need to learn how to interface, use and especially manage potentially distributed sensors for each individual sensing technology. Also, applications are hard to evolve, e.g. when a better sensing technology is available, the application must be modified so that it can interface with the new technology.

The objective of this chapter is to provide an overview of state-of-the art in context management and illustrate in a concrete case study how pervasive advertising applications can be developed more effectively by using this knowledge. This chapter is intended for

- **Practitioners in industry** that seek to integrate sensors in a cost effective way requiring a minimal level of expertise with the sensing technologies,
- **Researchers** that study pervasive advertising applications, e.g. usability, acceptance, privacy, novel ways of applications and interactions, and
- **Sensor Technology Providers,** i.e. researchers and businesses that develop sensors and sensing technologies and are interested in making their technologies available for easy use by pervasive advertising application developers.

Section 9.2 defines our terminology. In Sect. 9.3 we describe a targeted advertisement scenario with public displays. Based on this scenario we describe challenges associated to managing context and provide an overview of suitable solutions in Sect. 9.4. In Sect. 9.5 we describe a methodology that guides developers in integrating context in their applications. We describe our own context management framework (CMF) in Sect. 9.6, and in Sect. 9.7 we present a case study in which we realize the application scenario. Finally, we discuss our design decisions in Sect. 9.8 and conclude the chapter with a summary in Sect. 9.9.

9.2 What Is Context?

Our definition of context is based and closely related to Dey's definition that relates context to an entity such as people, places and things [7]. Furthermore, we use the term *context information* to explicitly relate to a concrete structured data set instead of the high level concept.

We consider this relationship to a real-world entity as an important property of context information: rather than describing raw sensor data and having knowledge about the related entity implicitly in the sensor and application, context information carries the relationship to the entity in the data itself. This way, applications know what the data relates to without making potentially wrong assumptions. For instance, a context information instance directly embeds the information that the noise level is related to a particular shop.

Context is typically related to information obtained from sensors that often provide potentially fast changing information about the physical world. In general we consider context information to be independent of the nature and usage of the data. For instance, static user profile data can also be considered as context information. When integrating context information in the application, it is however necessary to examine its origin, nature and use in more detail. This analysis and realization for pervasive advertising applications is the purpose of this chapter.

9.3 Guiding Scenario: Context-Aware Digital Signage

Based on our own experience [16, 32] with building pervasive advertising applications prototypes, collaborations with stakeholders and previous academic work in this area [20, 28], we choose a Digital Signage scenario to illustrate the importance of context management. In Digital Signage electronic displays are used for communicating to a potential audience. In connection with real-world knowledge they can help advertisers to better communicate and engage [18] with potential customers, e.g. by better targeting and measuring the impact of delivering advertising content and offer interactive applications such as games.

The tools and methods described in this chapter can easily be transferred to other forms of advertising, e.g. using other devices such as mobile phones [23], or modalities such as sound (see chapter 16) or even smell [6, 9].

For our scenario as depicted in Fig. 9.1, we assume that customers have opted in to the services described below and provide personal information such as preferences and privacy settings. We also assume that the services are able to learn preferences and detect situations in which content and services are most likely to be accepted both based on anonymous statistical data and on an individual basis, and by correlating other user data.

Displays in our scenario show targeted content depending on nearby individuals or groups of individuals. The content may be based on users' profile information,

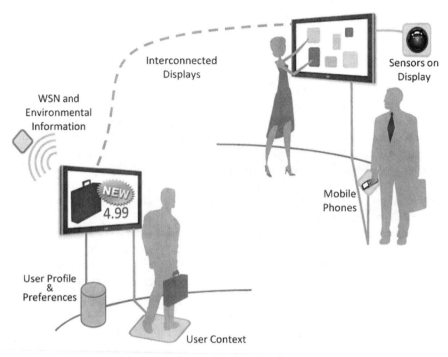

WSN and
Environmental
Information

Interconnected
Displays

Sensors on
Display

NEW
4.99

Mobile
Phones

User Profile
&
Preferences

User Context

Fig. 9.1 Context-aware Digital Signage Scenario using various context information sources

learned preferences, dynamic knowledge about users' current situation such as activity, environmental context of the display (weather, temperature, brightness, noise, etc.), or items on a public shopping list. The presentation of content is further influenced by application specific knowledge that provides information about the success rates of certain content for a specific situation, time and location [20]. For instance younger people may be more receptive to an interactive game than older people, or good weather may increase the likelihood of successfully advertising ice-cream, while rain may increase the likelihood for advertising umbrellas.

Content is augmented with QR codes, i.e. two dimensional bar codes, or Near Field Communication (NFC) tags [22] that allow customers to remember the content or access a secondary web page offering additional product information and services. Remembered content can later be accessed in an experience log that, among other functions, supports the purchase of the advertised product. Other services include buying the product on the spot, retrieving personalized discount coupons in the form of barcodes, and a navigation service that uses displays and mobile phones [29] to navigate customers to a destination, e.g. the place where they can buy the product. Such navigation itself may be weather dependent, e.g. to guide users in such a way that rain is avoided. The interaction with the display and later actions, e.g. purchasing the product, provide valuable audience measurement data for advertisers.

In addition to normal content, displays also offer interactive, product-related games. Players at different locations can interact by touch with a nearby display showing a collection of mobile phone models. The display prompts for a phone model that both players must touch at the same time in order to increase their scores. At the end of the game players receive a – potentially score-related – discount coupon. The game performance is used as a form of audience measurement, i.e. for determining which models are identified fastest and can provide valuable feedback about customer's product knowledge.

9.4 Context Management

In the last decade, after Dey et al. raised an awareness on the importance of context middleware [8], a myriad of systems have been developed that seek to simplify development of applications that rely on sensor and context information.

In this section we provide an overview of some recent approaches and relevant systems. In particular we point out that current research, as for instance carried out in the EU project SENSEI [30], shows that providing sensor and context information from distributed, heterogeneous sources is still a challenging task. Further relevant systems are for instance surveyed by Kjær [13].

9.4.1 Challenges of Developing with Context

The scenario described in the previous section raises questions regarding the acquisition, access and management of context information. We consider the following aspects of key importance for effectively supporting application developers:

- **Discovery of context information,** related to people, places and objects, e.g. identifying the passers-by
- **Discovery of mobile context sources** such as a mobile phone sensor close to a display
- **Providing unified, high level abstractions** for accessing heterogeneous context sources providing static and dynamic information about people, places and things. These abstractions make it easier to adapt and extend the pervasive advertising application to different environments.
- **Appropriate handling of distributed context sources**, e.g. sensors associated with displays, mobile phones or wireless sensor networks deployed in the environment
- **Efficient monitoring of changing context conditions,** such as passers-by approaching or leaving the vicinity of a display or display environment in order to display the right content

9.4.2   Context Management and Access Approaches

There are different approaches for gathering, managing and accessing context. These approaches range from libraries offering APIs to toolkits providing building blocks, to complete infrastructures through which local as well as distributed context information can be accessed [11].

Based on the challenges identified above, we provide an overview of frameworks and their characteristics that can in principle be applied to the domain of pervasive advertising (cf. Table 9.1).

Modern sensor APIs such as the Android Sensor API [1] or the Microsoft Sensor API [19] typically provide low-level access to local sensors but also provide a certain level of abstraction to the developer. Both systems provide a *SensorManager* class which allows requesting a sensor by its type. This is possible via a common driver model which has to be implemented by device manufactures.

A *LocationManager* class which uses the *SensorManager* to get location information from the available location sensor is provided by both APIs. Depending on the requested quality of the information, the *LocationManager* uses a predefined type of location sensor or tries to get the best result. For the discovery of new hardware sensors, the Microsoft Sensor API can use the driver model and the device discovery of Windows.

The Xensor System is a research targeted context system [33]. The main goal of Xensor is to allow researchers to acquire logged data about persons' behaviours without requiring them to attend a research lab. It provides clients for Windows Mobile 5.0 that gather sensor data and a logging repository to store the data. The Xensor client uses three types of *Xensor Modules* to gather context information that is provided as .NET objects to the developer. Module types include (1) *Experience Samplers* that are used to get direct input from a user, (2) *Usage Sensors* that are used to gather application usage data, and (3) *Context Sensors* that are used to gather information from the actual sensors of the device such as GPS, Bluetooth, etc. These modules are controlled by the *Xensor Engine* which loads and unloads modules dynamically on request.

Toolkits provide components that can be re-used when building applications. The Context Toolkit [8] offers widgets, aggregators and interpreters as components. Widgets provide access to context information, hiding the low-level details of sensor access. Interpreters are used to derive higher level context information. Components can be distributed and re-used by multiple applications, but applications need to be statically configured to use them. Information is modelled as programming language objects, but there is no underlying semantic model like an ontology.

Context infrastructures are intended to be used by multiple client applications. They can be local or distributed and differ regarding their scalability. In the Context Broker Architecture (CoBrA) [5] one broker maintains a context model for a certain space. This simplifies local reasoning as all information relevant to a certain space is available centrally, e.g. hosted by a powerful server. Clients can dynamically discover context information, but they need to find the right broker first and any

Table 9.1 Overview of approaches for context management and access

Approach	Structure and distribution	Discovery	Modelling abstractions	Processing and inference
Microsoft Sensor API (Microsoft 2011)	Local API	Type-based sensor discovery	C struct records	–
Android Sensor API	Local API	Type-based sensor discovery	Java objects	–
Xensor [33]	Mobile clients synching to a repository	–	.NET objects	–
Context Toolkit [8]	Distributed widgets	Static configuration	Programming language objects	Interpreters, aggregators
Context Management Service (CMS, [37])	Context domains with peered context brokers	Context broker as discovery service	UML or ontology model represented as PIDF or RDF	Context Reasoners: ontology reasoning and machine learning
IYOUIT [3]	Mobile phone clients, coordinated by a central server	Static configuration	Ontology concept instances	Ontology reasoning and other classification algorithms
CoBrA [5]	Multiple independent brokers	Broker directory, access through model kept by brokers	OWL ontology	Context reasoning engine in broker
C-CAST [14]	P2P distributed brokers	Broker based discovery of context providers	Entity-based context represented in XML	Context providers: aggregation, fusion, inference
Sensor Web [4]	Sensor access and management services	Supported by registry services	Sensor focused with semantic extensions	No specific support, can be provided as sensor
SENSEI [30]	Distributed components for discovery and context access	Peered directories for resource discovery	Integrated two level ontology for sensor values and context entities	Resources providing aggregation, fusion and reasoning

processing or reasoning about information from different brokers needs to be handled by the client. Context information is modelled using the Web Ontology Language (OWL).

The Context Management Service (CMS) developed in the Awareness project [37] is based on context brokers and context sources. The CMS is structured according to domains consisting of one context broker and multiple context sources. Context sources can be sensor-based, context reasoners, or context storage services. Context brokers can be peered through an inter context broker discovery protocol. The CMS assumes a context model with entities and context associated to these entities. As representations both an extended Presence Information Data Format (PIDF) and RDF are supported. Context sources support queries based on SQL and RDQL and subscriptions based on the Session Initiation Protocol (SIP).

IYOUIT [3] provides a social aspect to Context Management. It provides a client for Nokia S60 phones which collects information from the phone sensors (e.g., GPS), user input (e.g. mood) and derived data (e.g., weather at the location). The underlying context system is the CMS described in the previous section. The deployment, however, has a strong focus on semantically enriching information, making wide use of ontology reasoning and classification algorithms to ensure data consistency and infer new relationships among gathered information. For example, a day spent at home, work, a place of the type "restaurant", then work again and finally home, can be classified as a normal working day.

In C-CAST, a broker manages relationships between context providers and context consumers [14]. Aggregation, fusion and inference of context information is handled by context providers that have to manage their own inputs, possibly from other context providers. Clients can dynamically discover context providers through a broker and context information is modelled in ContextML. Context providers must support queries and may optionally support subscriptions.

The OGC Sensor Web Enablement (SWE) working group is defining a comprehensive set of web services for accessing sensor data [4]. SWE models sensors as processes providing geographically referenced observations and measurements. Sensors and their information can be discovered based on provided sensor descriptions rather than contextual information. Sensors can be freely distributed, but need to push their information to a Sensor Alert Service (SAS) in order to support subscriptions. The Sensor Web has been considered for use with pervasive advertising applications by Foerster et al. [10].

SENSEI [31] integrates Wireless Sensor Networks into a sensor framework and provides a context framework on top of it. For clients, the Semantic Query Resolver (SQR) provides a single point of access for discovering resources as well as directly querying or subscribing to context information. The SQR includes a planner that can dynamically create processing trees based on the currently available sensor and processing resources, which are used for aggregating, fusing and inferring context information. Information is modelled as an integrated two level ontology representing sensor information as well as real world entity-based context information.

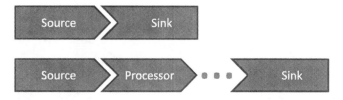

Fig. 9.2 Basic system model of a typical context management system. Sources produce context information, processor fuse or modify context and sinks consume information

9.5   A Methodology for Developing Context-Aware Advertising Applications

In this section we describe a simple methodology that helps researchers and practitioners to design and develop flexible context-aware advertising applications systematically and efficiently. The methodology presented in this section is generally applicable to context-aware applications and is extracted from the approaches described in the previous section and our experience in designing context-aware and pervasive advertising applications. As depicted in Fig. 9.2 it is based on a simple system model that considers a pervasive advertising application as distributed application consisting of context consuming (sinks), producing (sources) and processing components (processors). A processor is both a sink and a source.

The methodology follows a top-down approach for developing the application and consists of the following questions that must be answered step-by-step:

- What are the context sinks in my application?
- What information does each sink consume?
- How is the information modelled and described?
- What information sources, i.e. sensors and services, are used?
- How are sensors and other information sources integrated?
- How can sinks access context information?

As illustrated in the previous section many choices exist in particular with respect to modelling and accessing the information as well as distributing and structuring the components. For the remainder of this chapter we use our own middleware for demonstrating how answering these questions helps to realize our scenario.

9.6   The Context Management Framework

We developed the Context Management Framework (CMF) with the purpose of simplifying the development of context-aware applications. The Context Management Framework originated from the MAGNET project [24] and has been applied to many application areas – in particular to pervasive advertising and Digital Signage [32].

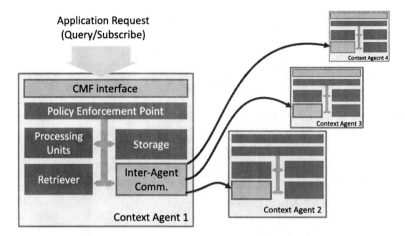

Fig. 9.3 High level architecture of the context management framework consisting of coordinating context agents

As depicted in Fig. 9.3 the CMF consists of multiple *Context Agents*. A collection of Context Agents is typically grouped in clusters and can further be organized in clusters of clusters. Each agent provides access to information stored locally and at connected agents. Agents also enforce policies that define which applications and other agents can access which entity/attribute pairs.

A *Context Agent* offers information to applications from any of the following three sources: sensors accessed by *retrievers*, persistent context available from the *storage* component and *processing units*. Indirectly applications are also context sources as they are able to modify information in the storage component. According to our system model in Fig. 9.2 processing units, storage components, and applications are also sinks.

Applications typically access the CMF using the *CMF Interface* on a local Context Agent, i.e. an agent deployed on the same computing node as the application. The CMF Interface offers access via a declarative *Context Access Language* (CALA) that is able to query distributed entity/attribute pairs. CALA provides query, subscribe, insert, delete, and update operations that operate on a cluster of *Context Agents*. Thus applications can access information in a fully declarative way and do not need to address individual agents directly. They are able to use a unified interface to access information generated by any sensor.

The CMF uses an entity/attribute based data model (see Fig. 9.4). Each piece of information is described as an entity that has an id and a type. An entity consists of one or multiple context attributes consisting of a name, type and value. Each attribute can be associated with metadata, e.g. for quality of information. In particular we use the metadata to annotate attributes with temporal information indicating in which time interval the attribute is valid.

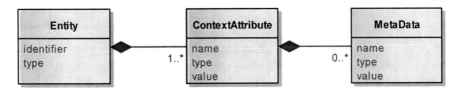

Fig. 9.4 CMF information model consisting of an entity, ContextAttribute and MetaData [2]

The CMF is OSGi based [26] and runs on most devices that support a Java virtual machine, ranging from regular computers to embedded PCs – as used in professional Digital Signage displays – to Windows Mobile and Android mobile phones, home gateways and set top boxes. The programming interface is based on XML-RPC, and its main concepts are currently being standardized as part of the Context API in the Open Mobile Alliance (OMA) Next Generation Service Interface (NGSI) [2].

9.7   A Case Study: Developing with the CMF

In this section we apply the methodology described in Sect. 9.5 to our Digital Signage scenario from Sect. 9.3. We use our CMF middleware as a tool that supports researchers and practitioners in realizing their applications. Using the example of our guiding scenario we answer each of the questions presented in Sect. 9.5 and use our CMF middleware as a tool to conceptualize and implement the scenario step by step.

9.7.1   What Are the Context Sinks?

Table 9.2 lists the identified sinks. The content adaptation component is responsible for showing the content based on the display context such as nearby users. Consequently it is realized as a CMF application.

The preference learning component learns preferences about users and content. User preferences include preferred content for a user or user group in a given situation. In contrast, content preferences indicate the preferred presentation context (e.g. environmental context, time, location) of a certain content or content type. Such preferences can be learned based on previously recorded attention times (how long has the audience looked at the content) or on actions resulting from watching the content (e.g. purchasing actions for advertisements). Learned preferences can thus be considered as context that is known before and constantly updated after the content is shown.

The preference learning component is realized as a processing unit that updates the preference database. The preference data base itself is realized with the storage component.

Table 9.2 Sinks extracted from the guiding scenario and their realization with the CMF

Component name	CMF realization
Content adaptation	Application
Preference learning	Processing unit
Preference database	Storage
Secondary content website	Application
Navigation service	Application
Mini game	Application
Context logging service	Processing unit
Context log	Storage
Experience log	Application

For a prototype realization selecting the CMF as preference database is the preferred choice as all information can uniformly be managed in one system using a single API. In a commercial deployment however, it is more likely that learned preferences are managed by an existing preference database external to the CMF and thus the preference learning component may be realized as application.

The secondary content website, navigation service and the mini game are all realized as applications using respective context information.

Finally, the context logging service records related context information, e.g. for audience measurement, later analysis and the experience log application. Similar to the preference learning service it is realized as processing unit that stores the result in the *Context Log* realized with the CMF storage component.

9.7.2   What Information Does Each Sink Consume?

The information consumed by each sink is listed in Table 9.3. The content adaptation sink component requires a considerable amount of context information in order to target the content to the current audience. Similarly, the preference learning component uses presentation context, audience measurement data (e.g. attention time, dwell time, interaction feedback, etc.) and other feedback in order to derive the user and content preferences. For instance the *opportunity to see (OTS)* is a common term to describe the number of passers-by that could have potentially looked at the content of the display [31].

The secondary content webpage only requires a launch trigger, i.e. the information that should be displayed. In our scenario secondary information is being displayed on the mobile phone. In an extended scenario this information could however also be displayed on any nearby display including the display on which the original advertisement is shown.

The navigation service requires information about the user's location, destination and display orientation in order to display the right directions.

Table 9.3 Context Information consumed by each sink

Context sink	Consumed context information
Content adaptation	Identity/number of passers-by, user profiles and preferences, user activity, environmental context, shopping list items, content preferences
Preference learning	Presentation context, audience measurement data, buying actions
Preference database	User preferences
Secondary content webpage	Launch trigger incl. display
Navigation service	User location, destination, display orientation
Mini game	Touch event
Context logging service	All of the above, game performance
Context log	All of the above, game performance

9.7.3   How Is Information Modelled and Described?

Figure 9.5 shows the domain ontology of the guiding scenario in form of a UML diagram. It captures the information produced and consumed by context sources and sinks as described in the previous section.

Audience Measurement information is captured in a separate entity and is linked to both the display and indirectly via *PresentationContext* to *Content* as at measurement time it is easier to relate audience measurement context statically to a display or a place rather than to dynamically changing content. This way it is easier to develop context sources as they do not rely on other context information. The relationship to content is inferred by processors such as the preference learning component or dedicated reasoners.

The relationships between *Product, ShoppingList, Person,* and *Content* further illustrate how the CMF can be used to capture, store and react to the context of a display. The shopping list contains a set of products that a user may eventually buy. The purchasing action is recorded in the *Person* entity. The *Product* entity is related to the content that advertised the product. The associated *PresentationContext* captures the context the advertisement was shown in. This way, user and content preferences (*preferredPresentationContext*) can be inferred and used to optimize the overall system behaviour.

Finally, we use a *WebApplication* entity to model our secondary web page. It uses the URL as identifier. The *launchState* attribute is inserted in the storage component to indicate that the application should be launched. This shows how the CMF can be used as distributed communication infrastructure.

9.7.4   What Context Sources Are Used?

Table 9.4 lists the context sources and their realization with the CMF. In order to fully implement the scenario, there must be a source for each CMF attribute. We only list the most important sources. Other sources are mostly CMF applications

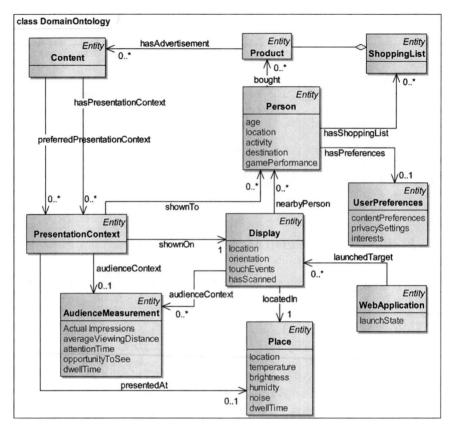

Fig. 9.5 An UML visualization of the domain ontology suitable for realizing the guiding scenario. Each class is a subclass of *Entity* and each attribute is an instance of *ContextAttribute*. Associations are also realized as *ContextAttributes*. The model is simplified only containing the most important entities and attributes. For instance it does not show basic user profile information

that provide static information, e.g. the location and orientation of the display or processors that infer new relationships, e.g. between the presentation context and audience measurement data.

We have only listed those sensors that we have integrated or are considering integrating in the CMF. Many other sensors could be used, e.g. body worn sensors for inferring user activities [36]. Figure 9.6 shows the resulting information flow between sources and sinks.

Shopping list items can in principle be provided by an application that uses the CMF as distributed database. If the shopping list application already exists it may be a better choice to access the shopping list by a retriever.

Most of the audience measurement data can be obtained by a camera attached to the display. Many commercial systems are available, e.g. the VISAPIX People

Table 9.4 Context sources and their realization with the CMF

Context source	CMF realization
User preferences	Storage, application, preference learning processor
Activity	Microsoft outlook calendar retriever
Environmental context (humidity, temperature, brightness, noise)	SUN SPOT retriever[a]
Shopping list items	Application or database retriever
Age, gender, attention time, actual impressions, viewing distance, OTS, dwell time	Camera retriever
Launch trigger	Barcode retriever/NFC retriever
Product purchased	Barcode retriever, reward scheme retriever
Location	Bluetooth ping retriever, barcode retriever, NCF retriever, GPS retriever, location system retriever
Display orientation	Application, location system retriever
Touch event	Application
Mini game score	Mini game application
Context history	Context logging processor and context log storage

[a]SUN SPOT Sensor Nodes Web Site, http://www.sunspotworld.com/ [accessed 31 Oct 2010]

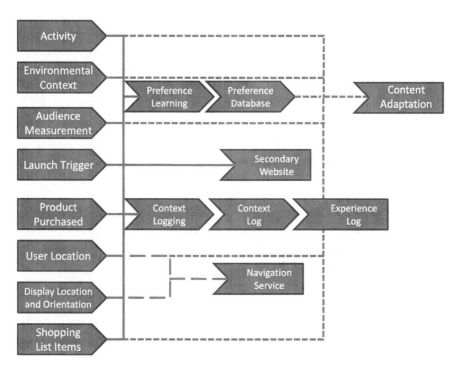

Fig. 9.6 Simplified view on the information flow between sources and sinks. Related information is summarized and some sources and sinks are left out for better readability. For instance the mini game application and related sources are not shown

Counter, [38] Trumedia's audience measurement systems [34], or the Field Analyst [21]. For obtaining opportunity to see measurements and dwell time we implemented our own source using the OpenCV programming library [26].

The launch trigger can be provided by an NFC or Barcode Retriever on a mobile phone. In our implementation [32] we used the QR code reader QuickMark [25] that is available for a vast range of mobile phones. While the above scenario does not require providing the launch trigger via the CMF, it is an easy way of extending the scenario with additional functionalities, e.g. launching the application on a different display than that of the device with which the barcode was scanned. The ZXing programming library (ZXing 2010) provides APIs for coding and decoding various barcodes that can be used as launch trigger retriever in our scenario.

The purchase of a product can best be monitored at the checkout. In our implementation we chose to integrate a retriever interfacing a commercial off-the-shelf barcode reader that is able to read personalized discount barcodes from a mobile phone. Such data collection requires the consent of users. Reward scheme infrastructures as offered by most larger European supermarkets could be used as alternative context source.

User location as required by the navigation service can easiest be obtained from any explicit interaction with the display, e.g. when scanning the barcode or NFC tag. In our own implementation we have used the scanning of the personal discount barcode to infer the position of the user.

For proactive content presentation it is necessary to obtain location information without explicit user interaction. Therefore we ping Bluetooth devices in a privacy preserving way [32]. For outdoor scenarios we have also integrated a GPS retriever for mobile phones. In indoor scenarios it would be necessary to equip customers with tags, e.g. integrated in loyalty cards or in trackable shopping carts ([15], Metro Future Store [17]). More importantly it requires the deployment of usually expensive indoor positioning system [35]. If available, such a system can also be used to obtain dynamic orientation information. We have experimented with an ultrasound-based system [39] and integrated a retriever in our CMF.

9.7.5 How Are Sensors and Other Information Sources Integrated?

Sensor information or extracted features of a sensor are typically integrated into the CMF by implementing a *source* and a *mapper* that together constitute a *retriever*. A source accesses the actual data and provides its data set over a well defined interface to a mapper. A mapper then transforms data representations, e.g. extracting the actual data out of encoded Bluetooth information.

Sources and mappers are independent components that are wired in a configuration file. A configuration file defines mappings to entity/attribute pairs as shown in the listing in Fig. 9.7.

```
entityId=display1
entityType=Display
retrieverName=BtPingRetriever
attributeName=hasScanned
attributeType=MACAddress
sourceClass=eu.neclab.[...].BtPingSource
mapperClass=eu.[...].ToBluetoothAddressMapper
```

Fig. 9.7 Listing of a retriever configuration. The configuration defines how BTPingSource is wired with ToBluetoothAddresMapper to deliver Display entities

The mapper extracts the MAC address from the data set provided by the source. Additional retrievers can be provided with even less effort: for instance if one would be interested in the Bluetooth friendly name, one could define a mapper that creates a *BluetoothDevice* entity extracting the MAC address and the Bluetooth friendly name. In this case the configuration would not contain an *entityId* property but the mapper could be written to provide the MAC address as entity id.

Processing Units are used to fuse context information and use a CALA-based interface to access and provide context information. They provide context information using update and insert operations. For instance we use a processing unit that subscribes to MAC address sightings provided by the retriever above and provides the location of a user. It uses a simple mapping between display ids and location, and a mapping between MAC addresses and user Ids.

Applications provide context information simply by using insert, update and delete operations on entity/attribute pairs.

9.7.6 How Can Sinks Access Context Information?

With our Context Access Language, CALA, single one-time queries can be expressed or subscriptions on entity/attribute pairs can be defined. CALA provides similar concepts to the SQL query language, but has been deliberately designed with limited expressiveness so that it can easily be evaluated in a distributed way. For instance CALA does not support join operations.

CALA supports the following language constructs both for queries and subscriptions:

- **Selectors** – selects the entity and attributes to be returned. Entities can be selected either only by types or type and identity
- **Restrictions** – defines constraints on the returned attribute values
- **Scopes** – restricts the search space. In the current implementation, network scopes are supported that allow to specify whether only values available in the local CMF agent or a whole cluster should be returned

Subscriptions also allow the specification of a monitored attribute and a trigger condition defining when notifications should be sent to the sink. For instance one can specify that a notification should be sent every few milliseconds or whenever

```
<Subscription>
    <EntityTypeSelector>
        <entityType>User</entityType>
        <attrib uteName>location</attributeName>
    </EntityTypeSelector>
    <OnChangeSubscriptionCondition>
        <attributeName>location</attributeName>
    </OnChangeSubscriptionCondition>
    <Scope>
        <networkScope>CLUSTER</networkScope>
    </Scope>
    <Options></Options>
</Subscription>
```

Fig. 9.8 Example of an XML representation of a CALA Subscription used by the content adaptation component to access location information

the attribute changes its value. The example in Fig. 9.8 shows an XML representation of a CALA subscription used by the content adaptation component to access location information.

9.8 Discussion

In our case study we have made certain design and implementation decisions that impact the implementation effort, maintainability and extensibility of the realized scenario. These are in particular decisions with respect to

- Distributed vs. centralized context management,
- Semantic and declarative access vs. service-based access, and
- Contextualized information vs. low level sensor information.

We decided for a decentralized architecture that allows dynamic peering of context sources and sinks. An alternative approach could have been to use central servers that store all context information (cf. CoBrA [5]). This approach works well for small scale installations and avoids the challenging task of distributed reasoning. But a major drawback is the required communication overhead as all information needs to be sent to the server, which may result in unacceptable latencies. Additionally, centralized approaches require a higher level of trust that context information is not misused.

Semantic and data driven context access as realized in CALA, enables the specification of *what* rather than *how* context information is accessed. This reduces the complexity for application developers as they do not need to care about which sources to access, nor use a directory service (cf. SensorWeb [4]).

Our case study also shows that even a comparatively simple scenario involves a large number of sources, processors and sinks (cf. Fig. 9.6). As the number of components increases it becomes increasingly hard to manage the relationship between the components. By its declarative approach the CMF takes away this burden both from application developers and developers of sources and processors.

Our data driven approach requires developers to carefully think about how they model the information. For instance, if we decided to configure a mapper to provide Bluetooth sightings directly as user location, we would not be able to derive other information easily. Likewise, application developers must be aware of what information is available in the system. We are considering providing an extensible ontology targeted at Digital Signage and Pervasive Advertising applications to reduce and simplify the data modelling effort.

By its entity/attribute model the CMF enforces contextualization of any provided data. This is in contrast to the sensor APIs described in Sect. 9.4. The entity/attribute model forces developers to think about the semantics and as a result provides richer and more meaningful data.

9.9 Summary

In this chapter we have presented state-of-the art in context management and applied it to the specific problems that researchers and practitioners face when developing Pervasive Advertising applications. Based on a Digital Signage application scenario, we motivated the challenges faced by pervasive advertising applications that rely on context information. We have provided an overview of existing solutions for context management including our own framework, the CMF, and presented a methodology for developing context-aware advertising applications. We illustrated how the methodology can be followed by presenting a case study using the CMF. Finally we have discussed design choices in our case study.

Acknowledgments The work described in this chapter has been partially funded by the SENSEI and Pervasive Display Networks (PDN) projects. SENSEI, contract number 215923 is partially funded by the European Union as part of the European 7th Framework Program. PDN is a joint project between NEC Europe Laboratories and NEC Display Solutions Europe GmbH.

References

1. Android developers site http://developer.android.com/ [accessed 12 Jan 2011]
2. Bauer, M., Ito, N., Kovacs, E., Schülke, A., Criminisi, C., Goix, L.-W., Valla, M.: The context API in the OMA next generation service interface. In: ICIN 2010 Weaving Applications into the Network Fabric, Berlin (2010)
3. Böhm, S., Koolwaaij, J., Luther, M., Souville, B., Wagner, M., Wibbels, M.: Introducing IYOUIT. In: Proceedings of the International Semantic Web Conference (ISWC'08), October 27–29, Karlsruhe. LNCS, vol. 5318, pp. 804–817, Springer Verlag, Heidelberg (2008)

4. Botts, M., Percivall, G., Reed, C., Davidson, J.: OGC sensor web enablement: overview and high level architecture. Available at http://www.opengeospatial.org/pressroom/papers (2007)
5. Chen, H., et al.: A context broker for building smart meeting rooms. In: Proceeding of the Knowledge Representation and Ontology for Autonomous Systems Symposium. AAAI Spring Symposium, Stanford (2004)
6. CrunchGear: NTT commercializes aroma-emitting Digital Signage system. http://www.crunchgear.com/2008/08/26/ntt-commercializes-aroma-emitting-digital-signage-system/ (2008). Accessed 12 Jan 2011
7. Dey, A.K., Abowd, G.D.: Towards a better understanding of context and context-awareness. In: Proceedings of CHI 2000 Workshop on the What, Who, Where, When, Why and How of Context-Awareness, Hague (2000)
8. Dey, A.K., Salber, D., Abowd, G.D.: A conceptual framework and a toolkit for supporting the rapid prototyping of context-aware applications. Hum.-Computer Interact. (HCI) J 16(2-4), 97–166 (2001). 16
9. Emsenhuber, B.: Scent marketing: subliminal advertising messages. In: Proceedings of the 2nd Pervasive Advertising Workshop, Luebeck (2009)
10. Foerster, T., Broering, A., Jirka, S., Mueller, J.: Sensor web and geoprocessing services for pervasive advertising. In: 2nd Pervasive Advertising Workshop, Lübeck (2009)
11. Hong, J.I., Landay, J.A.: An infrastructure approach to context-aware computing. In: Human Computer Interaction, vol. 6, pp. 287–303. Mahwah, New Jersey, USA (2001)
12. Intel: Intel unveils digital signage concept, Intel news release. Available at http://www.intel.com/pressroom/archive/releases/2010/20100111corp.htm (2010)
13. Kjær, K.E.: A survey of context-aware middleware. In: SE'07 Proceedings of the 25th Conference on IASTED International Multi-Conference: Software Engineering. ACTA Press, Anaheim (2007)
14. Knappmeyer, M., Baker, N., Liaquat, S., Tönjes, R.: A context provisioning framework to support pervasive and ubiquitous applications. In: 4th European Conference on Smart Sensing and Context, pp. 93–106. Springer, Berlin (2009)
15. Krüger, A., Spassova, L., Jung, R.: Innovative retail laboratory - investigating future shopping technologies. In: IT – Inf. Technology, vol. 52, nr. 2, pp. 114–118, Oldenbourg Verlag (2010)
16. Martin, M., Scott, J.: NEC and Instoremedia present Sensor enhanced Digital Signage Solutions. http://www.youtube.com/watch?v=ibqBtF3PGwU (2010). Accessed 12 Jan 2011
17. Metro future store website, http://www.future-store.org/ [accessed 12 Jan 2011]
18. Michelis, D., Send, H.: Engaging passers-by with interactive screens – a marketing perspective. In: Proceedings of the. 2nd Workshop of Pervasive Advertising, Lübeck (2009)
19. Microsoft sensor API, http://msdn.microsoft.com/en-us/library/dd318953(VS.85) [accessed 12 Jan 2011]
20. Müller, J., Schlottmann, A., Krüger, A.: Self-optimizing digital signage advertising. In: Adjunct Proceedings of Ubicomp 2007, Innsbruck (2007)
21. NEC field analyst video, http://www.youtube.com/watch?v=eh5zL30iSA0 [accessed 21 Jan 2011].
22. NFC forum, http://www.nfc-forum.org/home/ [accessed 12 Jan 2011].
23. Nguyen, Q.N., Hoang, P.M.: Push delivery of product promotion advertisements to mobile users. In: Proceedings of the Pervasive Advertising and Shopping 2010 Workshop, Helsinki (2010)
24. Nikolakopoulos, I.G., Patrikakis, C.Z., Cimmino, A., Bauer, M., Olesen, H.: On the personalization of personal networks – service provision based on user profiles. J. Univers. Comput. Sci. 15(12), 2353–2372 (2009)
25. Open CV website, http://opencv.willowgarage.com/ [accessed 06 Nov 2010].
26. OSGi alliance, http://www.osgi.org, [accessed 10 June 2010].
27. Quickmark QR reader web site, http://www.quickmark.com.tw [accessed 01 Nov 2010].
28. Ribeiro, F.R., José, R.: Timely and keyword-based dynamic content selection for public displays. In: International Conference on Complex, Intelligent and Software Intensive Systems. IEEE Computer Society, Washington, DC (2010)

29. Rukzio, E., Müller, M., Hardy, R.: Design, implementation and evaluation of a novel public display for pedestrian navigation: the rotating compass. In: 37th International Conference on Human Factors in Computing Systems, pp. 113–122. ACM, New York (2009)
30. SENSEI Consortium: The SENSEI real world Internet architecture. White Paper. Available at http://www.sensei-project.eu/. Accessed 12 Jan 2011
31. Spaeth, J., Singer, S., Hordeychuk, S.: Audience metric guidelines, digital place-based advertising association. Available at http://www.dp-aa.org/guidelines.php (2008)
32. Strohbach, M., Kovacs, E., Martin, M.: Towards pervasively adapting display networks. In: 1st Pervasive Advertising Workshop, Nara (2009)
33. ter Hofte, G.H.: What's that hot thing in my pocket? SocioXensor, a smartphone data collector. In: 3rd International Conference on e-Social Science (2007)
34. Trumedia company website, http://www.tru-media.com/ [accessed 31 Oct 2010].
35. Ubisense website, http://www.ubisense.net [accessed 01 Nov 2010].
36. Van Laerhoven, K., Berlin, E.: When else did this happen? Efficient subsequence representation and matching for wearable activity data. In: Proceedings of the 13th International Symposium on Wearable Computers (ISWC 2009), pp. 69–77 (2009)
37. Van Sinderen, M.J., Van Halteren, A.T., Wegdam, M., Meeuwissen, H.B., Eertink, E.H.: Supporting context-aware mobile applications: an infrastructure approach. IEEE Communications Magazine **44**(9), 96–104 (2006)
38. VISAPIX company website, http://www.visapix.com [accessed 01 Nov 2010].
39. Zhao, J., Wang, Y.: Autonomous ultrasonic indoor tracking system. In: IEEE International Symposium on Parallel and Distributed Processing with Applications (ISPA08), IEEE Computer Society Press, Los Alamitos, pp. 532–539 (2008)

Chapter 10
Social Networks in Pervasive Advertising and Shopping

Erica Dubach Spiegler, Christian Hildebrand, and Florian Michahelles

Abstract With the proliferation of digital signage in the retail environment and the simultaneous rise in social networks, a new opportunity presents itself to show social network comments in stores. This chapter provides an overview of social networks and its relation to word-of-mouth marketing and will then apply these concepts to the role of social networking in advertising and retailing, particularly focusing on digital signage. Further, a case study of an experiment is presented where a chain of small-space retail stores measured the sales data in a controlled field study. This chapter will show that stores with digital signage displaying comments from social networks were able to increase sales, though not as much as those showing traditional advertising. Additionally, the data revealed that displaying product-specific social network comments are more effective than showing general brand-related comments. The chapter concludes with recommendations for placing social network comments on digital signage.

10.1 Introduction

Social networks have entered the public consciousness and permeate many people's daily lives. Of these, Facebook is the most prominent social network, and by the end of 2010 had more than 500 million active users, half of whom log on every day and

E. Dubach Spiegler (✉) • F. Michahelles
ETH Zürich, Zürich, Switzerland
e-mail: edubach@ethz.ch; fmichahelles@ethz.ch

C. Hildebrand
University of St. Gallen, St. Gallen, Switzerland
e-mail: christian.hildebrand@unisg.ch

J. Müller et al. (eds.), *Pervasive Advertising*, Human-Computer Interaction Series, DOI 10.1007/978-0-85729-352-7_10, © Springer-Verlag London Limited 2011

in total spent over 700 billion minutes interacting with it per month [14]. The result is that every fourth web page accessed in the US was Facebook [29]. While there are many social networks, the next biggest ones are My Space with about half the size of Facebook and Twitter, again just under half as big as My Space [8]. With such large numbers of users and activities, it is no wonder that social networks have attracted the attention of advertisers and retailers, with estimates of 3.3 billion USD spent for advertising on social networks in 2010 [33].

This chapter introduces social networks and looks at the different aspects of social networks in the context of pervasive advertising.

10.2   Social Networks Overview

Online social networks are not new: they emerged in the early days of the world-wide web in 1994 and gained moderate public prominence first with Friendster in 1999 [32], which was eclipsed by MySpace soon after it launched in 2003. MySpace was able to hold on to the leader position of social networks until about 2007 when Facebook took the lead. Social networks can be defined as "web-based services that allow individuals to (1) construct a public or semi-public profile within a bounded system, (2) articulate a list of other users with whom they share a connection, and (3) view and traverse their list of connections and those made by others within the system." [3].

Pervasive computing by definition has a location component, so the recent development in social networks to add a location component needs to be watched closely. There is increasing prominence of location-based social networks that include a geographic element in the way their users connect to each other. The foremost example of this technology is Foursquare with 5 M users [16], followed by others such as Gowalla and over 120 other such services [31]. At the time of writing, the newly launched location-based application by Facebook called Facebook Places is being watched closely to see if it will by default become the dominant location-based social network application [21]. The users' interactions with these location-based social networks are very personal due to the information being accessed with their personal mobile devices, including all their logged statuses and preferences, as well as being very specific to time and location. These social networks deserve the particular attention of advertisers because of their link to physical spaces which overlap with the intentions of pervasive advertising and retailing.

Many social networks exist, and while Facebook is the focus of this article due to the size of its user base and its importance to advertisers, our goal is to keep the reported findings general enough so that they translate to other social networking sites that exist today or to ones that might surpass Facebook in the future.

10.3   Word-of-Mouth in Social Networks

The retailers' interest in online social networks is that they facilitate consumers discussing their products, a modern form of Word-of-mouth (WOM) which has been recognized as one of the most influential sources of information transmission since the beginning of human society [12]. Defined by Brooks already in 1957 as being on the rise among younger white-collar consumers because (1) they face many more choices and decisions regarding purchases than did their counterparts in the past, and (2) at the same time they have less contact with tradition. Thus the interpersonal network within the group serves a guiding function in the "delicate job of keeping in tune with the life style of the moment." [4].

These societal trends have only accelerated since then, and for retailers, WOM has become a particularly prominent feature on the Internet thanks to the ease with which people can transmit information [7]. The Internet provides numerous venues for consumers to share their views, preferences, or experiences with others, as well as opportunities for firms to take advantage of WOM marketing [35], to the point that the term "Word-of-Mouse" has been coined for WOM in virtual communities (e.g., [17]).

Other research supports this, showing that consumers prefer gathering information about their planned purchases first from friends and secondly from virtual communities above other sources, such as commercial information from salespeople, brochures and advertisements [23, 28, 38]. Social networks neatly give users access to information from their friends as well as communities of virtual strangers, so that, e.g., all the "Fans" of the "Nutella" spread share a passion for that brand and form a community around it.

Nearly six in ten adults (58%) in the USA have done research online about the products and services they buy, and about a quarter (24%) have posted comments or reviews online about the things they buy. On a typical day, 21% of adults search for product information online [22]. Given the dominance of social networks and the importance of WOM, it is not surprising that the retail industry is one among many that is trying to understand what this means for their business.

10.4   Retail and Advertising on Social Networks

Users of social network sites come into contact with advertising and retailers in two main ways: advertisements and "fan" pages. Taking Facebook as an example, advertisements are placed in the side-bar of the users' page, and they resemble any other online ad that is not specific to social networks. However, the advertising content might be better tailored to the user, since Facebook has access to extensive information about each user. These advertisements are relatively passive – relying on page impressions and click-throughs to measure success. In contrast, users can actively

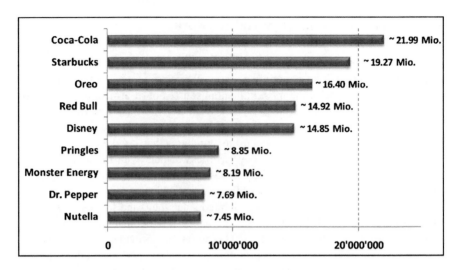

Fig. 10.1 Number of Facebook brand fans of various top brands (by January 2011) (Based on the number of Facebook fans per brand according to the listing at http://fanpagelist.com/)

become "fans" of company pages set up by retailers and manufacturer's brands thus allowing a direct communication between the sellers and consumers.

Companies make decisions on which brands they want to represent on the social networks. Some companies will show only their main brand e.g. the clothing store H&M has a Facebook fan page, but their sub-brand H&M Kids does not. In many cases, a company as well as the brands owned by the company are present, e.g. Nestlé as the company is on Facebook, as well as many of their brand pages such as Kit Kat or After Eight. Depending on the platform and the company strategy, the communication can have more of a broadcasting quality (e.g. Nestlé), or a more interactive one (e.g. Coca-Cola), or a mix, such as Audi where official communications are visible at the top level, and customer comments at a second level where photos of their cars or driving experiences are encouraged. Additionally, companies have the option of providing applications, running polls or hosting competitions within their Facebook fan pages. All of these activities and the users' responses to them are tied to fine-grained measurements and tools for analysis. Despite the various efforts from the companies and the general popularity of the medium, measuring the effectiveness is elusive [34]. Some small cases have been reported, such as the Houston bakery chain that increased customer frequency in their stores thanks to their carefully managed Facebook advertising campaigns [10], and an experiment regarding the effectiveness of company-driven WOM communication showed that it does increase sales [18].

It is an indication of the newness of this medium that many different forms of interaction are being experimented with, sometimes with great success. One example is Coca-Cola, which found a communication tone that helped it become the consumer brand on Facebook with the most fans (see Fig. 10.1).

By contrast, poor understanding of the medium at Nestlé noticeably damaged the brand when a consumer post about the destruction caused by palm oil forestation was answered by an official, but belligerent company representative. The resulting flood of consumer reactions in support of the original post caused the discussion to be much more widely broadcast than would have otherwise been the case, ultimately being transported to mainstream media [13].

The ability to interact directly with customers is an opportunity for marketers and is increasingly becoming a requirement for mass-market brands, though best practices are only just beginning to form. Different consumer brands and retail stores are handling this opportunity and these challenges in different ways. While many brand "fan sites" can be found that have been started by consumers themselves, notably cigarette brands, but also brands with strong followings, such as Coca-Cola, these "renegade" pages can present a problem for the brand owners. One issue is that the communication between the users and the brand is not under the control of the brand, and many of the users are probably not aware that this is not an official site. Another issue is the fragmentation of the fans, making the brand look weaker than it is. For example there are two official Nutella fan pages: one for Nutella International with 7.4M fans and one for Nutella Italy with 2.3M fans. They also provide an application that allows people to send each other virtual Nutella gifts [15]. But in addition to these official activities there are over 20 different Nutella fan sites, some of which have over 100,000 fans each. These are fans that cannot be reached by the company directly, which is one issue with the fragmentation of fan sites often found on social networks.

Regardless of the online activities, the goal is to increase sales. In general, this marketplace rewards more participatory, more sincere, and less directive marketing styles [9]. Consumers bring their online worlds and online social networks with them when they shop: increasingly, they can access this information on their mobile phone or see it on screens in retail stores. This is where the worlds of online social networks and pervasive advertising meet.

10.5   Social Networks and Pervasive Advertising

Pervasive advertising enables the kind of serendipitous advertising common on TV, radio and print, but with the added benefit of allowing new types of ads [30] such as user-generated comments.

The simplest form of pervasive advertising, in the context of social networking, is advertisements that are visible to the users when they access their regular social networking sites using their mobile phones. While these ads are targeted to the user's preferences and screen content, they are not tailored to the location. This is where the marketer's interest in location-based social networks such as Gowalla and Foursquare and Facebook Places come in, since consumers link to their network while being in a specific physical location which the social network (and thus the advertising algorithms) are aware of. Currently many retailers are experimenting with providing coupons based on the location of a consumer or giving awards to members that "check in" to a specific store location [1, 6]. One example is Starbucks, which gave a discount to the "mayor" of a given franchise, i.e. the Foursquare user who had checked into that franchise most often [37].

Highly targeted, social-network informed advertising on mobile phones is currently fertile ground for experimentation. A related topic is how to get social networks onto public advertising spaces. Retailers are investing more and more heavily in a better-understood pervasive technology to convey marketing messages: digital signage. These screens show advertisements, tailored content, brand-building information, etc. Translating this to social networks would mean showing Facebook "quotes" on a public display (i.e. statements provided by fans of a given brand or company page). This could either be done as "static" advertising where the content is defined by the marketing department ahead of time and broadcast the same way each time, or in a more dynamic fashion: updating the content on the display as the Facebook brand or company page receives a new comment. Research suggests that due to the customized nature of using content from social networking sites, the timeliness of the content is crucial. As such, information needs to be harvested, interpreted and consumed in the shortest possible time in order to be meaningful, since delays might invalidate the context [11].

Retail stores have a particular interest in better understanding the combination of digital displays and social networks, since they often function as meeting points and social hubs in the areas where they are located. However, many questions arise from this, such as how to show the comments from a Facebook wall on a public display so that people can relate without feeling that their privacy has been invaded. Also, our research indicates that the cognitive load on consumers viewing the displays is very high for the text-heavy Facebook content being shown, probably reducing its effectiveness.

The following chapter describes a field experiment which was designed to answer the question of the effectiveness of social media comments on digital displays and to measure the impact on sales. The background and method of the experiment are described and the results obtained are detailed.

10.6   Case Study: Social Network Comments Displayed In-Store

To better understand the effect of social networks on public displays, a field experiment [5] was conducted to measure the impact of social network comments on digital signage on consumers in retail stores. The experiment was set up in small-space retail stores, known as kiosks, that primarily sell press products (newspapers, magazines and books), cigarettes, candy and drinks and gambling (mainly lottery). See Fig. 10.2 for an example kiosk.

In 16 stores digital signage was installed, and for 5 weeks social network comments were shown and sales data were then analyzed to measure the effects of the experiment. The following sections describe the background of the small-space retail store, the method used in the experiment, and the findings and conclusions that can be drawn.

Fig. 10.2   Example kiosk at a busy traffic intersection

10.6.1   Kiosk: High-Footfall, Small-Space Retail Stores

The Valora retail holding company runs approximately 1,000 kiosks in Switzerland under the brand name "k kiosk", usually simply referred to as "kiosk" [36]. Kiosks are small or even micro-space retail shops that are characterized by their compact size, no larger than 60 m², selling convenience products – mainly press, cigarettes, candy, drinks and lottery – to a mass customer base at high-footfall locations. They are frequently located at public transport stops, intersections, pedestrian areas and train stations (20% of the kiosks are in train stations; Zürich main station alone has more than ten stores).

Kiosks come in three size categories with the smallest kiosk consisting of a simple window shop, the middle sizes are open-front shops, and finally the largest are walk-in shops. However, even the largest kiosks have a floor space of no more than 60 m² total (for both customers and employees combined). Depending on the size, the larger ones sell a variety of additional products such as phone cards, stamps, stickers and collectibles, gifts (vouchers, plush animals) and, in some, food (sandwiches, salads, coffee, etc.).

Kiosk customers span all demographic segments, though most of them are "on the go" and are looking for exceptionally fast service at very convenient locations. Accordingly, sales show high frequency at small volumes: kiosk serves 400,000 customers per day, who buy an average of between one and two articles and are on average 34 years old.

Customers help themselves (self-serve) to most products and hand them to the personnel for checkout and payment. However, higher-value items (e.g. phone cards or lottery tickets) and restricted items (such as cigarettes), are kept behind the counter.

10.6.2 Pervasive Applications in Kiosks

The current kiosk business model is projected to run into difficulties for various reasons. Press products are increasingly affected by the digitalization of media (mobile phones, e-readers, iPads, etc.); cigarettes are subjected to an increase in legislation, bans and taxation; candy and sugary drinks are harder purchases to justify in the larger trend towards a healthier life style; and, finally, gambling is increasingly moving online. However, the kiosk assets, such as competence in retailing press products and convenience foods, together with long-running leases of highest-value retail real-estate, make the kiosks valuable. For these reasons, Valora began a search for the future role of kiosks in an increasingly digital world, in terms of products on offer as well as services.

From a set of workshops with Valora and different industry partners (SAP, Siemens, Nokia) on the topic "kiosk of the future", the conclusion was reached that pervasive computing concepts are a good fit with the goals of Valora to take advantage of the superior locations of their kiosks. They aim to make kiosks an "information and service hub" [25] and provide customers with a bridge between the digital and the physical world. Pervasive applications have been identified as potentially being part of the answer in the search for their new role, especially in combination with social networks [26]. Valora's goal is to combine the kiosk strengths of consumer product retailing and convenience with the competition for printed press from the digital world, including "Web 2.0" technologies, and specifically from social networks. One direction taken was to show advertisements on digital signage, which provided the company with advertising revenue, intermixed with entertainment and information for customers (e.g. celebrity birthdays, horoscopes, weather, etc.). Combining these two goals meant showing online social network activities for kiosk products on in-shop digital signage, thus bringing the digital and analog worlds together.

10.6.3 Digital Signage in Kiosks

While the high-footfall kiosk locations offer any pervasive application exposure to many eyes, the challenges for pervasive applications in this kiosk environment are numerous: the customers are exceptionally mobile and usually in a hurry. The environment is often very busy with crowds of people, dense information signage (e.g. train time tables, direction signs), conventional advertising, and the shopping

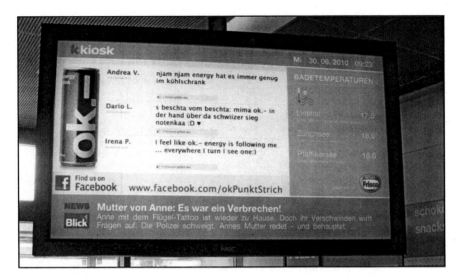

Fig. 10.3 Digital signage in the retail store displaying social media comments

environments. All this results in a very intense visual experience against which any pervasive application will need to compete.

Digital Signage allows for a broad range of content: from generic advertisements to responsive content [27] or interaction [19]. Displaying social network comments rests on the principles of "word-of-mouth" described above, with the aim to guide consumers, who are used to having a lot of choice and who place an emphasis on their social network. However, due to the customized nature of using content from social networking sites, the timeliness of the content is crucial; information needs to be harvested, interpreted and consumed in the shortest possible time in order to be meaningful to the consumer, since delays might invalidate the context [11].

In 2010 Valora conducted a digital signage experiment to understand the effects of digital signage in kiosks, involving a total of 50 kiosks. Of those, 16 contained large, 40 screens that were suitable for the field experiment and which the research team was able to use. The screen design featured an upper bar with time and date, a lower bar with news headlines, and a side bar with infotainment such as weather and horoscopes. The design was part of Valora's digital signage experiments and could not be changed for the field experiment (Fig. 10.3).

10.6.4   Social Network Content

In addition to gaining access to the digital signage, the research team required access to relevant Facebook comments to be shown on the display. For this, a "Fan Page" was set up after Valora approved the use of the "ok.-" brand and product range for this proposed field experiment. Using this private label brand allowed greater control

Fig. 10.4 Screen shot of Facebook Fan Page for the private label ok.-

over content creation and Facebook messaging to the "Fans" than would have been possible with a national or global brand.

The private label ok.- consists of approximately 130 quality consumer goods at low prices. The brand name ok.- is a play on the Swiss custom of using the notation of 10.- instead of 10.00 CHF. In May 2009 the ok.- energy drink was the first product to launch, priced at 1 CHF (0.67 €) and designed to compete directly with the Red Bull energy drink (priced at 3.50 CHF (2.37 €)). The customer response was very positive, and further products were successively introduced, including a calorie-reduced version of the energy drink, bottled water, chewing gum, etc. Due to the success of these items, household products were added (e.g. tissues, soap).

The Facebook Fan Page for the ok.- brand was set up in March 2010 (www.facebook.com/okPunktStrich) and since then has steadily increased in number of "Fans" to over 35,000 in January 2011 (see Fig. 10.4). The success of the Fan Page is reflected not just in the user numbers but also in other measures such as number of comments, "likes" and photo uploads. The comments provided by the fans were used as the content for the field experiment.

Transparency toward the customers has a high priority for Valora, and the intent to use the fans' Facebook comments for commercial uses – such as the digital signage experiment – was openly declared at the top level of the fan page. In a follow-on contest, users of the Facebook fan page were asked to mark posts with an asterisk

(*) if they wanted their posts to be published on the public displays. Approximately 80% of the comments posted during the week of the "ok.- star" contest were marked with an asterisk, indicating the high willingness of fans to have their comments used in public.

Another crucial part of the experiment setup was defining whether comments would be edited, shortened or censored. The decision was taken by Valora that the comments would not be edited except for length if they did not fit the public display template. Importantly, it was decided that comments that were merely negative would not be censored. However, a guideline of conduct was formulated for the posts, explaining that personal attacks and comments that violate the law would be removed. Correspondingly, the team defined an "escalation path" that would be taken if comments on the Facebook fan page violated these guidelines.

The content for the field experiment was taken from the live Facebook ok.- Fan Page every day at 8 pm. The three most recent brand comments and three most recent ok.- Energy drink comments were used for the next day's display. As described, the comments were not edited, and though guidelines were set up to exclude offensive content (including porn, racism, sexism, personal ads, etc.), no censoring of comments was necessary during the experiment. For privacy reasons, the user's photo and last name were removed before using their comment, though otherwise the Facebook look and feel was kept to indicate to passers-by where the content originated from.

10.6.5   Digital Signage Field Experiment

In trying to understand the different aspects of social networks on digital signage, a field experiment in a retail space is ideal, as the content of the digital signage can be manipulated and the effects measured using point-of-sale (cash register) information. The collaboration with Valora allowed us access to the necessary infrastructure, content and data.

10.6.5.1   Hypotheses

As companies like Valora conduct substantial investments in digital signage infrastructure, it is important to quantify the effect of such digitalization strategies and to test for measurable effects in terms of sales volume. Relying on findings that show the general awareness effect of digital signage in a retail environment [20], we argue that a particular and domain-related content is positively related to sales in contrast to unspecific random content. Thus, we hypothesize the following:

(H1) Showing specific domain-related content information leads to higher sales volume than random, unrelated content.

Furthermore, we argue that presenting specific product information reveals stronger effects on sales compared to more global brand-related content. The rationale behind this is related to findings from consumer behavior research that underline that the more specific the given information is, the better it can be mentally processed and lead to specific formative buying behavior [35]. Thus, we argue:

(H2) Product-related content yields higher sales than brand-related content.

Since many companies actively engage in community activities on social networking sites like Facebook [24], it remains unclear if presenting comments from members of a company-led community reveals specific effects on sales. We argue that in the case of a dynamic kiosk environment, consumer behavior is more time-pressured than time-abundant, more information overloaded than having a scarcity of visual information stimuli, and so forth. Therefore, we hypothesize that due to these retail environment conditions, the sales impact of traditional advertising will be stronger than social network comments, as these advertising stimuli can be processed faster and demand less cognitive effort.

We finally hypothesize:

(H3) Traditional advertising yields higher sales than social network comments.

10.6.5.2 Dependent and Independent Variables

Choosing which content to show in which location and at what time will be based on a completely randomized experiment design to minimize the impact of the different influences that come from the "natural" setting of this field study [26].

The independent variables are based on our experimental variations. Five different types of content were displayed on the in-store digital signage: within the first condition we varied product or brand specific content. Secondly, we either presented traditional advertising or social network comments of the day from the ok.- Facebook fan page. Overall, we have a final 2 (product vs. brand) ×2 (traditional advertising vs. social network comments) experimental design. See Figs. 10.5–10.8 for screen shots of each of the four conditions. In addition, every kiosk was treated with a control condition where no experimental manipulations were presented. Every kiosk was randomly assigned to one of the five conditions lasting for 1 week each.

The dependent variable is the financial data of daily sales, as captured from the cash register of each of the 16 experimental kiosks. Since we were only interested in the general sales effect during our experiment, and in order to control for any spurious effects of a possible underlying trend component, we applied common time series methods to trend-adjust the sales data first [2]. We ran a linear model on the longitudinal sales data and subtracted the least-squares trend, as a general procedure in time series analysis. All statistical models were applied to this final, trend-adjusted, stationary time series.

Fig. 10.5 Still frame from video advertisement for the ok.- brand

Fig. 10.6 Digital signage screen with social networking comments for the ok.- brand

Fig. 10.7 Still frame from video advertisement for the ok.- "Energy Drink" product

Fig. 10.8 Digital signage screen with social networking comments for the ok.- "Energy Drink"

10.6.5.3 Experimental Design and Procedure

In order to test our hypotheses we ran the field experiment with systematic manipulation of the presented digital signage content in 16 kiosks all over Switzerland, located in airports, hubs of public transport, shopping centers and in rural areas. Initially, Valora had assigned 16 parallel (twin) kiosks to act as a control for each experimental kiosk, but they were dropped as the matched pairing did not meet the requirements for a scientific study (analyses revealed major differences in terms of location, sales area size, sales volume and so forth).

The content was shown in stores for 5 weeks from 5th of May to the 8th of June 2010. Every experimental condition was run for 1 week, and the shown content was visible for 15 s within a 2 min loop. Figure 10.2 shows an example of the digital signage placed within the kiosk environment, displaying Facebook comments.

10.7   Results

In order to test our respective hypotheses, we applied a repeated measures linear mixed model (LMM). This model family expands more traditional model assumptions and allows us to model correlated and non-constant error terms over time and the underlying covariance structure explicitly. This is of major importance, as this additional flexibility in model specification allows us to account for inherent store-to-store variation and store heterogeneity within our field experiment, as well as to model repeated effects on single stores over time. The respective error terms are assumed to be independent among different stores. Since all stores can be assumed to be randomly

Table 10.1 Parameter estimates of effects from repeated measures LMM

Variable	β	S.E	t-value
Intercept	−22.67	15.47	−1.47[†]
Experimental condition[a]	24.5	12.06	2.03*
Brand presentation[b]	−33.88	10.89	−3.11***
Traditional advertising[c]	30.69	10.51	2.92**
Brand × traditional advertising	9.74	15.42	0.63
Small kiosk type[d]	−40.43	8.63	−4.68***
Sales location[e] = public transport	26.62	8.21	3.24**
Sales location[e] = local retail	21.04	15.95	1.32[†]
Sales location[e] = shopping mall	−1.57	17.00	−0.09
Urban area[f]	0.88	14.58	0.06

$*p < .05; **p < .01; ***p < .001; {}^{†}p < .20$
[a]Reference category = control condition
[b]Reference category = product presentation
[c]Reference category = facebook messages
[d]Reference category = large kiosk type
[e]Reference category = airport location
[f]Reference category = non-urban area

selected from a larger population, we specified the respective store as a random effect within our model. This is important as we are not interested in specific effects of single stores but rather the hypothesized effects of our experimental variations.

Additionally, since we have repeated measurements of single stores over time that will probably be correlated with each other (sales volume in 1 week is not independent of sales volume in the following week), we have to find the optimal covariance matrix first. Therefore we started with the most parsimonious first-order autoregressive covariance structure and expanded the model complexity by applying an autoregressive moving-average, a Toeplitz-based covariance matrix as well as a more complex unstructured covariance matrix. In order to choose the most appropriate model specification, we conducted likelihood-ratio (LR) tests between every nested model. Overall, the best fitting model was based on the unstructured covariance matrix and outweighs its higher number of to be estimated parameters (e.g., testing unconstrained (UN) vs. autoregressive (AR) model with a chi-square distributed LR test of $-2LL_{UN} = 842.25$ vs. $-2LL_{AR} = 890.66$, $\chi^2(13) = 48.41$, $p < .001$).

Table 10.1 summarizes our results. Our experimental variation of the panel content yielded a significant positive effect on sales in contrast to our control condition where only random and unspecific content was displayed ($F(1,91) = 4.12$, $p < .05$). This supports hypothesis one.

Furthermore, our experimental conditions revealed two significant main effects: in the first case, the strongest positive effect was found for product in contrast to brand specific content ($F(1,601) = 9.628$, $p < .01$), suggesting that product-related content reveals stronger and more behavioral stimulating and compulsive effects than brand presentations. Thus, hypothesis two is supported as well.

Most importantly, the second main effect revealed a strong negative effect for Facebook comments compared to traditional advertising ($F(1,357) = 28.641$, $p < .01$).

This finding has to be reflected with regard to the general nature of a kiosk: consumers tend to process given information selectively at the point-of-sale and due to consumers' time constraints, retailers have to choose digital signage strategies that allow for very fast information processing with low cognitive involvement. Actively reading given social network comments requires cognitive capacity as well as motivation to process textual stimuli, whereas easy to process visual cues of classical advertising are not dependent on this assumption. Hence, hypothesis three is supported. The revealed main effects were not qualified by a significant interaction ($F(1,206) = .399$, $n.s.$).

Regarding our control variables, we found a significant effect for the respective sales area ($F(3,1411) = 5.267$, $p < .01$). Follow-up contrasts revealed that the significant effect was attributed to the difference between airport and public transport locations ($M_{Airport-Public\ Transport} = -26.62$, $SE = 8.21$, $p < .01$). This effect suggests that retailers should strongly account for location specific effects that are dependent on the general target audience: while airport area stores are probably more frequented by international consumers who aren't familiar with a specific national brand, this effect is reversed for locations with a high local awareness, like local public transport areas or shopping centers. Most importantly, we found no significant effect for the degree of urbanity ($F(1,774) = .004$, $n.s.$). This finding underlines that the general effect of digital signage is not dependent on highly urban in contrast to non-urban areas.

Note that although airport locations are usually in more urban areas, the general effect between urban and less urban places is less crucial - thus, retailers promoting national brands should focus more on panel installations on the right target location regarding the sales place than on looking for or distinguishing between urban and less urban places. Finally, larger kiosks yield significant higher sales volume than smaller kiosks regarding the ok.- energy drink ($F(1,2947) = 21.936$, $p < .01$).

Overall, our results significantly underline the efficiency as well as the effectiveness of digital signage strategies that rely on social network comments. While we found that product-related cues yield stronger positive effects than brand-related presentations, the more important finding is the positive effect of social network comments, which nonetheless do not surpass the effects of traditional advertising. We believe that this finding is attributed to the higher cognitive requirements as well as time consuming processing of text-based messages in contrast to visual stimuli of classical advertising. Furthermore, the analysis of our control variables additionally revealed that the prevailing store circumstances are highly relevant for deriving effective retail strategies: while significant sales effects can be revealed by digital signage in local transportation areas, this effect is reversed for locations that are frequented by more international consumers.

10.7.1 Discussion of Case Study

The experiment described in this chapter allowed a comparison between standard advertising and displayed comments from a social network, both for brand-content and product-content. The effects were measured using sales data. From this, several core conclusions can be drawn:

- Digital signage showing comments from social networks increases sales, though not as much as advertising (but more than showing unrelated content).
- Displaying product-specific social network comments is more effective than showing general brand-related comments

While the qualitative findings offer a clear picture of sales, the qualitative findings from the experiment are worth consideration:

- The text-based nature of social network comments imposes an additional cognitive load on shoppers when compared to traditional advertising. This might be especially true in a busy retail environment. Screen design must take this into account and aim to minimize the cognitive load.
- Though not measurable, showing social network comments appears to add benefits of perceived "coolness" or innovation to the image of the brand or product.
- Industry constraints – e.g. regarding placement of displays, layout of content, other content on the public displays – must be planned for and built into the design.

The evident success of traditional advertising, as evidenced in this experiment and the omnipresence of advertising, indicates that a clever design would mix social media comments with traditional advertising. This would allow a brand or product to benefit from the experience of traditional advertising while adding the elements of innovation and word-of-mouth.

10.8   Summary

Advertising agencies and retailers are experimenting on how to use social networks in advertising, hoping to harness the new medium to increase sales. The trigger is the meteoritic rise of social networks and the large number of users active on these websites. With their trusted connections between users, and users placing a high value on word of mouth for making buying decisions, brands are increasingly ensuring and professionalizing their presence on social networks. In the context of pervasive advertising, social networks might influence buying behavior in two settings: (1) users may access social networks on their mobile phones while shopping in a store location. (2) Social network comments would be displayed either statically on digital signage in the store (e.g. selected by the marketing department) or actively updated as new comments arrive on the social network site.

To determine the effect of social network comments on digital signage, a field experiment was conducted which revealed new insights regarding the effectiveness of pervasive computing applications on digital signage. Our statistical analyses showed that the integration of social network comments on digital signage results in measureable effects in sales. This was true especially for social network comments on specific products but also for general brand-related comments, though to a lesser extent. Since traditional advertising content still trumped in this context of busy small-space shops selling low-involvement products, we conclude that the ability of customers to process textual stimuli in a shopping environment is limited. Thus the use of social network comments needs to be carefully evaluated. We strongly believe that the general effects of our analyses can be generalized for other situations: present product rather than global brand-related content and assess consumers' capabilities and motivation to process textual social network comments within a given in-store situation.

Beyond the effect on sales, the social network comments are likely to provide the consumer with an impression of innovation for the product or the brand in question, as well as for the retailers themselves. Thus, a carefully designed mixture of traditional advertising and social network comments would maximize the benefits of both advertising and social networks' ability to generate word-of-mouth.

References

1. Ailawadi, K.L., Beauchamp, J.P., Donthu, N., Gaurid, D.K., Shankar, V.: Communication and promotion decisions in retailing: a review and directions for future research. J. Retail. **85**(1), 42–55 (2009)
2. Box, G.E.P., Jenkins, G.M., Reinsel, G.C.: Time Series Analysis: Forecasting and Control. Wiley, New Jersey (2008)
3. Boyd, D.M., Ellison, N.B.: Social network sites: definition, history, and scholarship. J. Comput. Mediat. Commun. **13**, 210–230 (2008)
4. Brooks, R.: "Word of mouth" advertising in selling new products. J. Mark. **22**(2), 154–161 (1957)
5. Brush, A.J.: Ubiquitous computing field studies. In: Krumm, J. (ed.) Ubiquitous Computing Fundamentals. Chapman & Hall, Boca Raton (2009)
6. Bustos, L.: 110 ways retailers are using social media. GetElastic. http://www.getelastic.com/social-media-examples (2008). Accessed Dec 2010
7. Chevalier, J.A., Mayzlin, D.: The effect of word of mouth on sales: online book reviews. J. Mark. Res. **43**, 345–354 (2006)
8. Compete.: Monthly normalized metrics/Nov 2010. Compete. http://siteanalytics.compete.com/facebook.com+myspace.com+TWITTER.com/?metric=uv (2010). Accessed 23 Mar 2011
9. Deighton, J.A., Kornfeld, L.: Interactivity's unanticipated consequences for markets and marketing. J. Interact. Mark. **23**(1), 2–12 (2009)
10. Dholakia, U., Durham, E.: One Café Chain's Facebook experiment. Harvard Business Review, March 2010
11. Di Ferdinando, A., Rosi, A., Lent, R., Manzalini, A., Zambonelli, F.: MyAds: a system for adaptive pervasive advertisements. Pervas. Mob. Comput. **5**, 385–401 (2009)
12. Duan, W., Gu, B., Whinston, A.: The dynamics of online word-of-mouth and product sales - an empirical investigation of the movie industry. J. Retail. **84**(2), 233–242 (2008)
13. Economist.: The case against palm oil – the other oil spill. The Economist 24 June 2010 (2010)
14. Facebook.: Facebook: press room statistics. Facebook. http://www.facebook.com/press/info.php?statistics (2010). Accessed 23 Mar 2011
15. Facebook.: Facebook: Nutella International and Nutella Italy. http://www.facebook.com/Nutella and http://www.facebook.com/Nutella.Italy (2011). Accessed 23 Mar 2011
16. Foursquare.: Foursquare: how many users does foursquare have? Foursquare. http://foursquare.com/about (2010). Accessed 23 Mar 2011
17. Godes, D., Mayzlin, D.: Using online conversations to study word of mouth communication. Mark. Sci. **23**(Fall 4), 545–60 (2004)

18. Godes, D., Mayzlin, D.: Firm-created word-of-mouth communication: evidence from a field test. Mark. Sci. **28**(4), 721–739 (2009)
19. Hardy, R., Rukzio, E., Holleis, P., Wagner, M.: Mobile interaction with static and dynamic NFC-based displays. In: Mobile HCI 2010. ACM, New York (2010)
20. Huang, E.M., Koster, A., Borchers, J.: Overcoming assumptions and uncovering practices: When does the public really look at public displays? In: Pervasive 2008. Springer, Heidelberg (2008)
21. Janke, K.: Social media: Was Marketer über Werbung auf Facebook und Co wissen müssen. http://www.horizont.net/marktdaten/dossiers/pages/protected/show.php?id=96278&page=4&params= (2010). Accessed 23 Mar 2011
22. Jansen, J.: Attention shoppers: online product research. Pew Research Center publications. http://pewresearch.org/pubs/1747/e-shopping-researched-product-service-online (2010). Accessed Dec 2010
23. Jepsen, A.: Information search in virtual communities: is it replacing use of off line communication? J. Mark. Commun. **12**(4), 247–261 (2006)
24. MacInnis, D., Price, L.: The role of imagery in information processing: review and extensions. J. Consum. Res. **13**(4), 473–491 (1987)
25. Meier, M, D.: Warum die Kioske auf M-Budget machen. Tagesanzeiger 5.1.2010. http://www.tagesanzeiger.ch/wirtschaft/unternehmen-und-konjunktur/Warum-die-Kioske-auf-MBudget-machen/story/28369312 (2010). Accessed 23 Mar 2011
26. Michelis, D., Send, H.: Engaging passers-by with interactive screens – a marketing perspective. 2nd Workshop on Pervasive Advertising, Lübeck (2009)
27. Müller, J., Exeler, J., Buzeck, M., Krüger, A.: ReflectiveSigns: digital signs that adapt to audience attention. Proceedings of Pervasive Computing 2009, Nara (2009)
28. Nielsen.: Consumers trust real friends and virtual strangers the most. Nielsen wire. http://blog.nielsen.com/nielsenwire/consumer/global-advertising-consumers-trust-real-friends-and-virtual-strangers-the-most (2010). Accessed 23 Mar 2011
29. O'Dell, J.: Facebook accounts for 25% of All U.S. Pageviews. Mashable. http://mashable.com/2010/11/19/facebook-traffic-stats/ (2010). Accessed 23 Mar 2011
30. Ranganathan, A., Campbell, R.: Advertising in a pervasive computing environment. In: Proceedings of the 2nd International Workshop on Mobile Commerce, Atlanta, 28 Sept 2002 (2002)
31. Schapsis, C.: Location based social networks, location based social apps and games – links. BDNooZ. http://bdnooz.com/lbsn-location-based-social-networking-links (2010). Accessed Dec 2010 (2010)
32. Schiffman, B.: In praise of friendster. Wired Magazine 9 May 2008 (2008)
33. Schonfeld, E.: Worldwide advertising on social networks estimated to hit $3.3 Billion in 2010. Techcrunch. http://techcrunch.com/2010/08/16/advertising-social-networks-3-3-billion (2010). Accessed 23 Mar 2011
34. Shankar, V., Hollinger, M.: Online and mobile advertising: current scenario, emerging trends, and future directions. MSI Report 07–206 (2007)
35. Trusov, M., Bucklin, R.E., Koen, P.: Effects of word-of-mouth versus traditional marketing: findings from an internet social networking site. J. Mark. **73–5**, 90 (2009)
36. Valora.: Yearly report. Valora. http://www.valora.com/media/documents/english/reports/2009/valora_gb2009_en.pdf (2009). Accessed 23 Mar 2011
37. Van Grove, J.: Mayors of starbucks now get discounts nationwide with foursquare. Mashable. http://mashable.com/2010/05/17/starbucks-foursquare-mayor-specials (2010). Accessed 23 Mar 2011
38. Wang, M.C.H., Wang, E.S.T., Cheng, J.M.S., Chen, A.F.L.: Information quality, online community and trust: a study of antecedents to shoppers' website loyalty. Int. J. Elect. Market. Retailing **2**(3), 203–219 (2009)

Chapter 11
Adapting News and Advertisements to Groups

Berardina De Carolis

Abstract This chapter deals with adaptation of background information and advertisements, displayed in an environment, to the interests of the group of people present. According to research on computational advertising, it is important to develop methods for finding the "best match" between user interests in a given context and available advertisements. Accordingly, after providing an overview of the most popular group recommender approaches, this chapter looks at new issues that arise when considering group modeling in pervasive advertising conveyed through digital displays. The chapter first discusses general issues concerning group recommender systems, with particular emphasis on the acquisition of user preferences and interests. A system called GAIN (Group Adaptive Information and News) is then presented. This was developed with the aim of tailoring the display of background information and advertisements to groups of people.

11.1   Introduction

Today, many communal and shared places are equipped with large digital displays or other output devices typical of the particular environment. Examples include cardio-fitness machines in fitness centers, food dispenser displays, bus/train/plane notice-boards, etc. In contrast to online information seeking, such displays entail "encountering" the information while conducting another activity [9]. By "background information", we refer to content and news that are secondary to the main reason or tasks that led users to that particular environment [16]. Examples of background information are those that may be provided when people queue at an automatic coffee dispenser, at a bus stop, or in some social places, like fitness or shopping

B. De Carolis (✉)
University of Bari, Bari, Italy
e-mail: decarolis@di.uniba.it

J. Müller et al. (eds.), *Pervasive Advertising*, Human-Computer Interaction Series, DOI 10.1007/978-0-85729-352-7_11, © Springer-Verlag London Limited 2011

centres, where people go for reasons other than that of receiving information. However, in these places, people might be interested in reading some news and advertisements relevant to them, for instance, because it is boring to stand in a queue.

The information system used in a particular environment may, in turn, wish to recommend items or advertisements to users who may be attracted by ads that are peculiar to the place or the activity that brought the user there. In this context, it may be effective to mix appropriate background information with pertinent advertisements. Indeed, the display of background information of interest for people present in the environment may maintain their attention and increase the probability of looking at ads, thus becoming an opportunity for effective digital advertising. This is the approach discussed in this chapter.

According to the research on computational advertising, it is important to develop a method for providing relevant ads, by finding the "best match" between available ads and a given user in a given context [3]. Therefore, this problem may be approached, as in recommender systems, by filtering information according to user interests with the aim of providing interesting ads. Accordingly, an overview of the most popular group-recommender systems approaches is provided. We then discuss the importance of modeling group interests and of identifying the variables that influence the modeling process, in the context of advertising through public displays. Then, we show how GAIN (Group Adaptive Information and News) has been developed through this approach, and tested in a fitness center. In particular, we discuss the results of an evaluation experiment showing that (i) adaptation to the group is a promising way to improve the efficacy of information provided in daily life and that (ii) the display of adapted background information seems to be an effective way to convey situationally relevant advertisements. In the final section, some conclusions are drawn.

11.2   Group Recommender Systems

Computational advertising aims at providing relevant ads by finding the "best match" between available ads and a given user in a given context [3]. For this reason, effective computational advertising may be seen as a recommendation problem, in which the system, taking into account user interests, generates the most appropriate set of relevant ads. In addition, in environmental advertising, the system must consider that most recommendations must be directed to a group of people, rather than a single user. In the following subsections, we provide a brief introduction to recommender systems and to group modeling.

11.2.1   An Overview on Recommender Systems

A Recommender System (RS) applies search and information filtering techniques with the aim of providing users with personalized suggestions about a set of items belonging to a specific domain [1]. The starting point is available information about users and items. In this way, it is possible to overcome the information overload problem that may reduce user decision-making capabilities. Nowadays, many online shops in various domains utilize a recommender system. Examples of application domains are news, music, books, movies and services (i.e. travel, financial, wellness, etc.).

According to Adomavicius and Tuzhilin [1], a formal definition of a recommendation problem may be the following: let's denote with C the set users of the system and with I the set of items that can be recommended by the system. Each user can be described with a profile that may, in the simplest case contain only the user ID or it may include various characteristics (i.e. gender, age, profession, etc.). Also, items in I may be defined with a set of features. For instance, in the music domain, each song may be represented by its ID, title, genre, artist, etc. The cardinality of these two sets can be very large and, in order to reduce user's cognitive overload, it is important to filter these items for a given user. Therefore, it is necessary to define a utility function $u : C \times I \rightarrow R$, where R is a totally ordered set of values. This function measures how much a user liked a given item. Then, for each user, the system has to choose an item that maximizes this utility. A central problem in providing recommendations is that u is not defined completely in $C \times I$ but only into some subsets of this space. Typically, a user does not express a preference or a rating for each item in a catalogue. For this reason, an RS must also be able to estimate the values of u for the part of the data space in which the function is not defined, starting from the points of $C \times I$ in which it is defined. The objective is then to predict the rating, or the level of preference that a given user would accord to an item that has not yet been evaluated. In conformity with this objective, recommender systems may use various techniques to provide useful and appropriate suggestions to their users. Such systems are generally classified into the following main categories [5]: collaborative, content-based, demographic, knowledge-based and hybrid.

Collaborative recommender systems are probably the most widely used. Systems based on this method compute correlations between users, by recognising the affinity among user choices and considering their item evaluations. These systems predict product ratings for the current user, based on the ratings provided by other users who have preferences similar to the current one [12]. In this approach, all values of the utility function $u(c, i)$ of an item $i \in I$ for a user $c \in C$ that are unknown, are estimated considering the utilities $u(c_j, i)$ assigned to the same item by users c_j who is considered similar to c. In this way, it is possible to predict the rating that would be given by the active user to the product and to generate a set of *top N items* accordingly. A typical user profile of a system based on this approach comprises a vector of items together with their rating. This profile is updated continuously over time, according to the user interaction with the system. A great advantage of using a collaborative filtering approach is the independence from the specific domain and nature of the items to be recommended. However, since collaborative recommender systems depend on user ratings, some problems may arise when only a few users have rated the same items. In particular, when a new user interacts with the system, this approach does not produce recommendations, because they are generated from a comparison between the active user and other users based on the accumulation of ratings. Therefore, a user with few ratings becomes difficult to categorize. Usually, to cope with this problem users are required to rate a set of products or to state explicitly their interests or clickstream information is collected and interpreted as ratings [30]. Similarly, a new item that has not had many ratings cannot easily be recommended.

Content-based systems use only the preferences of the current user and predict ratings for an unseen item, based on the degree of similarity of its description to items that the user rated highly in the past [26]. The item description is usually a text and, using information retrieval techniques, a vector representation of relevant features of the item is derived, by identifying the most relevant keywords appearing in the text. With this approach the system learns which are the preferred items of users from their rating behavior. These preferences, usually expressed as a combination of item description and user preference, are stored inside their profiles. These are formalized differently, according to the evaluation method adopted by the RS. The most popular methods use decision trees, neural networks, fuzzy logic or probabilistic reasoning. According to the computed profile, the ranking produced by the system for a particular user is static and represents the best predicted ordering of items with respect to the relevance of those items for the user. In content-based RS, the value of the function $u(c, i)$ of the item i is predicted according to the values of $u(c, i_k)$ given by the same user to items i_k, considered "similar" to i. Content-based techniques also have a start-up problem related to new users. Moreover, content-based techniques are also limited by the features associated explicitly with the items they recommend.

Demographic approaches make use of stereotype reasoning. With this approach, the user is classified on the basis of personal attributes and information stored in the user profile and recommendations based on demographic classes usually formalized in stereotypes. These demographic features are used to generate initial predictions about the user [15, 25].

Knowledge-based systems use a knowledge structure to make inferences about user needs and preferences [4]. As with all knowledge-based approaches, for recommender systems as well, it is necessary to acquire the knowledge on which recommendations will be made. Therefore, it is necessary to formalize how a particular item meets a particular user need, as well as the relationship between a need and a possible recommendation. This constitutes the main disadvantage of the approach and the represented knowledge influences the range of possible recommendations. However, it does not suffer from a start-up period during which its suggestions are of poor quality.

Finally, *hybrid* systems combine two or more techniques in order to obtain better performance with a reduction in the limitations of the pure approaches [5]. For instance, collaborative systems have proposed a combination of content data with rating data. This may help to capture correlations between users or items, thus improving the accuracy of the recommendations.

11.2.2 *Acquisition of User Preferences*

This brief overview clearly demonstrates the need, when developing an RS, to formalize the user profile according to the requirements of the adopted recommendation approach. Since the system needs to know as much as possible about the user for generating the most relevant and appropriate set of recommendations, acquiring such information and constructing a valid and a reliable user model are extremely important.

The acquisition process may be *explicit, implicit* or a *combination* of the two.

With the *explicit* approach, preferences are acquired directly from the user. The problems associated with this approach are as follows: (i) most users do not want to provide much information or spend time answering questionnaires; consequently (ii) information gathered through this approach may be only part of what the user really needs and will correspond to the image that the user has of him/herself; (iii) users may not understand some of the questions and their underlying motivation.

On the other hand, with the *implicit* approach, the system observes user behaviour during the interaction and reasons behind it, in order to infer information about relevant user features and preferences. In fact, when users interact with computers, they provide a large quantity of implicit information, the interpretation of which facilitates profile building. This process is transparent for the user, but the resulting model may be imprecise, so that the personalization process may be not effective. Moreover, the inferred knowledge may be not reliable in every context, since users may have different goals, which may vary according to the context.

A good compromise is a *mixed approach* in which the system explicitly asks the user only a few questions and, from this information, tries to infer more details or new knowledge about the user.

A variation of this approach involves a natural language dialogue between user and system, in order to acquire relevant information about preferences. *Conversational Recommender Systems* (CRS) adopt this approach in order to build a reliable model of user preferences [29]. A variation of this approach entails criticizing items that the system recommended [21, 22]. The user is involved in a dialogue in which the system suggests items and the user provides an evaluation of one of the displayed items. This critique-based procedure enables the system to better understand user needs and preferences thus improving the quality and appropriateness of recommendations. In [27], it is shown that critique-based recommendations are particularly effective in supporting mobile users in product selection decisions.

11.2.3   Group Modeling

Most recommender systems address their recommendations to individual users. However, in specific application domains, users consult or interact with the system in a group. This is the case, for instance, with an environmental information system in which groups of people look at information and news on public displays.

The majority of group-adaptive systems employ strategies to synthesize a group model from the individual models of its members. In building the group profile, systems usually start from preferences and interests of individual users (generally computed according to one of the methods explained previously) and aggregate these data using variations of the average strategy. A survey of the strategies that may be employed for computing a group profile is presented in [18]. These strategies attempt to maximize group satisfaction and/or to avoid dissatisfaction of some member in the group or to privilege a group member. However, there are particular application domains in which the group profile is computed from a negotiation process. For instance, Jameson [13] emphasizes that, in particular applications, group recommendations require aggregating preferences on which all members have agreed, in order to reflect the preference of the group as a whole. Marreios et al. [17] address this problem in terms of an argumentation-based system, in which intelligent agents simulate the behaviour of individuals as group members who participate in a decision making process.

Let us now consider some examples of group recommender systems.

PolyLens [23], a component of MovieLens, is a system used to recommend movies according to inferences made from preferences expressed by each user of the system. Polylens uses an algorithm that merges individual user recommendation lists, and sorts selected movies in a decreasing degree of preference, by taking into account the minimum score given to every item in the list. This strategy seems appropriate for MovieLens since it tends to suggest movies that part of the group really wants to see.

MusicFx [19] is a system employed in fitness centers to choose music according to the preferences of the groups of users in different rooms. The strategy used by MusicFx is that of *Average without Misery*, which is based on the sum of normalized scores of all items in the list preference list. Since this strategy enables fixing a threshold (a minimum predefined value under which that alternative is eliminated from the final sequence of interests), it insures a minimum degree of satisfaction for each item in the final list of music songs. For this reason, the less favourable users can eliminate those pieces from the list that he/she dislikes, by giving them a zero evaluation score. However, this may constitute a problem since, if several users give a zero score to several items, the system will not be able to create a list, because all the preferences will be equal to zero.

Intrigue [2] helps guides in designing tours for heterogeneous groups of tourists. Intrigue creates a group preference model by aggregating the preferences of subgroups of homogeneous users (i.e. children, elderly, etc.). Intrigue uses a W*eighted Additive Utilitarian Strategy*, where the group model is a weighted average of the subgroup models, with the weights reflecting the importance of the various subgroups (e.g., the subgroup of disabled persons is considered especially important, because of the special requirements of its members).

CATS [21, 22] allows friends planning a vacation to reach a consensus in their travel decisions. This system offers a cooperative approach to group recommendation, by providing group members with some awareness of each other's activities as they explore vacation options, working simultaneously around a multitouch table.

Pocket Restaurant Finder [20] helps a group decide where to eat together, by recommending them a restaurant. Each user indicates his/her preference with respect to each of 15 types of cuisine on a 5-point scale ranging from "Definitely don't want . . . " to "Definitely want . . . ". Similar ratings are given for 17 possible restaurants, 3 price categories, and 3 ranges of travel time from the current location.

Starting from this data, the group preference arbitration algorithm is invoked to create a list of prospective restaurants, sorted in order of expected desirability (for a given group). The algorithm first computes each person's *individual preference* for each restaurant, then takes the average of these values to represent the *group preference* for each restaurant, and uses that single value to sort the restaurant list.

Flytrap [7] is a system that constructs a playlist which tries to please everyone in an active environment. Users' musical tastes are derived automatically from information about the music that people listen to on their computers. As in MusicFX, users are recognized by their active ID badges that inform the system when they are nearby. Using the preference information it has gathered from watching its users, and knowledge of how genres of music interrelate, how artists have influenced each other, and what kinds of transitions between songs people tend to make, the system finds a compromise and chooses a song. Once it has chosen a song, music is automatically broadcast and played.

Adaptive Radio [6] is a system that selects music to play in a shared environment. Rather than attempting to play the songs that users *want* to hear, the system avoids playing songs that they do *not* want to hear. Negative preferences can potentially be applied to other domains, such as information filtering, intelligent environments, and collaborative design.

11.2.3.1   Group Modeling in Smart Environments

When group modeling is applied in the context of ambient intelligence and pervasive computing, it is important to consider some other *dimensions* that influence the recommendation process. Apart from the approach used to compute recommendations, it is important to understand how to compute the information needs of people present in a communal space and some context features, such as the particular activity zone in which information is displayed, the time of the day and so on. In our opinion the following variables influence "who is the group" and "what" might impact on group interests in this application context.

Group formation: this may occur *intentionally*, when people join the group for a common purpose or in response to the preferences of one person, or *accidentally*. For instance, in MusicFX, Flytrap and Adaptive Radio group formation is accidental while in the other systems it is intentional.

Type of presence: we define as *persistent* the presence of a person who usually visit that particular place, and *occasional*, that of a person who does not usually frequent that place. For instance, a person who tends to take coffee at the same time at the same automated dispenser in the common facilities area of the same building, is considered as persistent, while a friend joining her for coffee on a particular day is occasional. Knowing the type of presence of people within the environment is important, since this may influence for instance, the group modeling strategy.

Amount of time people usually spend at the place: a person may attend the shared space for a *short* period (i.e. waiting at the bus stop or at the coffee machine, etc.) or for *longer* (i.e. training in a fitness center, shopping in a mall).

Context: certain types of information and ads may exert a greater impact when the user is in a particular context. Obviously, context features depend on the type of environment and on the activity that people perform there [24]. Examples of relevant contextual features are the current location, social situation, time of day, day of the week, as well as the activities of people and some events of that are of common interest.

Preferences and interests of the target population in the environment: in this case, adaptation requires a knowledge of the interests and informational needs of the group of people that is usually present at a particular time at a particular location. Targeting news and advertisements to groups, rather than of single users may also constitute an advantage in terms of privacy protection. Moreover, it is worth considering the social aspect of groups. That is, when a user is in a group, a discussion about the displayed items is more likely to occur. However, a problem associated with group modeling is related to the possibility that its members' preferences may be totally unknown or completely or partially known to the system, if the profiles of all or some of the users may be transferred to the environment. In our opinion, providing a solution to this problem requires a different approach to group modeling and adaptation to that used by web-based recommender systems. In such cases, the system identifies users who are logged into it, recognizes their interests they state explicitly, or builds their profile incrementally from the feedback or rating they provide using, for instance, a collaborative approach. Accessing user profiles or collecting user ratings is not always possible in a physical location in which the system may be not aware of all the people present. In fact, even if we assume that active badges or mobile personal devices will be used to interact with an active environment and therefore, the system will be able to understand who is present, we cannot assume that everyone will use this technology or give permission to use their data or to detect their presence in the environment. Therefore, it is reasonable to assume that, while modeling the group of people present at a given location, some or even all of them will be unknown to the environment.

In order to compute the profile of group interests in such a context, a *demographic* approach may be integrated with information about the interests of known users. The above mentioned variables can be relevant for targeting useful background information and ads, since they yield the most relevant demographic profile.

Another issue relevant in this specific application domain concerns the tuning and updating of the group model. One possible way may be to use implicit information that users provide during their interaction with the system. However, this is not possible when information is provided through a *non interactive wall display*, but it could be possible if the user has access to the same system through a *mobile device* such as a smartphone. In this way, the degree of interest in particular news or ads categories could be inferred. Moreover, individual user profiles could be integrated and enriched by mining the web (i.e. analysis of cookies, etc.) and social network data (i.e. profiles and posts on Facebook).

11.3 The GAIN System

In this section, GAIN (Group Adaptive Information and News) is presented as an example of a system that has tested the what proposed in the previous sections. The current version of the system is an extension of that presented in [8]. It was designed using a Service Oriented Architecture [10] and exploits the features of *web services* (WS) technology to enable flexibility and interoperability. The main components of the system are:

- *GAIN Web Application* (WA), responsible for filtering news and ads categories, according to the assumed interests of the group.
- *Group Modeling WS*, responsible for computing the preferences and interests of the group present in the particular environment
- *Ads and News Reader WSs*, responsible for selecting advertisements and news of interest.
- *Ads Manager WS*, which can be used by advertisers to compose and make available an advertisement through GAIN, by specifying its title, category, relevant keywords and description, and then making it available as an RSS (Really Simple Syndication) feed.

In the presence of people whose profile can be accessed by the system (*known group*), the Group Modeling WS, starting from information about their interests, computes the profile of the group by combining this data with the Demographic Group Profile (GP), a statistical forecast of the unknown group composition, as described in the next section.

User profiles in GAIN are formalized, using the situational statement language UserML from UbisWorld [11], since we use it in other user modeling components that we developed for other projects. UserML provides a language that represents the user model in considerable detail, by introducing information useful for contextualization. Furthermore, it seems appropriate for this kind of system. The following is an example of statements describing a situation in which a female user is very interested in reading news about "wellness" when she is in the locker room:

```
<situation id="101">
    <statement>
        <mainpart subject="User1" auxiliary="HasInterest" predicate="Topic"
        range="Text" object="WELLNESS" />
        <explanation confidence="0.8" />
    </statement>
    <statement>
        <mainpart subject="User1" auxiliary="HasLocation"
        predicate="locker room" />
    </statement>
</situation>
```

a   **b**

Fig. 11.1 (**a**) Application of GAIN in a fitness center. (**b**) The mobile application

Starting from the user profile, the system extracts the set of features necessary for information filtering as a vector of items and their score or confidence, selected according to relevant contextual tags (i.e. time slice, activity zone).

The Ads and News Reader Web Services select ads and news about a given topic on channels in the Internet, using the RSS feed technology. In this way, updated information about several topics can be provided to the group. Each RSS feed follows a standard syntax and consists of a set of news and ads, each with a title, a description, and a link to a web page where the news is located. A further tag describes the category of news or of the ads. This tag is important for filtering items according to group preferences (for more detail see [8]). News and advertisements can be part of the environment (*internal*) or sponsored by *external* advertisers.

The list of filtered items is sorted according to the interest score that the group-modeling component calculates for each topic of interest, and is used to periodically update the digital display.

As far as interaction is concerned, a non-interactive wall display (Fig. 11.1a). The user can interact with the same application through a mobile version of the system (Fig. 11.1b).

In order to test GAIN, we selected as a fitness center[1]. Such an environment correspond with the main objective of this research, since:

- people take out a contract with the center, and contextually, it is possible to ask them to complete a questionnaire about their interests;
- users are often provided with magnetic or RFID badges that can identify their entry into the environment;

---

[1] A.S.D. BodyEnergy, Mola di Bari, Italy.

- users are heterogeneous and have different interests. Furthermore for a certain period of time their presence is fairly stable, with some turn-over periods;
- the overall environment can be divided into different activity zones, in which people may well have different information needs;
- it is possible to forecast statistically how many and which categories of users are present in a particular activity zone at a given time, and therefore, to combine this information with the profiles accessible to the system.

Even if the system has been tested and evaluated in a fitness center, the proposed architecture is sufficiently general to be adapted to different domains. The system has been developed using standard protocols and languages. In addition, GAIN web services can be used as part of other applications that require that particular service.

11.4   Group Modeling Strategy in GAIN

In smart environments, group modeling may be more complicated than in other types of application domains, since the group may be heterogeneous and not share a common goal or task. Moreover, the system may have access only to the personal profiles of some group members. For this reason, in order to model the group, we assume that it can be split into two subgroups:

- the *known subgroup*, which includes the set of users (and their profiles) that are surely near the display for a certain period of time. For instance, they have a personal device that allows them to log transparently into the system;
- the *unknown subgroup* that includes users who cannot be recognized by the system, but who should be there statistically.

In GAIN, we formulated the hypothesis that, in order to improve the level of effectiveness of the adaptation process, a mixed approach to group modeling could be adopted, combining the statistical distribution of preferences of people who usually attend a particular location, with those of a subgroup known to the environment. In order to collect statistical data that could be used to build the demographic profiles, we conducted a study of the people distribution and the interests about news in each activity zone of a fitness center.

In particular, as shown in Fig. 11.2, the following activity zones were considered: the *reception hall*, the *male* and *female locker rooms* and the *fitness rooms*.

Groups in these places comprise people who spend a limited period of time (short or long) there and their formation is accidental. However, it is implicitly regulated by the type of activity that people performs there (i.e. group courses, individual training, and so on).

The study involved 170 subjects (a typical representation of the target users of our application during a given day) who usually spend some time at the fitness center.

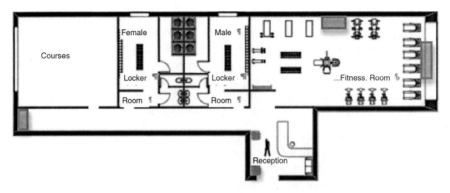

Fig. 11.2 Layout of the fitness center, *grey boxes* indicate displays

Subjects were requested to complete a questionnaire that was divided into three sections:

- *demographic data* about the subjects (gender, age, category);
- *frequency of attendance* (at *what time*, for *how long* and *how many days* during the week subjects were present) and in which activity zone subjects are supposed to stay at each time slice, according to the specific habitual activity. We identified 10 time slices, from 9.00 in the morning to 13.00 p.m. and from 16.00 to 22.00 in the evening.
- *topics* of interest, by asking subjects to score them in a list, using a 1–5 Likert scale (from 1: *I really hate it* to 5: *I really like it*) for each activity zone.

Due to space limitations, we do not show present the results of the study in full detail. However, from this data, we derived some information about the habits of each user, in term of the average number of minutes spent at each activity zone during a day, and about their distribution during each time slice, and about their flow in the environment, according to their activity program. Figure 11.3 shows the distribution of subjects interests, when in the fitness room around 10.00 a.m. and 18.00 p.m. These time slices were selected as quite relevant. In the morning, mainly women attend the fitness room, while in the early evening there are mainly male students. From this example, one might infer that the user's gender is the triggering feature of a stereotypical profile of group interests. However, gender is not considered as a trigger, in this phase of system development, for two main reasons: (i) the preliminary study showed that in another time slice (late in the evening) women have different interests (partially because they have a different cultural background); (ii) in our application domain, users are not always recognizable by the system and therefore, it might not have access to information about their gender. Therefore, we used these data to build the *statistical dataset* of our group modeling module. From this set of data, it is possible to identify that the time slice and the activity zone in which users were located. These are important factors for triggering different demographic interest profiles. For each zone and time slice the default confidences for a list of possible topics were then derived independently of personal data.

The group profile is then defined according to the formula described below in (1), where different weights may be assigned to the *known* and *unknown* groups,

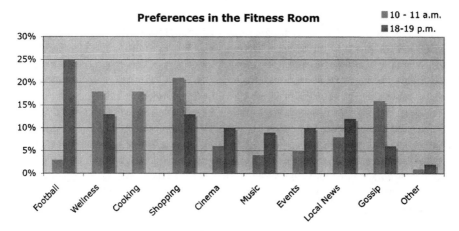

Fig. 11.3 Comparison of interests in two time slices

according to the relative importance one wishes to allocate to one group as opposed to the other. In the formula, we denote as:

- P_{SURE}, the weight (from 0 to 1) allocated to the preferences of known group.
- $P_{PROBABLE}$,[2] the weight (from 0 to 1) allocated to the preferences of the unknown group.
- K, the number of topics;
- UM_j^i the score for *topic j* in the activity zone A from *user i;*
- b the base of the votes; can be 1, 5, 10, 100, etc.
- N, the number of known users;
- M, the number of profiles that constitute the statistical dataset (initially, M was equal to the number of profiles collected in the preliminary study);
- f_i, the frequency of attendance for each user of the selected activity zone, calculated as the number of days attended by *user i* divided by number of working days;
- t_i, the average number of minutes in which the *user i* is in the activity zone in the considered time slice;
- $F_m = \sum_{m=N+1}^{N+M} \left(f_m * t_m \right)$, the frequency in the statistical dataset.

Then, C_j, indicating the confidence value for a topic j to be shown to the group in the activity zone A, is computed as follows:

$$\forall j \in \left\{1,...,K\right\}: Cj = 1/b \left[\frac{P_{SURE}}{N} \sum_{i=1}^{N} \left(UM_i^j \right) + P_{PROBABLE} \sum_{i=N+1}^{N+M} \left(UM_i^j * \frac{f_i * t_i}{F_m} \right) \right] \quad (1)$$

with $N>0$ and $M>0$ and $b <>0$.[3]

---

[2] We wanted to express the confidence of each topic as a percentage. For this reason, we set $P_{PROBABLE} = f(P_{SURE})$, f being a function that relates these two values to one another.

[3] This is valid if $P_{SURE} + P_{PROBABLE} = 1$, otherwise, it is necessary to divide the value of C_j by the value of $P_{SURE} + P_{PROBABLE}$ in order to obtain a result between 0 and 1.

This formula is a variation of the additive strategy [18], in which the weight for the unknown part of the group cannot be distributed uniformly, since people are present in a place with different frequencies. For computing, as accurately as possible, the confidence values for the unknown part of the group, news filtering considers the fact that some users are more likely to be in given activity zone at some times than others. This frequency in the formula (1) is calculated by considering $(f_i * t_i)/F_m$ that allows approximating the presence of users according to data in the statistical dataset. In particular, we used the data collected in the preliminary survey in order to calculate f_i and t_i as the average number of minutes that a *user i* spends in the activity zone, during the week, in the time slice in which the group modeling function is activated. Obviously, when $N=0$ and $M>0$, P_{SURE} should be set to 0 and $P_{PROBABLE}$ to 1. In the opposite case, when $N>0$ and $M=0$, $P_{PROBABLE}$ should be set to 0, and $P_{SURE}=1$. Once the list of preferences is computed by the group modeling web service, it is used to filter the news by means of the GAIN web application.

11.5   Updating the Group Model

In the context in which GAIN is applied, the group model can be updated in different situations: (a) in a *non-interactive* context in which users passively look at news on a wall display, (b) using a *personal interactive* version of the system in which the user may receive a personalized selection of news on his/her mobile device. In all cases, we believe it would be impractical to update the model by asking people to explicitly rate the relevance of background information, especially since they are actually there for a different purpose.

In GAIN, group model updating occurs when *new users* come into the activity zone or when the *next time* slice is reached, according to the statistical distribution explained previously. The system re-applies the formula (1) to calculate the new confidence value of all news categories. In order to avoid sudden changes in the topics list, scanning of known users is done every *n(A)* minutes. This time interval corresponds to the average time that subjects involved in the preliminary survey stated that they spend in each activity zone *A,* calculated for all time slices.

However, we can assume that some users interact with the system using a personal device. If so, the user whose personal profile has previously been transferred to the system, is considered part of the known subgroup and the group model is updated according to the user's clicking behavior. This information may be considered as a kind of implicit feedback, since we can assume that users do not click on news at random, but rather on issues that interest them [14]. Therefore, clicked links may be considered as positive samples, which match the user preferences from a statistical perspective.

Information on the clicking behavior of all known users in a determinate activity zone, together with information on the date and time, are used for updating and tuning the demographic profile of the group in that zone, for that time slice. To this end, a temporary profile for each time slice and for each activity zone is created. With *GIP(A)$_t$*, we denote the Group Interaction Profile for the activity zone *A* in time slice *t*. This profile has the same structure of UM(A)$_i$ and contains a list of the news categories of the considered domain, but with an initial confidence value of 0. The only difference is the lack of information about the average time spent in the shared place ($f_i * t_i$), because we consider it constant for the current time slice. Each time a user selects a news item belonging to a category *x*, this is denoted as positive feedback and the relative counter is increased. At the end of the time slice, the confidence for each category is updated by dividing the relative counter by the total number of selected news items. For example, if N is the number of all the news items selected by the users, and we consider K$_j$ as the counter of selected news for each category, the confidence value C$_j$ in the GIP(A)$_t$ for the category j, will be calculated as K$_j$/N. The temporary profile GIP(A)$_t$ is then used to update the group preferences for activity zone A in the given time slice, since it is added to the statistical dataset and used in the next computation, according to formula (1).

In this case, the number of profiles M, used to build the statistical dataset, is increased. This approach enables us to adjust the statistical profile, in order to achieve a situation that is closer to the real usage model of the system. However, a possible problem may arise with respect to the number of collected profiles (M), since they enrich the statistical dataset and are never discarded. In order to solve this problem, the idea is to stop this form of information gathering, when we have a sufficiently large number of usage profiles (around 1,000) and to use machine learning techniques to extract information for building stereotypes, relative to activity zones and time slices. With this new approach, the temporary profiles will be considered as new examples for updating stereotypes. Moreover, direct interaction through the personal device facilitates user identification and thus, the implicit feedback may also be used to update his/her personal profile.

11.6   Evaluation of GAIN

In order to validate our approach we performed two subjective evaluation studies aimed at testing: (1) the impact of adaptation on news presentation and (2) whether the display of adapted background information is an effective way to convey relevant advertisements. In both experiments, we used only the statistical demographic group profile. Accordingly, in the first experiment, we could assess the adequacy of this profile to the interests of people in the selected activity zone and time slice, and obtain a more accurate adaptation in the second study. In these experiments, the data is obtained from questionnaires. We are aware that combining this subjective evaluation with a more objective one could improve the accuracy of results, as for instance in [28].

11.6.1 First Study

This study aimed at assessing whether the user interest in the news differed, depending on whether or not the news presentation was *adapted* to the specific group.

The study involved *80* people who usually attend the fitness center. The test was conducted at about 10.30 a.m. on two different days in the fitness area.

We formed two groups of 40 subjects each. Each group comprised 15 males and 25 females, chosen randomly among users of the fitness center in that time slice (this distribution mirrored that of the preliminary study). Both groups were provided, for 30 min, with a set of news selected by GAIN. According to the preliminary study, this was the average time people stay in that activity zone in that time slice.

The interface used in the experiment was a non-interactive wall display. Both user groups could look at the news on three displays positioned at the center of each wall of the room (see Fig. 11.2), all displaying the same set of news simultaneously. The news was refreshed every 7 min.

Before the experiment both groups received a short description of the purpose of the experiment. The first group was then provided with news selected randomly from the following categories: Local News, News, Wellness, Cooking, Football, Music, Cinema, Gossip, Weather, Culture.

For the second group, the experiment was conducted under the same conditions and with the same procedure, except for the news selection method. In this case, news categories and the number of news items provided for each category were filtered and ordered according to the group interest profile, triggered by the activity zone and daytime (see the distribution of interests in Fig. 11.3).

At the end of the experiment, both groups were asked to complete a post-test questionnaire as accurately and honestly as possible. The questionnaire took no more than 5 min to be completed, after which participants were fully debriefed.

The questionnaire consisted of 15 items, some of which concerned demographic data, and other items aimed at understanding which categories they liked and disliked. The other items were aimed at assessing whether subjects: looked at news, were interested in the displayed content and found the content appropriate and adequate to the situation, needed more news categories, liked the service of providing background information on displays, would have liked to interact with the news on their smartphone. Table 11.1 summarizes the results of the most relevant questions for evaluating the effectiveness of group adaptation.

The results show that subjects in the 'adaptation' modality gave, on average, a higher evaluation score to questions Q2, Q3, Q4. These questions, in fact, aimed at assessing the impact of adaptation on individual satisfaction: the results indicate that adaptation seems to increase the *appropriateness*, *adequacy* and interest of information provided.

Answers to the fifth question indicate that there was almost no need for different news categories in the adapted condition. The table shows that, at least for these four questions, the p-value of the t-test is less or equal than 0.01, indicating that the difference between the two conditions can be considered significant.

Table 11.1 Analysis of results of the most relevant questions for evaluating the effectiveness of group adaptation (Scores expressed on a scale from 1 to 5)

Question	No adaptation	Adaptation	p-value
Q1: Look at news	3.9	4.3	0.19
Q2: Interest	3.0	3.9	0.01
Q3: Appropriateness	3.3	4.3	0.004
Q4: Adequacy	2.7	3.3	0.01
Q5: Need for more categories	3.2	2.5	0.01
Q6: Liking	3.4	3.9	0.176
Q7: Need for interaction	4.5	4.7	0.388

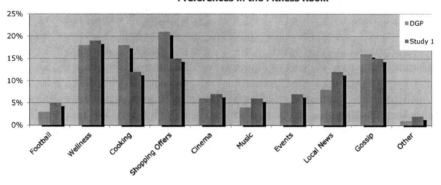

Fig. 11.4 Difference between the DGP and the results of Study 1

Answers to Q1 and Q6 show that people liked the service of background information provision and looked at news in both conditions. Moreover, for both conditions subjects would have liked to interact with the news, since the average score to question 7 is between 4 and 5.

As far as questions aimed at assessing which categories of news subjects liked and disliked, results summarized in Fig. 11.4 seem to confirm the distribution of preferences stored in the Demographic Group Profile (DPG), with a difference for cooking and shopping that change their position in the list of preferred topics.

11.6.2 Second Study

The aim of this study was to understand whether the display of adapted background information was an effective way to present ads.

The study involved 60 people who were in the fitness room at the same time and on the same weekdays as for the first study.

We formed two groups of 30 subjects each. Each group comprised 10 males and 20 females chosen randomly among people that attend the fitness center in that time slice.

Also in this case, before the experiment, both groups were given a short explanation of the experiment.

The first group was then provided with news and ads selected randomly, without adaptation to the group profile. In this second study, internal and external advertisements were added to the previous list of news categories.

For the second group, the experiment was conducted under the same conditions and with the same procedure except for the news selection method. In this case, categories were filtered and ordered according to the group interest profile triggered by the activity zone and daytime (see the distribution of interests in Fig. 11.3). The number of news items and ads provided for each category was proportional to their confidence value. In particular, in each category, the number of ads was in a 1:2 proportion to the number of news items on show. For instance if *7* was the number of news to show for a given category, then *3* advertisements were shown.

At the end of the experiment, both groups completed a post-test questionnaire that was structured in two main parts. As in the previous study, the first part of the questionnaire assessed the impact of adaptation on individual satisfaction. In addition, in this second phase, we wanted to measure the degree of recall. Therefore, we included questions on information recall of the ads messages. In particular we included recall questions about *words* contained in the advertising message or about the *topic category* to which the advertisement belonged. The answers to this form of question were formulated as a single choice (e.g., *Based on the news displayed, XXXX is a useful product for improving*: (a) teeth (b) skin, (c) heart, (d) muscles).

Subjects of both groups evaluated the service positively. However, the results show that the degree of recall was higher for participants who received adapted advertising. The proportion of correct answers given by the subjects, both for words and categories, was lower in the *non-adapted* condition than in the *adapted* one (71% vs. 90% for words and 60% vs. 83% for categories). Therefore, the results of the second study seem to confirm that adapting categories of news and ads to the group profile was effective in providing relevant advertisements and that the display of adapted background information was an effective way to present ads. However, in general, from specific recall questions, subjects from both groups showed a preference towards environment-related ads, rather than external ones.

11.7   Discussion and Summary of Results

In this chapter, we discussed how group modeling can be used to adapt background information and to make advertising on digital displays more effective. To this end, after having analysed the different group modeling strategies proposed in the literature, we implemented a group modeling service to compute the profile of group interests in situations where members can be totally unknown, or partially or completely known. This is an interesting situation in pervasive computing contexts, in which a potential use of personal devices, storing relevant information about the user, can be combined with environment computing facilities. In order to test this approach, we developed GAIN, a system that combines the features of a news aggregator with those of a recommender system, mixing news and advertisements adapted to group preferences. The results of two evaluation studies indicate that the group that received news adapted to its profile was on average more satisfied than the other group and that group-adapted news display may be an effective way to present advertisements of interest to the specific group.

Acknowledgements The author is grateful to Dr. Brian Bloch for his comprehensive editing of the manuscript.

References

1. Adomavicius, G., Tuzhilin, A.: Toward the next generation of recommender systems: a survey of the state-of-the-art and possible extensions. IEEE Trans. Knowl. Data Eng. **17**(6), 734–749 (2005)
2. Ardissono, L., Goy, A., Petrone, G., Segnan, M., Torasso, P.: INTRIGUE: personalized recommendation of tourist attractions for desktop and handset devices. Appl. Artif. Intell. **17**(8–9), 687–714 (2003)
3. Broder, A., Fontoura, M., Josifovski, V., Riedel, L.: A semantic approach to contextual advertising. In: Proceedings of ACM SIGIR Conference on Research and Development in Information Retrieval (SIGIR '07), pp. 559–566. ACM, New York (2007)
4. Burke, R.: Knowledge-based recommender systems. In: Kent, A. (ed.) Encyclopedia of Library and Information Systems, vol. 69, pp. 180–200. Marcel Dekker, New York (2000)
5. Burke, R.: Hybrid web recommender systems. In: Brusilovsky, P., Kobsa, A., Nejdl, W. (eds.) The Adaptive Web: Methods and Strategies of Web Personalization. LNCS, vol. 4321. Springer-Verlag, Berlin/Heidelberg/New York (2007)
6. Chao, D., Balthrop, J., Forrest, S.: Adaptive radio: achieving consensus using negative preferences. In: Proceedings of the 2005 International ACM SIGGROUP Conference on Supporting Group Work, Sanibel Island, 2005, pp. 120–123
7. Crossen, A., Budzik, J., Hammond, K.: Flytrap: intelligent group music recommendation. In: Gil, Y., Leake, D. (eds.) IUI 2002: International Conference on Intelligent User Interfaces, pp. 184–185. ACM, New York (2002)
8. De Carolis, B., Pizzutilo, S.: Providing relevant background information in smart environments. In: Proceedings of EC-Web 2009 LNCS. E-Commerce Web Technol. **5692**, 357–362 (2009)
9. Elderez, S.: Information encountering: a conceptual framework for accidental information discovery. In: Proceedings of an International Conference on Information Seeking in Context (ISIC), Tampere, 1997, pp. 412–421
10. Endrei, M., et al.: Patterns: Service-Oriented Architecture and Web Services. IBM Redbook (2004)
11. Heckmann, D.: Ubiquitous User Modeling. IOS Press, New York (2005)
12. Herlocker, J., Konstan, J., Riedl, J.: Explaining collaborative filtering recommendations. In: Proceedings of the 2000 Conference on Computer-Supported Cooperative Work, Philadelphia, 2000, pp. 241–250
13. Jameson, A.: More than the sum of its members: challenges for group recommender systems. In: Proceedings of the Working Conference on Advanced Visual interfaces, Gallipoli, 25–28 May 2004

14. Joachims, T., et al.: Accurately interpreting clickthrough data as implicit feedback, In: Proceedings of the 28th Annual international ACM SIGIR Conference on Research and Development in information Retrieval, Salvador, pp. 154–161. ACM, New York (2005)
15. Kobsa, A., Koenemann, J., Pohl, W.: Personalized hypermedia presentation techniques for improving online customer relationships. Knowl. Eng. Rev. **16**(2), 111–155 (2001)
16. Maglio, P.P., Campbell, C.S.: Tradeoffs in displaying peripheral information. In: Proceedings of Association for Computing Machinery's Human Factors in Computing Systems CHI 2000, The Hague, pp. 241–248
17. Marreiros, G., Ramos, C., Neves, J.: Multiagent approach to group decision making through persuasive argumentation. In: International Conference on Argumentation, Liverpool (2006)
18. Masthoff, J.: Group modeling: selecting a sequence of television items to suit a group of viewers. User Model. User Adapt. Interact. **14**(1), 37–85 (2004)
19. McCarthy, J., Anagnost, T.: MusicFX: an arbiter of group preferences for computer supported collaborative workouts. In: Proceedings of the ACM 1998 conference on CSCW, Seattle, 1998, pp. 363–372
20. McCarthy, J.: Pocket restaurantFinder: a situated recommender system for groups. In: Proceedings of the Workshop on Mobile Ad-Hoc Communication at the 2002 ACM Conference on Human Factors in Computer Systems, Minneapolis (2002)
21. McCarthy, K., Salamo', M., McGinty, L., Smyth, B.: CATS: a synchronous approach to collaborative group recommendation. In: Proceedings of the Nineteenth International Florida Artificial Intelligence Research Society Conference, (FLAIRS-06), Melbourne Beach, 2006, pp. 86–91
22. McCarthy, K., et al.: Group recommender systems: a critiquing-based approach. In: Paris, C., Sidner, C. (eds.) Proceedings of IUI 2006: International Conference on Intelligent User Interfaces, pp. 267–269. ACM, New York (2006)
23. O'Conner, M., Cosley. D., Konstanm, J.A., Riedl, J.: PolyLens: a recommender system for groups of users. In: Proceedings of ECSCW 2001, Bonn, 2001, pp. 199–218
24. Partridge, K., Begole, B.: Activity-based advertising. In: Müller, J., Alt, F., Michelis, D. (eds.) Pervasive Advertising, pp. 83–102. Springer, Dordrecht (2011)
25. Pazzani, M.: A framework for collaborative content-based and demographic filtering. Art. Intell. Rev. **13**, 393–408 (1999)
26. Pazzani, J., Billsus, D.: Content-based recommender systems. In: Brusilovsky, P., Kobsa, A., Nejdl, W. (eds.) The Adaptive Web: Methods and Strategies of Web Personalization. Lecture Notes in Computer Science, vol. 4321. Springer-verlag, Berlin/Heidelberg/New York (2007)
27. Ricci, F., Nguyen, Q.N.: Mobyrek: a conversational recommender system for on-the-move travelers. In: Fesenmaier, D.R., Werthner, H., Wober, K.W. (eds.) Destination Recommendation Systems: Behavioural Foundations and Applications, pp. 281–294. CABI Publishing, London (2006)
28. Schrammel, J., et al.: Attentional Behavior of Users on the Move Towards Pervasive Advertising Media. In: Müller, J., Alt, F., Michelis, D. (eds.) Pervasive Advertising, pp. 287–308. Springer, Dordrecht (2011)
29. Warnestal, P.: User evaluation of a conversational recommender system. In: IJCAI Workshop on K&R in Practical Dialog Systems, Edinburgh, 2005, pp. 62–67
30. Zanker, M., Jessenitschnig, M.: Case-studies on exploiting explicit customer requirements in recommender systems. User Modeling and User-Adapted Interaction, vol. 19, pp 133–166. Springer, Netherlands (2009)

Chapter 12
Deploying Pervasive Advertising in a Farmers' Market

Ian Wakeman, Ann Light, Jon Robinson, Dan Chalmers, and Anirban Basu

Abstract Farmers' markets are the source of a rich and pleasurable consumption experience. In this chapter, we report on our attempts to support and augment these experiences through the deployment of pervasive advertising. We describe the ethnographic approach we used to delineate the areas of enjoyment and pleasure, how narratives are weaved around and through the stalls and their products, and how trust is formed and maintained between the stallholders and the customers. We show how this understanding can be applied in the design of supporting advertising applications. We then evaluate the applications using the same ethnographic approach, uncovering problems which would not have been visible with other evaluation techniques.

12.1 Introduction

Elsewhere in this volume, there has been much discussion of how semiotics can be used to analyse the relationships between customer, advertisement and object. Van Waart et al. [19] have discussed how the touchpoints between a brand and the customer can be analysed across a number of dimensions, to ensure that the touchpoints offer an experience that enhances the relationship between the customer and the brand (see Chap. 3). In this chapter we show how the existing relationships between the customer and brand can be uncovered, so that the touchpoint experiences support and reinforce the brand.

I. Wakeman (✉) · J. Robinson · D. Chalmers · A. Basu
School of Informatics, University of Sussex, Brighton, UK
e-mail: ianw@sussex.ac.uk; D.Chalmers@sussex.ac.uk

A. Light
Northumbria University, Newcastle, UK
e-mail:ann.light@gmail.com

J. Müller et al. (eds.), *Pervasive Advertising*, Human-Computer Interaction Series, DOI 10.1007/978-0-85729-352-7_12, © Springer-Verlag London Limited 2011

In previous work we have developed computing support for a located shopping guide [15], and an augmented reality system for commenting on poster presentations [16]. The consequent research question that emerged was whether such technologies could be used to support located shopping areas, and in particular, whether such systems could be deployed with a limited fixed infrastructure such as a street market.

Street markets are commonplace all over the world. They are characterised by the temporary nature of the stalls, although some stalls are regular attendees, and used by a diverse range of customers. Farmers' markets are a particular form of street market, emerging from the movement to encourage local produce and connect food producers directly to their customers. The eponymous farmers run stalls providing vegetables, poultry, meat and other produce. Such markets are typically not restricted to farmers, but do emphasise local artisan producers such as chutney makers and pie bakers. The organisers of our local farmers' market were enthusiastic about cooperation in exploring the possibilities of our technology, and so the development began.

When we deploy pervasive computing systems, we are often deploying in situations which already function well. In such cases, we must ensure that the existing processes and interactions are supported and enhanced rather than interrupted and disturbed. The approach often promoted in the literature is to take an ethnographic approach, where the existing sets of interactions are observed, analysed and used as input to the design process. In developing our application we have taken a pragmatic approach to capturing qualitative data, utilising accompanied shopping trips with a researcher acting as participant/observer to gain an understanding of how the market functions, analysing this data to inform the design process, and then using more accompanied shopping to evaluate the effectiveness of our deployed applications.

From our observations, it emerged that *trust* was the fundamental concept underpinning the interactions between the consumers and the stallholders, and any pervasive advertising would have to build and support trust at a number of different levels. In the rest of this chapter, we will first provide a brief overview of the limited existing work in deploying to market situations, summarise the basic consumer behaviour understanding of markets, and our underlying theoretical approach to describing trust. We will then discuss how narratives, pleasure and trust relationships are manifested and developed within the farmers' market, based on the evidence from our observations. We will then describe the technologies we deployed within the market, and discuss the effectiveness of our deployments.

12.2   Related Work

Designers of pervasive computing systems have begun to consider retailing. In [13] the impact of a dynamic map on retail is explored, whilst in [14], the same group ask whether an interactive mannequin increases browse time at shop windows. Focusing on social dynamics, Heath et al. [7] report on quasi-experiments with an intelligent gavel, designed to link internet bidders at live auctions more dynamically into the auction-room action. Work at Limerick [2] specifically targets a market to examine the situated nature of the interactions taking place. They note that with "an ever evolving urban space and social activities, a careful approach is required for introduction of computational technology to conserve and enhance them." The final outcome of this work [12], the Recipe Station, allowed market users to access and share recipes that incorporated market produce. This took the form of an installation located in the market to which people contributed personalised recipes and from which they were issued to other shoppers triggered by RFID tools related to the ingredients bought. The author suggests that using the station over the 5 week pilot became interleaved with people's discussions about food and shopping.

12.2.1 Markets and the Shopping Experience

Categorising outlets in his ethnographic description of a flea market [18], the sociologist John Sherry challenges the view that shopping can be reduced to the analysis of purchasing and selling behaviour. He clusters marketplaces around two axes: formal/informal and economic/festive. Sherry characterises the economic function by notions of rationality and utility, whereas the festive function is hedonic and experiential in nature. Farmers' markets appear in the festive/informal quadrant. Further, he argues that sidewalk sales, auctions and farmers' markets exhibit greater dialectical intensity than other venues do – "That is, the counterpoised dimensions of the model are brought into such intimate association and are condensed so tightly that the resulting tension is palpable to participants and seems to energise them as well."

Market shopping preserves earlier relations between customers and clerks. Shopping at the local grocery store was an opportunity for shoppers to chat with each other while waiting in line to be served and comment on the clerk's remarks and the quality of the products. Markets date from the first days when surplus produce allowed people to exchange one kind of value for another. They have long been the social heart of a community or city as well as an economic and political hub, though in industrialised regions they are not as common or as extensively patronised as they were. But in a world of increasing internet commerce for standard or bulky items such as washing powder, books and electronics, the chance to buy food in the situated and occasional form of markets grows in appeal. And interest in local produce has fuelled a resurgence. Stalls trading on the pedigree of their goods are springing up in town squares and suburban car-parks. They are often distinguished by simple, rustic presentation of items.

The Common Cause Co-operative, which runs the farmers' market in this study, set up one of the first in Britain in October 1998. Now there are more than 500 in the UK and they are more common elsewhere. The co-op defines a *farmers' market* as one "where farmers, growers or producers from a defined local area are present in person to sell their own produce direct to the public. All products sold should have been grown, reared, caught, brewed, pickled, baked, smoked or processed by the stallholder"[3].

Given that farmers' markets appear only for a day a week/month, are usually open air and stock only a few of the goods that make up a typical monthly shop, they are not attended for their ease of use. Instead, the market fulfils a different role in meeting people's shopping requirements. Friends of the Earth [4] identify several reasons why shoppers might wish to use this source for produce, apart from the indirect benefits to farmers, the environment and the local economy: consumers enjoy the atmosphere and experience; they get fresh, healthy produce at competitive prices, often in areas where there are no alternative sources of this kind; and they can participate in building up social connections through shopping locally.

12.2.2   Theoretical Approach to Trust

In general trust is required within a transaction when there is the possibility of consequent loss or harm and the other party can influence whether the loss or harm is suffered. If the transaction proceeds, then the party at risk is *trusting* the other party will not intentionally cause harm or loss. Of course, within a farmers' market, the loss or harm is either a perceived monetary loss in feeling that the purchased item has been oversold – the same item is found significantly cheaper in a local shop – or the damage done to the fabric of everyday life when an item is found to be unfit for purpose – the special joint of meat bought for dinner turns out to be rotten.

Following the model of McKnight et al. [11], trust can be examined across a range of constructs: Dispositional Trust; Trusting Beliefs; System Trust; Situation Decision to Trust; Trusting Intention and Trusting Behaviour. Dispositional Trust refers to the intrinsic traits of an individual that predispose them to trust. Over the course of their experience, people develop expectations about how people behave in any given situation, and these expectations will be carried through into similar new situations, forming the basis for initial beliefs. As a particular situation unfolds, a person will develop from these initial beliefs into Trusting Beliefs about the other individuals. These trusting beliefs are themselves likely to be formed of judgements about the others' *ability* and competence to perform, the others' *benevolence* and good will to the believer's well-being, the others' *integrity* and principles on which the other acts, and the *predictability* and consistency of action in the given situation.

As well as the generation of trusting beliefs, an individual will be influenced by their beliefs about the systems and societal structures in place to support interactions. As long as the situation appears normal (as in Garfinkel's definition of "normality" [5]) and subject to such structures as the legal system, and local assurance criteria such as membership of trade associations, then the individual will also have *system trust* to support their trusting intentions. Further, if they have become accustomed to a particular sort of situation, and a particular trusting decision has become habitual, their intention will become affected by a situational decision to trust.

The combination of the above cognitive and affective states will influence the individual to decide whether to trust the other, and their intention to behave in a trusting manner. A trusting intention requires that the individual is willing to depend on the others with confidence, even though negative outcomes are possible, whilst the trusting behaviour is the actual act of committing to the transaction.

12.3 The ShoppingLense Framework

Connecting the physical and virtual worlds is a key goal of pervasive computing. One promising approach to linking location to its virtual shadow is through augmented reality (AR), where graphical anchors on patterns within displayed video provide links off to relevant websites and other services. To experiment with this approach within the shopping context, we developed a set of technologies to support the collaborative tagging of patterns within the environment, and to allow users to browse the patterns using specialised AR software based on the ARToolkit [1], or their own phone if we used QRCodes [9] as tags. In other words, we had the means to equip users to wander through the market finding tags linking to product-related materials stored remotely and which could, certainly with the AR device, be supplemented in situ. Our design question was then whether we might incorporate this into the market in such a way that it brought something of value to the shopping experience and avoided detracting from other aspects.

The underlying design of the tool reflects our belief that eventually it will be possible for everything and anything to be used as a pattern, and for everyone to both create patterns and add anchors to any pattern. In recognition of the sheer quantity of tagging that would ensue from this, the team has developed a trust-based means of prioritising information associated with patterns to help users manage the data, based on previous work in Wakeman et al. [21].

If information comes from a trusted source it is given more prominence in display than other material. This is achieved by ensuring that each pattern and anchor can be ranked by users according to their trust in the source of it, using a system of pseudonyms to give privacy while ensuring that the right trust rating is assigned. So at the heart of the tool are concepts of pseudonyms, patterns and a pattern registry. Mobile phones recognise QRCodes as a pattern. AR tools can do the same with a fiducial marker. The phone/AR tool is then able to look the pattern up in the pattern registry and retrieve data attached to the pattern, such as comments. We attempted to port our AR tool across to a mobile phone, but the phone available proved insufficiently powerful. Instead, the AR tool was used on a Ultra-Mobile Personal Computer (UMPC).

Given this framework, we set out to investigate the market, and to understand how best to design advertising applications to support the market experience.

12.4   Methodology

We first approached the market organisers explaining that we had a toolkit that
could support customers and stallholders in communicating to each other, and that
we wished to experiment within the market. The market is held monthly, so our
timetable was as laid out as follows:

February 2009   Initial visit: discussions with stallholders and market organisers.
March 2009   Pre-intervention: accompanied shopping ethnographic study of
                two separate shoppers.
April 2009   Deployment 1: accompanied shopping whilst using the
                ShoppingLense on a UMPC.
May 2009   Deployment 2: accompanied shopping whilst using a QRCode
                reader on a mobile phone.

The techniques used for data gathering were chosen to answer the questions:
What is the shopping experience? Which aspects are fun and should not be tam-
pered with adversely? What might the tool offer? For this reason, we adopted a
method that situated our informants as deeply in the experience we were researching as possible. Our trained ethnographer accompanied the participants whilst shopping, acting as a stimulus to provoke shopping behaviour and observe encounters
between our shopper and others. We collected accounts in two parts: a chat during
shopping and a reflective interview afterwards.

The sample we worked with was carefully picked. We chose four volunteers,
including one couple who volunteered together (I 44 years old, W 41 years old,
K 39 years old, H with partner, 22 years old) who like markets and shopping, who
are articulate, confident of their opinions, extrovert and fairly competent with ordinary technology like phones. Within this, we selected for variation in their priorities, so that some liked cooking, others food more generally, some were concerned
with buying local or a different ethical/social priority while others weren't. Since
we were testing out a tool that we specifically didn't want to use to interrupt the
better aspects of the shopping experience, it was important to us to work with participants for whom shopping was a pleasure in the first place, and who would then
be able to articulate the experiences they were having.

To collect data about the shopping experience, an interviewer shadowed each
participant for the duration of her encounter with the market. The interviewer
requested that the shopper give an account of the experience as it happened, using
the interviewer as a foil for comments, a potential source of answers to any questions that occurred to her and the recipient of a verbal protocol that corresponded
loosely to a think-aloud tour. This interaction was recorded as audio, as were any
incidental encounters that accompanied the shopping, such as hearing other shoppers or chatting to stallholders. Moments of encounter with others or with objects in
use (such as bags, money, goods, phones, etc) were captured with a camera. After
the shopping, the two sat down locally and the shopper was asked to reflect on the
shopping tour. During this phase, the interviewer asked questions about things
noticed during the previous stage and pressed for amplification of comments made

by the shopper at this time or during the interview. This was also audio-recorded. Just as this think-aloud tour used the market as a stimulus for accounts of shopping, similarly reflection was encouraged by use of photos of stalls as an aide-memoire for different points in the tour.

Each participant was given £25 to shop with. Although this might be understood to change the way that the participant went about shopping, it did not seem to impinge greatly on their processes. In fact, it could fairly be said to have become part of their housekeeping exercise, noted below, since they normally set out with an idea of budget and/or things to buy in mind. Instead, the incentive was uniformly regarded as fair acknowledgement of their time: they spent at least as long reflecting on their shopping with the interviewer as they did conducting it.

We chose aspects on which to focus before embarking on the accompanied shopping. These were:

- Indications of trust and relationship building with stallholders/other shoppers
- Patterns of encounter and particularly those that seemed to give pleasure
- Stories told about the products by the stallholders or the shoppers
- Points of interaction: shopper/stallholder, shopper/other shopper, shopper/objects

Using these emphases to guide us, we analysed the accounts and the visual material we collected in the first phase to inform the design. In the second phase, we used it to evaluate the design. The next section outlines our findings.

12.5 Setting the Scene

The market is laid out as in Fig. 12.1, with a mixture of stalls, ranging from simple tables (Fig. 12.2) through to refrigerated vans (Fig. 12.3). The stalls were used to display products, with the majority providing samples for tasting. Mobile network coverage within this street was mostly good, although we did notice occasional variation, and we were able to complement these networks through an ad-hoc WiFi network. The companies behind the stalls varied greatly in their embrace of the Internet for marketing. The butcher collected email lists and sends a weekly update of where he would be appearing, special offers and suggested recipes. All but two of the businesses had a web presence and some were able to offer online ordering.

12.5.1 Developing Trust

Our participants provided many insights into how the market and stall holders provide many different signifiers upon which to activate and build trust. Most significant was the development of conversations between the stallholder and their customers, both whilst negotiating at the point of sale, and from joining existing customers' conversations with the stallholder.

Fig. 12.1 Farmers' market view

Fig. 12.2 Simple stall

Fig. 12.3 Butcher's van

In one case, the stallholder of the pie stall invited other customers to join the negotiations of sale to provide *bona fides* of the quality of the product, and to discuss whether the product can be frozen. In consideration afterwards, the participant showed how these conversations can help induce trusting beliefs: "*So if French people think its good food then it really must be a recommendation*" (I). The other participant started a conversation with one of the couple currently being served by the butcher, exchanging tips about how to store roast beef. Such reassuring conversations help to generate trusting intentions about purchase decisions, developing trust that the decision will be well founded.

Overall, we found there were a number of subjects around which conversation formed. The most significant of these was the provenance of the produce, when customers would ask about the place and means of production. For instance, at a stall selling goats' cheese, we had the following exchange:

Do you have your own goats? (W)
Yes, its a full time goat dairy farm…with about 400–450 on the farm

The stallholders understand that the key attraction of the farmers' market is that it's local. As one of our participant's commented, the farmers' market consists of "*Real people who have put together their own stuff from farms, or stuff they've made. Authenticity is really important.*" To that end, the stallholders not only discuss the provenance of the produce, but provide the history of how the company came to be. One stallholder proudly talked of this year being the "*30th anniversary this year, and its our 8th year of doing farmers' markets*," whilst another stallholder told a vignette of they came to be selling on the stall:

> I'll tell you a little story about how I came to work for them. I went to a charity event and bid £27 for three pies. I bought them, put them in the fridge, ate them, they were so nice, and phoned him up went up to the farm, buying off them ever since, and eventually he says what do you do at weekends …and now you know and I'm here and that's how it all started.

Besides contributing to the social nature of the market, such exchanges help to develop trusting beliefs in the customer, reassuring them that the products are local, and are produced in line with their expectations.

Another key set of topics for conversation is advice on what produce to choose, and how to prepare the produce for eating. At all of the stalls our participants visited, there was discussion about what they were looking for, whether the produce was for a special meal, and advice on cooking or how to present, whether the produce was venison, pork, chutneys or goats' cheese. Such conversations promote trusting intentions prior to purchase by showing that the stallholders are both interested in making sure the purchase decision is correct, and that they are knowledgeable about their products. As one of our participants reflected, "*I trust them because they have investment in their produce*" (W). However, there are differences in motivation across shoppers – our other participant reflected on how trust was engendered with a greater emphasis on the product:

> [There's a] …genuine sense of enthusiasm from stallholders, enables trust in the stallholder and by proxy to the product. But products come first – they look yummy and good and homegrown. The stallholders then back that up. (I)

Such conversations have other positive effects. One participant noted that "*My self-esteem has gone up through having a conversation that we're both interested in*" (W).

Determining the *quality* of a product in food consumption is a subject studied by consumer behaviourists and others. Products from supermarkets rely upon the *uniform standards* of quality generated by marketing and the other trappings of a consumer society. However, within a farmers' market, these uniform standards don't apply, since the necessary signage is absent in packaging and other shop displays. Instead, as Kirwan describes [10], the quality of products in farmers' markets is negotiated contingent upon conversation and place:

> In the case of FMs, the producers and consumers concerned are engaging in face-to-face interaction in order to create conventions of exchange which incorporate spatial and social relations that can replace 'uniform standards'.

The display of materials is set up to differentiate between the farmers' market produce and that available at conventional shops and supermarkets. Packaging is less sophisticated, emphasising the artisan nature of the product and the small scale production, in contrast to the slick packaging of supermarket produce. Produce such as cheeses and chutneys are all available to try, rather than solely those on special offer, encouraging the belief that the producer is confident you'll find something to like. Our shoppers found this to help in forming trusting beliefs – "*You can try stuff out – its just all 'ere for you to have a go at"* (I) – and indeed found the unsophisticated presentation a key piece of evidence for the products' quality.

A monthly street market is by definition a transient opportunity for consumers. The very appearance and presentation of the stalls signify the temporary nature of the stall. Stalls typically use a lightweight awning, and a covered table. Signage is attached to the awnings using market clips. Even the vans used by the meat suppliers, enabling the use of refrigeration equipment show the consumer that there is a time limited opportunity to get access to the stall. This can be seen as part of the "charm" of the market. Our accompanied shoppers displayed the same positions:

> You can get that feeling that its real people selling their produce, actually because it quite thin, the displays are relatively thin. Its not absolutely piled up like a commercial thing

and that there are *"Banners hanging behind stalls, there's a sense of homemade quality, the higgledy piggledy look."* (I).

Kirwan also notes that the perception of quality is based upon "the build up of trust over time, which is facilitated by consumers being able to make direct connections with the place and nature of the good they are purchasing" [10]. In our observations, we found that customer I on her second visit to the stall was recognised and asked about how they had found the chutney they had bought previously, which was followed by the descriptions of similar chutneys.

Finally, there is an element of system trust. The norms of the farmers' market are primarily created by the organisers of the market. Producers who apply to run a stall within the market are required to fill out a form explaining their provenance chain, showing that their produce is primarily local[1] and are subject to inspections by the market organisers. The organisers also work closely with the local agricultural college to promote organic and ethical production. Producers admitted to the market are therefore aware that they are in the market because of the origin of their produce and production ethics. Although the organisers conscientiously place small fliers describing the organisation and ethos behind the market, these are almost always ignored. However, in our observations, one stallholder described how stalls had to be certified to be in farmers' markets to one of our participants. Such system trust is reinforced as shoppers become more aware of the origins of the stalls and the market.

12.5.2   Shopping as Fun

We observed several common behaviours in our shoppers. The following list features particularly those aspects we deemed to have given pleasure, based on the valence of descriptions in the accounts:

---

[1] The emphasis is on locality of produce but obviously producers of chutney can make use of ingredients sourced outside of the locality.

Our shoppers all started by surveying the market, by walking through to savour experiences to come, assess the range of produce available and decide where and how to begin.

> Can I just wander round and look at everything first? A relatively quick wander down and then turn round and come back up again...I'll walk the other way and take a much deeper look. What I often do, if I've got somewhere I really want to look at, I often delay it, I save it up rather than rush to it, to spin it out a little bit. (K)

This "pre-consumption" activity did not involve specific planning. Instead, they approached shopping with a mix of loose intentions (getting chutney) and situated inspiration (trying venison). *I really enjoyed that, just nosing around and having a look.* (I) Another feature was pleasure in contact with others:

> It is all about the relationship with the stallholder and they are very practised at engaging and judging somebody. And I was being quite chatty and they were happy to go along with that. Thinking about the encounter with the couple at the pie shop, it would be fun to have a bit more of that. (I)

Not only were these encounters pleasant, but the shoppers relished the inspiration that contact with others provided in deciding what to buy. Recordings show people delighting in endorsing the quality they had appreciated. In some cases they made a point of telling the stallholder that they had returned to make a repeat buy. Buying in this respect can be seen as a collaborative activity, not only with those known to the shopper but at the point of assessing the goods, by the deliberate courting and/or appreciative reception of input from others present.

> He prompted them to say something and they were really enthusiastic, quite spontaneously enthusiastic. And really pleased to say how much they liked it and give us the history of buying the pies and saying they've been back, that they've moved and that they came back specifically to this stall...Anyone who can build a relationship with his customers like that must be worthwhile.

A further activity was tasting the small samples made available at the stall to demonstrate taste and quality:

> It's something about having little bowls of things out: "just try it": there's no commitment. It feels very generous. "We want to share it, we want to hand it out to you" ...this encouragement to just dip in and taste things. It gives a sense it's his own stuff, he made it so he can give it out and you get a sense that it's a privilege to be sharing it. (I)

> Even if it's just the opportunity to taste them. (W)

In [10] there is an analysis of how markets are distinct from conventional shopping arenas in that they provide a temporary space for consumption. Indeed, they are often as much about theatre and participatory entertainment as about locating necessary items of consumption [8]. In Gregson's analysis of car boot sales [6], the market space is described as:

> one where people come to play, where the conventions of retailing are suspended and where the participants come to engage in and produce theatre, performance spectacle and laughter.

Whilst the farmers' market is not quite so anarchic as a car boot sale, the interactions between stallholder and customers can be viewed as creating a spectacle. For instance, as part of a conversation with four other customers, the stallholder selling pies started singing loudly to the tune of Don McLean's *American Pie*

> Bye, bye, my lovely steak pies.
> Have a pastie, have a pork pie, give my game pie a try
> They're really good and they're lovely to buy…

Whilst this obviously entertained the immediate customers, it also generated interest from other passers-by, and thus attracted custom.

Beyond intentional entertainment from the stallholder, the spectacle of the selling process/environment also induces pleasure:

> The first thing that you look at is the product and you see these gorgeous yummy things laid out. And then when the person behind the stall is enthusiastic about them too and tells you stories, that's actually reinforcing that first impression of variety, tastiness and difference. …I think if there had been someone just standing there, arms crossed, bored behind the thing, you'd probably say "that's really nice chutney or whatever, I'll have some of that", but it wouldn't have been as interesting. (I)

12.5.3 Narratives and Stories

Narrative is so much part of selling that the commentators who have recently observed the rise of narrative marketing do so with a certain embarrassment, e.g. [17]. Brands have stories attached to them to build their identity while individual products have blurbs on their packaging to enhance their meaning to those buying. The use of narrative in an informal setting differs from the marketing of big business, but, in Sherry's words, "[d]ealers impart meaning to their goods, providing cultural biographies for objects, which many consumers believe enhance their value. In fact, these "stories" or "histories" are sought by some consumers as avidly as the objects themselves" [18].

Common Cause has its narrative, on its website, as a form of authentication/ promotion: "*Fruit and vegetables sold at a farmers' market will have been harvested the day prior to, or even on the very morning of the market.*" And the producers are forthcoming with tales, such as the story from pie man of coming to work for the stall in Sect. 12.5.1, or from the man with the goats' cheese stall:

> How many goats does it take to make this much cheese? Well, we have about 400, 450 on the farm. Oooh! We have obviously a full time diary staff to look after the goats. They are obviously not milked by hand: we can put 36 in there at any one time and milk them. It's actually our 30th anniversary this year and our eighth at farmers' markets.

Hearing stories made a big impression on the shoppers: *They've got really good stories: so it's either genuine or they've been well primed. It felt like you'd sat down next to them in a pub and you'd got chatting, rather than sales patter* (I) The shoppers' accounts build on the producers' stories:

> One has this vision of a wonderful 1920s farm kitchen. You know, you want it to be like that but it's probably not. You would quite like it not to be some industrial processing centre, so I was trying to work out where this food might be on that sort of scale, from jolly Mrs Beeton kitchen to the other end some dank neon-lit warehouse kind of thing. I don't know, I'm now imagining that everything is a jolly family business. (I)

This, in turn, affected the accounts of purchasing. It is no longer a transactional event but an exchange of gifts; payment as an act of gratitude that someone is providing food with this level of care:

> It makes it feel less like a transaction: less like "I'm coming to purchase your goods" and more like "Ooh, you produce lovely stuff. Isn't that nice? Can I have some?" "Why don't we exchange some money and you can have some." It feels a lot more friendly somehow. (I)

So producers' and others' stories can be seen to add to the fun of events and, both directly and indirectly, to relations built through them. Of course, how the stories are told is important: not just as 'sales patter' but like something one might hear in the pub. This emphasis on sharing stories points to both opportunities and incipient problems in developing a tool: there is an important flow of information that can be augmented, but at the same time, it is situated in a vulnerable place, at the heart of face-to-face interaction.

12.6 Application Design

As can be seen above, it would be possible to offer a tool that gave information on the territory, pointing out places to visit and what was on sale. It could support planning what to buy and balancing the budget. However, the information that seemed particularly valuable took its shape out of the incidental communication: the stories told about people and products of production, cooking and other uses, and of consumption and special tales of delight or mishap. These were shared producer/shopper(s) and shopper/shopper(s). Only some of this informing occurred through direct interaction; much also came from 'listening in' on others. As people watched the spectacle of selling from around the stalls or, indeed, from a point in the queue, they were honing their judgements about what to buy through listening as well as observing and tasting. So, we conceived the tool to provide forms of 'listening in' to others. We decided to harness the 'remembered consumption' phase.

As for when to provide it, there seemed to be a natural slot both in physical and experiential terms. Physically, this occurred when approaching a particular stall, either to examine goods or to queue. Experientially, the moment was when others' stories intersected with the shopping narrative, just before and influencing purchase. A factor favouring this moment in socio-technical design terms was that it attached data to stalls, allowing us to fix markers to them and work directly with a single stallholder for each set of contents.

But to whom should the shoppers 'listen in' when using the tool? If just the stallholders, this would create a marketing tool, influencing to buy or arousing scepticism. We decided to experiment with two distinct sets of voices.

One reason we had focused on trust in our analysis was because the underlying technology of the tool allowed us to prioritise information from trusted sources. As a default (and a courtesy), the stallholders were set up as most trusted source in an application which we called AskUsAbout and which held news and information about a stall's products. However, we had witnessed alternative sources of information that were as entertaining and potentially more customer-focused than that supplied by producers (who might be expected to give a positive gloss to any enduring materials, even if their on-the-spot banter is more nuanced). Another source for trustworthy information would be the stories of other shoppers, and particularly those personally known to the shopper and/or whose preferences are known. In the absence of independent reviewers, this source might come to be a highly trusted source, as we see with recommender sites and user reviews.

For this reason, we made a separate application called VisitorBook, to which everyone could contribute their opinions and anecdotes. Separating the two functions to encourage real-time interaction with the trader and to offer asynchronous interaction among shoppers allowed us to avoid some politics of deployment (by simultaneously making producers' information trusted and distinct) and to draw attention to the subtlety of behaviours, described above, that supported the development of relations in the market. Being clear about these distinctions, we hoped we would be able to offer a tool that was more trusted itself, rather than regarded as a marketing tool by shoppers.

12.6.1 AskUsAbout

As the name suggests, this application was conceived as a means of stimulating dialogue between the producer and the shoppers at the stall. Placed near the point of sale but set back from the counter, it showed news and product information when users pointed their mobile device at the code/fudicial marker. This offered a talking point for shoppers as they reached the front of the queue, alerting them to new or unusual stock to ask about or order. For instance: *We have pet mince and free bones available. These are excellent value and really loved by dogs. Just £1.50, with reduced prices for regulars.*

12.6.2 VisitorBook

By contrast, the visitors' book was intended to be a space for customers to share experiences across time. Comments left by shoppers could be read by later users, some known, some unknown. In this way, recommendations (and friendly warnings) of the kind that shoppers interacting at a stall might share are preserved. We anticipated that the effect of VisitorBook would be quite different from that of the AskUsAbout function because of the different source of information. For instance: *We had some pork chops from David back in February, and they were delicious. Not only did they have the porkiest taste since we had Dotty down in Devon, they were cut so large that they were almost a roasting joint in their own right.*

12.7 Evaluation

Our evaluation comes from observing two of our participant shoppers (I and K) using the ShoppingLense (seen in Fig. 12.4, left hand side), and then one month later observing another two (W and H) using a mobile phone with a QRCode reader (a screen shot of this is seen in Fig. 12.4, right hand side).

It appeared both applications worked. Across all four participants, conversations were cued from reading the AskUsAbout information. The pattern would typically be that the shopper would read out the information to their accompanying shopper, when the stallholder would overhear and confirm the information. Discussion would then ensue. One shopper believed that the information helped increase her confidence in talking to the stall by providing her with background – its the "*Kind of thing that's useful when you don't really know [the stall] at all.*" (H).

For the visitors' book, both K and H were prompted to buy products they wouldn't otherwise have purchased:

> And I would, as I said earlier I think, have probably bought chicken or sausages because that's what my son likes to eat, but the fact that the kit mentioned pork chops made me think he really likes pork chops and I don't very often buy pork chops, so, yeah, just raised that possibility like you say (K)

and similarly

> Its good, if I go to that [the application] first before looking at this [stall], then I'm immediately drawn to the pork chops, which is something I wouldn't normally buy …I suppose this is really good marketing (H)

H then reasoned that the application worked because it was "*A review at point of use which you wouldn't normally get in any other way.*" Given that a trusting belief is generated from the comment that is converted to a trusting intention of the purchase, it can be argued that the applications directly influenced the cognitive trust of the shoppers.

There were usability issues with both the ShoppingLense and the QRCodes. Although the UMPC is small, it still requires both hands to manipulate. Once the shopper was encumbered with bags, using the UMPC or paying became a struggle to coordinate all the necessary placing of bags. Although this became easier as the shoppers became accustomed to the kit,

> But it didn't feel like a difficulty at that stall. I mean, I guess that was the third stall that I'd bought something at and I think I'd kind of…I don't know why it was easier there, I can't remember now. Because that was the, the one stall where I didn't need to, I didn't think about it. (K)

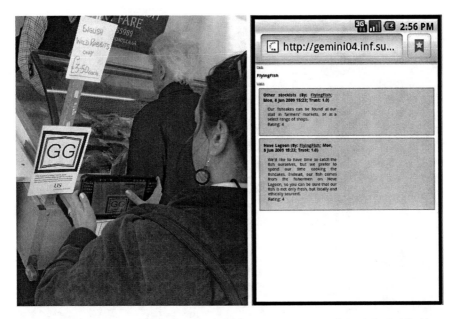

Fig. 12.4 A participant using the ARToolkit browser and a browser view of the AskUsAbout application

it was noticeable that the phone was easier to use – *"This is really intuitive – I don't know this phone, but taking a photograph is really good"* (H). Underhill noted in [19] that when the hands are too full, the shopping spree is over. If we expect the shopper to then manipulate gadgets whilst holding bags, we will encounter problems. Indeed, the ballet of placing bags and kit on the stall to dive for the money to pay almost resulted in the UMPC being left behind – see Fig. 12.5.

We had problems with sunshine producing glare on the screen making it difficult to angle the UMPC so as to see the display – *"I can't see anything here. Hmm, I'm really struggling because of the sunlight to make it work."* (K), with the shopper later referring to the need to move backwards and forwards to find a visible angle as "the dance." This may prove a major hurdle for the deployment of augmented reality in outdoors settings, since the UMPC has to be continuously pointed at the pattern to be viewed in real time. The QRCode deployment didn't suffer from these problems, since once the picture was taken, the returned HTML pages could be viewed in the shade of the stall, or by turning to position the body correctly.

Internet connectivity for our phones was occasionally problematic, and we were at the mercy of the idiosyncrasies of particular browser implementations. During the shop, one phone stopped getting 3G connectivity, so we had to switch to an alternative phone, with a different browser, and thus different approaches to scrolling the screen.

Whilst our focus has been on delivering the technical solution to facilitate communication between stallholders and queueing customers, it became obvious from our deployment that the content of the comments is all important.

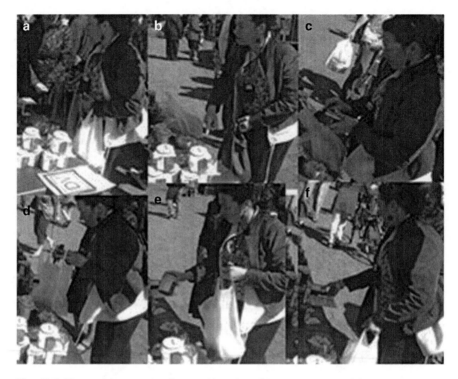

Fig. 12.5 The participant tastes chutney (**a**), points (**b**), extracts money (**c**), puts away purse (**d**), takes product (**e**) and retrieves AR tool (**f**). Note the fudicial marker visible in a

> Wasn't the [information] the cue for you to have a conversation with the stallholders? (interviewer)

> No, it wasn't…it felt like the information from the stallholder was, em, telling me something to persuade me to buy something, whereas I feel as though my conversations with stallholders usually are about, em, getting information that I want rather than information that they want to impart. (K)

The most successful comments contained the copy that was most informal, aligning itself with the authenticity of the market.

Positioning of the patterns could also present problems. The patterns had to be placed so that they were easily visible to the queueing customers, which could be difficult when queues would form irregularly.

One shopper raised a problem about whether the visitors' book was intended for comments about the experience of shopping and interacting with the stall, or about the experience of consumption. Our naive answer was that it was for both, but we plan to investigate in future work how to capture and provide comments at the appropriate time.

Finally, we saw several examples of the problems of combining the virtual world with a located market. Our shoppers wanted to talk to the stallholders and found the applications to be a hindrance, especially when they weren't accustomed to the gadget:

> Hmm, I guess it kind of it feels more awkward for me, yeah, em, normally I would, my focus would be to try something and then probably talk to the stallholder and em, be more interpersonally focused than elsewhere which I feel focused elsewhere today

We saw suggestions that this may be a digital divide between how the younger and older shoppers would use the kit, where the younger shoppers would naturally explore the virtual world before conversation – "*I don't know what they sell – I'm going to check out the bar code thing to see if that's any help*" (H) – whereas the older shoppers all expressed a preference for conversation if possible – "*My attention split between stallholder and the kit.*"

12.8   Conclusion

The investigation showed a complex system of trust and engagement between stallholders and shoppers in farmers' markets. The nature of these markets focuses on honest, even rustic, products and direct contact with producers. This first deployment went some way to exploring the use of technology to support the pervasive advertising needs of such markets. We found that there was a desire from stallholders to open up new ways of being in touch with their customers and that customers were generally interested in exploring the technology. However, in using technology care must be taken to blend into the existing experience.

In use, the application's interaction with the shopping experience, and the normal building of trust and selection of products, was mixed. The direct interaction with stallholders at a market is important to shoppers and their understanding of quality and the nature of products. In some cases the applications added to this, suggested a change from routine or prompted interaction. In other cases the way comments were written felt out of place. Static text failed to have the subtlety of direct contact, and so the marketing side of such a system seemed better limited to factual, e.g. provenance and prices, when direct interaction was still possible. On the other hand feedback from other customers would be harder to obtain without such a system, unless a repeat customer happened to be ahead in the queue. An enduring virtual connection to the products might also be of interest away from the market as an aid to discussing the purchases.

The adding of comments presented a conceptual challenge for future work – separating the experience from the product. Both are important to shopping, beyond the purely utilitarian, but commenting on the product most naturally occurs away from the point of sale and the tags of this application. Entering comments was found to be harder than browsing existing comments.

Pervasive computing has deployment issues for outdoor markets – glare on screens, use of hands when shopping and familiarity barriers. It may be that other form factors will have an advantage over UMPCs/phones. However, the simple and familiar (QRCodes and phone) was largely found to be usable and familiarity was quickly built.

The tools described here should translated to other forms of market, e.g. permanent or weekly general markets and other markets selling clothes and other specialised items. In the first case utility and price are more prominent, which may create a greater need for evidence of quality and less for providence. In the latter the association with youth culture may give rise to a stronger desire to understand social perceptions of products and benefits from a willingness to blur the real and virtual divides.

Acknowledgements This work was carried out with the support of the EPSRC, grant number EP/D077052/1.

References

1. Billinghurst, M., Kato, H.: Collaborative augmented reality. Commun. ACM **45**(7), 64–70 (2002)
2. Ciolfi, P.L., Deshpande, B.L.: Understanding place as experience: augmenting Human activities in context. In: Yi-Fu, T. (ed.) Space, Place and Experience Workshop at INTERACT 2005. Giuseppe Laterza, Italy (2005)
3. Common Cause Website: http://www.commoncause.org.uk/ Accessed 23 Mar 2011
4. Friends of the Earth: Farmers' markets. RDA Briefing **2**, (2000)
5. Garfinkel, H.: Studies in Ethnomethodology. Prentice Hall, Englewood Cliffs (1967)
6. Gregson, N., Crewe, L.: The bargain, the knowledge, and the spectacle: making sense of consumption in the space of the car-boot sale. Environ. Plann. D **15**(1), 87–112 (1997)
7. Heath, C., Luff, P., Vom Lehn, D., Yamashita, J., Kuzuoka, H.: Enhancing remote participation in live auctions: an 'intelligent' gavel. In: CHI '09: Proceedings of the 27th International Conference on Human Factors in Computing Systems, pp. 1427–1436. ACM, New York (2009). doi: http://doi.acm.org/10.1145/1518701.1518918
8. Holloway, L., Kneafsey, M.: Reading the space of the Farmers' market: a preliminary investigation from the UK. Sociol. Ruralis **40**(3), 285–299 (2000)
9. ISO (ed.): Information technology – automatic identification and data capture techniques – QR Code 2005 bar code symbology specification, 2nd edn. No. 18004 in IEC, ISO/IEC, Geneva (2006)
10. Kirwan, J.: The interpersonal world of direct marketing: examining conventions of quality at UK Farmers markets. J. Rural Stud. **22**(3), 301–312 (2006)
11. McKnight, D.H., Chervany, N.L.: The meanings of trust. Tech. Rep. 94-04, Carlson School of Management, University of Minnesota, Minneapolis (1996)
12. McLoughlin, M.: The recipe station: technology facilitating social interaction in a public environment. In: Proceedings of Create 2008. Golightly, D., Rose, T., Bonner, J., Davies, SB (eds.). The Ergonomics Society, London (2008)
13. Meschtscherjakov, A., Reitberger, W., Lankes, M., Tscheligi, M.: Enhanced shopping: a dynamic map in a retail store. In: UbiComp '08: Proceedings of the 10th International Conference on Ubiquitous Computing, pp. 336–339. ACM, New York (2008). doi: http://doi.acm.org/10.1145/1409635.1409680
14. Reitberger, W., Meschtscherjakov, A., Mirlacher, T., Scherndl, T., Huber, H., Tscheligi, M.: A persuasive interactive mannequin for shop windows. In: Persuasive, p. 4. ACM, New York/Claremont (2009)
15. Robinson, J., Wakeman, I., Chalmers, D., Basu, A.: The North Laine shopping guide: a case study in modelling trust in applications. In: Proceedings of IFIP Conference on Trust Management, pp. 183–197. Springer, Boston (2008)

16. Robinson, J., Wakeman, I., Chalmers, D., Horsfall, B.: Augmented reality support for poster presentations. In: TruLoco 2010: The Joint International Workshop on Trust in Location and Communications in Decentralised Computing, Morioka (2010)
17. Rolfe, B.: Making marketing a narrative. In: B&T. Reed Business Information, Chatswood. http://www.bandt.com.au/news/ac/0c0182ac.asp (2003)
18. Sherry, J.F.J.: A sociocultural analysis of a midwestern American flea market. J. Consum. Res. **17**(1), 13–30 (1990)
19. Underhill, P.: Why We Buy: The Science of Shopping. Simon and Schuster, New York (2008)
20. van Waart, P., Mulder, I.: Pervasive Advertising, Chap Meaningful Advertising. Springer, London (2011)
21. Wakeman, I., Chalmers, D., Fry, M.: Reconciling privacy and security in pervasive computing. In: 5th International Workshop on Middleware for Pervasive and Ad-Hoc Computing (MPAC07). ACM, New York/Los Angeles (2007)

Chapter 13
Rural Communities and Pervasive Advertising

Nick Taylor and Keith Cheverst

Abstract Digital signage is most commonly seen in urban environments targeting large groups of viewers. We believe that there is also a role for pervasive technology in smaller communities, including in rural areas that are typically late to receive the benefits of new technologies. This chapter describes a recent pervasive advertising display deployed in Wray, a village in North West England, which was developed with the involvement of community members and evaluated 'in the wild'. Our research contributes an exploration of rural communities as a site for pervasive digital signage, including our experiences relating to the design of the display and findings relating to its use in the community.

13.1 Introduction

As the technology required to realise pervasive displays becomes readily available and affordable, digital signage has become a common sight in urban areas, particularly when used for advertising purposes. However, this proliferation of pervasive technologies has largely omitted rural areas; while many rural residents are finding that technology can help to solve issues caused by their remote location in a society that is increasingly centred on large cities, the technologies readily available elsewhere are not always accessible. This is most apparent in the case of broadband Internet, which is often unavailable in rural areas, but also extends towards technology research: the vast majority of research into pervasive technologies

N. Taylor (✉)
Culture Lab, School of Computing Science, Newcastle University, Newcastle, UK
e-mail: nick.taylor@newcastle.ac.uk

K. Cheverst
Lancaster University, Lancaster, UK
e-mail: kc@comp.lancs.ac.uk

J. Müller et al. (eds.), *Pervasive Advertising*, Human-Computer Interaction Series,
DOI 10.1007/978-0-85729-352-7_13, © Springer-Verlag London Limited 2011

takes place in urban areas, university campuses and workplaces, and the fruits of these labours may take many years to reach rural areas, if at all.

To address this disparity, our work is primarily concerned with how digital signage in public spaces can be utilised to help support the community in a rural village by displaying community-generated content, which might be used to promote a sense of community and awareness of events in the village. Over a 4 year period, we have worked closely with Wray, a village in North West England with a keen interest in technology, where we have engaged the community in the development of a series of iterative prototypes to explore the domain. Initially, deployments took the form of a photo display used to show a community-generated collection of photographs in a public location, but feedback led us to consider the use of such a display for other types of content—namely, for advertising and event listings. This has led to the development of WrayDisplay, a public display that allows residents to share event listings, advertisements and photos with other members of the community via two displays in public spaces.

In this chapter, we explore the process of engaging the community that led to the development of this display and describe results from a 6 month period of deployment. We present WrayDisplay as a case study to illustrate numerous insights into the role of pervasive advertising displays in rural communities and factors to take into consideration when developing such displays.

13.2 Background

Our work builds upon a wealth of public display research, much of which is aimed at supporting community in some way. This section will briefly explore related work in the field, including existing research into community displays in both the workplace and more social environments, and introduce our own previous work in Wray that led to the development of WrayDisplay.

13.2.1 Community Displays

Digital signage has formed part of the pervasive computing vision since its inception. However, it is only within the last 10 years that the technologies required to realise large, public displays have become commonplace. Since then, many digital signage projects have emerged supporting community, initially based in the workplace and typically with the ability to post content that might be of mutual interest to colleagues [2, 5, 10, 16]. Although these displays each had different means of submitting, displaying and bringing content to the attention of passersby, each found that displays quickly became valuable additions to the workplace community.

Outside of the workplace, a number of more recent projects have begun to explore digital signage as a means of supporting neighbourhood communities. These have included both urban and suburban social spaces [3, 15] and rural areas in developing nations [4, 9]. Typically these displays have been deployed in public social spaces, such as cafés or community centres, often described as 'third places'—locations distinct from the home and workplace where people gather and socialise [13]. Deployments in the wild rather than in the researchers' own workplace naturally introduces new complexities and a need to better understand deployment environments, and several of these projects have thus sought to engage community members in the design process by various means, including participatory methods.

13.2.2 The Wray Photo Display

WrayDisplay builds on the Wray Photo Display [17, 19], a previous public display developed for Wray that centred on sharing community-generated photographic content between residents, deployed in the village's post office/shop over a period of over 3 years since August 2006. This was intended as a technology probe [7], designed to help us understand the rural environment while allowing behaviour to emerge over time and providing residents with a concrete example of the technology in action in their community to inspire feedback and suggestions. Our approach to working in Wray has been to use a participatory methodology to engage residents in iteratively improving these prototypes, in order to create a useful technology for the community while improving our own understanding of the issues surrounding rural technologies [18].

The Wray Photo Display was initially deployed as a simple application for displaying photos uploaded by residents. Following deployment, we observed usage in the community and logged interaction with the display, as well as collecting feedback through various means, including a comments book, meetings with residents and deployments at public events. Based on feedback from participants, the display's functionality slowly developed to meet the community's needs and the content of the display grew to include over 1,500 photos depicting both the village's history and recent events. We discovered that digital signage had a clear potential for supporting a sense of community spirit and awareness by sharing content in public spaces.

Despite the overall success of photos on the display, feedback consistently pointed towards news and events as a possible area for expansion. In this sense, the Photo Display had succeeded as a technology probe in demonstrating the potential of public displays and eliciting feedback on how they might be used, leading us to begin designing a replacement display with a wider range of content.

13.3 Designing the Display

Throughout the process of iteratively designing and evaluating public displays in Wray, we have attempted to engage the community in the process as much as possible, drawing requirements for the display's functionality directly from discussion with residents and revising prototypes based on feedback collected through a variety

Fig. 13.1 An existing noticeboard outside the village hall in Wray

of channels, including group meetings with participants. The following sections describe the process of developing a new display following repeated expressions of interest in news and advertising content from residents, from surveying existing noticeboards in the village to probing the possibilities of digital displays and gathering feedback leading to the development of a new display.

13.3.1 Survey of Existing Displays

While photo sharing behaviours were not prevalent in Wray prior to the introduction of the Photo Display, the same could not be said of news and advertising content. Existing public noticeboards were located outside the village hall (Fig. 13.1), church and both outside and inside the post office. Although some were locked and reserved for official notices, others were freely accessible and widely used to post advertisements, typically for small local businesses, items for sale and upcoming events within the village. Other notices on display showed information about local services, maps, wildlife and activities, as well as information about health services and charities that may be of interest to residents. This was often highly localised, not only to the local area, but also to the vicinity of the display: for example, the display outside the church was used exclusively for church information, while a series of displays near footpaths outside the village showed information about walks and wildlife. The village was also served by the Wrayly Mail, a monthly newsletter edited by a volunteer and distributed to residents, which mostly contained very brief adverts and event listings for the coming month.

However, residents had reported issues with the use of existing noticeboards and newsletters within the village. For example, several participants had told us that the noticeboards were filled with expired notices that made it difficult to identify new and relevant content. Furthermore, those living outside the main village on farms—who were still considered to be part of the community—were unable to see the content on a regular basis without making a lengthy trip into the village. The monthly distribution of the newsletter also meant that information had to be submitted far in advance, which was not always possible. Many of these problems seemed to indicate that a digital display might be capable of augmenting the distribution of community information to address these issues.

13.3.2 Working with the Community

Based on feedback from community members and problems identified in the previous section, a meeting was held with residents to determine exactly what features might be desirable on a digital noticeboard. This was aided considerably by two events that had recently occurred in the village: in the first, a suspected con artist had visited Wray and sold an elderly resident £1,000 of frozen fish, a significant event that quickly passed around the village as people encountered each other on the street, or as they arrived at our meeting; in the second, a consultation meeting for a new wind farm development in the area was advertised in the newsletter, but had been forgotten by the time of the meeting and was missed by several interested residents. Both these events were used to illustrate possible scenarios for use of the display, such as distributing urgent news that could not wait until the next issue of the newsletter, or bringing notices to the attention of residents as relevant dates approached.

In response to these requirements, a modified Photo Display was rapidly developed that added a news ticker along the bottom of the display (Fig. 13.2). Items could be scheduled to appear on the ticker between two set dates by the designated administrator, our primary contact in the village, and other residents were able to email submissions to her for inclusion on the display. Like the original Photo Display deployment itself, this was not intended as a fully-functional feature, but as a very basic function that would help residents to explore issues surrounding news submission and generate feedback to inform the design of subsequent displays.

This modified prototype was trialled in the village post office for several months, during which a total of 44 messages were posted. However, despite generally positive feedback, it appeared that few residents had taken notice of the new addition, suggesting the need for a more salient means of displaying news content, and it was decided to proceed with a display that would combine the existing Photo Display's content with more prominent news content.

However, as the Photo Display was well-established and used by this point, we were somewhat hesitant to dramatically alter it in ways that might prove unpopular.

Fig. 13.2 A modified Wray photo display with news ticker

To address this, residents were presented with several suggestions for a redesigned display to judge their reaction and gather input. We were particularly interested in how much display space for photos participants would be willing to sacrifice in favour of notices, and the designs presented were intended to provoke comments on the division of photo content and notices, the proportion of each type of content and navigation between them.

Contrary to our expectations, residents wanted the majority of the display to focus on news content rather than photo content. Where our designs had featured one third news, it was instead suggested that this should be reversed. One participant explained that he and other residents had already seen most of the photos, which were not time-sensitive, and it was more important to see notices and advertising on a regular basis.

13.4 WrayDisplay

A revised display based on design input from the previous meeting, dubbed WrayDisplay, was developed to replace the existing Photo Display. This combined the existing photo content with notices that could be posted by members of the community and displayed this content in public locations in the village.

Fig. 13.3 WrayDisplay home page showing photos and notices

The main component of WrayDisplay was a touchscreen display running a full-screen application, which showed the top three current news items along with the most recent three photographs submitted to the display (Fig. 13.3). Each news item comprised a headline, short summary and optional image, which were shown on the front page, with an optional text field for further details that could be accessed by touching the news item to open it. Each news item had a start date and end date, between which it would be shown as an active news item, and an optional 'reminder' date on which it would receive renewed prominence by returning to the top of the news queue. Users were also able to post comments on notices using an on-screen keyboard, or send notices as an email to themselves or others. In addition to current notices, it was also possible to browse through archived news items by month.

WrayDisplay's content was stored on a central server, which allowed multiple individual displays to share the same content by synchronising their content with this server, caching local copies to reduce reliance on an Internet connection. Residents could submit content to the server using a web application, but were also able to email the administrator directly and request that she input a notice. All notices were checked and approved by the administrator before appearing to the public, due to strong feedback in meetings indicating that this was necessary.

Displays were deployed in two locations in the village. The first deployment replaced the existing Photo Display in the village post office, located near existing paper noticeboards (Fig. 13.4) and utilising a 21″ portrait touchscreen display. Shortly after this deployment, we began discussing the possibility of a second deployment with the owner of a local café that had been identified by residents as a

Fig. 13.4 WrayDisplay in the village post office

suitable location. After the owner responded positively, this was deployed on a smaller, 19″ display, initially on a trial basis.

Upon deployment, there was interest from both business proprietors in having a dedicated section on the display for their own content. As a preliminary means of exploring this requirement, the display was modified slightly to ensure that the latest news item submitted by each proprietor would always be displayed in the top-most notice slot on their respective displays. We also received feedback from the café's owner suggesting that she might like to be able to moderate content herself in addition to moderation conducted centrally by the administrator. A need for this later became evident when an advert for a new coffee machine in the post office was shown on her display, which was reportedly perceived as competition by a displeased café owner.

Other feedback from both the café owner and residents suggested an advertisement feature, although it had been intended that the existing features would perform this function. The ambiguous term 'news' had been used on the display to indicate that any type of content could be posted, much like a normal noticeboard, but a large number of event listings had been posted early in the deployment (further detailed in the next section), leading residents to believe that this was the purpose of the new features. This eventually led to notices being separated into 'adverts' and 'events', where adverts operated as before and events were listed chronologically as a village calendar.

13.5   Usage and Content

WrayDisplay was deployed in the post office in February 2010 and installed in the café 1 week later, where they are both still deployed as of January 2011. During this period, 190 individual notices have been posted, a number which continues to grow, and both displays have seen regular use by village residents and visitors. The following sections describe the type of content posted by users and analyses usage levels of the two displays.

13.5.1 Adverts and Events

Despite the apparent desire for a digital noticeboard, posting of content was initially somewhat lacklustre. Initially, the vast majority of content was posted by our contact, who imported the listings directly from the Wrayly Mail as she received each copy. Although it had been expected that she would add any information submitted for inclusion on the village website she ran, it had not been anticipated that she would copy Wrayly Mail content across en masse, but this meant that a wealth of potential content was already available without requiring any extra effort from the originator, including content from those who might not otherwise have used the display.

Overall, 148 (78%) of the notices posted were event listings, compared to only 42 (22%) that were adverts, largely because the majority of the notices in the newsletter were event listings and our contact was particularly interested in the use of the display as a village calendar. As described in the previous section, this appeared to have the effect of discouraging other types of content, such as advertisements, until the notices were split into two distinct categories. Prior to this split, advertisements accounted for 17% of the notices posted, but 33% of the notices posted afterwards when alterations to the display encouraged use for advertisements.

Event listings typically included a date and title in the headline, with a brief description including the venue and any entrance fee. Where they had been copied from the Wrayly Mail this was usually the only information available, as the newsletter only had brief listings, but those community members who added their own events normally included a longer listing. The following examples show typical events posted on the display:

> **Mon 22nd Feb, Ewecross Historical Society**
> High Bentham Town Hall, 7.30 pm, Mark Rand 'The Settle-Carlisle railway'.
> Membership £5 a year, visitors £2 per evening.
>
> **Fri 26th Feb Domino Drive 7.30 pm**
> Wray with Botton Sports Committee in Wray Institute. Refreshments provided.

Groups within the village, such as the Women's Institute and Over 60s group, regularly used the display as a means of advertising their activities both by listing upcoming events and by posting photographs of past events. At evaluation meetings, both these groups felt that the display was useful for advertising their events to a wider audience, where previously they had typically been spread by word of mouth.

Following the addition of an explicit advertisements section, use of the display for this purpose grew considerably. One resident posted numerous advertisements for her homemade jewellery business and later posted a hen hut she was attempting to sell that was quickly purchased by another resident. Further items for sale have subsequently been posted by this user and others, including a successfully sold tumble dryer, and even a car. The following advertisements are typical of content posted into this section of the display:

Part Time Job Vacancy
There is a part time job vacancy at Bridge House Farm Tea Rooms.
Come and be part of the team at Bridge House Farm Tea Rooms. We have a part time job available. This is just for one day a week at the moment but possibly more hours available as the season becomes busier. The job will involve general front of house duties. For more information contact…

Hen hut for sale
Wooden hen hut, about 6 years old, wind and water tight, perch, water feeder - £50

Interestingly, the photo section was also used for advertising during this period, where it had not been in the past. The resident who had posted adverts for her jewellery business also created a photo category on the display and uploaded photos of her goods. We had always been slightly surprised that the Photo Display had not been appropriated in this way, particularly given the obvious desire for advertising content, and it appeared that the addition of advertising functionality encouraged this behaviour.

13.5.2 Display Usage

In addition to the content itself, both displays logged all interaction, allowing us to track use of the prototype and the relative popularity of different types of content and different locations. Based on logs running for 6 months from deployment, the display amassed some 33,497 touches spread across 784 individual sessions (where a session is defined as a series of interactions after the display has been dormant for at least 10 min). While many of these interactions related to the existing photographic content on the display, there were also a total of 736 notice views in 370 sessions—very roughly four notice views and two sessions each day. This might seem to be a somewhat low number, but given the size of the community, the possibility of peripheral awareness and the fact that the display is only one of many information sources in the village, we believe this represents a satisfactory number of direct interactions.

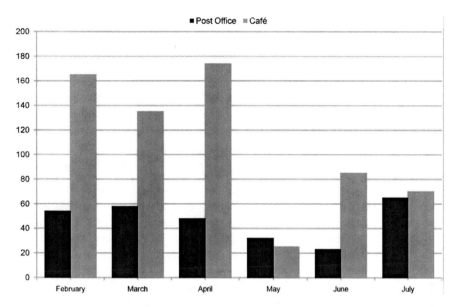

Fig. 13.5 Notice views in the post office and café

Figure 13.5 shows the number of notice views per month in each location: in the first 3 months, it is clear that use of the new café display far surpassed the existing post office display. Clearly this is at least partly due to novelty, as the café installation was new while the post office display had been in place for several years, and usage did appear to level out during the second 3 months. However, the café could certainly be considered to be a location more conducive to interaction, given that customers are likely to spend time relaxing and socialising there. Conversely, the post office display might be considered to better support more peripheral engagement, due to the higher number of people passing the display, albeit only briefly.

When talking to the owners of the post office and café, both said that the display saw use on most days, and the post office owner reported that people would often enter discussion around it. Although our logs show that a majority of sessions were primarily made up of photo viewing, it is important to remember that usage logs do not tell the entire story: many listings visible on the front page of the display convey all the necessary information without the user needing to open the notice or physically interact with the display, possibly to the point of enabling peripheral awareness. For this reason, the proprietors' observations are particularly useful.

From our own anecdotal observations, both locations appear to be well-used, particularly given the village's location. The post office is usually busy during our visits, and on one occasion when we spent half an hour inside the café, at least one group of customers was seen using the display in that period alone as they entered the building and waited to be served.

13.6   Discussion

Following 6 months of deployment in the wild, we have been able to use WrayDisplay to illustrate a number of insights into the role of digital signage in rural communities. This section discusses these findings, including methods of engaging the community in the design of such displays and design considerations for future displays.

13.6.1   The Role of Advertising Displays in Rural Communities

Even before the deployment of WrayDisplay, local advertising played an important role in village life, including advertising upcoming events, local businesses and available services, as well as facilitating small, local transactions such as items for sale. This is demonstrated by the prevalence of existing noticeboards, newsletters and websites serving the community—services that exist in many other similar villages and neighbourhoods.

Despite this, there certainly seemed to be a role for digital signage in the village as well. Naturally, we do not wish to replace any of these existing means of advertising with digital alternatives, but to augment them to improve the distribution of this content through the community. Input during the design stage showed that there were a number of issues that could be addressed by digital displays, such as outdated content, the need for timely 'breaking news' and reminders, and better support for those outside the village proper. Selling items in a local newspaper was also reported as being problematic, due to the distance that people in nearby towns had to travel to collect goods, and participants had felt that the ability to advertise goods on a very local scale would be helpful.

WrayDisplay did not simply inherit existing behaviours surrounding the sources of information it was augmenting. Although the post office display was located adjacent to existing noticeboards used to post items for sale and local services, it developed its own identity as a place for events listings, taking on the role of a village calendar. These unique aspects of a digital display were further evidenced by the contentious coffee machine advert: it is unlikely that the post office owner would have attempted to post such a notice alongside other adverts in the café's window, but the distributed nature of the system led to unexpected results. Other features unique to the display proved to be more beneficial: in one case, the commenting features were used to mark an item for sale as sold, something that would not be possible on a newsletter listing.

The display was also particularly useful for those outside the village, including residents of nearby villages and farms. Many who could be considered to be part of the Wray community did not pass paper noticeboards regularly and consequently could miss important information. Our contact, for example, lived on a farm close to the next village and was heavily involved in community activities in Wray, but complained that she had no way of regularly seeing noticeboards without travelling to the village hall or post office. For these residents, as well as those further afield, such as expatriates who still wish to remain abreast of events in the village, this is a valuable resource.

13.6.2   Engaging the Community in Designing Displays

Rather than a general-purpose display suited toward widespread deployment for advertising purposes, this project has sought to develop a display tailored to the needs of an individual community through the use of a participatory approach and the iterative development of prototypes. This process of deploying functional prototypes, collecting feedback and improving the deployments has proved to be very successful in creating a technology that is well-suited to its deployment environment. Although we designed to support certain types of behaviours that we expected would occur based on our fieldwork, our prototypes have been flexible enough to allow behaviour from the community to emerge over time. The approach also appeared to create a sense of ownership of the display by the community, and one participant in an evaluation meeting said that the village was proud to have a facility that their neighbours did not, suggesting the café display itself acted as an advertisement for the entire village when seen by visitors.

This approach has also made frequent use of our primary contact as a "human access point" [8], an individual who is a part of the local community but also comfortable with technology who can act as a bridge between researchers and participants, as well as promoting the technology and helping people to use it. Although we must be careful not to be too reliant on this individual, it proved to be an excellent means of accessing the community. Our contact also served as a curator and moderator for the display, ensuring that nothing unsuitable was posted and importing listings from other sources. While this role could have been fulfilled by a researcher, having a member of the community acting as an administrator meant content was far more likely to be appropriate and grounded in the community's needs.

Although our approach has meant the development of the display has been centred on Wray, it is reasonable to expect that other communities and neighbourhoods, particularly rural villages, will have similar requirements. Further study would be required to determine to what extent our observations hold true in other communities and how suitable the technology developed for Wray is elsewhere, but we believe WrayDisplay could be easily adapted to other environments.

13.6.3   Harnessing Existing Flows of Information

Previous work with digital signage has identified the importance of fitting in with existing routines to ensure users were able to integrate displays into their existing practices with as little personal cost as possible [1], and this proved to be equally true of advertising displays in Wray. But whereas this previous work found that particular technologies, such as email and instant messengers, were important in harnessing these practices, we also found that particular individuals could act as gateways to existing information. Our contact, for example, was already a gate-keeper for information on the village website and this role further allowed her to acquire early copies of the Wrayly Mail from its editor (who otherwise eschewed attempts to update her methods of creating and distributing the newsletter) in order to ensure its content was also added to the display.

Although it had not been anticipated that content from the Wrayly Mail would be imported wholesale, this did ensure that there was always current content on the display to ensure it remained useful. However, as the display was designed with occasional individual posts in mind, large batches of content meant that some items would be immediately pushed off the front page. This also led to an ebb and flow of content on the display, as large amounts were posted at the beginning of the month but gradually expired towards the end prior to the next batch being posted. Future displays might be designed to better support this behaviour.

Our contact had also previously expressed concerns about what would happen if she were unable to continue acting as a moderator for the display, fearing that it was too dependent on her—a common problem identified by Redhead and Brereton [14] in their survey of community communication. For these reasons, community systems should make use of key individuals, but not rely on them alone.

In terms of technology, a web application was a suitable means of submitting content for many residents, as using simple web applications was part of their exist-ing computer use. For others, unfamiliar applications were a considerable barrier to use. Even those who embraced technology were often only familiar with particular applications that they used regularly—such as their webmail—and were not confi-dent using new services. For this reason, we intentionally stressed that news could be submitted via our contact due to her existing role in distributing this type of con-tent. This meant that those unwilling or unable to use the display's website were still able to submit their content by email instead, a medium that most in the village appeared to be comfortable with. For those who weren't, notices could naturally be submitted by non-technical means as well.

13.6.4 Importance of Location

It should come as no surprise that location was an important factor in the deploy-ment of displays. The effect of location on the usage of displays, in terms of both volume of interactions and type of content, is well represented in public display research and the "interaction between technology and its location" [12] is central to our understanding of public displays. Our experiences confirm the findings of past research, particularly the observation that 'waiting' spaces attract use [2], but also note that different locations bring differing audiences and senses of appropri-ate content.

At the simplest level, the impact of location was visible in the usage statistics. The original Photo Display was briefly deployed in the village hall prior to being moved to the post office, where it subsequently saw far greater levels of usage due to its increased visibility by the large number of residents passing through the shop. Likewise, the deployment of a second display in the café initially showed higher levels of usage than the post office, likely due to the novelty of having a display in this location and the more varied audience who are less likely to have seen the display before, although usage did flatten out after several months.

The display's audience also differed significantly by location. While the post office reached an audience that was mostly local, the café received far more visitors from other villages and further afield. Although we had initially feared that this might make the café display less useful, feedback from residents indicated that reaching a wider audience was seen as a welcome effect of this deployment, suggesting that it might be advantageous to intentionally harness this effect to target adverts at particular audiences. For example, some groups might only want to advertise their events to residents within the village, while others might be actively trying to encourage visitors from elsewhere to use their services. The suitability of different locations for adverts targeting different groups is something that community members appeared to be well-equipped to judge for themselves.

Beyond this, appropriate content also varied between locations, again exemplified by the coffee machine advert. While this was perfectly acceptable in the post office, it was not appreciated in the café due to the perception that it was promoting their competition. The differences in appropriate content across locations is also reflected in existing paper noticeboards in the village by a noticeboard outside the church, which was unlocked but only contained church-related material. In this case, either residents recognised that posting other content was inappropriate or any unauthorised notices were taken down. This is behaviour that could be replicated in a digital display by allowing notice posters to choose which displays their content would be shown on, or by allowing individuals in the deployment venues to remove items on a local basis, rather than rejecting them from the entire system.

13.6.5 Terminology and Signifiers

One of our more interesting observations was the way that established content appeared to influence subsequent usage despite the display being intentionally designed to support any type of notice content, as demonstrated by requests for a 'classifieds' section so that residents could post advertisements. The high number of event listings posted to the display relative to other types of content when the display was first deployed appeared to give the impression that this was the only appropriate type of content. Furthermore, although we had used the term 'news' on the first prototype as a catch-all term for noticeboard-type content, a term that originated in discussion groups with residents, once deployed this term appeared to suggest content exclusive of advertisements.

Fig. 13.6 A refrigerator and whiteboard appropriated as community noticeboards. The presence of notices indicates to others that this is acceptable

Norman used the term 'signifiers' to suggest that "we know how to behave by watching the behaviour of others, or [...] the trails they leave behind" [11]. This certainly appeared to be occurring in this case, highlighted by the sudden influx of advertisements when the content was divided into events and adverts, signifying that this content was permissible and appropriate. This relates to Harrison and Dourish's [6] concept of 'spaces' and 'places', in which interactions are governed by both the physical space in which they are situated and the cultural expectations associated with that particular place.

There are many further examples of noticeboards dependent on signifiers to indicate appropriate behaviour, both in Wray and elsewhere (Fig. 13.6). We have often been drawn to one noticeboard in the post office, located very close to our own display, where notices have been attached to the side of a branded drinks refrigerator, subverting the refrigerator's original secondary purpose as an advertising device for the drinks company and appropriating the surface to display community content. At some point, the surface was used to post a notice for the first time, indicating to others that it was 'okay' to post notices there. In a similar example, a whiteboard in our department kitchen went unused for many years until a single message was written on it, after which the board quickly became used for doodling, banter and notices.

13.7 Conclusions

This chapter has described our work developing a digital noticeboard for use in Wray, based on input from community members themselves and deployed in the village for an extended period of time. From this experience, we have gained a number of insights into the use of digital signage in rural settings and the process of engaging a community in designing displays tailored to their needs, as well as factors to consider in the design of such displays.

Our observations have included areas in which Wray was not already well-served and where digital interventions could augment existing practices to address issues that exist, and the value of fitting in with existing information flows and carefully considering display locations with the village. We were also surprised by the extent to which early content on the display influenced its later usage and perceptions of appropriate content by residents.

Above all, our research has shown that there is clear potential for appropriately designed digital signage in rural communities. While public displays are often deployed in urban and workplace environments, such pervasive technologies are rarely investigated elsewhere. Work in Wray has demonstrated that displays can be successful in rural environments as well, suggesting a need for further research to explore digital signage, and pervasive technologies in general, in this area.

Acknowledgments This work was supported by a Microsoft European PhD Scholarship. We would also like to thank Chris Conder and the continually helpful and enthusiastic residents of Wray.

References

1. Cheverst, K., Dix, A., Fitton, D., Rouncefield, M., Graham, C.: Exploring awareness related messaging through two situated-display-based systems. Hum. Comput. Interact. **22**(1), 173–220 (2007). doi:10.1080/07370020701307955
2. Churchill, E., Nelson, L., Denoue, L., Murphy, P., Helfman, J.: The plasma poster network. In: O'Hara, K., Perry, M., Churchill, E., Russell, D. (eds.) Public and Situated Displays: Social and Interactional Aspects of Shared Display Technologies, pp. 233–260. Kluwer, Dordrecht (2003)
3. Churchill, E.F., Nelson, L., Hsieh, G.: Café life in the digital age: augmenting information flow in a café-work-entertainment space. In: CHI '06 Extended Abstracts on Human Factors in Computing Systems, Montreal, pp. 123–128. ACM, New York (2006)
4. Frohlich, D.M., Rachovides, D., Riga, K., Bhat, R., Frank, M., Edirisinghe, E., Wickramanayaka, D., Jones, M., Harwood, W.: Storybank: mobile digital storytelling in a development context. In: CHI '09: Proceedings of the 27th International Conference on Human Factors in Computing Systems, pp. 1761–1770. ACM, New York (2009)
5. Greenberg, S., Rounding, M.: The notification collage: posting information to public and personal displays. In: CHI '01: Proceedings of the SIGCHI Conference on Human Factors in Computing Systems, Seattle, pp. 514–521. ACM, New York (2001)
6. Harrison, S., Dourish, P.: Re-place-ing space: the roles of place and space in collaborative systems. In: CSCW '96: Proceedings of the 1996 ACM Conference on Computer Supported Cooperative Work, Boston, pp. 67–76. ACM, New York (1996)
7. Hutchinson, H., Mackay, W., Westerlund, B., Bederson, B.B., Druin, A., Plaisant, C., Beaudouin-Lafon, M., Conversy, S., Evans, H., Hansen, H., Roussel, N., Eiderbäck, B.: Technology probes: inspiring design for and with families. In: CHI '03: Proceedings of the SIGCHI Conference on Human Factors in Computing Systems, Ft. Lauderdale, pp. 17–24. ACM, New York (2003)
8. Marsden, G., Maunder, A., Parker, M.: People are people, but technology is not technology. Phil. Trans. R. Soc. A **366**(1881), 3795–3804 (2008). doi:10.1098/rsta.2008.0119

9. Maunder, A., Marsden, G., Harper, R.: Making the link – providing mobile media for novice communities in the developing world. Int. J. Hum. Comput. Stud. (2011). doi:10.1016/j.ijhcs.2010.12.009
10. McCarthy, J.F.: Promoting a sense of community with ubiquitous peripheral displays. In: O'Hara, K., Perry, M., Churchill, E., Russell, D. (eds.) Public and Situated Displays: Social and Interactional Aspects of Shared Display Technologies, pp. 283–308. Kluwer, Dordrecht (2003)
11. Norman, D.A.: The way I see it – signifiers, not affordances. Interactions 15(6), 18–19 (2008). doi:10.1145/1409040.1409044
12. O'Hara, K., Perry, M., Churchill, E., Russell, D. (eds.): Public and Situated Displays: Social and Interactional Aspects of Shared Display Technologies. Kluwer, Dordrecht (2003)
13. Oldenburg, R.: The Great Good Place: Cafes, Coffee Shops, Community Centers, Beauty Parlors, General Stores, Bars, Hangouts, and How They Get You Through the Day. Paragon House, New York (1989)
14. Redhead, F., Brereton, M.: A qualitative analysis of local community communications. In: OZCHI '06: Proceedings of the 18th Australia Conference on Computer–Human Interaction, Sydney, pp. 361–364. ACM, New York (2006)
15. Redhead, F., Brereton, M.: Designing interaction for local communications: an urban screen study. In: INTERACT 2009, Berlin 2009. LNCS, vol. 5727, pp. 457–460. Springer, Heidelberg (2009)
16. Snowdon, D., Grasso, A.: Diffusing information in organizational settings: learning from experience. In: CHI '02: Proceedings of the SIGCHI Conference on Human Factors in Computing Systems, Minneapolis, pp. 331–338. ACM, New York (2002)
17. Taylor, N., Cheverst, K.: Social interaction around a rural community photo display. Int. J. Hum. Comput. Stud. 67(12), 1037–1047 (2009). doi:10.1016/j.ijhcs.2009.07.006
18. Taylor, N., Cheverst, K.: Creating a rural community display with local engagement. In: DIS '10: Proceedings of the 8th ACM Conference on Designing Interactive Systems, Aarhus, pp. 218–227. ACM, New York (2010)
19. Taylor, N., Cheverst, K., Fitton, D., Race, N.J.P., Rouncefield, M., Graham, C.: Probing communities: study of a village photo display. In: Proceedings of the 18th Australasian Conference on Computer–Human Interaction (OZCHI '07), Adelaide, pp. 17–24. ACM, New York (2007)

Chapter 14
Attentional Behavior of Users on the Move Towards Pervasive Advertising Media

Johann Schrammel, Elke Mattheiss, Susen Döbelt, Lucas Paletta, Alexander Almer, and Manfred Tscheligi

Abstract In this chapter we analyze the attention of users on the move towards pervasive advertising media. We report the findings of two multi-sensor eye tracking studies designed to provide a better understanding of the actual attentional behavior of users on the move in different public environments. In the first study 106 participants were equipped with eye tracking technology and asked to use public transportation vehicles equipped with information and advertising screens. In a second study 16 participants were asked to stroll through a shopping street for about 15 min, and during this time different indicators for their behavior and focus of attention (eye tracking, movement and pose tracking) were captured. Motion and pose data was correlated with eye tracking data to identify typical patterns of attention. We report the results of these studies, then discuss the implications of the main findings for pervasive advertising and finally reflect on the used research methodology.

J. Schrammel (✉) • E. Mattheiss • S. Döbelt
CURE Center for Usability Research & Engineering,
Vienna, Austria
e-mail: schrammel@cure.at; mattheiss@cure.at; doebelt@cure.at

L. Paletta • A. Almer
JOANNEUM RESEARCH Forschungsgesellschaft mbH,
Graz, Austria
e-mail: lucas.paletta@joanneum.at; alexander.almer@joanneum.at

M. Tscheligi
ICT&S, University of Salzburg, Salzburg, Austria
e-mail: manfred.tscheligi@sbg.ac.at

J. Müller et al. (eds.), *Pervasive Advertising*, Human-Computer Interaction Series,
DOI 10.1007/978-0-85729-352-7_14, © Springer-Verlag London Limited 2011

14.1   Introduction

Measuring the attention towards different kinds of advertising media is of high interest in marketing research. Most existing research in this area focuses on a person's attention towards indoor advertising media like printed advertisements and in-store placement. The more uncontrolled environment of outdoor advertisements has not been targeted and analyzed in detail yet, mainly due to limitations of available methods for tracking the user's focus of attention.

Different investigators try to overcome the methodological difficulties of unrestricted situations by using virtual representations of the real world. This approach allows studying a person's attention in a controllable way. However, due to the rather artificial situation concerns regarding the external validity arise, i.e. whether the results obtained in the virtual representation are comparable to those in real life situations.

To investigate the characteristics and mechanisms of successful outdoor advertisement design reliable data and knowledge about the detailed visual attention of users on the move is needed. By knowing how people perceive different kinds of advertisements in a realistic outdoor setting, the impact of pervasive marketing approaches can be increased through better design and placement of advertising media.

In this article we describe two studies aiming to advance the current knowledge and methods in the field of visual attention on advertisement media of users on the move. We investigated the participants' visual fixations on digital displays in public transport (study 1) and on brand logos while walking through a pedestrian shopping street (study 2). With the results of the studies' explorative field trials we want to answer basic questions about the perception of these outdoor advertisement media. The data can also act as a reference for further research about visual attention in public spaces.

14.2   Related Work

In this section we present previous work related to our studies. The main focus is on visual attention, eye tracking technology and attention to public displays and advertisement.

14.2.1   Special Importance of Attention in Pervasive and Mobile Computing

Mobile computing technology allows having electronic devices available whenever and wherever we want. However, designers and developers of mobile applications like palmtop computers, PDAs, and mobile phones have to face unique challenges, because location and environment are usually less predictable than in desktop applications [3]. Similar restrictions apply also to public displays. Furthermore mobile computing devices have the common problem of rather small visual displays and limited input techniques, wherefore performance is often substantially worse than in the desktop context (e.g., [29]). Multitasking and support for task interruption are of high relevance, since in a mobile context the frequency of distracting events is much higher than for a desktop application [12] and tasks with interruptions take longer to complete on a mobile device than with a desktop application [28]. Therefore special interest is on the increased competition with regard to attracting the users' attention and on interaction as a non-primary task in a certain context – which is also an issue for public displays.

14.2.2 Human Visual Attention and Perception

Humans are continuously confronted with a vast amount of information and stimuli, but they are not able to process all of it in parallel. Therefore it is believed that the human information processing includes a bottleneck where attentional systems decide which information an individual processes. In visual attention this bottleneck is quite obvious defined by the fovea, an area of the retina with the highest resolution. In foveal vision humans tend to fixate objects which they are attentive to. However humans are also able to attend objects which are in their peripheral visual field and 24° distant from the fovea [34]. The spotlight metaphor considers visual attention as a kind of spotlight which can be moved around to focus different objects in the visual field. The size of this spotlight can vary [13] and the smaller the attentional area is the higher is the processing capacity for that area. When an individual wants to attend another object in the visual field the "spotlight" has to be moved. Is a person involved in a visual search task, the feature integration theory [38] postulates the existence of a pre-attentive subsystem, which at the earliest stage of visual processing decomposes a visual stimulus into its elementary features. At a more focused attentive level, these independent basic features are recomposed in order to obtain an integrated perception of an object and the world.

14.2.3 Development of Eye Tracking Technology

To analyze a person's gaze behavior is not a new idea. Research on eye tracking is conducted since over 100 years. In the last decades a strong focus was on eye movement recording systems, with the aim to gather objective and quantitative data of a person's visual attention [11]. Early eye tracking methods were quite invasive, e.g. electro-oculographic techniques or contact lenses covering cornea and sclera [33].

Today we can look back to a variety of eye tracking systems, differing in terms of their appearance and their eye detection techniques and algorithms [16]. Basically eye tracking can be infrared-based, i.e. the different reflection of infrared light between cornea and pupil is used to determine the line of sight (e.g. [33]) or appearance-based, i.e. computer vision techniques are used to find the eyes and their orientation (e.g. [37]). Furthermore eye trackers can be head-mounted, build into the computer screen, and – since about the last decade – even portable. The development in the direction of more and more non-intrusive and mobile eye trackers enables researchers to observe close to natural behavior unaltered by limitations of the technical equipment. With mobile eye trackers it is possible to go into the real world and gather data in realistic settings [19].

Eye tracking technology is further developed towards more light-weight and low-cost systems (e.g. [1]) which enable eye tracking in various situations and activities and to make it affordable for the general public. Most recent developments try to expand the application of eye tracking to infants, for whom the portable eye trackers for adults are ill-suited [15].

14.2.4   Eye-Tracking in Public Spaces

The development of portable and less intrusive eye trackers enables attention measurements in the public space. However, only a rather small body of research exists using eye tracking in real environments. This probably can be explained by two factors. Firstly, investigations with mobile eye tracking imply a reduced controllability of the setting and consequently difficulties to realize an experimental design arise. Secondly, it is a big challenge to deal with the free movements of head and body. These movements make it harder to map eye tracker coordinates onto world coordinates, and often require a laborious, manual processing of the data [22]. Thus, many researchers rely on virtual environments simulating a real setting (e.g. [27, 35]) to investigate visual attention in an environment as natural as possible but nevertheless allowing experimental control. In this regard Hayhoe and colleagues [20] pointed out the necessity to validate performance in virtual environments by investigations in real environments and – the other way around – to use gaze behavior in the real world to generate hypotheses tested in a virtual environment.

Early attempts to obtain measurements of eye movements in a natural context and with free head and body movements typically concern everyday activities like driving a car [17, 24], playing golf [14], washing hands [32], or making a sandwich [21].

More recent research also targets the visual attention in public spaces mainly with explorative field trials. For example Wessel and colleagues [40] investigated the gaze behavior of science museum visitors to examine which eye movements are related to exploration behavior and cognitive elaboration. The authors could identify a common pattern. All participants first scanned each exhibition wall as a whole, and then explored single exhibits in their vicinity. Results show an initial quick skimming of pictorial information, which is a rather automated process, followed by processing like reading text – an elaboration pattern commonly assumed in research.

Gaze patterns usually depend on the given task of a person. This was shown by Droll and Eckstein [10] who investigated gaze and memory for objects while walking around a building with the aid of a mobile eye tracker. Participants being told that they will be asked about what they saw following their walk were much more likely to notice exchanged objects along their path. They also fixated objects longer prior to the change than participants being simply instructed to walk around the building. The authors state that this result suggests task demand to have an influence on gaze control. Another study [18] investigated natural gaze behavior while ascending and descending a hill in an urban environment for two different terrains (street with constant slope and irregularly spaced sidewalk steps). The conditions resulted in different gaze distributions and the authors claim that the task strongly affects gaze behavior even when instructing participants and environment are kept identical.

Concrete implications for the placement of wayfinding information in nursing homes could be drawn by a mobile eye tracking study of Schuchard and colleagues [36]. The authors investigated wayfinding in a nursing home of older adults with mild dementia. They could support earlier findings that participants look mainly at the floor and lower part of hallway, and therefore rarely look at areas where wayfinding information is usually placed.

The various insights in gaze patterns in public spaces are only possible due to the evolving mobile eye tracking technology. Although authors point out constraints like limited conclusions on cognitive processing, obtrusiveness of measurement, limited temporal and spatial accuracy, and laborious data analysis [40], mobile eye tracking has the potential to explore eye movements in a more natural setting than every other technology before.

14.2.5 Attention in Guidance Systems and Driver-Environments

The user in public spaces who is typically on the move in public transport or car traffic has to face the challenge of filtering out the relevant information from the large number of available information. To facilitate this filtering process the design of signs in guidance systems (like platform numbers or speed limits) is essential. Early studies in this regard are concerned with differential effects in traffic sign perception, like smaller reaction times for warning than for regulatory signs [8] and longer reaction times for extravert participants [26]. More recent research in this field [4] could show that ergonomic design principles play an important role in the comprehension of traffic signs. The results show a strong relationship between the comprehension level and the three principles of compatibility, familiarity, and standardization for drivers of different cultural backgrounds. Ng and Chan [30] considered the participant's experience with icons. They identified semantic closeness as being most important for signs not learned before, and that sign features determining sign usability change as the experience with the sign grows. The authors conclude from this result that designers of traffic signs should consider different user groups.

Research was also conducted on how the attention of drivers can be distracted from relevant information like traffic signs, e.g. by advertisement. Since for the advertising industry it is desirable that roadside advertisements gain a lot of attention, it can be a seen as source of distraction, increasing the complexity of drivers' visual environment [39]. In the worst case this can result in a fatal accident. An interesting question in this regard is how much attention different kinds of roadside advertisements really attract. A driving simulation study found that roadside advertisements increase mental load and eye fixations and can distract the attention from more relevant road signage [41]. However, the visual attention on ads is high especially in situation which are monotonous and with a lower workload. Another driving simulation study investigated differences between static and video adverts [6]. The authors found that video advertisements cause a significantly greater impairment of driving performance than static ones (indicated for example by longer and more fixations and a greater variation in lateral lane position). Besides the type of advertisement also placement seems to be an influencing factor for amount of attracted attention. Crundall and colleagues [7] used eye tracking of participants watching a video clip to study the influence of different locations of adverts. They found that adverts placed at the height of bus shelters attract and hold attention at inappropriate times compared to adverts placed in 3 m altitude. The findings have direct implications for the representation of roadside billboards as means of marketing. Nevertheless they shouldn't be a risk for car drivers.

14.2.6   Attention in Advertisement

The question how people attend advertisements in general has concerned many researchers in the fields of marketing, psychology and neuroscience. Research was done for all kinds of media including print advertisement in magazines and papers, in-store marketing and outdoor advertisement.

Effects of the placement and appearance of advertisement on the amount of visual attention of observers is a frequently researched topic in printed advertisement. A study investigating eye movements while choosing businesses from yellow pages [25] could show that 93% of the consumers notice quarter page display ads but only 26% of the plain listings, and that color ads are noticed before and viewed longer than non-color ads. Furthermore consumers spent 54% more time viewing ads they end up choosing than ads they didn't choose, which demonstrates a certain relationship between visual attention and choice behavior. A study by Drèze and colleagues [9] investigated the consumer choice for brands on different shelf levels in the context of in-store marketing. The authors found brands on shelves near the eye or hand level being chosen more often than brands on the lowest shelf. Similar results were found with a study applying eye tracking technology [5]. Investigations of the visual attention of (potential) observers of outdoor advertisement are also often about whether and how long the observer looks at specific aspects of boards, brands, banners, or posters. Basically outdoor posters catch a lot of attention, e.g. in a study of the OAAA [31] 70% of outdoor posters in the visual field of the subject were seen, and 63% of these were likely to be read. Maughan and colleagues [27] found a correlation between the fixations of participants on advertisements and whether they liked the advertisement or not. Interestingly there is a strong relationship between increasing number of fixations and increasing preference for the advertisement, though nothing can be told about the direction of causality – i.e. which factor is the cause and which the effect.

To provide passengers of public transportation systems with advertisements on digital displays is a rather new advertisement medium, thus there is still a lack of research investigating the mechanisms of this type of advertisement. Research on attention towards public displays in general provides valuable information also for digital displays in public transport. Huang and colleagues [23] for example state that attention towards public displays is difficult to attract and hold, and define valuable design recommendations regarding e.g. positioning and content format.

14.2.7   Methods of Attention Measurements in Advertising

As measurement of the effect of specific marketing strategies, researchers frequently rely on recall and recognition as a measure of attention to the advertisement in question (e.g., [2]). This approach follows the rational that objects gaining more attention will also be remembered more likely. But the relationship between attention and recall is not unambiguous as was shown by a series of studies of the OAAA [31]. The studies reveal that people tend to recall only a third of outdoor boards they looked at and also recall boards which were never shown. This is why the authors claim unaided recall not being the best method to assess ad effectiveness, and consider aided recall and recognition as more accurate. Another possibility frequently used in marketing is to measure brand choice or numbers of sales (e.g., [9]). On the one hand these measures seem comfortable in the context of outdoor advertisement, since they are a simple assessment and deliver valuable insights about the effectiveness of pervasive advertisement. On the other hand it is questionable if these rough measures can really teach us detailed about the person's attention in a complex advertising situation including many factors moderating between attention and memory (and respectively purchase). Justifiably, researchers claim for better marketing metrics of visual attention than self-reported recall or number of sales [5].

In the context of advertisements eye tracking is a promising and increasingly used method, since it supplements subjective measures like questionnaires with objective data, telling if people really look at specific objects in their visual field. Eye tracking provides rich data about the gaze behavior, more accurate than questionnaires and can't be easily manipulated by the person [40]. Considering the little amount of research using mobile eye trackers in a realistic context, much work has to be done in technical and conceptual regards to advance findings in this field.

14.3   Attention in Public Transport Towards Digital Displays (Study 1)

The driving idea behind the first study was to investigate human attentional behavior towards digital displays (so-called info-screens) in urban public transport with the aid of mobile eye tracking under natural conditions. More specifically the focus was on the attention, awareness, attitude and memory of people related to such displays, as well as the influence of different content-types, like advertisements and news.

14.4   Method

Field Study Context. The info-screen is a display mounted in trams in the city of Graz in Austria (see Fig. 14.1a). Four info-screens with a size of 17 in. are installed in each tram (two in the middle of the train and two in the front part). They are either pointing against the driving direction or sideways, wherefore their visibility and the viewing distance varies depending on the observers' location in the tram. The info-screen is broadcasting its content in cycles that get repeated every 14 min, which is about the length participants were in the tram in one direction. The content-types forming a cycle at the time of the experiment were advertisement, news, culture, entertainment, sports/weather, event-tips and passenger information.

Participants. A random sample of 106 people (51 female, 55 male) with a mean age of 30 years took part in the study. Participants were located in Graz and had different educational (bachelor, master) and professional (apprenticeship, teacher) backgrounds. Due to technical problems (malfunction of the information displays in the tram and problems with the mobile eye tracking system) six participants were excluded from the data analysis.

Material. The eye tracker used in the experiment was an iView X HED mobile eye tracker of the *company* SMI, consisting of a size adjustable, lightweight helmet, tablet pc (carried in a daypack), and a sampling rate of 50 Hz (see Fig. 14.1b).

After the eye tracking in the public space a questionnaire consisting of 22 questions was provided, which includes the following topics: subjective measurement of

Fig. 14.1 (**a**) Placement of two info-screens in tram either pointed against the driving direction or sideways. (**b**) Mobile eye tracking system

how long participants paid attention to the info-screen; inconvenience by the helmet and the daypack; attitude about the info-screens; likability of the content-types; likability of different kinds of advertisement media; and demographic data. Furthermore recall and recognition of content shown on the info-screen was assessed. As a recall test participants were asked to tell in no specific order which content they had seen during their ride. Then participants were asked to recall which specific ads, logos and brand names they could remember. For measuring recognition participants' were provided with a textual list including ads actually being broadcasted and ads that were not shown on the info-screen.

Procedure. Participants were informed about the general aim of the study to measure attentional behavior in public spaces, but not that the focus lies on the attention towards the info-screens. After presenting the mobile eye tracking system participants could decide if they still wanted to participate in the study.

The actual testing procedure started with the calibration of the eye tracker once subjects had the helmet on. The calibration was done using a five-point calibration target. Then participants were asked to carry out the simple task to bring back books and magazines to the return box of a public library located about 25 min away from the starting point, and then to come back. With a detailed description of the route, a ticket, a mobile phone (in case they have additional questions), and an umbrella (to protect the eye tracker in case of sudden rain), participants left. The calibration was checked again when the participants left to go to the public library and when they came back to see if the helmet had gotten out of place. In total participants were on their way for about 50 min.

When the participants returned the questionnaire, presented in electronic form, was filled out by the facilitators with the participants providing the answers, because some participants were not familiar with the computer technology.

Data analysis. The data from the eye tracker, consisting of the scene video and the data of the eye movements, was recorded on the tablet pc that had been carried in the daypack. The operators of the info-screens provided the corresponding time-stamped log-files. The quantitative data set (with the log-files and the eye tracking data) enabled to determine on a frame by frame basis if the info-screen was in the visual field of a participant and which content was displayed. With the questionnaire it was possible to compare whether a participant's memory and self-assessment regarding length of attention towards the info-screen was consistent with the quantitative data.

14.5   Results

Participants' attitudes towards testing and advertisements. First of all we investigated how inconvenient participants felt because of the testing equipment. Overall participants reported in the questionnaire that they were not bothered very much by the helmet and the daypack (23% of the participants were not disturbed at all, 70% were disturbed a little bit, 5% felt severely disturbed by the equipment). Furthermore

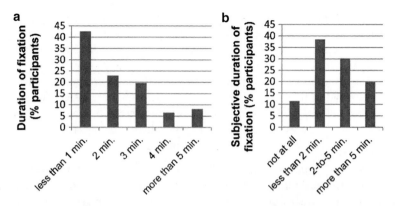

Fig. 14.2 (**a**) Percentage of participants' duration of fixation on the info-screen over the whole time spent in the tram. (**b**) Participants' estimation about the overall duration of fixation

most participants reported that they didn't feel nervous (64%) during the ride at all, 34% felt a little nervous and only 1% reported having felt very nervous. Regarding the participants attitude towards the info-screen two thirds of the participants rated the presence of the info-screen as being good, 20% where indifferent and 10% didn't like it at all. The preferred advertising media in general assessed with the questionnaire were television and posters.

Attention towards the info-screen. The eye tracking data reveals that of the 100 subjects included in the data analysis 61% fixated the info-screen at least once. The respective data from the questionnaire is not in line with the eye tracking data since 88 participants reported to have seen the info-screen.

From the 48.7 h all participants together spent in the tram, 23.06% of the time the info-screen was in the visual field of the participants, and in 3,64% of the time attention was directed towards the info-screen – i.e. the info-screen was fixated. Participants focused on the info-screen between some seconds and 9 min – on average for 104 s (see Fig. 14.2a for the frequency of fixations durations overall participants). Subjects were also asked in the questionnaire to measure their subjective feeling about the attention-span towards the info-screen. Most subjects thought about their attention-span being up to two minutes (see Fig. 14.2b), which corresponds to the measured average value of attention-span.

Differential effect of content-type. One of the main questions in this research was to investigate the visual attention on different types of content. Analyzing the fixation-time of different content-types shows that "news" got most fixation-time (4.54% of the overall testing time) followed by "sports/weather" (3.98%) and "entertainment" (3.81%). The remaining categories got around 3% except for "culture" which got 2.65% of the overall testing time. A further analysis with the distributions of the number of fixated frames on the info-screen for each participant and content-type, shows no significant differences between the content-types (p=0.39).

The differential effect of content-type was also addressed in the questionnaire by asking the participants whether one content-type is of interest for them or not.

Fig. 14.3 Percentage of participants rating the different content-types as interesting in the questionnaire

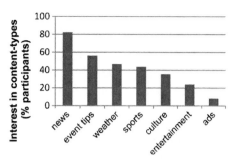

Fig. 14.4 Mean duration of fixation on the info-screen (in percent of the whole testing time) of participants' at different daytimes

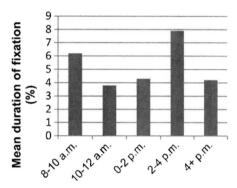

The (due to an organizational error left) 96 participants rated "news" and "event-tips" as most interesting, followed by "weather" and "sports" (see Fig. 14.3). These differences in interest towards the content-types can't be found in the eye tracking data in terms of a higher number of fixations.

Differential effect of daytime. The investigation of the attention towards the info-screen at different daytimes shows the longest mean fixation times between 8 and 10 a.m. and between 2 and 4 p.m. (see Fig. 14.4). A possible explanation for this might be the fact that in the morning participants' interest for news is higher than during the rest of the early day hours. The even higher peak in the afternoon could result from a relationship between the daytime and the number of travellers in the tram, which is in the early afternoon probably small.

Recall and recognition of the info-screen information. From all participants 80% were able to recall categories, and on average participants recalled three different categories. Twenty-seven percent were able to recall specific spots and logos and 18% recalled brand names. In the recognition task 43% of the participants were able to recognize spots correctly, but they only recognized between 1 and 4 advertisements (mean 1.37).

The correlation between fixation time on the info-screen and recall/recognition was tested next. The results show no significant correlation between number of frames fixated and number of content recalled ($r = 0.102$) and respectively content recognized ($r = 0.341$).

14.6 Discussion

The results of this study show that according to eye tracking data more than half of the participants did focus on the info-screen, and nearly nine out of ten reported to have noticed the screen. Therefore the info-screen gains a considerable amount of attention of the participants – even under the given free-exploration condition.

The content-type seems not related to the length of fixation time. For example few participants found "advertisement" interesting, but nevertheless the fixations on "advertisement" did not differ from any other content-type. A possible explanation for this could be the fact that fixation time on the info-screen does not imply that participants' were actively following the presented content. Or maybe participants' have the mental model of ads being not interesting.

Further, no significant correlation between duration of fixation on the screen and recall/recognition exist. One explanation for this result might be the experimental setup that participants had no idea about the purpose of their ride and no order to look at the info-screen. Another explanation could be the fact that – as already mentioned above – fixating the eye tracker does not implicitly mean perceiving its content.

Considering the fact that participants did not know about the aim of the study and the natural environment, those results are very interesting because of their explorative character. We learn from this study that fixation time on digital displays in public transport seems not to depend on content-type. Also, fixation time per se does not seem to be a suitable indicator for content-memorization.

The findings from this study can serve as a basis for future research, e.g. if we can actively and reliably catch people's attention in a natural environment like this one (or any other urban environment) and how we can optimize content for such a form of advertising to improve content memorization. Despite their similarities with TVs digital displays like the info-screen do miss audio as a channel for communicating with its audience, which requires separate considerations for pervasive advertisement.

14.7 Attention in Shopping Streets Towards Logos (Study 2)

In this section we describe the second field study which aimed to better understand, which areas and objects receive attention by pedestrians in an urban setting (shopping street). The basic research question was whether there is a significant influence of the users' movement on the direction of attention. Additional research questions address the influence of context variables (e.g. daytime and frequentation) on the relation of motion and attention and the effects of the relation of motion and attention on memory.

14.8   Method

Field Study Context. The study was conducted in the inner city of Graz (Austria) in a pedestrian shopping street, which represents a realistic urban setting.

Participants. 20 participants – males without contact lenses or glasses (to ensure a stable recording of eye tracking data) – were recruited. A financial allowance as a compensation for the participants' effort was offered. Because four of the participants could either not be tested because of bad weather or cancelled their participation, 16 study participants remained.

Material. The same mobile eye tracking system as in the first study was used to capture gaze movement data and scene video. Additionally built-in sensors of the Google Nexus One smartphone were used to capture GPS-position data. The position fixing component of the device is a GPS receiver, which is integrated directly within the chipset. The device is also equipped with integrated accelerometers and a tilt compensated magnetic sensor. Only the GPS-data will be used as the sensors do provide more accurate data. The conducted questionnaires include questions regarding e.g. demographic data, familiarity with the test area (Herrengasse), and free recall of shops in the test area.

Procedure. The study started with a detailed briefing. The aim of the study to investigate the visual attention in a shopping street was not revealed to the participants – instead of that they were informed that the study focuses on the improvement of eye tracking equipment. The participants were asked to act as natural as possible and try to ignore the eye tracking equipment as far as possible. Test participants signed a consent form and were asked to fill out a pretest-questionnaire. Then participants were equipped with the technical test setup and accompanied by a test facilitator on their way through the inner city of Graz. Participants were asked to follow a specific route (to reference GPS data tracks). Overall time of data capture per test person was about 15 min. Then the technical equipment of the participants was demounted and the data was saved. Participants were asked to fill out a final post-questionnaire and the financial allowance was paid.

Data Analysis. The main focus of this study is the relationship between eye tracking and motion tracking data. Therefore the synchronized data was investi-gated according to correlations between eye and body movement metrics. But also the general visual attention while walking through the shopping street was analyzed by considering how many fixations participants had in different areas of their visual field and on commercial logos.

14.9   Results

Visual attention and orientation while walking through a shopping street. The first part of the data analysis focused on the attention on different areas of the visual field based on the eye tracking data. Without considering the body orientation this – of

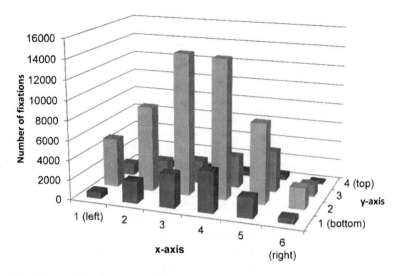

Fig. 14.5 Number of fixations over all participants at different areas of the visual field from left to right and bottom to top (752×480 pixels)

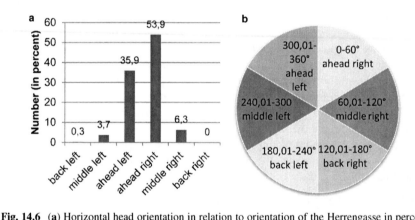

Fig. 14.6 (**a**) Horizontal head orientation in relation to orientation of the Herrengasse in percent from back left to back right. (**b**) Categorization of the horizontal orientation data

course – doesn't tell anything about the concrete direction of visual attention. As can be seen in Fig. 14.5 most times the gaze of participants falls in the horizontal middle in a somewhat lowered position. This result indicates that participants direct their eyes most of the time towards this default position so to say.

Also the horizontal head orientation of the alongside the shopping street moving participants is mostly aligned centered (see Fig. 14.6a, b), with a stronger orientation towards the right side (where the shops of the street in our test scenario were located). For this analysis the orientation of the street was taken into account. Regarding the vertical alignment of the head of pedestrian users (see Fig. 14.7a, b)

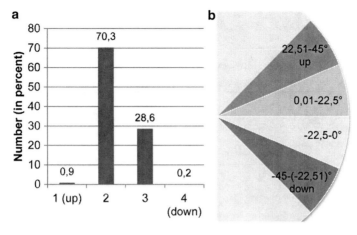

Fig. 14.7 (a) Number of vertical head orientations in percent from up to down. (b) Categorization of the vertical orientation data

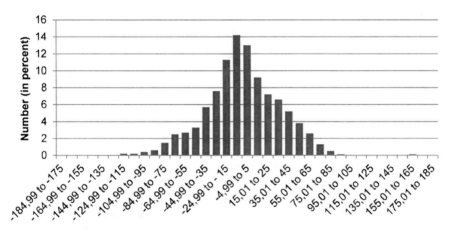

Fig. 14.8 Relative horizontal head orientation (difference between head and body orientation) expressed in degrees across all test participants

the average orientation is directed towards a slightly elevated position (mean = 4.10°), and there is more orientation towards the upper sphere than the lower sphere.

Relationships between head and body orientation data. The relationship between head and body orientation was analyzed with the data of the two motion sensors. The results show a distribution of orientation as might be expected: In the majority of cases the head orientation is aligned with the body orientation, with decreasing numbers for relative orientations to the sides (see Fig. 14.8).

Relationships between situational factor, visual attention, and motion. The relationship between the number of people on the shopping street (categorized into "few" and "many"), the motion speed of participants', the number of fixations on commercial

Table 14.1 Pearson correlations between the situational factor "number of people on the street", the attentional factor "fixation on logos" and the motion factors "motion speed" and "horizontal deviation of the head"

	Motion speed	Horizontal deviation of the head	Number of people on the street	Fixation on logos
Motion speed	1	−0.26	−0.05	−0.05
Horizontal deviation of the head	–	1	−0.02	−0.03
Number of people on the street	–	–	1	−0.02

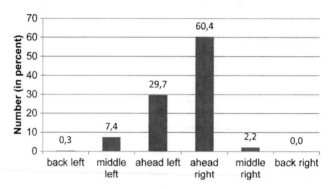

Fig. 14.9 Head orientation over all participants while they fixated on logos

logos and the horizontal centrality of the head orientation was calculated. The results (see Table 14.1) show an interesting correlation between motion speed and horizontal deviation: higher speed is associated with a smaller deviation from the centered orientation ($r=-0.26$, $p<0.01$). The other correlations (although also statistically significant) are rather small, but indicate e.g. that a lower motion speed is related to the fixations of logos and a higher number of people on the street. A subsequent comparison of means shows a significant difference in motion speed while fixating a logo and fixating something else than a logo (0.92 compared to 0.99 m/s) and between few and many people on the street (1.00 compared to 0.97 m/s).

Attention to logos. Besides its relationship to other variables (see previous section), the attention on advertising media in the shopping street was investigated also in general. The fixations on logos were annotated by means of the scene videos, and it was coded for each frame if the participants fixated a logo or something else. The results show that big size logos in the shopping street received a considerable amount of attention, because about 4% of the fixations are on them (89.5% are on something else, than logos and 6.5% couldn't be assessed in the videos). In 60.4 % of the logo fixations the head orientation of participants was ahead right, which means that they looked at logos on the same street side in front of them and didn't turn their heads too much to look at logos (see Fig. 14.9). 29.7% of the logo fixations were on the other side of the street.

14.10   Discussion

The investigation of pedestrians' attention and motion with the aid of mobile eye tracking delivers initial results relevant for advertisement strategies in a shopping street. The eye, head, and body orientation of the participants may indicate how advertisement should be placed. The eye gaze of participants were in average on a slightly lowered position, whereas the head was a bit elevated from straight ahead ($4.10°$). This can easily be explained by the needs of pedestrians to navigate between other pedestrians, the usage and consultation of personal devices (e.g. looking on the watch, consulting written materials, using electronic devices, etc.) and watching objects of interest in shopping windows, for which the head orientation doesn't need to be necessarily lowered. Interestingly 4% of fixations are directed to logos, and these fixations tend to relate slightly with the lower motion speed of participants', which is again related to the number of people on the street. Furthermore people tend to show less variation in their horizontal head orientation when they move faster. Since participants' fixated mainly logos which were straight ahead of them, and didn't look at logos beside of them, it may be advantageous to place logos so that they can be seen from more distance.

14.11   Attention on the Move – Summary of Findings

The two presented studies investigated the attention on advertising media in two different situations: within a digital display in public transport and towards logos in a pedestrian shopping street. The results show that the attention towards advertising media is in both situations not negligible. 61% of the participants fixated the info-screen at least once, and 3.64% of the time the participants' attention was on the display, although they could only see at the displays at certain positions in the tram. Similarly 4% of the visual attention of pedestrians in a shopping street was targeted on advertisement logos. The results also indicate that daytime and crowdedness (which are probably related to each other) may have an impact on the visual attention on advertisement, but for clear results this has to be investigated in a more systematic way. Interesting are the main orientations of attention of participants walking through a shopping street, which lies in position horizontally centered, and vertically lowered for eye gaze and respectively elevated for head orientation. While walking along shops, participants mainly looked at advertisement logos which were distant in front of them, so that they didn't turn the head to the side much. Furthermore logo fixation has been found related to a slower motion speed.

14.12   Implications for Pervasive Advertising

Initial implications for pervasive advertising in public spaces can be drawn from the presented studies. Digital displays installed in the public transportation systems evoke a decent amount of visual attention; regardless of the actual content (news,

Fig. 14.10 Shopping street
"Herrengasse" with logos
mounted at right angle to the
house walls

entertainment, advertisements etc.) they are transmitting (study 1). This result is even more interesting considering the fact that participants were not instructed to stand near by the displays to have the possibility to look at them. For plain advertisement logos the location and placement seems to be of high relevance, since people fixate logos located in front of them (study 2). Therefore logos which are mounted at right angle to the house walls might be seen better from their perspective (see Fig. 14.10) than those mounted parallel. The results of study 2 also indicate small relations between the logo fixation, motion speed, and number of fixations. A slower motion speed as well as fewer people on the street, slightly relates to logo fixations. This instance seems reasonable, since on the one side pedestrians with a higher motion speed have to be concentrated more on where they are walking and on the other side viewing logos could decelerate them. Furthermore people on the street could block the view on logos. However, because of the field design of the study, with many uncontrolled variables, the correlations are (although significant) very small. To clarify causality the relation between speed and logo fixation has to be investigated more systematically, within an experimental setting. The eye tracking and motion data of the pedestrians' reveals the ideal placement of logos at medium height, since most eye gazes and vertical head orientations are at this level. For future research it would be interesting to analyze the relationship between eye and head/body movements.

14.13 Discussion of Research Methods for Analyzing Attention

The used method of mobile eye tracking to investigate the concrete visual focus of participants in public situations has a great potential for researching perception and attention processes. Only by tracking the participants' eye gaze and motion valuable data about the actual attention and orientation towards advertisement can be assessed. However, the procedure needs a further development of tools for automatic processing, because so far the data handling is quite laborious. Also less obtrusive technology would be very much desirable to minimize possible influences of the tracking equipment on the users' behavior.

Even though these are two serious methodological issues, we still think eye tracking provides very valuable research data as they have the chance to also provide situational and not only out-of-context and summative data (as recall and recognition rates), therefore this method allows studying the involved perception processes in much more detail.

In future work we plan to develop formal models of the users' attention behavior to be able to quickly and cheaply estimate attention distributions in virtual models of the environment, thereby allowing considering these data already in the design phase of buildings and public spaces.

14.14 Limitations of the Studies

As for all research, for understanding the results the limitations of our two studies should be considered. Whereas the number of user was very high in the first study the results of the second study need to be interpreted more carefully as the number of users was much smaller. However, with regard to mobile eye tracking studies the number of users is still on the top of available research.

Another limitation that should be considered is possible effects of the used tracking technology on the movement pattern of the users. As the equipment is very well visible people might have behaved differently compared to casual situations. Users were asked after the tests whether the technology had an influence on their behavior or not, and a majority of users replied with minimal to no effect.

References

1. Babcock, J., Pelz, J.: Building a lightweight eyetracking headgear. In: Proceedings ACM SIGCHI: Eye Tracking Research and Applications, pp. 109–114. ACM, New York (2004)
2. Barlow, T., Wogalter, M.S.: Alcoholic beverage warnings in magazine and television advertisements. J. Consum. Res. **20**, 147–56 (1993)
3. Barnard, L., Yi, J.S., Jacko, J.A., Sears, A.: Capturing the effects of context on human performance in mobile computing systems. Pers. Ubiquit. Comput. **11**(46), 81–96 (2007)
4. Ben-Bassat, T., Shinar, D.: Ergonomic guidelines for traffic sign design increase sign comprehension. Hum. Fac. J. Hum. Fac. Erg. Soc. **48**(1), 182–195 (2006)
5. Chandon, P., Hutchinson, J.W., Bradlow, E.T., Young, S.H.: Does in-store marketing work? Effects of the number and position of shelf facings on brand attention and evaluation at the point of purchase. J. Market. **73**, 1–17 (2009)
6. Chatttington, M., Reed, N., Basacik, D., Flint, A., Parkes, A.: Investigating driver distraction: the effects of video and static advertising. Published Project Report PPR409. Transport Research Laboratory, London (2009)
7. Crundall, D., Van Loon, E., Underwood, G.: Attraction and distraction of attention with roadside advertisements. Accid Anal Prev **38**, 671–677 (2006)

8. Dewar, R.E., Ells, J.G., Mundy, G.: Reaction time as an index of traffic sign perception. Hum. Fac. J. Hum. Fac. Erg. Soc. **18**(4), 381–392 (1976)
9. Drèze, X., Hoch, S.J., Purk, M.E.: Shelf management and space elasticity. J. Retail. **70**(4), 301–326 (1994)
10. Droll, J., Eckstein, M.: Gaze control, change detection and the selective storage of object information while walking in a real world environment. Vis. Cogn. **17**(6/7), 1159–1184 (2009)
11. Duchowski, A.T.: A breadth-first survey of eye-tracking applications. Behav. Res. Meth. Instrum. Comput. **34**(4), 455–470 (2002)
12. Dunlop, M., Brewster, S.: The challenge of mobile devices for human computer interaction. PUC **6**, 235–236 (2002)
13. Erikson, C.W., St James, J.D.: Visual attention within and around the field of focal attention: A zoom lens model. Percep. Psychophy. **40**, 225–240 (1986)
14. Fairchild, M.D., Johnson, G.M., Babcock, J., Pelz, J.B.: Is your eye on the ball?: Eye tracking golfers while putting. Unpublished manuscript, Rochester Institute of Technology (2001)
15. Franchak, J.M, Kretch, K.S., Soska, K.C., Babcock, J.S., Adolph, K.E. Head-mounted eye-tracking of infants' natural interactions: A new method. In: Proceedings of the 1020 Symposium on Eye-Tracking Research & Applications, pp. 21–27. ACM, New York (2010)
16. Hansen, D.W., Ji, Q.: In the eye of the beholder: a survey of models for eyes and gaze. IEEE Trans. Pattern Anal Machine Intell. **32**(3), 478–500 (2010)
17. Harbluk, J.L., Noy, Y.I., Eizenmann, M.: Impact of cognitive distraction on driver visual behavior and vehicle control. Paper Presented at the 81st Annual Meeting of the Transportation Research Board, Washington, DC (2002)
18. Hart, B.M., Einhäuser, W.: The effect of terrain on eye movements while walking in the real world. Perception 38, ECVP Abstract Supplement, pp. 24–24 (2009)
19. Hayhoe, M., Ballard, D.: Eye movements in natural behavior. Trends Cogn. Sci. **9**(4), 188–194 (2005)
20. Hayhoe, M.M., Ballard, D.H., Triesch, J., Shinoda, H., Aivar, P., Sullivan, B.: Vision in natural and virtual environments. In: Proceedings of the 2002 Symposium on Eye Tracking Research & Applications, pp. 7–13. ACM, New York (2002)
21. Hayhoe, M.M., Shirvastava, A., Mruczek, R., Pelz, J.B.: Visual memory and motor planning in a natural task. J. Vis. **3**, 49–63 (2003)
22. Henderson, J.M.: Eye movements. In: Senior, C., Russell, T., Gazzaniga, M. (eds.) Methods in Mind (171–191). MIT Press, Cambridge (2006)
23. Huang, E.M., Koster, A., Borchers, J.: Overcoming assumptions and uncovering practices: When does the public really look at public displays. In: Proceedings of Pervasive 2008. LNCS, vol. 5013, pp. 228–243. (2008)
24. Land, M.F., Lee, D.N.: Where we look when we steer. Nature **369**, 742–744 (1994)
25. Lohse, G.L.: Consumer eye movement patterns on yellow pages advertising. J. Advert. **26**(1), 61–73 (1997)
26. Loo, R.: Individual differences and the perception of traffic Signs. Hum. Fac. J. Hum. Fac. Erg. Soc. **20**(1), 65–74 (1978)
27. Maughan, L., Gutnikov, S., Stevens, R.: Like more, look more. Look more, like more: the evidence from eye-tracking. J. Brand Manag. **14**(4), 335–342 (2007)
28. Nagata, S.: Multitasking and interruptions during mobile web tasks. In: Proceedings of the Human Factors and Ergonomics Society 47th Annual Meeting, pp. 1341–1346. Mira Digital Publishing, St. Louis (2003)
29. Neerincx, M.A., Streefkerk, J.W.: Interacting in desktop and mobile con-text: emotion, trust and task performance. In: Proceedings of EUSAI Conference. Springer, Eindhoven (2003)
30. Ng, A.W.Y., Chan, A.H.S.: The variation of influence of icon features on icon usability. Ind. Eng. Res. **4**(1), 1–7 (2007)
31. OAAA (Outdoor advertising association of America).:. The PRS eye tracking studies: Validating outdoor's impact in the marketplace. Retrieved online from: http://www.truckads.com/pdf-bin/EyeTrackingStudy.pdf (1999–2000). Accessed 15 Sept 2010

32. Pelz, J.B., Canosa, R.: Oculomotor behavior and perceptual strategies in complex tasks. Vision. Res. **41**, 3587–3596 (2001)
33. Poole, A., Ball, L.J.: Eye tracking in human-computer interaction and usability research. In: Ghaoui, C. (ed.) Encyclopedia of Human Computer Interaction, pp. 211–219. Idea Group, Hershey (2005)
34. Posner, M.I., Snyder, C.R.R., Davidson, B.J.: Attention and the detection of signals. J. Exp. PsycholGen. **109**, 160–174 (1980)
35. Rothkopf, C.A., Ballard, D.H., Hayhoe, M.M.: Task and context determine where you look. J. Vision. **7**(14), 1–20 (2007)
36. Schuchard, R.A., Connell, B.R., Griffiths, P.: An environmental investigation of wayfinding in a nursing home. In: Proceedings of the 2006 Symposium on Eye Tracking Research & Application, pp. 33–33. ACM, New York (2006)
37. Tan, K.H., Kriegman, D.J., Ahuja, N.: Appearance-based eye gaze estimation. In: Proceedings of the Sixth IEEE Workshop on Applications of Computer Vision (WACV'02), pp. 191–195. IEEE Computer Society, Washington, DC (2002)
38. Treisman, A.M., Gelade, G.: A feature-integration theory of attention. Cognit. Psychol. **12**, 97–136 (1980)
39. Wallace, B.: Driver distraction by advertising: genuine risk or urban myth? Municip. Eng. **156**, 185–190 (2003)
40. Wessel, D., Mayr, E., Knipfer, K.: Re-viewing the museum visitor's view. In: Workshop Research Methods in Informal and Mobile Learning, Institute of Education, London (2007)
41. Young, M.S., Mahfound, J.M.: Driven to distraction: determining the effects of roadside advertising on driver attention. Ergonomics Research Group Report. Brunel University, Uxbridge (2007)

Chapter 15
Ambient Persuasion in the Shopping Context

Wolfgang Reitberger, Alexander Meschtscherjakov, Thomas Mirlacher, and Manfred Tscheligi

Abstract In this chapter, we give an overview on the use of pervasive computing to persuade customers in the shopping context and therefore present novel approaches towards Pervasive Persuasive Advertising. We synthesize the results of three studies, each of which lasted several days and was conducted with situated prototypes in actual shopping environments. The aim of these prototypes was to influence the customers' shopping behavior by means of persuasive strategies and to ultimately improve the overall shopping experience. Based on these studies, we give a characterization of the shopping context and propose a contextually adequate persuasive strategy based on striking the balance between engagement and unobtrusiveness.

15.1 Introduction

The transition of the retail environment towards the creation of an increasingly sophisticated shopping experience [1] opens up a great potential for Pervasive Computing applications in general and specifically Pervasive Advertising in this context. Providing customers with an ambient shopping environment can raise the customers' awareness of the shop, enhance the overall efficiency of the shopping process, support the delivery of different messages to the customers, and ultimately improve the overall shopping experience. Specifically, Ambient Persuasion Technologies can be used as advertising means and to help customers to make more advantageous buying decisions. They lead to an increased customer engagement and allow combining the benefits of online shopping with those of "real" shops.

W. Reitberger(✉) • A. Meschtscherjakov • T. Mirlacher • M. Tscheligi
University of Salzburg, Salzburg, Austria
e-mail: wolfgang.reitberger@sbg.ac.at; alexander.meschtscherjakov@sbg.ac.at;
thomas.mirlacher@sbg.ac.at; manfred.tscheligi@sbg.ac.at

J. Müller et al. (eds.), *Pervasive Advertising*, Human-Computer Interaction Series,
DOI 10.1007/978-0-85729-352-7_15, © Springer-Verlag London Limited 2011

In this chapter, we give an overview on three consecutive case studies of Ambient Persuasion prototypes in the shopping context. The aim of these studies was to deploy Pervasive Advertising applications and to enhance the shopping experience in real life. In order to create a new shopping experience, retail stores were equipped with Pervasive Computing technologies, especially Ambient Displays. The results of these studies are synthesized in order to give HCI researchers and practitioners insights about the design, deployment, and user experience of such applications. Based on these results, future possibilities and challenges for applying Ambient and Pervasive technologies towards Pervasive Advertising within shopping environments are discussed.

15.2 Background

Persuasive Technology is defined as "any interactive computing system designed to change people's attitudes or behaviors" [6]. One of the key prerequisites for a successful persuasive intervention is to interact with the user at the right time and place. According to Fogg, important strategies for Persuasive Technologies are social facilitation, persistence, and simplicity [7]. Complementary to Fogg's strategies, Cialdini [3] names six basic tendencies of human behavior, such as reciprocity or scarcity, that can be utilized for persuasion. Two different fundamental persuasive routes (central and peripheral) are laid out in the Elaboration Likelihood Model (ELM) [13, 14]. The central route to persuasion involves the presentation of arguments, which are central to the issue at hand and require careful thinking and deliberation on the side of the recipient or persuadee. On the contrary, the peripheral route requires much less cognitive processing and relies more on aspects like the attractiveness of the source, the message length and the presence of positive or negative stimuli in the context in which the message was presented.

Whereas the first two presented case studies describing an ambient store map use the central route of persuasion, the case study third case study about an interactive mannequin is based on applying the peripheral persuasive route.

15.2.1 Ambient Persuasion

The term Ambient Persuasion refers to the use of Persuasive Technologies that rely on context sensing and a network infrastructure, to enable the delivery of context sensitive system behavior and persuasive content, personalized for the user, at the right time and at the right place [18]. This opportune moment is also referred to as kairos [6]. A persuasive intervention, which takes place at this opportune moment, has an increased persuasive potential, i.e. a Persuasive Technology is more likely to change a user's attitude or behavior when the principle of kairos is taken into account. Ambient Persuasion constitutes an innovative synthesis of the paradigms of Ambient/Pervasive Computing and Persuasion. The Ambient Intelligence system uses implicit and explicit input to make inferences about the state of the user and the environment and thus enables the delivery of a contextually adequate persuasive message or interaction.

The concept of Ambient Persuasion was also discussed as an element of societal interfaces, which are advanced interaction approaches that are explicitly designed to solve or improve specific societal problems by utilizing HCI to create a more socially and ecologically sustainable society and to support the quality of life [24]. There are applications that have already employed Ambient Persuasion successfully in order to change peoples' attitudes and behaviors regarding environmental sustainability [8], to support proper posture in the work place [12], and to foster a more physically active lifestyle [4].

15.2.2 Shopping Context

The shopping context in particular is a challenge for the design of Pervasive Interfaces. In shopping malls, advertisement messages and other distractions are omnipresent. Therefore, designers have to find a middle compromise between the unobtrusive nature of Pervasive Interfaces, and the necessity not to be overlooked by the user who is already confronted with an information-rich environment.

Underhill [25] claims that there are three important benefits which can only be offered in "real shops": Firstly, sensory perception like grasping, trying on and trying out, smelling and other sensual stimuli; secondly, immediate gratification; and thirdly, social interaction. Therefore, the shopping experience in retail stores is completely different to the experience shoppers get when buying in online stores. By integrating pervasive technologies into real stores, they can be enhanced without sacrificing the benefits that these stores offer already.

Several researchers within the HCI community [2, 10, 27] have conducted research on public displays. Schmidt et al. [22] discuss how to improve the user experience by tailoring advertisements and to improve the understanding of the advertising space. Researchers in the field of pervasive computing have already investigated how digital signage can be integrated into the shopping experience in retail stores. Recently, these displays and other pervasive computing applications have been exploited within the shopping context.

Pinhanez and Podlaseck [15] applied their studies on frameless displays to the shopping environment. They designed and implemented projections within the retail environment to attract shoppers or inform them about special products.

A similar approach is followed by Sukaviriya et al. [23]. In their study, text, and imagery projection into physical environments as well as vision systems and sensors for user interaction are used to design a retail store. An interesting approach on how public displays can augment shop windows is presented by van Loenen et al. [26]. The Intelligent Shop Window (ISW) is a public display that reacts to the presence of users in two modes. In the signage mode, it displays advertising images related to the shop. In the interaction mode, it provides additional product information whenever a person looks into the shop window or touches the screen.

The introduction of Persuasive Technologies in a retail setting was studied by Russell [21]. The paper specifically discusses the use of video displays depicting advertising messages and their persuasive effects on the customers. They conducted a field study by comparing customer exit interviews in various retail stores, which showed that the customers noticed the displays, recalled the content, and were influenced towards the desired effect.

Typically, researchers try to improve the online shopping experience to compensate for what is missing compared to shopping experiences in "real shops". The approach presented here employs the opposite strategy: to enhance the shopping experience by merging the advantages provided by online shops with the benefits of shops in the real world.

15.3 Situated Prototype Studies of Ambient Persuasion

The first two studies presented in this paper are based on the perCues framework [17] which enables the individual users to relate their actions to those of a larger group of users, enabling them to adjust their behavior based on this newly formed awareness. Specifically for the context of shopping, the purpose was to make the users aware of the collective behavior of other customers over a certain period of time. The ultimate aim was to influence their shopping behavior by enabling them to make more informed decisions based on the collective intelligence of the previous shoppers. In this case, the global factor is the shopping behavior of all customers in a shop over a certain period of time, e.g. all customer activity in a shop over the last week.

The collective behavior is a rather elusive factor, which cannot be easily grasped by the individual without the help of a perCues application. Yet again, this factor can have a profound impact on the shopping behavior of the individual user. Through awareness of this factor, the user can discern the popular areas of the shop from the not so popular areas and adjust his behavior accordingly, being able to make more informed and hopefully intelligent decisions. Giving the individual user information about the collective behavior of other customers empowers the individual in a context where more or less subtle forms of manipulation are usually the norm. Instead of manipulating the user into behaving in a desired way or creating false desires in order to make him buy a product that he ultimately might not even need, the perCues application puts the individual in the center of the decision process. It does not manipulate the user to change his behavior, on the contrary, it only presents further information which was previously not visible to him and leaves it to the user how he ultimately acts on this information.

The third study included a prototypical application that aimed to address the user at an earlier stage in the shopping process, when he is still outside of the store. Rather than presenting information to the user, this application, an interactive

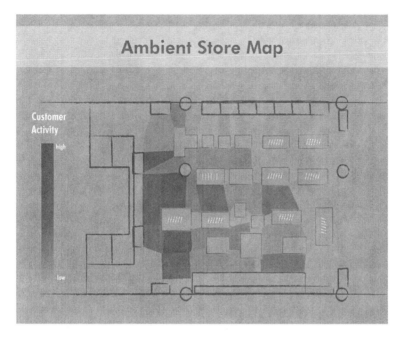

Fig. 15.1 Digital signage prototype entitled "Ambient Store Map" as deployed in a sporting goods store. Dark areas (originally colored *red*) show increased customer activity

mannequin in a store window, aimed to engage the user and catch his attention. This design decision was made based on the lessons learned from the first two studies. There it was found out that in order to benefit from ambient applications like the ones outlined above, the customer needs to be made aware of their existence, a task that is not trivial in an environment like the shopping context which is saturated with media and full of distractions.

15.3.1 Case Study 1: Enhancing the Shopping Experience with Digital Signage

Usually researchers try to improve the online shopping experience to compensate for what is missing compared to shopping experiences in "real shops". The approach presented here employs the opposite strategy: to enhance the shopping experience by merging the advantages provided by online shops with the benefits of shops in the real world.

For this case study [16], we equipped a retail store with a digital signage (see Fig. 15.1) by using the metaphor of a store map. One reason for this decision was that an exploration of the mall where the application would be deployed showed that static maps were already used to give customers an overview of the mall and its shops.

Fig. 15.2 Digital signage prototype as deployed in a sporting goods store, where the study took place

Additionally, using this metaphor we could build on the previous knowledge of the users and their existing experience with maps. The use of darker and lighter colors to indicate different levels of activity also follows the standard map conventions in other contexts, where e.g. darker colors indicate higher altitudes or higher temperatures.

The figure shows a map of the sporting goods store, where the application prototype was deployed. The areas colored in different shades of red (in the figure visible as darker areas) indicate the customer activity in the particular parts of the shop. This design integrates the awareness of the activity of other customers, a feature that was previously limited to online shopping, with the qualities of real world retail shops such as sensual perception, social interaction and immediate gratification.

In order to research our application, we deployed a prototype in a single brand sporting goods store where we conducted a 3-day field study (see Fig. 15.2). The study was carried out during the regular opening hours of the mall. Therefore, we were able to recruit a considerable number of participants. The results of the study indicate potentials and challenges for an improvement of the shopping experience with pervasive computing technologies.

To evaluate the prototype, we combined three different methods. Firstly, 400 customers in the shop were directly observed. In this way, social interactions with companions or shop personnel as well as products and areas of special interest, and the usage of technologies such as mobile phones could be investigated. The particular focus of these observations was targeted towards the perception of the digital signage, the duration of fixation as well as towards the following actions. The second method was to conduct short in situ interviews with 50 customers, who had just investigated the digital signage. This way, we aimed to find out if the customers understood the information delivered through the digital signage. Furthermore, they were asked for suggestions on how to improve the prototype. Finally, video material recorded through a spectacles camera worn by 37 customers was evaluated and utilized in the study.

The findings indicate that the data presented in the map was easy to interpret and to understand for most users. 46 out of 50 customers who were asked in short in situ interviews understood the information delivered through the digital signage. It was one of the design challenges to find the right balance between a short and long time interval as basis for the displayed customer activity. The actual setup of our application displays the collective behavior of the shoppers over a period of 30 min. The result was a map, which only changed gradually over time based on the collective customer activity.

During the field study, it was discovered that the users liked to see their own impact on the map as well. This was the case when we set the time interval to 1 min or less so that the individual activity could change the map easily. The users immediately became more interested in the map, since the map reacted instantly to their behavior. This finding indicates that the display of the individual position is a key affordance also of an ambient store map, just like the "you are here" signs on traditional public maps. One challenge for future development of the ambient store map concept will be the integration of the individual impact with the collective impact. The user should be able to grasp the collective activity and yet see the impact of his own behavior as well.

Additionally, the user feedback indicated that the information richness of the visualization adds to its perceived usefulness. Some users e.g. suggested adding information such as the contents of a particular shelf. These findings were especially useful for the redesign of the map presented in the next section.

15.3.2   Case Study 2: A Dynamic Map in a Retail Store

The prototype we developed for the second case study was based on the results we obtained from the first study described above. It consists of a digital signage (see Fig. 15.3) showing an enhanced store map [11], which combines the dynamic visualization of customer activity (e.g. hot-spots, sales ranks) with conventional map elements (e.g. product locations, promotions). On the right side of the figure, a list with iconic representations of the different products on sale is displayed. These icons are used to mark the locations of these items in the map. The top left part of the display pictures bestseller items, which are also emphasized by a visual cue (animated glowing). In the bottom left corner on the screen is a legend for the color scheme, which is used in the map to dynamically indicate the customer activity.

In order to research our prototype map in the context of shopping, we deployed it in a retail store and conducted a 3-day in situ study. The study consisted of a structured interview based on a two-part questionnaire divided into open questions and

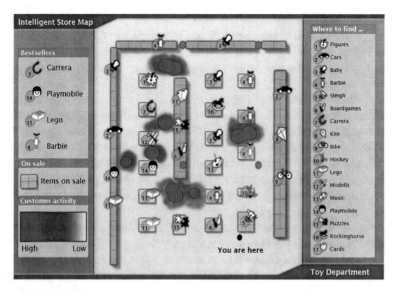

Fig. 15.3 Iterated version of the digital signage including a bestseller list on the *left side* and a store directory on the *right side*

statements. Since the study took place in the busy shopping environment, we decided not to hand out the questionnaire but to conduct a guided interview with 47 customers to increase the rate of return.

The study results indicate that customers immediately understood benefits in areas where we used concepts already established in the shopping environments (e.g., promotions). The reaction to less conventional concepts like customer activity information was mixed. Information about bestsellers was valued highly, whereas the information about frequently visited areas was valued lowly. Our findings show that the assigned value for customers is related to the personal value and to the size of the mapped area. In general, the study revealed that the context of shopping is a promising but challenging area for pervasive computing.

15.3.3 Case Study 3: A Persuasive Interactive Mannequin for Shop Windows

This case study outlines an interactive mannequin [19] for persuading bypassing customers to extend the time they stay in front of a shop window (see Fig. 15.4).

The mannequin was designed and prototyped to be seamlessly integrated into a real shop window, constituting an Ambient Persuasion Interface. The design concept of the virtual mannequin is based on actual "real world" mannequins. Based on implicit input from the customers, the mannequin reacts on their presence by

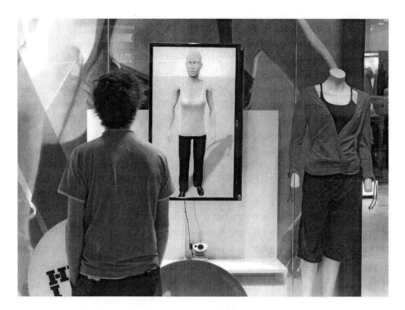

Fig. 15.4 Interactive mannequin deployed in a shop window

looking into their direction. We implemented a prototype of the Persuasive Interactive Mannequin (PIM) as a 3D model, visualized on a large LCD, and deployed it in a retail store within a shopping mall.

In a 3-day field study with 102 participants, we evaluated this prototype of the PIM, by gathering data for incremental development steps, validating preliminary design assumptions, and obeying user feedback. In order to study the prototypical implementation, we conducted a series of structured interviews. Like in the second case study, the main reason for this methodological choice was the increased compliance we expected from an interview as opposed to questionnaires.

In general, participants had positive feelings towards the Persuasive Interactive Mannequin (mean 3.26, SD = 1.28). 45.5% of the participants were very pleased or pleased with the PIM.

The study also revealed that the PIM could attract the customers' attention. Regarding this persuasive effect of the PIM prototype, our results show that the PIM prototype lead to an increased perceived duration of stay in front of the shop window. In sum 75.2% of the participants agreed that they remained longer than normally in front of this particular shop window, whereas only 17.9% stated that the PIM did not change their duration of stay. This assessment is further supported by our observation. The discovered effect can be explained through the customer's implicit interaction with the PIM. As soon as the PIM has gained the customers' attention, the challenge is to shift from implicit to a more explicit form of interaction in order to engage the customer. To accomplish this, the next version of the PIM will include the most frequently requested additional features. This could comprise the possibility to change the type and color of its clothes using gesture input. Additional information such as price (in particular special offers), fabric, available sizes, and colors could be displayed gradually based on the length of stay. Personalized recommendations could be visualized based on information stored on a customer's loyalty card (e.g. suitable shoes based on the customer's shopping history), which could be implemented for instance through near-field communication technologies (NFC).

15.4 Implications from the Ambient Persuasion Field Studies

The above mentioned field studies took place over a period of 3 years and lead to a deeper understanding of the design of Ambient Persuasion Interfaces in the shopping context. The main questions we want to address based on these field studies are as follows:

(RQ1) What are the most relevant context factors to inform the design of Ambient Persuasion in the shopping context?
(RQ2) Is Weiser's vision of calm computing, which stands as a paradigm for Ambient Technologies, still an appropriate means for guiding the design of Pervasive Technologies in the shopping context?
(RQ3) What is the adequate persuasive strategy to influence customers in the shopping context?

In the following sections, we will discuss these research questions.

15.4.1 Characterizing the Shopping Context (RQ1)

Based on the three studies and the experiences we gained by designing, implementing, and researching Ambient Persuasion Interfaces in the shopping context, we were able to identify five universally relevant context factors to inform the design of such interfaces. This characterization strives to demonstrate that there is not one monolithic shopping context but rather different distinct shopping contexts with diverse characteristics. Firstly, there is the aisle of the mall (see Table 15.1), which constitutes a large open space, inviting customers to leisurely stroll from one shop window to the next. Finding your way in this space is a task of medium complexity.

The single brand sporting goods store has a higher level of physical obstruction by medium height shelves and tables with goods on display. Customers are still able to overlook the space fairly easily and the limited number of products makes finding a particular desired item not too complicated. Contrarily, the large national chain grocery store where the second case study was conducted constitutes an environment with a much higher level of complexity. This is due to the large selection of

Table 15.1 Context factors in the shopping environment

Context factor	Shopping mall aisle (CS1)	Sporting goods store (CS2)	Grocery store (CS3)
Physical structure	Large open space, mid-grade difficult navigation, medium complexity	Mid-size semi obstructed space, easy navigation, medium complexity	Large obstructed space, difficult navigation, high complexity
Stress/time constraints	Leisurely strolling, few time constraints	Relaxed browsing, some time constraints	High stress factor, little time to spare
Motivation	Spending time, entertainment, enjoyment	Buy something nice to have	Fulfill basic needs
Attention level	Particularly high level of distraction by competing cues	Broad focus on different goods on sale and on branding elements of the store	Focus on getting the job done
Social factors	Diverse range of customers	Younger, mostly male shoppers, alone, couples, or groups of friends	Wide range of customers, comparably more families and children

products and the considerable size of the store, which is structured in a labyrinthine way with high shelves that block the view of the customer. Most customers in this environment focus their attention on getting the task of buying the desired groceries done, and do not react favorable to any distractions.

For an Ambient Persuasion application to be useful, the context in which it is needs to be sufficiently complex, as there is little need for additional information if all relevant aspects of the context can be easily understood by the user without the help of technology anyway. For example, a tiny local grocery store consisting of one main retail space can be easily grasped by the customer without the help of technology, whereas in a large hypermarket the customer can benefit from the introduction of an Ambient Persuasion application that would support him mastering the complexity of this situation.

15.4.2 Striking the Balance Between Being Engaging and Being Unobtrusive (RQ2)

In the context of shopping, it is necessary to aim for designs that strike the balance between being engaging and being unobtrusive. Often, Ambient Displays are used to provide information peripherally. Their unobtrusive nature makes it sometimes uncertain whether a person notices the information displayed or not. At the same time, Ambient Displays should not distract persons from their main tasks.

Consequently, a major design challenge for such interfaces is the shift of information from the periphery to the center of the users' attention. This transition from the background to the foreground has to be performed in a cognitively adequate way, in order to make an Ambient Display helpful and efficient instead of distracting and annoying. The findings of the two studies of prototypes of enhanced store maps in different retail stores indicated that while they were able to attract the attention of the majority of the customers, for some customers the design was not engaging enough to be noticed. Based on these results, we decided to move on from the notion that merely an Ambient Display is perceived which implies a certain passivity of the interface design. The resulting design consists of an interactive mannequin, which does not require active input on the behalf of the user since it implicitly reacts to his presence, but still actively tries to engage the user precisely through this reaction. Instead of waiting for the user to incidentally perceive this interface, the design aims to actively lure the user in order to shift the focus of his attention towards the display.

15.4.3 Developing a Contextually Adequate Persuasive Strategy (RQ3)

Based on our experiences in the shopping context, we developed a multi-step persuasion strategy. Fundamentally, there is a difference between micro- and macrosuasion. Microsuasion has the goal of achieving only small and incremental behavior and attitude changes, whereas macrosuasion aims at a comprehensive change in behavior and attitude. In the shopping context, traditional methods aim at an outcome at the level of macrosuasion, ultimately leading to a buying decision. With Pervasive Technologies, we aim to foster a discrete microsuasion strategy, aiming for a sequence of minor persuasive effects. Each step builds on the success of the previous persuasive intervention. The sum of these small steps ultimately results in the desired behavior.

When looking at the interaction process of how customers interact with ambient persuasion applications in the shopping context, we identified a sequence of persuasive steps. Firstly, the ambient persuasion application has to attract the attention of the customer. Hereby, the application has to compete against a variety of other attractions within the shopping context in order to stand out. Secondly, once the digital signage has acquired this attention, the second step is to retain the focus as long as possible (engagement). Thirdly, additional information, e.g. about the products in the store, and further persuasive cues can be presented to the customer. The first step focuses on the creation of awareness, which is difficult in the shopping context, because of its distractive nature where the user is constantly subjected to persuasive cues. Henceforth, it is necessary to create an interface that stands out and attracts the customer's attention.

With our first study about digital signage in a sporting goods store, we aimed to tailor the public display to the shop design to integrate it as unobtrusively as possible. The study results indicated that this approach was too unobtrusive for some users, because it was too calm and too abstract. In the next step, we designed an iterated version of the map for a retail store where we made the map metaphor as clear as possible and less abstract than before. The map contained specific useful information such as bestsellers, items on sale, and location information. In our third study, with the interactive mannequin we employed a different persuasive approach. Like in the first studies, the digital signage was seamlessly integrated into the shopping context, again using a familiar and appropriate metaphor – that of a mannequin. The mannequin was not designed to gain attraction merely by its presence, but rather aimed at gaining the awareness of customers already looking into the shop window. By actively reacting to implicit input from the customer, we actively created a new situation, which we could use to further guide the user. Now that the first microsuasive step of creating awareness was achieved, the next step was to provide additional interesting information and try to engage the customer to actively interact with the Ambient Persuasion Interface. In this way, the user's attention is secured and he can be subjected to further persuasive cues. The sum of the microsteps described above, together fulfills the aim of influencing the user to either enter the shop or make a buying decision.

15.5   Conclusion and Outlook

We have presented how technology can be used to influence customer behavior in order to foster Pervasive Advertising. Based on our results in this context, we argue that the design principles of ambient and pervasive interfaces in shopping environments need to evolve from Weiser's original notion of calm computing [28]. In agreement with Rogers [20], we propose to move on from calm computing and replace it with the new aim of creating engaging user experiences with ambient and pervasive technologies. This is particularly necessary because in the shopping context there is a fierce contest for the awareness of the user from all sides.

In this attention economy [5] all stakeholders compete for one scarce resource: the attention of the customer. Ambient interfaces that follow this new design approach may be ambient in the sense of the word, which means that they are integrated into the environment of the user and surround him, but they are not unobtrusive or disappearing in the sense of the original vision for such interfaces. Rather, they have to actively react to the presence of the user, finding the right moment for maximal engagement based on implicit input about the situation and the context of the user. Further research regarding a deeper understanding of contextual attention and specifically the underlying factors that influence the attention of users is needed to inform the design of digital signage in the shopping context.

Considering our findings, digital signage in the context of shopping does not need to be designed to be perceived actively and consciously. It just needs to be tightly interwoven into the environment so that it can be perceived peripherally and unconsciously, thus also reducing the cognitive load of the user. In this way, it is also possible to introduce a new interface as an addition to the already overloaded and noisy shopping environment without overly disturbing or annoying the user.

Our future work will take observations in the area of Neuromarketing by Lindstrom [9] into account, which state that 85% of the time people's brains are on what he calls autopilot. Whereas Lindstrom specifically points out that he only wants to study what goes on in people's brain on an unconscious level when they make buying decisions, our approach would go one step further by subliminally persuading the users and influencing them at the tipping point (kairos) of their buying decisions.

References

1. Bäckstrom, K., Johansson, U.: Creating and consuming experiences in retail store environments: comparing retailer and consumer perspectives. J. Retail. Consum. Serv. 13(6), 417–430 (2006)
2. Brignull, H., Rogers, Y.: Enticing people to interact with large public displays in public spaces. In: Proceedings of INTERACT'03. Ios Press, Zurich (2003)
3. Cialdini, R.B.: Influence: Science and Practice. Allyn & Bacon, Boston (2000)
4. Consolvo, S., McDonald, D.W., Landay, J.A.: Theory-driven design strategies for technologies that support behavior change in everyday life. In: CHI '09: Proceedings of the 27th International Conference on Human Factors in Computing Systems. ACM, Boston (2009)
5. Davenport, T., Beck, J.C.: The Attention Economy: Understanding the New Currency of Business. Harvard Business School Press, Boston (2001)
6. Fogg, B.J.: Persuasive Technology: Using Computers to Change What We Think and Do. Morgan Kaufmann Publishers Inc., San Francisco (2003)
7. Fogg, B.J.: The six most powerful persuasion strategies. In: Persuasive 2006, vol. 3962. Springer, Eindhoven (2006)
8. Gustafsson, A., Gyllenswärd, M.: The power-aware cord: energy awareness through ambient information display. In: CHI '05: CHI '05 Extended Abstracts on Human Factors in Computing Systems. ACM, Portland (2005)
9. Lindstrom, M.: Buy-Ology: Truth and Lies about Why We Buy. Doubleday, Garden City (2008)
10. McCarthy, J.F., Costa, T.J., Liongosari, E.S.: UniCast, OutCast & GroupCast: three steps toward ubiquitous, peripheral displays. In: UbiComp '01: Proceedings of the 3 rd International Conference on Ubiquitous Computing. Springer-Verlag, Atlanta (2001)
11. Meschtscherjakov, A., Reitberger, W., Lankes, M., Tscheligi, M.: Enhanced shopping: a dynamic map in a retail store. In: UbiComp 2008: Proceedings of the 10th International Conference on Ubiquitous Computing, vol. 344. ACM, Seoul (2008)
12. Obermair, C., Reitberger, W., Meschtscherjakov, A., Lankes, M., Tscheligi, M., et al.: perFrames: persuasive picture frames for proper posture. In: Øhrstrøm, P. (ed.) Persuasive Technology. Lecture Notes in Computer Science, vol. 5033, pp. 128–139. Springer, Berlin/Heidelberg (2008). doi:10.1007/978-3-540-68504-3_12
13. Petty, R.E., Cacioppo, J.T.: Attitudes and Persuasion: Classic and Contemporary Approaches. Westview Press, Boulder (1996)
14. Petty, R.E., Cacioppo, J.T., Strathman, A.J., Priester, J.: Persuasion: Psychological In-sights and Perspectives, pp. 81–116. Sage, Thousand Oaks (2005)
15. Pinhanez, C., Podlaseck, M.: To frame or not to frame: the role and design of frameless displays in ubiquitous applications. In: UbiComp 2005: International Conference on Ubiquitous Computing. Springer, Berlin/Heidelberg (2005)
16. Reitberger, W., Obermair, C., Ploderer, B., Meschtscherjakov, A., Tscheligi, M.: Enhancing the shopping experience with ambient displays: a field study in a retail store. In: AmI 2007. Springer, Berlin/Heidelberg (2007)

17. Reitberger, W., Ploderer, B., Obermair, C., Tscheligi, M.: The perCues framework and its application for sustainable mobility. In: Persuasive 2007, vol. 4744. Springer, Palo Alto (2007)

18. Reitberger, W., Tscheligi, M., de Ruyter, B.E.R., Markopoulos, P.: Surrounded by ambient persuasion. In: CHI 2008: Extended Abstracts on Human Factors in Computing Systems. ACM, Florence (2008)

19. Reitberger, W., Meschtscherjakov, A., Mirlacher, T., Scherndl, T., Huber, H., Tscheligi, M., Mirnig, N., Pöhr, F.: A persuasive interactive Mannequin for shop windows. In: Persuasive 2009. ACM Press, Claremont (2009)

20. Rogers, Y.: Moving on from Weiser's vision of calm computing: engaging UbiComp experiences. In: UbiComp 2006: Proceedings of the 8th International Conference on Ubiquitous Computing, vol. 4206. Springer, Orange County (2006)

21. Russell, M.G.: Benevolence and effectiveness: persuasive technology's spillover effects in retail settings. In: Persuasive 2009. ACM Press, Claremont (2009)

22. Schmidt, A., Alt, F., Holleis, P., Müller, J., Krüger, A.: Creating log files and click streams for advertisements in physical space. Adjunct Proceedings of UbiComp 2008 (2008)

23. Sukaviriya, N., Podlaseck, M., Kjeldsen, R., Levas, A., Pingali, G., Pinhanez, C.: Augmenting a retail environment using steerable interactive displays. In: CHI 1992: Proceedings of the Conference on Human Factors and Computing Systems. ACM, Monterey (1992)

24. Tscheligi, M., Reitberger, W.: Persuasion as an ingredient of societal interfaces. Interactions 14(5), 41–43 (2007)

25. Underhill, P.: Why We Buy: The Science of Shopping. Simon & Schuster, New York (2000)

26. van Loenen, E., Lashina, T., van Doorn, M.: Interactive shop windows. In: Ambient Lifestyle: From Concept to Experience. BIS Publishers, Amsterdam (2006)

27. Vogel, D., Balakrishnan, R.: Interactive public ambient displays: transitioning from implicit to explicit, public to personal, interaction with multiple users. In: UIST '04: Proceedings of the 17th Annual ACM Symposium on User Interface Software and Technology. ACM, Santa Fe (2004)

28. Weiser, M., Brown, J.S.: The Coming Age of Calm Technology. Xerox PARC, Palo Alto (1996)

Chapter 16
Interacting with Sound

Max Meier and Gilbert Beyer

Abstract In this chapter we present future opportunities for using sound within pervasive advertising. We focus on current trends of interacting with sound, which we believe will have a strong influence on sound branding in the near future. We start giving an overview on the topics of sound branding and music making. Then we outline requirements, application areas and design issues for interactive music systems from an advertising and musicological perspective. From the advertising point of view, the benefit of music is that it is a strong vehicle to convey a memorable message to the target group. Originally used as jingle in radio and television ads or as background component in shopping malls, nowadays sounds are also used within interactive media in the internet and in digital signage. Yet, there have been only very limited attempts to include sound itself to the interactive experience. We describe in detail an approach that enables users to control advertising sounds by the interaction, utilizing a novel technique of algorithmic composition based on soft constraints. That followed, we present a public display prototype for interactive advertising music, and close with first results from a user study.

16.1 History of Sound Branding

John Groves, a pioneer in the field of sound branding, proposes that, from a historical point of view, the church constitutes the first truly integrated corporate identity [8] that would have, besides a corporate structure, a corporate behavior and a visual logo, also a brand sound: the bell. The use of music within advertising media began

M. Meier • G. Beyer (✉)
Ludwig-Maximilians-University, Munich, Germany
e-mail: max.meier@ifi.lmu.de; gilbert.beyer@ifi.lmu.de

J. Müller et al. (eds.), *Pervasive Advertising*, Human-Computer Interaction Series,
DOI 10.1007/978-0-85729-352-7_16, © Springer-Verlag London Limited 2011

in the twentieth century with jingles in radio and television commercials as well as music playing statically in the background at the point-of-sale or sales events. With the emergence of the Internet, sounds used in the branding context became attached to interactive elements. Sounds in such dynamic and interactive media are used in different marketing contexts and appear in various forms. The most important are:

Sound Logo. A sound logo is a short, distinctive melody or tone sequence with a length from 1 to 3 s. It can be seen as the acoustic equivalent of a visual logo and, in the ideal case, establishes a symbiosis with it. It is mostly played along with the visual logo at the beginning or ending of a commercial [26]. Famous examples for effective sound logos are Intel's "Intel inside" tune and Deutsche Telekom's "T-Mobile" tune [9].

Advertising Jingle. Advertising Jingles are short songs that are often played along with lyrics, to convey an advertising slogan. They distinguish themselves from sound logos by not only transporting associations, but functioning as mnemonic for the slogan. Thus they often follow known and memorable folk songs in melody, rhythm and tone, and integrate other brand elements like the brand name [26]. Famous examples are Pepsodent's "You'll wonder where the yellow went" jingle [9] and Haribo's jingle [26] used with slogans in different languages.

Background Music. Background Music in most cases is purely instrumental. Its purpose is to create a certain atmosphere, thus functioning just as a supplement to other stimuli such as voice or images. An example is accordion music, eliciting convenient associations to an advertisement for French wine [6, 26]

Sound Objects. In the case of product design, so-called sound objects are connected to activities like the closing of a car door [16]. In the case of interactive media, acoustic signals connected to certain events like a mouse click on a graphical element are also referred to as sound objects. They are sometimes part of metaphors of the used graphical interface itself (e.g. the sound appearing when moving an element to the recycle bin of the desktop metaphor), but also connected to virtual products in online advertising material like banner ads. An example is a banner ad from Apple where you can choose different colors of the iPhone, and a sound appears when the user hovers the mouse cursor over one of the items.

In literature, many more types and subtypes of sound branding are described, such as *Brand Songs, Soundscapes, Sound-Icons, Brand Voice* or *Corporate Song* [26]. Most of the sound branding elements are used in different application areas and have been transferred to various platforms, e.g. you can find a sound logo, jingle or sound object today as well in television, the internet, the mobile phone or even when unpacking a real or virtual product. As diverse are proposals for possible future applications of sound branding, including areas such as multi-sensory communication, the use of interactive sounds in packaging or at the point of sale [9]. In the following, we take a look at interactivity in advertising and outline the trend of interactive music that we suggest has been neglected so far in conjunction with sound branding.

16.2   Current Trends: Interactivity in Advertising and Music

In the last years, a trend to interactive advertising media can be identified. Examples are casual games in the web, appearing as banner on the logout page or inside a news portal, as well as interactive wall or floor displays in the out-of-home domain. Contents of these media are sometimes small games, such as a goal kicking game, but often also interactive plays [1], i.e. invitations to less structured activities that imply creative or participatory elements. Such media often allow manipulating visual objects that are constituent parts of the brand identity, like a brand logo that can be moved along the display surface by hands or feet (see Fig. 16.1).

For some reason however acoustic events do not appear at all or play only a secondary role in these interactive advertisements: often they are delimited to sound objects supplementing the visual interaction or statically playing background music. Nevertheless, the identity of many brands is defined by both a visual and acoustic appearance. On the other hand, beyond the advertising context interactive music systems have become increasingly popular: with social music games like *Guitar Hero*, popular songs can be re-played together, and easy-to-use musical applications (e.g. for the iPhone) give everyone the possibility for musical expression, even without having any musical knowledge (see Fig. 16.2).

The great commercial success of such interactive musical applications shows, that many people have fun playing with them. Yet, for some reason, such musical applications have barely been employed for advertising purposes so far, even if they are quite popular. A reason may be that they are rather new. We propose that the trends of interactive advertising and interactive music making will successfully combine in the future, producing new advertising media that will enable customers not only to play with, but also manipulate and shape brand melodies by means of interactive control mechanisms. Generally this may include sound logos, jingles as

Fig. 16.1 Point-of-sale display where users can play with visual brand elements

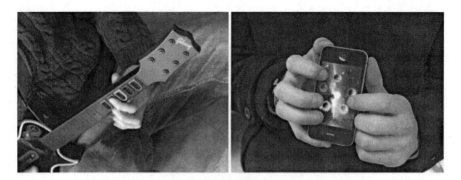

Fig. 16.2 Trend of interactive music making with Guitar Hero and the iPhone

well as background songs. Thinkable vehicles for such applications are interactive displays in shopping malls and outdoor environments, the internet, mobile devices or gaming consoles.

In this chapter, we present an approach which brings together interactive advertising and interactive music systems. When combining advertisements and music systems, the question arises how the given acoustic brand identity can be integrated in a suitable way. With our approach for creating musical advertisements, it is possible to create music in many different styles. For example, music can be generated in such a way that it resembles the melody of a well-known sound logo. This way, it is possible to develop interactive music applications which match a brand's acoustic identity.

16.3 Requirements of Interactive Music in Advertising

The functions of music in advertising are manifold. Sounds are used to gain or hold the attention of the listener [15, 17], to influence the mood of consumers, to structure the time of an ad or to persuade consumers by using rhetorical elements like rhythm, repetition, narrative, identification or location [25]. The benefits are a more effective information reception, memorization and an enhanced user experience by the use of multisensory branding [26], as well as the fact that the acoustic sensory channel is harder to ignore by the audience. But brand melodies are also subject to specific requirements. For example, according to John Groves the characteristics of an effective sound logo include memorability, distinctiveness, flexibility, conciseness and brand fit [9, 26]:

Memorability. Memorability is the most important quality of a good sound logo. It strongly depends on the sound designer's ability to create a "mini hit" or catchy tune. Memorability includes the recognition and recall of the sound logo, where the latter is more difficult to achieve. The advantage of memorable elements is that they help to quickly evoke associations when communicating a product or service.

Distinctiveness. A good sound logo has to be distinctive, otherwise it may not be recognized or confused with a competitor. For this reason an unmistakable sound characteristic has to be found. This is usually done by analyzing the market sector and how competitors deal with music and sound.

Flexibility. For a sound logo, two kinds of flexibility are advantageous, musical and technical flexibility. Musical flexibility means that a melody can be combined with different contexts and emotional situations of different advertisement, by recording it with different instrumentations or styles. Technical flexibility means, that the sound can be perceived cross-platform (e.g. via phone, computer speaker or television) without impairments.

Conciseness. A good sound logo has to be short, with tone combinations usually only lasting seconds. That is because they are often combined with visual logos, which also appear only a few seconds. A good sound takes less than two seconds to communicate the brand message.

Brand Fit. Brand fit means that a sound logo is a benchmark that should reflect the brand's values and communicate its attributes on the acoustic level. It can be very adverse, if the sound identity contradicts or obviously overstates the brand's attributes.

These are strong constraints an interactive musical advertisement has to conform to. To comply with such requirements, we make use of a novel technique that allows generating music in real-time with respect to certain *preferences* that express 'how the music should sound'. With this approach, it is possible to automatically derive preferences from existing melodies: this way, well-known melodies can be used in interactive applications and their characteristic properties can be preserved up to a certain extent (e.g. distinctiveness or brand fit). With this kind of preferences, it is possible to flexibly alter given melodies based on user interaction. Not only can the musical context of a melody be varied (e.g. instrumentation or style), also the melodic material itself can be subject to dynamic changes.

We use three kinds of preferences: First, we use preferences which are derived from user interaction, e.g. a touch display or a motion tracking system. These preferences reflect how the user wants the music to sound, for example 'I want to play fast notes with a high pitch'. The actual transformation of raw sensor readings to preferences depends strongly on the chosen user interface and interaction paradigm. The second type of preferences expresses general melodic rules: With this kind of preferences, it is possible to make the music consistent with a certain musical style (e.g. Hip-hop or Jazz). Furthermore, it is also possible to make the resulting melodies comply with a brand's distinct acoustic identity, e.g. a certain advertising jingle. In most cases, the preferences derived from user interaction will be concurrent to an advertising jingle, i.e. the user interaction does not fit to the jingle with respect to both tonality and rhythmics. Since a certain amount of control over the music is assigned to the user, it is inherently not possible to exactly play a given melody note by note. Nevertheless, it is possible to generate melodies which are similar to it by using note pitches as well as tonal and rhythmic patterns appearing in the brand's distinct melody. This way, melodies can be generated considering both interactivity and brand recognition. At last, we use preferences that coordinate several instruments playing simultaneously, for example a single player with static background music or multiple players among each other. This coordination is made by preferring harmonic intervals between different instruments. Furthermore, it is also possible to coordinate multiple instruments such that they play similar rhythmic patterns.

16.4 Related Work

In this section we present existing work on some basic domains that affects our concept of using an interactive music system for sound branding, and that constitutes the basis for our technical solution for combining user interaction and music composition. Of interest to our work are theoretical works on sound branding and interactive sound branding. There exist many articles on specific sound branding issues in classical and digital media, but they do not cover the field of user-controllable brand music. No work so far focused on how to control the brand music itself within the interactive experience, while the same is often done with visual elements of the brand identity. For a general survey on the topic of sound branding we refer to [9] and [26]. A good overview on algorithmic composition is provided by Essl [7] and Nierhaus [20]. Examples for interactive music composition and generation systems are *Electroplankton* [13] or *Cyber Composer* [12].

Approaches for imitating musical styles are related to our work: typical techniques for dealing with this problem are based on musical grammars or statistical models (see e.g. [7]). *The Continuator* [23] combines style imitation and interactivity. The purpose of this system is to allow musicians to extend their technical ability with stylistically consistent, automatically learned material. Based on a statistical model, the system is able to learn and generate musical styles as continuations of a musician's input, or as interactive improvisation back up which makes new modes of collaborative playing possible.

Our approach for generating music is based on constraint satisfaction problems. Several related approaches have been proposed where constraint programming is employed in a musical context. Especially in the field of musical harmonization, constraints are widely used: automatic musical harmonization deals with the problem of creating arrangements from given melodies with respect to certain rules. For example, a typical automatic harmonization problem is to generate a four-part arrangement of a fixed melody based on several rules e.g. from the era of Baroque. F. Pachet and P. Roy made a detailed survey on musical harmonization with constraints [24]. This work gives a short introduction to the problem of automatic music harmonization and refers to relevant works in this area.

To our knowledge, there is currently no work describing the combination of music generation and interactive advertisements. In [21], a system for musical performance is patented based on user input and stored original music data representing a music piece. A user's physical actions and physiological state are acquired and used to alter the stored tones. Similarly, in the patent [28], sensors are used to assess a user's physical condition which alters a stored piece of music. This gives constant acoustic feedback to the user and helps him to achieve a certain desired behavior in a training or therapy context. Another tool targeting the same application context is described in [14]: pressure-sensitive controls allow even people with severe disabilities to control the generation of music. The system introduced in [4] uses a performance device (e.g. based on hand proximity) to interactively control several aspects of a composition algorithm. When no input is provided, the system proceeds automatically to compose music and produce sound. A general-purpose position-based controller for electronic musical instruments is described in [27]. The position signal may be used for generating music or for applying effects to the output of another instrument.

Our approach for generating music is based on a reasoning-technique called soft constraint which allows dealing with soft and concurrent problems in an easy way. Bistarelli et al. [2] introduced a very general and abstract theory of soft constraints based on semirings. Building on this work, in [10] monoidal soft constraints were introduced, a soft-constraint formalism particularly well-suited to multi-criteria optimization problems with dynamically changing user preferences. Soft constraints have successfully been applied to problems such as optimizing software-defined radios [29] or orchestrating services [30]. We introduced a soft-constraint based system for music therapy in [11], giving us basic proof of concept in composing music with this technique.

16.5 Application Areas in Pervasive Advertising

Along with the emergence of interactivity in common media, advertising has also become interactive, for example in form of interactive internet banners, advertising in video games or public installations. Today, there exist a variety of platforms which are potentially suitable for advertising involving user-controllable music. In general, we see two different approaches for using interactive music in advertising: On the one hand, it can supplement other content, e.g. as part of a company's web page or an interactive application running on a public display. In this case, interactive music has the function to enhance the overall experience. On the other hand, an interactive music application can also be the primary part of an advertisement, for example in the form of a free application for mobile phones which is fun to play with and hence will be used voluntarily by people. We see a variety of application areas where interactive music can be employed for advertising:

Online Advertising. In the World Wide Web, all kinds of *Rich Media* advertising material [3] such as interactive banners, rectangles, skyscrapers, floating ads or streaming banners are thinkable to integrate interactive applications where users can control visual and acoustic brand elements via the mouse cursor. Last but not least

Fig. 16.3 Prototype for an application on the iPhone, where musical parameters like tone pitch can be controlled via the positions of the planets

the enrichment of ads by sound and interactivity is already common in online advertising. *Microsites* are usually intended to display a product, sweepstakes, seasonal advertisements (on Christmas or Easter) or the invitation to a promotional event [3]. Due to being self-contained web presences, they can provide a suitable interface for controlling music. Of course not all formats provide the convenient spatial and temporal environment for playing with music or interactive content in general. For example, peel backs or interstitial ads might be clicked away too quickly before the user understands he can interact with music.

Mobile Advertising. Interactive music applications can also run on platforms like mobile devices. These provide many possibilities for designing user interaction: from common controls like buttons or multi-touch displays to specialized functionality like acceleration sensors or global positioning. Musical applications are very popular and there exist a large number of applications for all common platforms. There are professional applications designed for musicians and, much more interesting for advertising, simple applications targeted at non-musicians. Figure 16.3 shows a prototype for an iPhone application which we currently port from an existing version for the Microsoft Surface table. With this application, music can be intuitively composed by arranging planet constellations. The user has much control over the music: for each planet, it is possible to control its speed (slow/fast) as well as the note pitches (low/high). Furthermore, the user can continually control how harmonic the music should sound. Musical applications on mobile phones have already been used for advertising purposes: for example, Audi gives away an app for the iPhone which is a combination of car racing and rhythmic games. For Procter and Gamble's Pringles potato chips there exists an app where one can play on virtual drums.

In-Game Advertising. Advertisements in console and online games are an expanding market. Common formats of in-game ads are virtual billboards in sports or role-playing games and product placements (e.g. usage of car brands in racing games [19]). While these classical forms of in-game advertisements might provide possibilities for interactive music, a more obvious field of application are video game soundtracks, traditionally contributing considerably to the gaming experience and in some cases being even the primary purpose of the game. Classical platform games like *Super Mario Bros* or *Sonic the Hedgehog* constitute a good example: if the player characters collect some treasure items (such as food containers or special equipment) or lose life energy, also the background music changes to a more positive or dramatic sound. Thinkable is to combine special abilities the characters get by collecting an item with interactive brand music.

Out-of-Home Advertising. Besides applications for devices owned by the user, interactive music could also be used on public displays. We developed a prototype of an interactive music application running on a large display where music can be intuitively played by hand movements; a detailed description of this prototype will be presented in the following sections.

This list of application areas can only cover a part of advertising opportunities for interactive music systems, and may be completed with many others. Also, there might be types of advertising or sites, where interactive music or music at all do not make sense or are inappropriate. Many people have fun with musical applications, but they can also be annoying in some situations. It is much harder to ignore sounds than visual stimuli and hence, one has to take care of maintaining a moderate level of loudness and avoiding sound pollution, especially in out-of-home applications (e.g. on public displays). Another issue is that interactive musical applications should not be misplaced. Music is first and foremost entertainment rather than information, and should only be employed where the user can expect at least entertaining content. Imagine a guerilla marketing campaign, where interactive music appears when waiting at an automated teller machine for drawing money; the audience might not be amused by such an advertisement.

16.6 How It Is Realized: Composing Music with Soft Constraints

To realize interactive, user-controllable music systems within advertising we developed a technical solution for real-time music generation that helps to coordinate the different characteristics of user interaction, the acoustic identity of a brand and the general harmonic and rhythmic concordance of instruments.

We make use of a framework for algorithmic composition of music which is based on a reasoning technique called *soft constraints* [11, 18]. With this framework, music can be interactively generated in real-time by defining so-called 'preferences' which express 'how the music should sound'. As an example, a typical preference for a single instrument would be 'fast notes with a high pitch'. Besides preferences for single instruments, it is also possible to coordinate multiple instruments with additional preferences. These global preferences typically involve harmonic or rhythmic relations between several instruments, e.g. 'play together in harmonic intervals and in a similar rhythm'. All preferences can also be generated dynamically while playing, for example based on user interaction: this way, music can be composed interactively in real-time by continually defining preferences which reflect 'how well the music matches the user interaction'. Furthermore, it is possible to define preferences which express that the generated music should resemble a given melody in order to make it fit to a musical style or a given brand melody.

In general, a soft constraint expresses how well an assignment of values to variables (a valuation) matches a desired result. A valuation is a function from variables to values:

$$Valuation = (Variable \rightarrow Value).$$

The extent to which this valuation is desirable can be expressed in various ways. The cited theory introduces a very abstract and elegant way of rating valuations with a set of grades and several operations e.g. for combining or comparing grades. Many concrete kinds of grades can be used, for example based on numbers or Boolean values. A soft constraint assigns a grade to each valuation:

$$SoftConstraint = (Valuation \rightarrow Grade).$$

Typically, one is interested in the best possible valuation which can be computed with a general solver for soft constraints. In our application of soft constraints for generating music we want to assign actions to voices: each voice corresponds to a certain sound (e.g. a piano, guitar or synthesizer sound); actions are for example 'play a note' or 'pause'. When an instrument should be polyphonic (i.e. it can play multiple notes at the same time), it has to have an according number of voices. We use soft constraints to rate action assignments:

$$(Voice \rightarrow Action) \rightarrow Grade.$$

At certain time intervals, each instrument is being asked to state preferences for its own notes. These preferences from all instruments are then extended with global coordination preferences and combined to a single constraint problem. This problem is being solved, yielding an action for each voice which satisfies the preferences best. In the next section, we will introduce a prototype where hand gestures are used to control music. Based on an optical tracking system, we derive two parameters from a user's movements: the total amount of movement (corresponding to the rate of played notes) and the average vertical position of all movements (corresponding to pitch). Based on these two parameters, preferences are generated reflecting the desired speed and pitch. For example, when the user makes fast movements and lifts his hands up, the music should also be fast and have a rather high pitch. Vice-versa, when the user is moving slowly and his hands are down, the music should be slow with a low pitch.

The music should fit the user interaction on the one hand, but we also want it to fit to a given sound brand on the other hand. This is realized with an additional preference reflecting 'how well the music matches a jingle's distinctive melody'. This preference is generated based on a timed transition model representing the

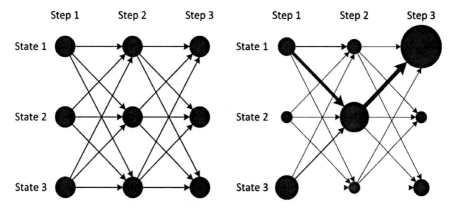

Fig. 16.4 Transition model visualization (*left*: empty model, *right*: trained model)

jingle's note pitches and rhythmic patterns as well as transitions between notes (e.g. 'C is often followed by E or another C'). Our approach is based on a custom transition model which represents sequences of events aligned upon a structured metric grid. Intuitively, the model represents (1) how often an event occurs at a certain metric position and (2) how often other events follow this event at this position. Following typical terms from the closely related area of probability models, the 'events' are called states. The discrete metric positions (representing 'time') are called steps:

$$State$$
$$Step = \{0, \ldots, n\}$$

In each step, each state has a certain weight for a given voice. This weight represents how often the state occurs at the given step:

$$stateWeight_{Voice}: \; Step \times State \to \mathbf{R}$$

The transitions between states at a given step are represented with the following function. The first two arguments define the original step and state – the third argument defines the next state. Transition weights are always defined for subsequent steps; the state in the third argument is implicitly assumed to be on the next state.

$$transitionWeight_{Voice}: \; Step \times State \times State \to \mathbf{R}$$

The following figure visualizes a timed transition model with three steps and states. State weights are visualized with black circles: the bigger the circle, the higher the weight. The transition weights are visualized with arrows (a thicker arrow indicates a higher weight). When the model is untrained, all weights are the same. Training the model modifies the weights; the right picture visualizes a trained model with shifted weights (Fig. 16.4).

Fig. 16.5 Concurrent
preferences

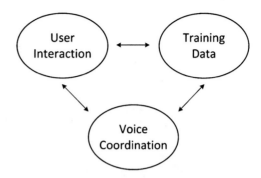

The actual states can be modeled in several ways: the simplest way is to directly use the existing set of actions as states. However, there would be a little disadvantage: if note pitches are directly used within the states, it is not possible to play a model in another tonal scale. If this is desired, it is better to use abstract stages in a tonal scale rather than concrete note pitches. Now, we define a constraint which expresses 'how well an action matches the data represented in the model'. Given the last step and the last actually executed state (the state corresponding to the last action chosen by the constraint solver), we can compute a total weight for each state on the subsequent step. This is done by just summing up the transition weight and the step weight itself:

$$totalWeight_{Voice} : Step \times State \times Step \times State \rightarrow \mathbf{R}$$
$$totalWeight_v (lastStep, lastState, step, state) = transitionWeight_v$$
$$(lastStep, lastState, state) + stateWeight_v (step, state)$$

The constraint itself for a certain voice $v \in Voice$ is constructed based on the last step, the last executed action and the current step. When the sets of actions and states are identical, the constraint can be defined like this:

$$modelConstraint_{Voice} : (Step \times Action \times Step) \rightarrow ((Voice \rightarrow Action) \rightarrow \mathbf{R})$$
$$modelConstraint_v (lastStep, lastAction, step)(val) = totalWeight_v$$
$$(lastStep, lastAction, step, val(v))$$

To sum it up, we have preferences based on user interaction (1) as well as preferences reflecting the similarity to a jingle (2) and – in most cases – these preferences will be concurrent among each other. Furthermore, it is also possible to coordinate several instruments among each other with additional global preferences (3). In our prototype, we define a global constraint which maximizes the amount of musical harmony between the interactive instrument and the background music.

Soft constraints are very appropriate for dealing with such problems and allow accommodating several concurrent preferences in an easy yet expressive way. When the preferences have been stated, a soft constraint solver can be employed for computing the best possible notes with respect to all preferences (see Fig. 16.5). We use a soft constraint solver which was originally prototyped in Maude [29, 30] and that we later implemented in a more efficient version in C#, making it possible to use it in a soft real-time environment. For more detailed information about composing music with soft constraints, we refer to [11].

16.7   Prototype: Interactive Music on Public Displays

To test how people can interact with brand music, we developed a prototype system within the application area of digital signage. The scenario is an interactive public display installed at a preferably quiet public place. A primary objective was to test a system that allows manipulating music by novice users in a public setting with no previous training period or musical expertise, and to explore which gestures users would use to control such an application. The prototype is based on a large public display where users are also able to interactively play music with hand movements. The system consists of a hardware setup and a software solution, which are described in the following.

The hardware of our system consists of a wall of luminous plasma displays (four 42‰ seamless displays arranged to a 16:9 screen of 1.85 m width and 1.05 m height, with a resolution of 1706 to 960 pixels) and a high resolution camera attached above the screens for detecting user postures and gestures. We see a vision-based sensing framework to be the most convenient technology in this scenario, as it allows collecting information about passerby's movements and gestures in an unobtrusive way. For testing reasons the sensing is realized using marker-based techniques. We attach two colored markers to a user's hands for analyzing his hand movements. The next planned step is to use marker-less body tracking involving the detection of individual body parts.

The software of the system is developed in .NET with C# and integrates several software components: We use the marker-based vision framework Touchless SDK [5] for tracking the hands with markers. The music is generated with the soft-constraint framework for interactively composing music described in the previous section. To conduct user tests with the system we developed several sample applications where the note pitch of the music can be controlled by up-and-down movements of the hands and the rate of played notes by the velocity of hand movement. The visualizations of these applications were developed with Microsoft's XNA framework and the Mercury Particle Engine. For example, we created an advertisement for a soft drink that allows users to control the brand sound by hand movements (see Fig. 16.6).

Depending on the passer-by's movements, notes are played and are visualized by bubbles, each note corresponding to one bubble. When someone starts to interact with the system, he can realize the connection between his movements and the notes he hears: When the movements become faster, the notes will also play faster – not moving at all leads to silence. The resulting melodies do not only fit to the person's movements, they are furthermore being generated in a way that they comply with the company's brand melody.

Fig. 16.6 Sample advertisement for a soft drink on our public display prototype that allows users to control brand sounds by hand movements

To explore how users would use a public display where they can interact with the music, we conducted a user study. First of all we found it important to figure out if users understand that they can control music, and second, how people would interact with a display where they can control the music. Generally, applications on public displays can be controlled by finger touch, hand gestures, body movements and postures, or also by changing body positions in a simple, unobtrusive way. With our vision-based system, we were especially interested in hand gestures. We already knew, based on informal observations of colleagues, that hand movements in front of our displays are understood and accepted quite quickly if the visual feedback is accurate enough, and developed different techniques for interacting with the system and controlling the music with hands. From these, we chose to compare three techniques in the study that had shown promise in pretests:

The first interaction technique is a gesture-based technique where the user can control visual elements and acoustic events only with *one hand at a time*. The note pitch of the music is controlled by up-down movements, and the rate of played notes is controlled by the velocity of movements. The second gesture-based technique allows the user to control the visuals and the music with *both hands*, and for computing note pitch and the rate of played notes the mean values of both the hand vertical positions and velocity are taken. The third interaction technique extends the second technique by allowing the user to control the acoustic events (note pitch and rate of played notes) with *separate hands*, i.e. one hand controls the note pitch and the other hand controls the rate. User observations on the understanding of our musical advertisement and on the different interaction techniques were conducted at our lab over the course of 3 days (see Fig. 16.7). For the study we prepared a room which contained the interactive display prototype. For the observation we used 4 cameras (allowing for detecting user behavior from different angles) and recorded to a synchronized, time-stamped video file using OpenCV [22]. In total, 21 people participated in the study (12 males, 9 females). The average age was 30 years; participants were students, employees, technicians, web designers, marketing managers, assistants and housewives. We started with an initial briefing of the participants,

Fig. 16.7 Recordings of the user study on our interactive musical advertisement. In the *left* image the user controls a *red* particle visualization with one hand, and a *yellow* particle visualization with the other hand. The *left* hand is used to control the rate of played notes, and the *right* hand controls the pitch. In the *right* image a test run with one-hand control is seen

where we also explained to them the setting of the study. Participants were told that there was a room containing a public display, but we did not tell if or how they could interact with the display. To be able to sense the movements of the hands with our marker-based system we asked them to put on colored gloves (after the study we surveyed if participants felt constricted by the gloves in any way). After the initial briefing we guided the participants to the room where our sample music content with one of the three described interaction techniques was running. We surveyed the people via webcams and did not interrupt them during the study. When they came out, we conducted a semi-structured interview with them. For all 21 subjects synchronized and time-stamped videos were recorded and predefined user behavior regarding hand movements and gestures was transcribed.

Even without any previous instructions, most users were aware that they have control over the music. Only 2 out of 21 people did not recognize the connection between their hand movements and the music they heard. No user stopped interacting while standing in front of the system for longer periods, and the average user made hand gestures for over 90% of the time which gives us further confidence that people understood the basic interaction paradigm. Based on the videos, we analyzed how long it took until people interacted in the way we intended, i.e. when they started to primarily make hand gestures which are relevant for the music generation. The variant based on only one hand took 132 s on average, the variant based on the mean values of both hands took 118 s and the third variant (separate hands for both parameters) took 92 s. Most users seemed to interact in a rather intuitive way but interviews revealed that not everybody did consciously identify the variable parameters ("pitch" and "rate of played notes") and how they can be controlled: 12 out of 21 people stated that they used up-and-down movements to control the music and only 10 out of 21 people could tell how note pitches can be controlled; only 2 users understood how they can vary the rate of notes. Nevertheless, the results of this study make us confident that public displays are an appropriate platform for advertising based on interactive music and that hand gestures can be used for interacting with music without any previous training. We are confident that additional visual clues or context-sensitive help instructions can greatly help in understanding how the system works: we observed that users were able to understand the system if we gave them only few initial instructions.

This prototype gave us basic proof of concept for intuitively interacting with music on a public display. We also plan to conduct a comparative study on recall of content: we want to figure out if the manipulation of acoustic events leads to a better memorization of presented visual elements. Further, it would also be interesting to see how users would interact with music in public places.

16.8 Conclusion

In this chapter we presented an overview of the topic of sound branding, and proposed how current trends of interactive music will open up new opportunities in this field of advertising. We described the requirements of interactive music in advertising, outlined possible application areas and limitations and presented related research on design and implementation issues of musical systems used for advertising.

We further introduced a general approach for developing sound branding applications, where advertising sounds are controlled by the interaction. To make sure that the resulting music complies with both the requirements of interactivity and brand recognition, we made use of a novel technique of music generation based on soft constraints. First user tests with our prototype with large advertising displays showed that algorithmically composing music with soft constraint solving works quite well, giving the user the impression of control over the music while producing quite recognizable sound. There exist a large number of platforms where applications involving interactive music could be employed, for example the internet, mobile devices, video games or out-of-home media. The evaluation of our prototype makes us confident that public displays are generally suitable for musical advertisements. We want to improve this prototype and experiment with other application concepts. We also plan to deploy the system in a real situation and evaluate how people interact with the system in public. We are further interested in developing and assessing new user interfaces and interaction paradigms for other platforms. At the moment, we work on an interactive musical advertisement for the iPhone.

Many people have fun with musical applications, but they can also be annoying in some situations. Thus, one has to take care to avoid sound pollution. It would be interesting to find criteria which indicate whether musical applications are appropriate in a certain context. Sound is a powerful tool which has to be employed with care. Within interactive advertising media, it can have various functions. For example, background music can create a certain atmosphere or sound objects can enhance user interaction. Interactive music applications are a rather new trend and allow interacting with music in an expressive way, enabling control over the melodic material itself. We think that combining musical applications with interactive advertisements will be fruitful in many regards.

References

1. Adamowsky, N.: Homo Ludens – Whale enterprise: Zur Verbindung von Spiel, Technik und den Künsten. In: Poser, S., Zachmann, K. (eds.) Homo faber ludens: Geschichte zu Wechselbeziehungen von Technik u. Spiel. Peter Lang Verlag, Frankfurt (2003)
2. Bistarelli, S., Montanari, U., Rossi, F.: Semiring-based constraint satisfaction and optimization. J. ACM **44**(2), 201–236 (1997)
3. Buss, A.: Internet-Marketing: Erfolg planen, gestalten, umsetzen. Markt & Technik, München (2009)
4. Chadabe, J.: Interactive music composition and performance system. US Patent 4526078 (1985)
5. Codeplex Website: http://touchless.codeplex.com/. Accessed 23 Mar 2011
6. Diederichs, F.A., Stonat, C.: Musik und Werbung. Marketing mit Emotionen. In: Moser, R., Scheuermann, A. (eds.) Handbuch der Musikwirtschaft, p. 416. Josef Keller Verlag, Starnberg und München (2003)
7. Essl, K.: Algorithmic composition. In: Collins, N., d'Escrivan, J. (eds.) Cambridge Companion to Electronic Music. Cambridge University Press, Cambridge (2007)
8. Farbood, M., Schoner, B.: Analysis and synthesis of palestrina-style counterpoint using Markov chains. In: Proceedings of the International Computer Music Conference, Havana (2001)
9. Groves, J.: A short history of sound branding. In: Bronner, K., Hirt, R. (eds.) Audio Branding – Entwicklung, Anwendung, Wirkung akustischer Identitäten in Werbung, Medien und Gesellschaft, pp. 40–51. Nomos Verlagsgesell, Baden-Baden (2009)
10. Hölzl, M., Meier, M., Wirsing, M.: Which soft constraints do you prefer? In: Proceedings of Workshop on Rewriting Logic and Its Applications (WRLA 2008), Budapest (2008)
11. Hölzl, M., Denker, G., Meier, M., Wirsing, M.: Constraint-muse: a soft-constraint based system for music therapy. In: Proceedings of Third International Conference on Algebra and Coalgebra in Computer Science (CALCO'09), Udine, pp. 423–432. Springer, Heidelberg (2009)
12. Ip, H., Law, K., Kwong, B.: Cyber composer: hand gesture-driven intelligent music composition and generation. In: Proceedings of 11th International Multimedia Modelling Conference (MMM '05), Melbourne, pp. 46–52 (2005)
13. Iwai T, Indies Zero, Nintendo (2005) Electroplankton. Nintendo
14. Jubran, F.: Sound generating device for use by people with disabilities. US Patent 2007/0241918 A1 (2007)
15. Kellaris, J., Cox, A., Cox, D.: The effect of background music on ad processing: a contingency explanation. J. Market. **57**(4), 114–125 (1993)
16. Kilian, K.: Von der Markenidentität zum Markenklang als Markenelement. In: Bronner, K., Hirt, R. (eds.) Audio Branding – Entwicklung, Anwendung, Wirkung akustischer Identitäten in Werbung, Medien und Gesellschaft, p. 66. Nomos Verlagsgesellschaft, Baden-Baden (2009)
17. Kroeber-Riel, W., Esch, F.-R.: Strategie und Technik der Werbung. In: Diller, H., Köhler, R. (eds.) Verhaltenswissenschaftliche Ansätze, vol. 6. Kohlhammer, Stuttgart (2004)
18. Meier, M., RechNet, GmbH: Musiksystem. German Patent DE102009017204A1 (2009)
19. Nelson, M.R.: Recall of brand placements in computer/video games. J. Advert. Res. **42**(2), 80–92 (2002)

20. Nierhaus, G.: Algorithmic Composition. Springer, Heidelberg (2008)
21. Nishitani, Y., Ishida, K., Kobayashi, E., Yamaha Corporation: System of processing music performance for personalized management of and evaluation of sampled data. US Patent 7297857 (2007)
22. OpenCV website: http://opencv.willowgarage.com/. Accessed 23 Mar 2011
23. Pachet, F.: The continuator: musical interaction with style. In: Proceedings of the International Computer Music Conference, Goteborg, pp. 211–218. ICMA, Gotheborg (2002)
24. Pachet, F., Roy, P.: Musical harmonization with constraints: a survey. Constraints **6**(1), 7–19 (2001)
25. Scott, L.: Understanding jingles and needledrop: a rhetorical approach to music in advertising. J. Consum. Res. **17**(2), 223–36 (1990)
26. Steiner, P.: Sound Branding – Grundlagen der akustischen Markenführung. Gabler, Wiesbaden (2009)
27. Wheaton, J.A., Wold, E., Sutter, A.J., Yamaha corporation: position-based controller for electronic musical instrument. US Patent 5541358 (1996)
28. Wiest, P.: Verfahren zur Akustisierung körpereigener physikalischer Werte und Vorrichtung zur Durchführung des Verfahrens. German Patent 19522958 C2 (1999)
29. Wirsing, M., Denker, G., Talcott, C., Poggio, A., Briesemeister, L.: A rewriting logic framework for soft constraints. In: Proceedings of Workshop on Rewriting Logic and its Applications (WRLA 2006), Vienna (2006)
30. Wirsing, M., Clark, A., Gilmore, S., Hölzl, M., Knapp, A., Koch, N., Schroeder, A.: Semantic-based development of service-oriented systems. In: Najm, E., Pradat-Peyre, J.-F., Donzeau-Gouge, V.V. (eds.) FORTE 2006. LNCS, vol. 4229, pp. 24–45. Springer, Heidelberg (2006)

Chapter 17
Scent Marketing: Making Olfactory Advertising Pervasive

Bernadette Emsenhuber

Abstract Store chains and service providers beguile customers with a pleasant shopping atmosphere often realized by installing scent diffusers to evaporate overwhelming fragrances. Such systems are becoming a standard interior of commercial locations as well as public places and are gaining in importance for human computer interaction. A historical, physiological and psychological overview shed a light on different aspects of scent marketing. Current scent marketing technology puts the relevance of olfactory communication for pervasive advertising and human-computer interaction up for discussion and constitutes prospectively technological challenges for olfactory human-computer interaction.

17.1 Purpose

Like other media-based business, the advertising industry is increasingly confronted with the problem of information overload. Penetrating this *information bulk* and reaching customers with advertising messages becomes correspondingly difficult. An important issue for advertisers is finding new methods of persuading consumers to purchase their goods and services. The first that come to mind in connection with the word *advertising* are posters, newspaper ads, commercials on TV or radio, etc., that is, visual and auditory media. However the advertising industry does also use

B. Emsenhuber (✉)
Johannes Kepler University, Linz, Austria
e-mail: bernadette.emsenhuber@catalysts.cc

J. Müller et al. (eds.), *Pervasive Advertising*, Human-Computer Interaction Series, DOI 10.1007/978-0-85729-352-7_17, © Springer-Verlag London Limited 2011

consumption-raising instruments like scents to manipulate consumer behavior by unconsciously raising emotions and consequently manipulating purchase decisions. The marketing expert Martin Lindstrom writes on his website:

> Did you know that currently 83% of all commercial communication appeals only to one sense – our eyes. That leaves a paltry 17% to cater for the other four senses. This is extraordinary given that 75% of our day-to-day emotions are influenced by what we smell, and the fact that there's a 65% chance of a mood change when exposed to a positive sound. This is a long way of saying that the importance of our senses has been completely overlooked in the brand-building business… until now.

Smell-supported advertising is called *scent marketing* [2], and relies on the neuropsychological effects of olfactory stimuli – emotionalization and recall by smell. The area of research analyzing the neuropsychological effects of advertising and commercial activities on the consumer is referred to as *neuroeconomics*. The term *scent marketing* came up in 2002, and defines a subarea of neuroeconomic research and should to be distinguished from *scent advertising* defining perfume advertisements. Designing fragrances and installing scent-dispensing systems for scent marketing purposes is called *air design.*

Olfactory perception allows a distinctly subliminal communication between human beings and their environment, through a direct connection of the olfactory system to our emotional center. Pam Scholder Ellen, marketing professor of Georgia State University states:

> With all of the other senses, you think before you respond, but with scent, your brain responds before you think. [50]

In the mid-1990s, psychologists examined the effect of scents on purchase behavior and confirmed that perfumed sales rooms contribute to increase sales [45]. Therefore, marketing experts did not hesitate to use the olfactory communication channel as a medium for subliminal messages [15].

Scent marketing is implemented in various shops, hotels or recreational facilities and has affected consumer's behavior for nearly 20 years, and with considerable impact: However, this is not always positive. Scents are interpreted very subjectively and can quickly annoy people. In cases where consciously perceive olfactory advertising messages, they sometimes fear injurious effects on their health [23]. Fearing miasma and the beguiling of people are known reactions to smell and can be found through the ages. It is necessary to avoid such reactions by respecting people's preferences and individualizing olfactory advertising messages, this requires the implementation of more intelligent and pervasive Scent Marketing systems.

17.2   The Historical Background of Scent Marketing

Scent marketing is not merely "a child" of the 1990s and was already used in ancient days. The first scent marketers to use were scent traders who sold fragrant goods like fresh bread, fish, cheese or flowers. These products disseminated their smell throughout the market square and lured people to the various different stands. This raises the question of non-fragrant products can be sold? These can be scented with perfume, for example. In the ancient world people used perfume to sell themselves, such as prostitutes, or their estate like their house or their slaves. However, the relevance of smell, perfume and olfactory perception has varies according to the historical with and culture, as the analysis and investigations of historians and philosophers demonstrate. For instance Alain Corbin speaks of an "*olfactory revolution*" in the eighteenth century, which was influenced by the French Revolution and a new standing of hygiene. Todays scent marketing is intensifying the relevance of olfactory perception and is compelling us to learn about the perception of odors once more. A brief retrospective review of the historical and cultural background of scent marketing is revealing:

Human perception was already of interest to ancient philosophers, but olfaction was neglected until the last decade. Why do the senses of sight and hearing gain so much more attention nowadays and why did researchers fail to the sense of smell until the last decade?

Walter Benjamin considered changes in the social relevance of perception, as people's adaption to new technical media [31]. Accordingly, the hegemony of visual and acoustic perception is due to the rise of telegraphy, photography, film, radio and television. However, as Paech [37] wrote in her article *Das Aroma des Kinos*, after the first cinemas had opened their doors, the first experiments with *scent movies* where also conducted. These pioneering efforts demonstrated the beginnings of new media on the one hand and resistance on the other hand, involving psychological effects, which would be discovered only a hundred years later.

In evolutionary terms, the sense of smell is the first form of perception, as demonstrated by German researchers who identified the reaction of sperm cells to the aroma of lily of the valley [20] and the fact that the olfactory bulb is situated within the oldest part of our brain [11]. In prehistoric times when visual and acoustic amplifiers did not exist, perceiving odors was crucial to survival. Studies on indigenous peoples and feral children indicate the relevance of olfactory perception far from civilization [20]. With respect to contemporary history, a decreasing impact of smell corresponds to increasing civilization.

Ancient advanced civilizations like those of Mediterranean area or in the Middle East invented perfume. Ancient people used scents to render homage to gods. Hygiene and sanitation were an important part of cohabitation and bad body odors were considered unacceptable. Accordingly, higher castes, which could afford these luxury fluids and scenting themselves and their home with perfumes. Body odor came to indicate class differences and was a symbol of social distinction as a consequence.

Scent also found its way into religions like Christianity or Buddhism as a spiritual instrument. In both religions, incense occupied a central position in communicating with god in both persuasions. Generally, Asian cultures have a special relationship to smell and especially to body odor. On the one hand, Asian people have almost no own body odor [8], On the other hand, hygiene and fragrances play an important role in their social coexistence and led to the development of a bathing tradition. In the early Middle Ages crusaders brought this tradition to Europe and consequently introduced the installation of bathhouses. Increasing plague epidemics and sexually deviant behavior in these bathhouses supported the church's opinion that personal hygiene makes people sick and encourages degenerate behavior. Accordingly, bathhouses were closed and bad smells were a daily occurrence.

A lack of understanding of personal hygiene existed for several centuries. In *The Foul and the Fragrant,* Corbin describes the olfactory situation in the eighteenth century in France [10].. Before the French Revolution, baroque society not only suffered from political instability and excessiveness, but also from unbearable sanitary conditions and diseases. Because of their ignorance, scientists ascribed the spread of disease to the malodor in the air and appealed for an improvement of public hygiene. As protection against miasma, people used a plethora of perfumes and scented powders, which contributed both to olfactory excesses and to the development of capitals of perfume like Grasse. It's is therefore surprising that Süskind chose that period of time and that location for his bestselling novel *Perfume* [47]. Only such an environment could constitute the perfect background for an olfactory genius like the character Jean-Baptiste Grenouille. Ultimately, the olfactory situation was so unbearable that philosophers of the Enlightenment had also stressed the importance of personal hygiene. With the French Revolution, says Corbin, there was also an *"Olfactory Revolution"*. The installation of sewerage systems and another manifestations of hygiene also manifested the prominence of smell. People became more sensitive to miasma, but also to fragrance and began to prefer light scents [44]. Enlightenment philosophers again raised the issue of a hierarchy of senses and labeled the sense of smell as unworthy of mention. Smells were undesirable and olfactory perception was classified as animalistic and *ignoble* [29]. The invisibility, immeasurability and subliminal perception of smell were the main reasons why scientists abandoned the concept of olfaction.

As already mentioned, Asia occupies a special position in the cultural history of smell. Smells, body odor and personal hygiene play an important role in the traditions, medicine and daily life in the Far East. This has its roots in an early understanding of hygiene and awareness that scents have a healing effect. In contrast to Western cultures, the peoples of Eastern Asia preserve their ability to smell and do not ignore olfactory incentives to date. They regard smells and the sense of smell as a natural part of their daily lives and there are no inhibitions in this context.

A comparison of civilized cultures shows how Enlightenment philosophers effectively influenced the perception of smells in the Western world. The olfactory Revolution led to an increasing disapproval of smells until they became a real taboo in European societies and an unsuitable topic for discussion. Only good old perfume *survived* the era of *"deodorization"* [10]. The commercial launch of Chanel No. 5, the first perfume consisting of artificially produced fragrances, initiated another olfactory revolution, because perfume was no longer a luxury good and was now achievable to everyone. Being scented no longer constituted a social class distinction. However, this was not the last milestone in the cultural history of smell. Indeed, it would seem we are going through a third olfactory revolution right now. Scientific success in olfactory research, such as the decoding of the first olfactory receptor by Linda Buck and Richard Axel [20], discussions about olfactory disturbance caused by cigarette smoke and biogas plants [49], the development of the first smell recorder and smelling mobile phones in Japan [10], and the increasing use of scents for marketing purposes, indicate a new relevance of odor.

17.3   The Sense of Smell

Without the special characteristics of olfactory perception, scent marketing would not work. Smell differs from other perceptions in the ability of the perceiver to respond and recall without thinking. Olfactory stimuli are almost instinctively processed in the human brain, in contrast to other sensual impressions [11]. Over the last few years, the mystery of smell could be unraveled more and more and will surely keep researchers busy the next years. The following discussion provides an overview of current research results, which constitute only the beginnings of olfactory research.

Skepticism about the significance of smell in social and cultural history is rooted in a lack of understanding of the smelling process. As the cultural history of olfaction reveals, there has never been a rational explanation of smelling. People were ashamed of this animalistic behavior, which was led by that incomprehension of the sense of smell. However, scents were always much sought-after for their emotionalizing and overwhelming effect. Since the end of the twentieth century, researchers, especially neurologists, psychologists and biochemists have attempted to explode the myth of olfaction.

The neurological olfactory center is situated in the earliest part of the human brain to form and a foetus's nose already develops at between 11 and 15 weeks [53]. Olfactory perception also includes the sense of taste, because tasting without smelling is almost impossible, a familiar effect of colds. Therefore, the perception of aromas can be defined as just one sense.

In comparison to other senses, smelling assumes a special position within the modalities of perception. The process of perceiving volatile components is characterized by spontaneous recall, inevitableness, unfiltration, unconsciousness and emotionality. As researchers have found out over the last few years, primarily neurological factors account for these characteristics, which give customers the potential to perceive highly emotionalizing advertising messages.

However one problem remains: The interpretation of odors can be very subjective and related to individual emotions. The recognition of odors is based on a learning process starting in the embryonic phase [42] and entails perceiving odors and saving them in combination with memories, incidents and emotions, forever stored in the long-term memory. Perceiving a known odor is essentially an odor-related memory recall. Accordingly, the sense of smell should constitute a perfect interface with the human brain, eternally depositing information and recalling it by means of "re-perception".

Perceiving a smell starts with a biochemical process based on a lock and key principle at the upper end of the human nose. The olfactory epithelium is located there and consists of about ten million olfactory receptors, which are sensitive to about 350 different volatile components. In 2006, Linda Buck and Richard Axel were awarded the Nobel Prize for decoding the first olfactory receptor. Meanwhile, another three receptors or sensory neurons have been decoded [20, 41]. In comparison, a dog's epithelium consists of about 220 million receptors. If an odorant molecule docks to the right receptor, an impulse is sent to the olfactory nerve, also called an olfactory bulb, which is the connector to different cerebral areas. The discovery of these neuronal connections explains the extraordinary characteristics of olfaction.

Evolutionarily and neurologically, the sense of smell is our fundamental instinct and also bears this functionality today. Odors can yield information about good or bad food, toxicity, or whether something is burning. Generally, we use this functionality every day and can identify at least 16 different scents. Specialists as perfumers or gourmets train their olfactory tool and can isolate up to 1,000 fragrances. Yet, the Sense of Smell Institute determined that the average human being could potentially recognize approximately 10,000 different odors [3]. This aptitude shows that we don't usually use our sense of smell to its full capacity.

Perceiving odors occurs spontaneously and is only avoidable by stopping breathing. This unavoidable nature is caused, on the one hand, by a lack of an *olfactory palpebral* and on the other hand, by the direct connection between the olfactory epithelium and long-term memory. Olfactory signals are processed without any filtering by our brain. Any perceived odor is saved in the long-term memory, in combination with the current smell situation, which includes locations, plants, persons, emotions, etc. Smelling such odors promptly recalls that particular situation, including various details. Researchers refer to this phenomenon as an "*olfactory memory*" or the "*Proust Phenomenon*", which obtained its name from Marcel Proust's explanations of sensual impressions in his work *In Search of Lost Time* [22].

We are always exposed to smells, but often they are too diffuse for conscious perception and we perceive them subliminally, which is a kind of protection measure. Odors can cause positive as well as negative emotional reactions, which are due to close links between the olfactory and the limbic system, our emotion center. How the perceiver is emotionalized depends on his or her memorized impressions. The combination of inevitability of perceiving odors and the emotionalization could be dangerous relating to psychological effects. The human olfactory system is equipped, more so than other senses with a habituation function. It rapidly habituates if the same smell is present for a longer time. Accordingly, it is almost impossible to identify one's own body odor or that of close relatives. Also, a constant environmental odor is no longer perceptible by habitants; only foreigners such as tourists or visitors will notice it [12]. The intensive emotionalizing effects of smells are the determining factors for a faster olfactory than visual or auditory habituation. The nostrils can not be closed instinctively, in contrast to eyelids. Olfactory habituation can serve as a protective mechanism that keeps us from having to constantly bear smells, which we can not escape and which could otherwise cause emotional harm.

The perception of pheromones another subliminal perception of volatile components is. Both humans and animals exude pheromones sensed by the veromonasal or Jacobson organ, so as to cause instinctive reactions within their species, which is also called olfactory communication. Most recently, there was a debate on whether humans have such an organ and generally communicate via pheromones [52]. Through numerous tests, scientists have now established that the human species is capable of perceiving and reacting to pheromones. After the discovery of the human Jacobson organ at the internal nasal septum, the first human pheromone was also extracted [46]. The sex steroid Androstenone, which could previously only be isolated from the saliva of boars, can in fact be found even in the male armpit sweat and urine [4]. Another argument supporting the existence of veromonasal communication is the ability of women to identify whether a man correlates genetically to her own DNA by checking his body odor, including pheromonal information [52]. Pheromones also play a role when mothers recognize their babies through smelling its body odor [52]. However it is also known that pheromones of other species can influence humans. Perfume components like cibet or musk are animal scents, which contain sexual pheromones from the male cibet cat and musk deer. Women find a small amount of such animal scents appealing, but do not instinctively react to them [52].

By understanding the human smelling process, the psychological effects of special fragrances can also be explained. An area of expertise concerned with these effects is Aroma-Chology ®, a term created by the Sense of Smell Institute [51]. This scientific group accumulates established knowledge of olfactory perception and deals with the relevance of smell to behavior, emotions and mood.

Food designers were among the first to explicitly apply fragrances for sales-promotion. The food industry relies on color-odor associations to inform consumers about the taste and smell of products. Heinrich Frieling, a color psychologist and expert for color associations, explains how colors influence consumption and why different sensory stimuli can complement another [17]. Table 17.1 shows colors and the associated odors or tastes used for food packaging and advertising. The tasting process is actually a smelling process, because the olfactory epithelium determines flavors through the internal channel to the pharynx. Tasting and smelling are almost the same perception process, an important fact for food producers. Color-taste and color-odor associations are derived from individual experiences affected by general factors like nature, culture and habitat. Therefore, it would be counterproductive to produce, for example blue sweets in the shape of a bear with orange flavor. However, such associations can diverge in different cultures, which forces producers to adapt their products according to the market in question. Air designers are also geared to color-odor associations and the aroma therapeutic effect of fragrances, when they develop perfumes for scent marketing.

An exceptional quality of olfactory perception is a direct connection between our smelling system and the hypothalamus, a neurological area, which controls the autonomic nervous system. This connection facilitates an influence on the viscera by perceiving odors and is the reason why aromatherapy really works and why some scents can affect consumer well-being.

Table 17.1 Color-odor
associations according to
Frieling [17]

Colour	Odour
Pink	Sweet, mild
Lavender	Sweet, unerotic
Magenta	Heavy, narcotic, charmingly, sweet
Indigo	Scentless
Blue	Scentless
Mint	Juicy, fresh to salty
Green	Fresh, fragrant, perfume with green fragrance
Olive	Musty
Lime green	Sour, dry, fresh, bitter
Yellow	Perfume, flower
Orange	Hearty
Red	Sweet hefty, hot
Gold	Sweet, good, stunning
Ocher	Sourly, neutral
Brown	Aroma, musty
White	Scentless
Grey	Bad

Physiological and psychological research are increasingly expanding into the field of sense of smell and accordingly developing from a scientific background for scent marketing and the unique impacts of smell on human behavior. However, this research is in its infancy and many elements of the smell phenomenon remain unexplained.

17.4   Scent Marketing

Scent marketing relies on the neuropsychological processing of olfactory stimuli in the human brain. It utilizes the effects of smell on human behavior and the Proust Phenomenon. The creation of a pleasant atmosphere for clients is a general objective of scent marketing. The aim is to ensure that customer remain in stores as long as possible and enjoy the ambiance, so that they buy more products and consume more [3327, 33]. However improving store atmosphere is not the only aim of scent marketing. Bradford and Desrochers differentiate between three forms of scent marketing, depending on how scents are used [3]: the *marketer scent*, the *product scent* and the *ambient scent*. Marketer scents are used for product or service promotion and form part of a promotion campaign. If the scent itself is the product, as with perfumes or air fresheners, Bradford and Desrochers refer to it as product scent. They refer to the original purpose of scent marketing, as an enhancement of the retail environment, as ambient scent.

It seems likely that product scents are only a form of scent marketing, when used in the form of marketer or ambient scents, or to promote themselves as product.

For example, EPAMEDIA, a European public space advertising company, equipped some of their illuminated panels with move-detecting perfume dispensers as olfactory support for perfume advertisements [27, 33]. Therefore, scent marketing generally means supporting the sale of products and services with odors.

Ambient scent was an early form of scent marketing. Decades or even centuries ago, bakeries, coffee houses and restaurants often worked unintentionally with scents as attractants. Their chimneys and ventilation systems released enough aromas that made people's mouths water. Today, such shops work systematically with synthetic fragrances in order to provoke similar reactions.

Improving the ambience of essentially negative locations like hospitals or dental practices is another form of ambient scent. It is a social impact of the western world that people become uneasy when they smell chlorine-camphor and phenol, which give disinfectants their typical smell. In order to cope with this pattern, dentists sometimes attempt to improve the atmosphere of their practice by using a so-called *doctor's fragrance* intended to put patients at ease [32].

A logo or corporate scent is a variation of marketer scent. Customers will hopefully perceive these shopping scenarios as pleasant and relaxed, which is due to the already mentioned Proust phenomenon. Customers use the recall of autobiographic memories as described in [22]. This effect entails the idea of using fragrances as part of the corporate identity of stores, hotels and service chains. Each time a client perceives the unique perfume of the chain, he or she will recall the shop, the situation and the pleasant atmosphere [34]. In 2006, hotel chains like Weston, Sheraton, Omni, Four Points and Hyatt incorporated special fragrances as part of their brand image [26].

As history shows, the scent of goods plays a relevant role in the sales process. Not only must food aroma meet one's expectations, other products are also liable to smell-related associations and connotations. For example, new cars do not smell of plastic and metal as one might expect. They are sprayed with an oil or leather fragrance, which is more appealing and familiar to drivers. However the RAC Foundation established that these odors can lead drivers, especially old men, to over-estimate their own capabilities, because they feel younger and more energetic, leading them to take more risks when driving [35]. Nonetheless, some producers experiment with such associations and perfume their products with unexpected aromas, in order to achieve a unique selling proposition or to cheer up their customers. Products like scented writing utensils, socks, CDs, USB-sticks, papers, etc. have already been introduced into the market.

Marketing strategies often include promotional events, such as advertising platforms and presentations of provider individuality. Event managers use the latest entertainment forms to compete for visitors and publicity. Thus, scents also capture the attention of event management and it is not surprising that there is a new occupation called "*Aroma Jockey*", with the aim of lifting the audience's spirit through *compositions of fragrance* [13]. The aroma jockey sets fragrances free, rather like a disk jockey plays songs. Affecting moods changes by using special fragrances may also assists in social interchanges, like meetings or classroom situations [26]. Researchers have noted that some fragrances contribute to improving the ability to think and enhance powers of retention [25]. This effect can also be used for marketing purposes.

All these forms of scent marketing have a common problem – they treat all clients
the same. Each person who enters a shop is confronted with the same fragrance,
often exuded mindless electronic dispensers, which evaporate one scent in fixed
intervals and do not respond to individual preferences. Currently, scent marketing is
inflexible and not adapted to custom tastes as formed by their culture and individual
experiences. Therefore, scents can affect customer behavior in the wrong way, with
dysfunctional consequences. There is no guarantee that each individual correctly
understands a scent-borne, olfactory message.

17.5   The Olfactory Medium – Transmitting Information
Through Smell

Like pictures or music, smell conveys information, which can be transmitted from
sender to receiver; we can communicate via smell and therefore, it is a medium [15].
As explained above, olfactory perception allows a very special form of communication, which is almost impossible to compare with other interaction modalities. No
other sensory stimuli are so impossible to ignore and perceived unconsciously so.
No other information affects our moods more intensively than odors. Odors can
have a special meaning and invisibly and spontaneously transmit information, which
other media cannot. Odors can bear information like emotions, warnings or memories, and also genetic information through body odor or pheromones.

The communication process through a medium can be formulated as a communication model, as in Shannon and Weaver (Fig. 17.1) [21]. According to Shannon's

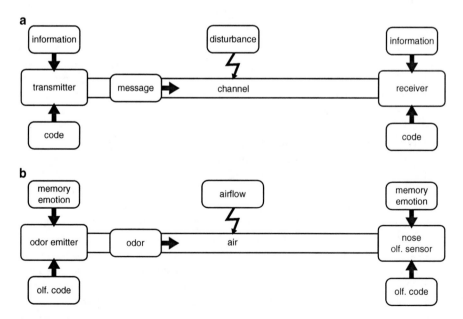

Fig. 17.1 Communication model by Shannon and Weaver

information theory, each message requires syntax, semantics and pragmatics, in a word: a language, which is spoken by both the sender and receiver. However, there is no unique olfactory language. Syntax, semantics and pragmatics vary, depending on culture and individual experience, but also on profession such as perfumer, food designer or wine steward.

According to Shannon's paradigm, a scent dispenser (the transmitter) and consumer (the receiver) should have the same understanding of the dispensed scent (the message). In order to ensure that in retail environments, where there is a high fluctuation of people and consequently a rapid change in tastes and olfactory languages, scent marketing systems must adapt dispensed scents to individual preferences as quickly as possible. In short, they need to detect consumers' olfactory language, before disposing their olfactory message – they have to become *smart*.

17.6   Olfactory Technologies and Interaction Within Pervasive Environments

General scent diffusers like scent candles, fragrance lights or other kinds of air fresheners work mechanically, without electricity. However, in the last few years. more and more electric scent gadgets were developed and tend to replace the analog models. Additionally to smell-sending devices, chemists are developing smell-detecting systems and *e-noses*. Devices that disseminate odors or detect volatile components can be categorized as *olfactory technology*. These components can act as *olfactory displays or sensors*, as human-computer interfaces and allow a bidirectional communication between them via smell. Thus, the technology for making scent marketing smart already exists, but the implementation stage still needs to occur. The following section provides of current olfactory technology for sending and sensing and how it is used.

17.6.1   Sending and Sensing Olfactory Information

Most scenting systems in sales rooms are integrated in to the air conditioning, but there are also heat-based standalone devices. The first commercially available air design systems could not adjust their running time, fragrance or scent volume; they ran continuously and led to a suboptimal flood of fragrances. Modern systems offer both time and volume adjustment, as well as the option of changing between various fragrances.

Not only advertising takes advantage of odors, olfactory communication is receiving more and more attention in human-computer interaction. Today, digitally controlled odor diffusers are not only applied for advertising purposes, they are increasingly used as ambient indicators, such as an olfactory display in HCI-systems. For instance, Keye [30] describes an ambient olfactory reminder system. The integration of an augmented reality application, with an odor machine for improving on the reality experience, is presented in [14]. NTT Communications developed a smell machine called *Aroma Geur*[36], laying the foundation for the first olfactory emails in 2004. This device was also used to create an ambient smell when listening to Tokio FM. In 2005, TriSenx launched their *ScentDome*[48] to enable websites to emit scents. The special smoothness of olfactory interaction spaces was the central subject of the *Space-of-Scent* project [19].

For the telecommunication industry, smell has been introduced successfully as a new sensory modality for interactions between human and mobile devices. The first "smelling" mobile phones were placed on the market in 2008. The Sony Ericsson SO701i is scented with an aromatherapy fragrance to enhance relaxation during stressful phone calls. In order to satisfy different preferences, the mobile phone is available with 8 different fragrances, which can also be useful for advertising purposes and tagging personal items like mobile phones with corporate scents. The Hyunday MP280 integrates an individual refillable scent diffuser, which acts as *smelling tone*. Samsung [7, 18] also hold patents for smell phones. German inventors have already patented a mobile phone with a smell chip, which can send and receive *smell messages* [9]. These mobile devices could be the future of mobile advertising – they offer a new method of sending not only informative, but also emotional advertising messages.

Odor diffusing facilities provide odors for static as well as mobile smart installations. Current scent marketing systems treat customers' homogeneously individual preferences into account. Making such systems intelligent responds to these preferences as well as to the consumers' psychological state, as aroma therapists do. The combination of emotion recognition, referred to [39] as *emotional computing*, and the use of smart olfactory technology can be a powerful advertising instrument.

Not only is the output of olfactory information an increasingly subject important for information technology research, but also the use of volatile substances as input for digital communication is becoming increasingly useful. Gas sensor arrays and electronic noses are especially useful for forensic investigations, for the detection of explosives, and for medical science as a means of diagnosing diseases like cancer. Today, they are used increasingly to control digital systems. For instance, the Japanese *Hanahana*-installation can manipulate flower-animations with ten different perfumes. Wyszynski et al. have even sent a recorded odor by email and reproduced it for the receiver [54].

Researchers of the Austrian Konrad-Lorenz-Institute are currently developing a system for recognizing individuals by their body odor, which reflects the identity like a fingerprint [38]. Body odor is the volatile state of sweat whose components are influenced genetically. Emotions like fear can also manipulate the sweat composition and contribute to the production of cold sweat [6]. Ackerl et al. ascribe this manipulation to a release of fear pheromones [1]. According to this theory, body odor has the potential to become a new data source for intelligent systems, enabling them to recognize individuals, as well as their emotions. It can be expected that in future, human pheromones will be measurable as animal pheromones are now [43].

Sensing odors could be a useful instrument to enable advertisers to find out more about their clients, especially their emotional states. Other useful elements include individual odor preferences, which could be examined by identifying their body odor or personal perfume. The development of body odor detection and analysis through gas sensors and artificial noses, is a current challenge for scientists.

17.7 Olfactory Zones of Interaction

The recognition and manipulation of emotions are basic instruments of advertising. The olfactory information channel allows both the detection of emotions by body odor analysis and the stimulation of emotions by means of aroma therapeutic scents or pheromones. In the near future, smart advertising systems may be able to react to individual emotional states and manipulate them at the same time. Such bidirectional communication via odor would function within unconventional zones of interaction.

Generally, we can define smells as ambient media, because of their subliminality and inertia. Therefore, olfactory interaction operates in the ambient interaction zone [28]. However, communication via odor operates within an unconventional ambient zone of interaction. Each smell-emitting human being or object is surrounded by a distinct vapor, constituting an olfactory aura, defined as *Olfactory Interaction Zone* [16]. This zone can be extended dynamically from a square meter size to a square kilometer scale. Consumers are often able to detect the aromas of nearby bakeries or restaurants over several meters leading them from the street to their salesroom as an *olfactory direction sign.* Within an olfactory interaction zone, the information priority is defined by the intensity of an odor and the odor itself. As an example, the odor of fresh bread is not so important as that of smoke.

Raab was concerned with the current sociology of odor [40]. He renders this unconscious communication modality explicit and defines interaction zones for olfactory interaction between humans, based on Erving Goffman's territories of the self (Fig. 17.2).

The body defines the individual odor and is a source of the most familiar fragrance. An individual's personal space encloses the body and varies in impact depending on olfactory sympathy. The unpleasant body odors of interaction partners can maximize the extensions of personal space and pleasant ones can minimize it. Special smells constitute a social identity, an affiliation to a social group, which defines the social space. Smells associated with regions, localities or goods define the public space as interaction zone. Such smells are more acceptable than *foreign* ones in the personal space, because they entail a communal territory, apart from the box territory. They form a private territory in public space, which is occupied by an individual and its individual fragrance, such as a table in a restaurant or a seat in a train.

Raab's olfactory interaction territories are comparable with interaction zones used in HCI, apart from the fact that one interaction partner is replaced by an intelligent computer system. Therefore, Raab's territories of interaction constitute another principle for olfactory interaction zones in Human-Computer Interaction.

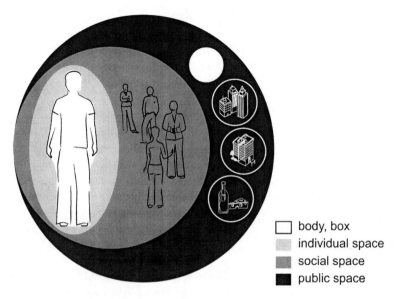

Fig. 17.2 Olfactory zones of human-to-human interaction according to Raab and Goffmann

An olfactory communication process can only be acceptable for a person, if the computer sends smell information without violating the human interaction territories. This needs to be kept in mind when planning scent marketing concepts and developing Scent Marketing systems.

17.8   Make Scent Marketing Pervasive

The current use of odors in human-computer systems, especially for scent marketing purposes, is based on the psychological knowledge of olfactory perception on the one hand, but also enters unfamiliar territories. There has not yet been sufficient psychological investigation to analyze the full range of mental effects of olfactory stimuli. However, in the near future, we have to content not only with visual and acoustic information overload, but also with olfactory information overload. Given that we suffer from excessive visual and acoustic impressions every day, nobody knows what mental damage numerous waves of fragrance could cause. Olfactory information overload could lead to two different scenarios: Scenario A describes a complete habituation of olfactory perception and a complete loss of our sense of smell. Scenario B would constitute another olfactory revolution, as in the eighteenth century, when miasma became overwhelming and intolerable [10]. In order to avoid such scenarios, users of the *smelling* medium must dose olfactory information very carefully, which requires respect for individual preferences and sensibility.

The highly subjective interpretation of olfactory stimuli requires an adaption of olfactory messages to the individual. Therefore, olfactory systems must *know* such preferences – they need to become more intelligent, or *smart*. Room-scenting product lines like Brise Sense & Spray or AirWick FreshMatic are the first sensor-controlled mass-market scent diffusers. Fragrance and intensity can be adjusted individually by hand. In public spaces, especially for scent marketing, such systems need more flexibility, because fragrance and its intensity must be autonomously adapted to people's preferences or moods. In the near future, smart scent marketing systems may be able to react to individual emotional states and manipulate them with aroma-therapeutic scents. Mobile *smelling* devices like smell phones offer a further possibility for mobile advertising – they offer a new method if sending not only textual, but also more emotional smelling advertising messages.

Whereas digital scent diffusers have already been brought to market, the development of gas sensors and artificial noses is still a topic of fundamental research. Especially for HCI-systems, there are not useful gas-sensing interfaces yet. Various interviewed computer scientists pointed to this aspect as a reason why smell is seldom used for Human-Computer Interaction [15].

A second problem is the social acceptance of such systems. At present, consumers are often unaware of these scents, which should potentially affect their mood. Maybe they cannot perceive them, because they are not trained to perceive smell, or they ignore them because they do not recognize odors as relevant information. Therefore, scent marketing is currently a productive advertising tool, which unknowingly effects customer behavior. Whether or not this is ethically acceptable, is discussed by Bradford and Desrochers [3]. They argue that only an objective ambient scent, which can be recognized by the consumer, is ethically acceptable. A covert objective ambient scent "*is developed to motivate an action or influence consumer behavior below the consumer's absolute threshold of consciousness*". Therefore, the consumer cannot avoid the manipulation, as would be possible in the case of listening or not listening to shopping mall music. Bradford and Desrochers [3] refer to Brehm [5], who described consumers' negative reactions to the loss of freedom to make a choice, as "*psychological reactance*". Raab's olfactory interaction zones could support the social acceptance of olfactory scent marketing systems. Also, a technological system has to respect olfactory borders and personal spaces. An HCI-system should not cross these borders by, for example emitting a flood of fragrances.

The Shannon-Weaver model implies that both sender and receiver need to have the same knowledge about the meaning of a message in a digital communication process. This meaning, code or language is a connotation of information to a word, number, picture, sound or smell and must be conveyed within such systems. In human-to-human interaction spoken languages are restricted to countries or culture groups. Olfactory languages like the aroma classifications of perfumers or the terms used by oenophilists, and also the meaning of smells within indigenous groups, are even more localized. Therefore, scent marketing systems need to know the user's cultural affiliation and his or her individual olfactory preferences. The future challenge for computer scientists and other developers or designers of scent marketing systems will be the spontaneous detection of individual preferences and the individualization of olfactory advertising messages.

Today, we can detect user preferences in different ways. Especially online marketing works with user profiles, such as Amazon, Facebook or Google. These user profiles include precisely individual such preferences, which can also be used for scent marketing and the adaption of scents to customer taste. Mobile devices like mobile phones or gadgets with a digital ID, facilitate identification of customers and their preferences, wherever and whoever they are. However, this can lead to a violation of privacy. Therefore, users need to agree with the process and accept it. Alternatively marketers can take the next step and allow customers to design their own individual shopping environment by means of a customizable preference profile saved on their mobile device, which, for instance contains color, sound and scent preferences.

Another way to individualize scent marketing is changing by scents, depending on customers' current emotional states and using the aroma-therapeutic effect of scents. Thus, shops and public places can adapt their shopping environments to that what people currently need and not that what they want. Depending on the general mood, they can calm people down or awake them up by using special scents like lavender or coffee aroma [24].

Sensing odors can also support advertising, which can be a useful instrument for finding out more information about people, especially about their emotional states, such as fear. Individual odor preferences, which could be examined by identifying body odor or personal perfume, are valuable data for pervasive advertising systems. Such preferences can refer to color preferences via color-odor associations, which could be useful for, e.g., fashion style suggestions in fashion stores, to give but one example.

Reacting to one person and adapting olfactory marketing messages to his or her taste should not be a problem for scent marketers. After all, every day perfumery employers, who scent each customer with different perfumes, do just this. But how can crowds be handled, how can a mass of people with different tastes be satisfied by that one *right* scent? As already mentioned, smell is a very inert medium, and cannot be changed in milliseconds, not even in a few seconds. It takes minutes to exchange olfactory messages. Therefore, pervasive scent marketing systems need to manage the preferences of people and groups, especially demographic groups, in order to satisfy the majority.

Current olfactory technology allows only a restricted form of intelligent scent marketing. Depending on how fast olfactory technology will be improved scent marketing can become more and more pervasive. However, first of all smell has to be accepted as serious communication channel for developing pervasive scent marketing systems.

Acknowledgments This work is supported under the FFG Research Studios Austria program under grant agreement No. 818652 DISPLAYS (Pervasive Display Systems).

References

1. Ackerl, K., Atzmueller, M., Grammer, K.: The scent of fear. Nero Endocrinol. Lett. **232**, 79–84 (2002)
2. Bartzos, F.: Duftmarketing – Eine spezielle Form des Neuromarketings. Master thesis. University of Vienna, Vienna (2008)
3. Bradford, K.D., Desrochers, D.M.: The use of scents to influence consumers: the sense of using scents to make cents. Springer J. Bus. Res. **90**, 141–153 (2009)
4. Brand, G., Jacquot, L.: Gehirn und Geschlecht. Springer, Berlin/Heidelberg (2007)
5. Brehm, J.W.: Theory of Psychological Reactance. Academic, New York (1966)
6. Chen, D., Katdare, A., Lucas, N.: Chemosignals of fear enhance cognitive performance in humans. Chem. Senses **31**, 415–423 (2006)
7. Cho, W., Lee, S., Won, J., Choi, S.: Mobile phone having perfume spraying apparatus. US Patent and Trademark Office. No. 7622084 (2006)
8. Classen, C., Howes, D., Synnott, A.: Aroma – The Cultural History of Smell. Routledge, Oxon (1994)
9. Convisual (2008) Deutsche Erfinder entwickeln Dufthandy-Anwendung. http://www.isi-goettingen.de/pdf/PI_Dufthandy_080428.pdf. Accessed 23 Mar 2011
10. Corbin, A.: The Foul and the Fragrant: Odor and the French Social Imagination. Harvard University Press, Cambridge (1988)
11. Dennis, C.: The sweet smell of success. Nature **428**, 362–364 (2004)
12. Deshmukh, S.S., Bhalla, U.S.: Representation of odor habituation and timing in the hippocampus. J. Neurosci. **235**, 1903–1915 (2003)
13. Emotion: Ein dufter Job. Emotion **06**, 94–99 (2008)
14. Emsenhuber, B.: Integration of olfactory media and information in pervasive environments. In: Proceedings of the First International Doctoral Colloquium on Pervasive Computing, Linz (2006)
15. Emsenhuber, B.: Das olfaktorische Medium – Die Integration olfaktorischer Information in die Mensch-Maschine-Kommunikation. Ph.D. thesis. University of Art, Linz (2010)
16. Emsenhuber, B., Ferscha, A.: Olfactory interaction zones. In: Adjunct Proceedings of Pervasive 2009, Nara (2009)
17. Frieling, H.: Farbe hilft verkaufen. HansenMuster-Schmidt, Northeim (2005)
18. Greco, P.M., Hunt, S.D., Seuck, J.W.: Communication device having a scent release feature and method thereof. US Patent and Trademark Office, No. 20040203412 (2008)
19. Haque Design and Research.: Scent of space. http://www.haque.co.uk/scentsofspace.php (2007). Accessed 23 Mar 2011
20. Hatt, H., Dee, R.: Das Maiglöckchen-Phänomen. Piper, Munich (2008)
21. Herczeg, M.: Interaktionsdesign. Oldenbourg, Munich (2006)
22. Herz, R.S.: A naturalistic analysis of autobiographical memories triggered by olfactory visual and auditory stimuli. Chem. Senses **29**, 217–224 (2004)
23. Herz, R.: The Scent of Desire: Discovering Our Enigmatic Sense of Smell, Reprint edn. Harper Perennial, New York (14 October 2008) (this is the english version of this book)
24. Herz, R.S.: Aromatherapy facts and fictions: a scientific analysis of olfactory effects on mood, physiology and behavior. Int. J. Neurosci. **119**, 263–290 (2009)
25. Herz, R.S., Schankler, C., Beland, S.: Olfaction, emotion and associative learning, effects on motivated behavior. Motiv. Emotion **28**, 363–383 (2004)
26. Higgins, M.: Figs? Coconut sunscreen? Hotels choose their scents. The New York Times. http://travel2.nytimes.com/2006/04/09/travel/09transhotel.html (2006). Accessed 23 Mar 2011
27. Hirt, R.: Multisensory.de – Der Blog zum Thema Sensory-Branding (2009). www.multisensory.de Accessed 27 May 2009
28. Ishii, H., Ullmer, B.: Tangible bits: towards seamless interfaces between people, bits and atoms. In: Proceedings of CHI 97, March 1997, pp. 234–24. ACM Press, Atalanta (1997)

29. Jütte, R., Lynn, J.: A History of the Senses: From Antiquity to Cyberspace. Polity, Cambridge (2004)
30. Keye, J.N.: Symbolic olfactory display. Master thesis, MIT, Massachusetts (2001)
31. Kloock, D., Spahr, A.: Medientheorien: eine Einführung. Wilhelm Fink Verlag, Munich (2000)
32. Lehrner, J., Marwinski, G., Lehr, S., Johran, P., Deecke, L.: Ambient odors of orange and lavender reduce anxiety and improve mood in a dental office. Physiol. Behav. **86**, 92–95 (2005)
33. Michell, D.J., Kahn, B.E., Knasko, S.C.: There's something in the air: effects of congruent or incongruent ambient odor on consumer decision making. J. Consum. Res. **22**, 229–238 (1995)
34. Morrin, M., Ratneshwar, S.: The impact of ambient scent on evaluation, attention and memory for familiar and unfamiliar brands. J. Bus. Res. **49**, 157–165 (2000)
35. Nicholson, S., Forrow, S., Delaney, K.: The scent of danger. http://www.carpages.co.uk/news/car-smell-part-1-05-06-05.asp (2005). Accessed 23 Mar 2011
36. NTT Communications.: Movie enhanced with internet-based fragrance system. NTT Com Press Release. http://www.in70mm.com/news/2006/new_world/index.htm (2007). Accessed 23 Mar 2011
37. Paech, A.: Das aroma des Kinos. http://www.uni-konstanz.de/FuF/Philo/LitWiss/MedienWiss/Texte/duft.html (1999). Accessed 23 Mar 2011
38. Penn, D.J., Oberzaucher, E., Grammer, K., Fischer, G., Soini, H.A., Wiesler, D., Novotny, M.V., Dixon, S.J., Xu, Y., Brereton, R.G.: Individual and gender fingerprints in human body odour. J. R. Soc. Interface **4**(13) (2007)
39. Picard, R.W.: Affective Computing. MIT Press, Cambridge/London (1997)
40. Raab, J.: Soziologie des Geruchs. UVK, Konstanz (2001)
41. Rasche, S., Toetter, B., Adler, J., Tschapek, A., Doerner, J., Kurtenbach, S., Hatt, H., Meyer, H., Warscheid, B., Neuhaus, E.: Tmem16b is specifically expressed in the cilia of olfactory sensory neurons. Chem. Senses **353**, 239–245 (2010)
42. Rouby, C.: Olfaction, Taste, and Cognition. Cambridge University Press, Cambridge (2002)
43. Sauer, A.E., Karg, G., Koch, U.T., De Kramer, J.J., Milli, R.: A portable EAG system for the measurement of pheromone concentrations in the field. Chem. Senses **175**, 543–553 (1992)
44. Stafford, B.: Body Criticism: Imaging the Unseen in Enlightenment Art and Medicine. MIT Press, Cambridge (1993)
45. Stöhr, A.: Air-Design als Erfolgsfaktor im Handel. Deutscher Universitäts-Verlag, Wiesbaden (1998)
46. Sturmheit, T.: Sex findet doch nicht im Kopf statt. http://www.welt.de/wissenschaft/article1083519/Sex_findet_doch_nicht_im_Kopf_statt.html (2008). Accessed 23 Mar 2011
47. Süskind, P.: Perfume. Penguin, London (2006)
48. TriSenx.: ScentDome. http://asia.cnet.com/crave/scent-dome-62100206.htm. Accessed 23 Mar 2011
49. Umweltbundesamt für Mensch und Umwelt.: Duftstoffe: Wenn Angenehmes zur Last werden kann. http://www.umweltdaten.de/publikationen/fpdf-l/3550.pdf (2006). Accessed 23 Mar 2011
50. Vlahos, J.: Scent and sensibility. The New York Times (2007)
51. Warren, C., Molnar, T.: Sense of smell institute (2010). www.senseofsmell.org/ Accessed 2 June 2010
52. Watson, L.: Jacobson's Organ: And the Remarkable Nature of Smell. W.W. Norton, New York (2000)
53. Wilson, D.A., Stevenson, R.J.: Learning to Smell. John Hopkins University Press, Baltimore (2006)
54. Wyszynski, B., Yamanaka, T., Nakamoto, T.: Recording and reproducing citrus flavors using odor recorder. Sens. Actuators B Chem. **1061**, 388–393 (2005)

Index

CPSIA information can be obtained at www.ICGtesting.com
Printed in the USA
LVOW030135081211

258381LV00005B/28/P